The Definitive Guide to Southern and Central California

www.californiawaterfalls.com

Extremely Important! You must read this.

While all of us love and cherish the great outdoors, at all times we must remember that many vast dangers are found in our precious rural lands. Many sites in this book require hiking on trails, places where there is no trail or the trail is no longer maintained. Many of these trails require stream crossings that are both simple and very complex, as well as treks through snow, climbs over mountains, both with stable and loose structures. Although we have strived to our greatest ability to point out the dangers you'll encounter, both the author and publisher of the book urge you to use the highest respect of carefulness while being in the outdoors, and does not assume liability or responsibility for any loss due to injury and or death that occur in the outdoors or while traveling to, or visiting any site in the book. Keep in mind that rivers, creeks and lakes fluctuate in an instant. Unstable and unsafe weather, water and road conditions can create harmful and deadly hazards. Hikers and anglers drown or are seriously injured due to the use of poor judgment and because they over estimate their human capabilities. Jumping, diving, sliding off rocks and walking the streambed can be dangerous. You are responsible for checking the depth of the water and locating submerged structures. Please use extreme caution at all times. In certain locations in this book the line between public and private property can be very vague. Do your best to respect all private property and obey all no trespassing signs.

With all this in mind, please have a great time, be safe and please remember to pack in and pack out.

This book could not have been done without the help and support of several people. A special thank you goes out to Dan and Cheryl Lezak for their tremendous support, both personally and financially. Without them, this book would be just an idea. Also, a thanks to Christian Perez, Tony Abel, Blake Lezak, Todd McLean, Scott Wiessner, Stephen Wiessner, Brandi Koerner and Brett Ross for assisting me on many of the long and extensive trips required to complete this book. To the US Forest Service, California State Parks and National Park Service employees who gathered information to help make this book a success, specifically, your help and thoughts are priceless. David Del Bourgo and Nicole Shaffer, you did a fantastic job editing this book.

Printed in Altona, Canada

Edited by David Del Bourgo and Nicole Shaffer

Maps by Joel Shangle

Book Design and Production by Chris Shaffer

Book Distributed by American West Books, Pacific Books, Hendrix and Sunbelt Publications

Send all questions and comments to Shafdog Publications by email to:

cshaffer@californiawaterfalls.com

Or visit us on the web @
www.californiawaterfalls.com
www.fishingcalifornia.net

All photos Copyright Chris Shaffer except:
p. 61 (top) Tim Shew, p. 137 (left) and 136 Tony Shaffer, p. 132 David Savage, p.160, 174,189 Stephen Wiessner and p. 386 Brett Ross

Three boys were playfully tossing a Frisbee in a large, open meadow on the right. A woman rode her bicycle alongside Southside Drive while her three kids followed a short distance behind. A father and son each peered curiously through binoculars, admiring the sheer cliffs below Sentinel Dome, which loomed overhead on the right, and a newlywed couple cuddled in a wool blanket in Leidig Meadow absorbing the crisp fresh air along the bank of the calm Merced River. Lupine, vibrant wildflowers, and lush green grasses submerged at the riverbank and clinging to fertile soil in the meadow brought the meadow to life. The scenic setting lured car passenger's eyes to the scene.

While scanning the road for hazards I was processing all these actions, trying desperately to maintain the posted 25 mph speed limit. This two lane, one-way road was beginning to crowd.

It was 9 am, late May, and tourists were beginning to flock to Yosemite National Park, one of the world's most popular national parks. I was eager to reach the parking area at Curry Village, lock up my car and head into the backcountry, enthusiastic to dodge the anticipated daily spring crowds. The sun had yet to dry the dew off flower petals or send the deer looking for shelter from the heat. Nor had it wakened all the campers from their tents, preserving that rare sense of serenity seldom found in California's busiest national park.

The serenity couldn't have lasted a second longer. My pleasant morning nearly took a turn for the worst.

Dodging disaster, my drink holder could not contain my ice tea as I was forced to slam on the breaks, responding to a chain reaction of tires screeching in front of me. I didn't hear a crash, but after feeling the whiplash that occurred it sure felt like we were in one. With traffic now stopped in the left lane, I jumped out of my car to make sure everyone ahead of me was ok.

I ran straight for the first car, four cars ahead of me, which halted the rest of the line.

"Sir, are you ok?" I said to the driver who appeared to be in great shape, not shaken up at all and putting a new role of film in his camera. His wife and kids also appeared unblemished.

"Yeah, why?" he said to me, curiously wondering why I was standing at his window. I glanced back at the cars behind me to make sure I was sane. Slamming on his breaks in the middle of the road this guy nearly caused a major accident. There was a left shoulder by the way. A few other drivers had left their vehicles to check on the situation.

"Are you crazy?" said a man in a British accent, wearing a Leeds United t-shirt. "You could have killed us. Why did you stop like that? I didn't see anything in front of you. The road was clear."

"It's not the road. Don't you see that?" said the man who nearly caused the accident. He was now out of his car opening the side door of his caravan to let his kids out. His car was still on the road. "That is the best waterfall I've ever seen. I can't believe it. This place is amazing!"

I remember my instructor warning the class of potential road hazards, you know, ice, snow, children running in the street and other accidents. Nevertheless, they never mentioned anything about watching out for waterfalls in traffic school!

I reckoned a coyote or deer darted across the road or one of the kids missed a Frisbee and ran into the street, but none of that happened. This guy stopped to see Yosemite Falls, Yosemite National Park's most popular tourist trap. I mean yah, it is the tallest cataract in North America and the fifth tallest waterfall in the world, but in LA where I live drivers don't stop for pedestrians, red lights or obey speeds limits. Heck most wouldn't even stop if they hit somebody!

Whether big or tall, powerful or gentle, waterfalls always have a way of overwhelming people, and in this case, prompting citizens to ignore the basic laws of

Yosemite Falls

the road.   *Mist Falls*

    When it comes to the wonders of water, and its descent to ultimately find a way back to the Pacific Ocean this scene happens more than you would think. This book was written to uncover many of the state's unknown waterfalls, while at the same time highlighting those that are well known.

    Yosemite Falls is one of more than 265 waterfalls in this book. While many go sadly unobserved, waterfalls are an integral part of California's natural lands. Populations increase daily, fires scar hillsides, floods destroy houses and create billions of dollars of damage, clogged freeways add to the region's smog and the state's budget yo-yos up and down. However, our waterfalls remain.

    The area we call home may be referred to as a giant megalopolis to the rest of the country, yet this vast metropolitan area is surrounded by hundreds of alluring waterfalls. Revealing how and where to find them, this book does the work for you.

    Sitting at the base of a refreshing waterfall along the cold sand of California's Central Coast, getting drenched with mist while walking the Mist Trail to Vernal Falls, admiring the cool, calm, fern-filled canyon of Berry Creek Falls, the crystal clear pool below King Canyon National Park's Roaring River Falls and studying the sun's rays as they break through the reflection of a twin rainbow at Rainbow Falls, waterfalls put a sense of awe in our hearts. They have a majestic way of

Mist Trail, Yosemite National Park

healing the soul and transform their audiences to an unfamiliar state where time stands still. Whether a dazzling freefall like Bridalveil Falls, a thunderous cascade such as Wapama Falls, or a faint sliver of water like Ribbon Falls; the soothing sound of water crashing against rocks is a heart-felt feeling that stamps a lasting impression in our blood forever.

Intriguing at it may be no two waterfalls ever look the same. While it may appear identical with each pass, the water is in a constant state of change, always falling, twisting, turning, twirling and weaving in different shapes. It requires its critic to balance power and beauty, elegance and grace.

Visiting waterfalls is more than just a chance to enjoy and appreciate nature; it's an opportunity to bring out your adventurous side and explore the wilderness while rekindling camaraderie with a group of old friends. A satisfying mean for exercise or a way to keep the family together for a day, the journey to a waterfall gives us a reason to set out into our wilderness areas. Hiking to waterfalls give people something to work for, a challenge, a destination, and offers a prize at the end of a long, hard hike.

With more than 265 waterfalls spanning from San Jose east along Highway 108 over Sonora Pass, down south to Mexico, The Definitive Guide to the Waterfalls of Central and Southern California makes even the most avid hikers and outdoor lovers salivate. This book contains detailed descriptions and directions to 65drive-to waterfalls, more than 775miles of hiking trails to waterfalls and a few boat-in waterfalls.

This book has been more than a career, it's been an honor to explore our state's crowded and secluded wilderness areas in search of majestic waterfalls. I've had a blast compiling all the data needed for you to plan a memorable trip to many of the state's best waterfalls. I hope you have as much fun as I did on your escapades.

In closing, please treat these areas with respect and pick up all trash whether you left it on not. These areas need to be persevered for our grandkids and their grandkids. With all this in mind, don't forget to have a blast!

Chris Shaffer
Author

The author at Snoopy Rock near Glacier Point

Lower Salmon Creek Falls in the Kern River Drainage

Rick Spadaro at Peppermint Creek Falls in the Giant Sequoia National Monument

How to use this book

The Definitive Guide to the Waterfalls of Central and Southern California has been carefully designed to aid you in finding your ideal waterfall easily. First, it helps you to plan your destination to fit your particular tastes and life-style, and to provide you, your family and friends with the most enjoyable outdoor experience possible. Once you've chosen a location, the rest is easy. Each article is written and structured in a user-friendly format that provides you with quick, fun and easy reading.

This book has been broken down into 16 geographical regions to allow those who prefer choosing their desired waterfall location by general vicinity to do so with ease. After selecting the region you wish to visit, turn to the map preceding that particular region. Here you will find a list of all the waterfalls in that area. Next, simply decide which waterfalls interest you and flip to the corresponding pages to obtain more information.

If you already know which waterfall you would like to visit, open to the table of contents, locate the waterfall and turn to the corresponding page.

The book is set up with 10 different categories containing valuable information about each waterfall. The structure is as follows…..

Name of Waterfall
Rating
How Short?
How Easy?
Best Time to View
Contact Information
Waterfall Information
Directions
Tips For Making the Trip
Nearby Attractions

Name of the Waterfall

Rating:
Even though this book covers only waterfalls in Central and Southern California, the ratings are based upon a comparison with all the waterfalls in California. In essence, a "ten" is the best possible score and "one" is the worst. A "ten" qualifies it as one of the top 10 waterfalls in the state. All of the ratings are based on the average amount of seasonal rainfall and factor in size, volume, uniqueness and grandeur.

How Short?
This tells you how short the round trip mileage to the waterfall is. This includes only trail miles, not miles accumulated when driving to the waterfall or to its trailhead. If no hiking is required it will say "Drive-To", which means you can drive right to the waterfall with your car. In some instances the words "Boat-In" are written. In this case the waterfall can only be reached with watercraft, unless otherwise specified. In some instances a waterfall can be both a drive-to and a hike-to waterfall. This can occur when

there is a drive-to overlook in addition to hikng to the waterfall or the waterfall is comprised of two or more tiers where the bottom tier is drive-to and the upper tier is reached via hiking. In this case both drive-to and a mileage will be listed.

How Easy?

This tells you what you should expect in terms of difficulty degree when setting out on your journey to the falls. The scale range is from one to five, with one being the easiest trip and five being the toughest. The scale is based on several factors, including mileage, the degree of difficulty the mileage is, whether or not there is an established trail, elevation gain and stream crossings. A "one" is doable by those of all ages. On the other hand, a "five," is only recommended for those in excellent physical shape, as these include long, challenging, strenuous hikes.

Best Time to View:

The best time to view these waterfalls has been recorded to enable you visit these waterfalls when their feeder rivers and streams are at peak flow and the waterfalls are most impressive. Keep in mind; these suggestions are based on the average amount of rainfall per year. Some years, precipitation is above average making the waterfall spectacular much longer than normal. On the other hand, a rainy season with below average precipitation may cause some waterfalls to dry up long before traditional periods, and others to not flow at all.

Contact Information:

The "Contact" section is dedicated to providing you with valuable phone numbers to help you plan your trip. This section includes numbers to check on updated weather and road conditions, as well as to find lodging, camping and tourist information at your destination.

Directions:

No need to bring along a ton of maps. All the directions tell you how to get to your chosen destination from a major city. These directions are listed to the nearest one-tenth of a mile in most instances.

Waterfall Information:

The "Waterfall Information" section can be found in the body of each write-up. It tells you everything you need to know about the waterfall you are planning to visit. This includes information about how to reach the waterfall, its height, descriptions of the

surrounding area, historical information, wildlife to look for on the path and much more. In addition, occasionally I will add in tidbits of interesting and humorous personal experiences to help bring these destinations to life.

Tips For Making the Trip:

One of the most helpful sections is called "If You Plan to Make the Trip." This covers the "plan ahead" stage, warning you of obstacles and/or hazards you might want to prepare for prior to visiting these various destinations. For example, some destinations may require chains in the winter; day-use fees may be charged; some streams dry-up by summer; and roads to certain locations are often closed by heavy rains, snow or torrential flows. Other questions that might arise are also answered. For instance, where can you buy supplies? Do you need to keep an eye out for rattlesnakes? If four-wheel drive is required, or if the roads are poorly maintained, that information will also be discussed in this section.

Nearby Attractions:

Some sightseers might want to spend a whole day in the general vicinity of the waterfall, instead of just a few hours, and may want to bring the family along. No problem. Listed in the "Also Nearby" section are ideas for places to take your family, including amusement parks, fishing sites, other waterfalls, hiking trails, historic sites, shopping and more.

Table of Contents

Big Todd McLean uses a log to cross the raging Tenaya in May of 1999 in Yosemite National Park

1

Stanislaus National Forest/ Sonora Pass

Tulloch Lake Falls
Rainbow Pool Falls
Diana Falls
Sonora Pass Falls
Sardine Falls
Leavitt Falls

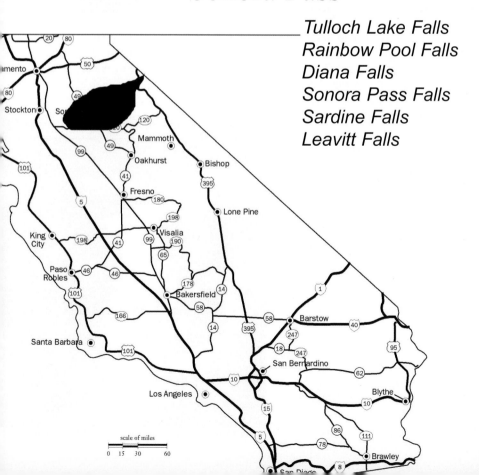

Tulloch Reservoir Falls

Rating: 7

How Short? Drive-To

How Easy? 1

Best Time to View:
Year-Round

Need Information?
Contact: South Lake
Tulloch RV
Campground and
Marina (209) 881-0107
or (800) 894-2267,
Tulloch Lake
(209) 785-3838

Tulloch Reservoir Falls would be a grand waterfall, except for one problem: it's artificial. Yes, it's not a natural waterfall. Tulloch is created by releases from Tulloch Reservoir; it can be turned on and off with the push of a button. Isn't that convenient? Luckily, when I was there the switch was on, so I didn't have to ask nicely for the lake operators to turn the waterfall on. (As if they really would have.)

If you can overlook the dam in the backdrop, Tulloch is actually a decent waterfall. Located at 500 feet in rolling foothill country, less than a half-hour drive west of Sonora, Tulloch is in a pretty setting. The hills are sprinkled with pines, oaks and other trees; the grass grows tall (but dies by May); and the lake can be seen directly behind the falls. I know it doesn't sound like the ideal place. But take my word for it, it's not bad.

Tulloch is actually three different waterfalls, one next to the other, fed by two different sets of release gates. The best waterfall is on the far right, closest to the road. It's a 150-foot cascade that creates a thunderous roar as it crashes down on the reddish-brown rocks that lean against the dam. Fifty yards to the left of this cascade, there is a more sloping drop that is fed by water from the same gates. Because much of the water is depleted by the first falls, this waterfall is not as powerful.

In reality, the third drop to the far left is not a waterfall at all. It may look like one from your vantage point, however, if you look more closely or use a pair of binoculars, you'll discover a pump plant above it. This third waterfall is created by water that is forced out of the bottom of the lake. It doesn't do anything interesting, such as crash onto rocks, freefall, or cascade. It just comes bursting out of pipes.

On a more positive note, Tulloch Falls is turned on most of the year. Because the waterfalls feed the main channel of the Stanislaus River, the water is needed to keep the river at levels sufficient for salmon and steelhead runs.

If you plan to make the trip, supplies are available at South Lake Tulloch Marina.

Also nearby are New Melones Reservoir, Don Pedro Reservoir, and Woodward Reservoir.

Directions: *From the 99 Freeway in Modesto, take Highway 108 east to Oakdale. At the junction of Highways 108 and 120 in Oakdale, drive 15 miles east to Tulloch Road. Turn left and drive approximately 4.5 miles to a dirt pullou on the left.*

Tulloch Reservoir Falls with Tulloch Dam in the backdrop.

Rainbow Pool Falls

Rating: 6

How Short? Drive-To

How Easy? 1

Best Time to Visit:
Year-Round

Need Information?
Contact: Stanislaus
National Forest
(209) 962-7825

Rainbow Pool Falls is located near the 3,000-foot mark in the Stanislaus National Forest. Although the falls is not comparable with any of the state's more spectacular waterfalls, one of California's best swimming holes can be found here. This large, deep pool is warm enough to swim in during the summer months and feels much like a YMCA pool, without the lifeguards, of course. It's a popular spot, and because it's part of the South Fork of the Tuolumne River, Rainbow Pools Falls flows year-round.

Only a 20-minute drive from Yosemite National Park, on hot summer days Rainbow Pool can get as crowded as the park itself. Because it's so easily accessible, many of Yosemite's visitors have heard about it. In fact, I can't think of a better swimming hole in Central California, and you can get to this one simply by walking 20 yards from your car.

With families picnicking and teenagers playing loud music, this place reminds me of a Southern California beach. Besides swimming, visitors read books in lounge chairs or lie on towels trying to catch some rays. Rainbow Pool is perfect for everyone.

And there's more. Rainbow Pool is also a popular fishing spot. Each spring and summer, the California Department of Fish and Game stocks the pool below the falls, as well as the stream above the falls, with rainbow trout. There are plenty of trout to be caught, as long as you fish in the morning or evening when people aren't jumping off the waterfall, freaking-out the fish.

Although the Forest Service keeps the day-use area clean, wear shoes in and around the water. I saw a lot of broken glass. The waterfall is a mere 20 feet tall, but can be powerful in the spring.

Rainbow Pool Falls

If you plan to make the trip, supplies are available in Groveland. The South Fork of the Tuolumne River is closed to fishing from November 16 to the last Saturday in April.

Also nearby are Carlon Falls, Middle Fork of the Tuolumne River, Yosemite National Park and Hetch Hetchy Reservoir.

Directions: *From Modesto, drive approximately 50 miles east on Highway 120 to the junction with Highway 108. Veer right, staying on Highway 120, and continue to Groveland. From Highway 120 in Groveland, drive east 13 miles to the Rainbow Pool turnoff. Continue a quarter-mile to the river.*

Diana Falls

Rating: 5

How Short? 1.0 Mile

How Easy? 1

Best Time to Visit:
February to September

Need Information?
Contact: Stanislaus
National Forest
(209) 962-7825

When anglers think of Bean Creek, they think of a place that used to provide great springtime trout fishing; that is, before the California Department of Fish and Game stopped stocking it in 1996. When waterfall lovers think of Bean Creek, they think of little Diana Falls.

Diana is a small waterfall, almost exclusively visited by locals, at 3,000 feet in the Stanislaus National Forest, near Greeley Hill, Coulterville and Groveland. Although the waterfall is on the way to Yosemite National Park, most of the park's visitors don't even consider a trip to Diana, not when they can drive another 45 minutes east and see Yosemite, Vernal and Nevada, some of the world's best waterfalls.

Diana Falls in early summer

The locals are happy Diana Falls isn't a main tourist attraction. It gives them a chance to enjoy their own little waterfall, without having to put up with the lines and traffic found in Yosemite National Park.

The hike to Diana Falls is effortless. Walk from your car through the gate and follow the North Fork of the Merced River a little more than four-tenths of a mile. Where Bean Creek meets up with the Merced, make a right, following Bean Creek. In less than 100 yards, Diana Falls will be on the left.

Diana Falls is an 18-foot drop off a granite ledge, fed by a stream that flows year-round. It's not the world's fifth tallest waterfall like Yosemite Falls, but if you need a quiet place in the outdoors to relax, it'll work. Just make sure not to show up after school gets out, because it's tough to unwind with kids splashing around in the water.

If you plan to make the trip, supplies are available at Greeley Hill Market.

Also nearby are Jordan Pond, Bull Creek and Rainbow Pool Falls.

Directions: *At the junction of Highways 49 and 132 in Coulterville, take Greeley Hill Road (Road J-20) east 10 miles. Stay on Greeley Hill Road as it bears south, splitting off from Road J-20. Drive 4.2 miles on Greeley Hill Road stopping just before you come to a one-lane bridge. Park in the pullout on the left side of the road. Cross the road and pick up the trailhead behind the gated dirt road.*

Sonora Pass Falls

Rating: 7

How Short? Drive-To

How Easy? 1

Best Time to View:
May to July

Need Information?
Contact: Toiyabe
National Forest
(760) 932-7070

With a 26 percent grade, Sonora Pass is the steepest paved pass in California. Runner up only to Tioga Pass, Sonora is also the second highest pass (9,624 feet) in the state. This winding passageway, which Highway 108 meanders through, marks the boundary of Tuolumne and Mono Counties, and is also quite rich in history.

The Sonora Pass Route, also known as the Old Emigrant Trail, was first traversed in 1852 by a wagon train known as the Clark-Skidmore Company. This was one of the few available routes for early settlers migrating west over the Sierra.

While there are many notable landmarks in the vicinity of the pass, few sightseers, if any, know about one of the most graceful points of interest. Unnamed and not shown on most maps, Sonora Pass Falls has a short lifespan, and because of its limited resources of watershed, you wont be able to find it if you arrive after July. Regrettably, the stream will most likely have dried up.

Viewing the waterfall is effortless. Your car does the hard work and elevation gain. Because there is no roadside parking on the south side of the road, you'll need to park on the north side where there is enough room for about three vehicles. Then, carefully walk across Highway 108 and you'll have no trouble locating the 40-foot freefall as it spills off the mountainside dropping below your view.

If you plan to make the trip supplies are available in Bridgeport and Dardanelle. Highway 108 closes in the winter and early spring. Call ahead for updated road conditions.

Also nearby are Sonora Pass, Leavitt Falls and Sardine Falls.

Directions: From Highway 395 in Bridgeport, drive 17 miles north to Highway 108 and turn left. Continue 14.7 miles to a dirt pullout on the right.

The Stanislaus River flows through Leavitt Meadow a short distance from Sonora Pass Falls.

Sardine Falls

Rating: 6

How Short? Drive-To

How Easy? 1

Best Time to View:
May to July

Need Information?
Contact: Toiyabe
National Forest
(760) 932-7070

Time is always of essence, and in the case of Sardine Falls you need to make a quick decision on how much of it you have to spare. Sardine can be seen two ways; from afar along Highway 108 or from its base, requiring a short, yet rewarding hike. The decision is entirely up to you.

If you choose to take the easy way out and snap a few photos from your car, there are two great spots to stop. The first is a pullout along Sardine Meadow, exactly 12.4 miles from the turnoff to Highway 108 from Highway 395. A more elevated perspective can be attained by continuing three-tenths of a mile west to another pullout. Don't expect to be awed from these pullouts. Keep in mind you are at least one mile from Sardine.

For those who enjoy flat strolls through the wilderness a trip to Sardine's base is a must. If not for the 70-foot waterfall, come for the wildflowers and lush forested surroundings. Although a few stream crossings are required, the walk at 9,000 feet in the Toiyabe National Forest is an easy one and best of all; you don't have to worry about getting lost because you can see the waterfall from the road. To reach Sardine, walk through Sardine Meadow, cross Sardine Creek and continue towards the waterfall. There are several paths that lead towards the falls, take any of them. The next landmark to look for is Mc Kay Creek because Sardine Falls is on Mc Kay, not Sardine Creek. Once you reach Mc Kay continue upstream to the falls.

If you plan to make the trip, supplies are available in Bridgeport and Dardanelle. Highway 108 closes in the winter and early spring. Call ahead for updated road conditions.

Also nearby are Sonora Pass, Leavitt Falls and Sonora Pass Falls.

Directions: *From Highway 395 in Bridgeport, drive 17 miles north to Highway 108 and turn left. Continue 12.4 miles to a dirt pullout on the side of the road.*

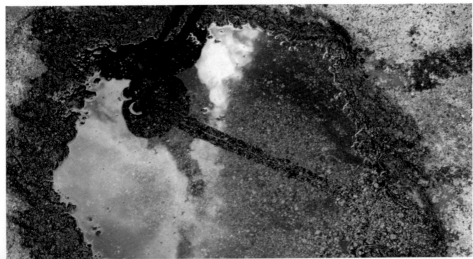

Reflections near Sardine Falls can be remarkable.

Leavitt Falls

Rating: 7

How Short? Drive-To

How Easy? 1

Best Time to View:
May to September

Need Information?
Contact: Toiyabe
National Forest
(760) 932-7070

At 7,700 feet in the Toiyabe National Forest just east of Sonora Pass, Leavitt is a dramatic freefall, plummeting more than 400 feet off a rugged, steep and rocky mountainside. Unfortunately, only about a 100-foot section of the falls can be seen. Much of the rest is hidden beneath pines and comprised of dozens of smaller cascades.

The fortunate thing about Leavitt Falls is that it's a drive-to waterfall and no hiking is required to view it. However, the unfortunate thing is that from the waterfall overlook Leavitt appears to be just average.

Leavitt is much better than your average waterfall. However, the only way to realize this is with a telephoto lens or a pair of binoculars. Don't get me wrong, it's still worth a trip, yet if there were a trail creeping you closer to the falls, this waterfall would be rated a nine.

A tributary to the West Fork of the Walker River, Leavitt Creek is supplied by a medium-size watershed, therefore keeping a sufficient amount of volume year-round. Snowmelt originates at the 11,569-foot Leavitt Peak and with aid from overflow out of Leavitt, Ski, Koenig and Latopic Lakes the creek gains volume and descends toward Highway 108, where it gains capacity when Sardine Creek pours into it. Two miles downstream of this point, Leavitt makes its' dramatic plunge.

If you plan to make the trip supplies are available in Bridgeport and Dardanelle. Highway 108 closes in the winter and early spring. Call ahead for updated road conditions.

Leavitt Falls in November of 2002.

Also nearby are Sonora Pass, Sonora Pass Falls and Sardine Falls.

Directions: *From Highway 395 in Bridgeport, drive 17 miles north to Highway 108 and turn left. Continue 8.8 miles to the signed turnoff for the falls. Turn left into the parking area.*

Region 2 Central Coast (North)

Uvas Park Falls
Tip Toe Falls
Pomponio Falls
Castle Rock Falls
Sempervirens Falls
Silver Falls and Golden Cascad
Berry Creek Falls
Maple Falls
Five Finger Falls

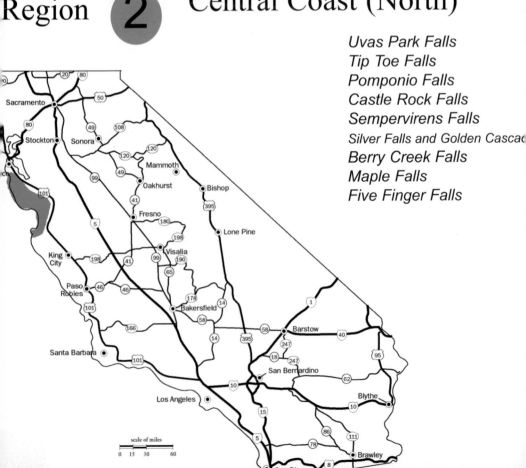

Uvas Park Falls

Rating: 5
How Short? 1.0 Mile
How Easy? 1
Best Time to View: December to May
Need Information? Contact: Uvas Canyon Park (408) 779-9232, Santa Clara County Parks and Recreation (408) 358-3741

If you have children who aren't able to endure long hikes, about 20 minutes from Morgan Hill, Uvas County Park is a perfect destination. By taking the fairly easy one-mile loop that follows Swanson Creek the entire way, you'll pass three small waterfalls. This short trail will hold your children's attention without tiring them out. For a brief afternoon outing in the wilderness, this hike can't be beat.

Shaded by a canopy of oaks, Douglas firs and laurels, the hike begins on a dirt road adjacent to Black Rock Group Area. It gradually ascends about 100 yards before coming to a fork. The left fork leads to Alec Canyon and Triple Falls. Stay right, continuing on the Waterfall Loop Trail that becomes a single-track trail.

The path crosses the stream and makes a pit stop at Upper Falls, a 15-foot cascade, before arriving at Basin Falls. Also a cascade, but fed by a different creek, Basin is only about 50 yards to the right of Upper Falls and is about 10 feet taller. The largest waterfall along the loop is Black Rock Falls.

After passing Basin, the path guides you downhill past Black Rock Falls. The falls is on the right, however, from this point, you can only see the lower portion, an unimpressive 20-foot cascade. Follow a trail spur up the canyon on your left, and 10 yards beyond the lower section, Upper Black Rock Falls spills 30 feet over a dark rock face. Because it's nearly a vertical drop, this waterfall is the most impressive on the loop.

Black Rock Falls

The path loops back to Black Rock Group Area, but there are two other waterfalls in the park for those who can handle a little more hiking. Triple Falls is a mile uphill from the group area, and downstream is Uvas Falls, but a landslide covered most of this waterfall.

If you plan to make the trip, supplies are available in Boulder Creek. There is a day-use fee.

Also nearby are Uvas Reservoir, Chesbro Reservoir and Calero Reservoir.

Directions: *From the 101 Freeway in Gilroy, drive north to Morgan Hill and exit Cochran. Turn left on Cochran to Monterey Highway and turn left. Drive to Watsonville Road and turn right. Take Watsonville to Uvas Road (G8) and turn right. Drive past Uvas Reservoir and turn left on Croy Road. Continue 4.4 miles to Uvas Canyon Park.*

Tip Toe Falls

Rating: 3

How Short? 1.3 Miles

How Easy? 1

Best Time to View:
December to June

Need Information?
Contact: Portola
Redwood State Park
(650) 948-9098

If you're planning a trip to Portola Redwood State Park for the sole purpose of viewing Tip Toe Falls, you won't be satisfied. If you're interested in a relaxing day among a redwood grove, however, the trip is well worth it.

Tip Toe Falls is listed and classified as a waterfall, yet its lack of size would typically keep it out of this book. Why did I decide to include the six-foot Tip Toe? For two reasons: first, the state park includes the waterfall on their park maps, and many visitors come here expecting to see a waterfall. Secondly, by inviting you to see this waterfall, you'll be able to enjoy the redwood grove that surrounds it.

Setting aside Tip Toe's lack of merit as a waterfall, the hike through the redwood forest is quite rewarding. It gives you glimpses of giant redwoods and a chance to see banana slugs that can grow up to four inches long. Although there are several trails that lead to the falls, I'm going to send you the shortest, easiest way. For longer loop trips, stop by the visitor center and pick up a park map.

Driving into the park, continue past the visitor center, following signs to the campfire center. Park in the dirt lot between the picnic tables and the campfire center. To get to the trailhead, walk along the service road past the campfire center to the signed path for Tip Toe Falls on the right. The Tip Toe marker is a few yards past a sign on the right side of the service road that reads, "Service Area, Authorized Vehicles Only,".

Shaded by oaks, redwoods and Douglas Firs, the trail begins with a brief uphill climb, before winding to the right and descending to Pescadero Creek. During the winter and spring, you'll have to rock-hop across the creek. In the summer, the park installs footbridges to aid in crossing the stream. The stream crossing is a half-mile from the campfire center, and after traversing it, you'll be faced with a decision. Veer away from signs to the park office, which puts you on the Iverson Trail. Take the left fork and go a tad more than one-tenth of a mile to the falls, crossing Mill Creek once along the way.

Tip Toe Falls

Located on Mill Creek, Tip Toe Falls cascades into a clear pool. The rock walls on both sides of the falls are dotted with ferns and various kinds of moss. The falls is shaded by tall trees that also keep the streambed cool.

Just upstream, there is another waterfall about the same size as Tip Toe. I wouldn't

waste any time climbing up the right side of the falls to reach it, though. The view of the upper falls, which is about eight feet tall, is obstructed by at least a half-dozen fallen trees. When I last visited in mid-April, a swarm of mosquitoes attacked me near the base of the upper falls, so I didn't make it any further upstream.

If you plan to make the trip, supplies are available in Saratoga. There is a day-use fee.

Big Basin Mule Deer

Also nearby are Pomponio Falls, Castle Rock Falls, San Lorenzo River, Loch Lomond Reservoir, Berry Falls, Golden Falls, Cascade Falls, Silver Falls and Sempervirens Falls.

Directions: *From the junction of the 101 and 17 Freeways in San Jose, drive south on the 17 Freeway past Campbell and exit Highway 9 (Saratoga Avenue). Follow Highway 9 through Saratoga to Highway 35 (Skyline Road). Turn right and continue to Alpine Road. Turn left and drive to Portola State Park Road. Turn left and drive to the state park.*

Banana Slugs are common on the path to Tip Toe Falls.

Pomponio Falls

Rating: 5

How Short? 0.25 Miles

How Easy? 1

Best Time to View:
December to May

Need Information?
Contact: Memorial
Visitor Center (650)
879-0212, San Mateo
County Parks
(650) 363-4020

Coastal redwoods thrive along the West Coast's fog belt, which stretches from Southern Oregon down to California's Central Coast. There are hundreds of parks along the coast where redwood groves can be seen. Most of them attract large crowds who come solely to be awed by the giant trees.

Set in a redwood grove along Pescadero Creek, Memorial County Park doesn't get mobbed the way many of the other state parks in the region do. Bay Area residents looking for a few hours respite from nearby city life, or even for a weekend camping trip, account for most of the park's visitors. And they are often satisfied. Not just by the redwood grove, but by Pescadero Creek and Pomponio Falls, as well.

If you're used to seeing a lot of waterfalls, Pomponio probably won't put a sparkle in your eye. Most Bay Area folks, however, aren't accustomed to waterfalls. And since their main purpose here is to see redwoods, viewing Pomponio's 30-foot cascade as it spills off a steep rock face into Pescadero Creek is often a delightful surprise.

There are a few ways to reach the falls. The easiest is by driving along the park access road towards Sequoia Campground. Just after driving over Pescadero Creek, park off the road. (When the rangers won't allow you to park alongside the road, leave your car in the amphitheater parking lot and walk down to the access road.) Roughly 30 yards uphill, a trail spur guides you down the hill on the right. Follow the spur 20 yards to Pescadero Creek. The waterfall is directly in front of you, across Pescadero. In the winter and spring, when the water levels are high, plan on getting wet crossing the creek.

To reach the brink of the falls, start at the entrance kiosk and walk two-tenths of a mile west, where Pomponio Creek crosses under the highway. You can drive here, but no parking is permitted along this stretch of the road. Just past where the Pomponio flows under the highway, there is a trail that works its way to a bridge at the falls' brink. The trail can be picked up on the south side of the road. There are also several loop trails within the park that pass by the falls.

With a visitor center, campgrounds, picnic areas, showers and hiking trails, Memorial County Park is an ideal family destination. There are a few noteworthy sites to look for while in the park. Where Pescadero Creek crosses under the park's access road, there is a fish ladder that enables steelhead to continue their seasonal runs upstream. Also, the high watermark from the El Nino season in 1998 can be seen 20 yards upstream from the ladder. It's amazing how high the water levels rose.

If you plan to make the trip, supplies are available in La Honda. There is a day-use fee to enter the county park.

Also nearby are Castle Rock Falls, Tip Toe Falls and Sempervirens Falls.

Directions: From Highway 1 in Santa Cruz, drive north to San Gregorio and turn right on Highway 84. Take Highway 84 to Pescadero Road and turn right. Drive 5.4 miles to Memorial County Park on the left.

Castle Rock Falls

Rating: 4

How Short? 1.6 Miles

How Easy? 2

Best Time to View:
December to May

Need Information?
Contact: Castle Rock
State Park
(408) 867-2952

When it comes to state parks, the Santa Cruz Mountains between Monterey Bay and the San Francisco Bay are full of them. Most of these parks, however, aren't known for stunning waterfalls. Instead, outdoor lovers come for the redwood groves, and hikers, mountain bikers and horseback riders enjoy hundreds of miles of trails.

Though each park has one or two waterfalls, few of these falls compare to the state's best. What the parks lack in the waterfall category, however, they make up for with spectacular views. Located in Castle Rock State Park, less than an hour from both the Monterey and San Francisco Peninsulas, the view from the brink of Castle Rock Falls is one of the best in the region.

Because you can only hike to the brink of the falls, it isn't an awe-inspiring experience, at least not from that vantage. What attracts visitors here is the great view from the wooden platform at the falls' overlook, a short and easy eight-tenths of mile walk from the parking area. This overlook offers a spectacular panorama of the San Lorenzo Valley and the rolling hills that surround it. Best of all, it doesn't take an entire day to complete the hike. It can be done in as little as 30 minutes.

Because there is a walk-in campsite 2.8 miles in, hikers and backpackers share the trail to the falls. But a "must" trip for those who have the time and energy is the 31-mile one-way hike to Waddle Beach, which is along the shore of the Pacific Ocean near Big

Basin State Park.

The single-track dirt path to the falls is much shorter. In the parking lot, there is a signed trailhead for the Castle Rock and Saratoga Gap Trails. Follow the Saratoga Gap Trail through a heavily shaded wooded forest, populated with Douglas firs,

Pomponio Falls from across Pescadero Creek

Steep cliffs make reaching the base of Castle Rock Falls difficult

31

madrones, bay laurels, canyon live oaks, coastal oaks and tanbark oaks.

A few-hundred yards in, a trail spur breaks off to the left, heading towards Castle Rock, three-tenths of a mile away. Stay on the main trail, continuing along a streambed on the right, which will either be dry or nearly dry. In fewer than 10 minutes, the stream merges with another stream that flows down from a canyon on the right. This stream forms the headwaters of Kings Creek and is also responsible for creating Castle Rock Falls.

Shortly after this confluence, comes to the first and only stream crossing. Using a footbridge to cross the five-foot wide streambed, you'll arrive at the final trail junction. The right fork winds to Goat Rock. Stay left, following the signs for Castle Rock Falls, two-tenths of a mile away. After a gradual descent, the trail flattens out as it nears the overlook. About 25 yards from the junction, there is a lone redwood tree along the path. Continue past it to the overlook.

Kings Creek flows year-round, spilling off a sandstone rim and cascading nearly 70 feet down the face. A signboard in the parking lot lists the height of the falls between 60 and 80 feet, which looks to be right on target. Don't think about attempting to scramble to the base without rappelling gear. The cliffs are nearly vertical and impossible to scale without proper equipment. Remember, you came for the view, not the falls.

If you plan to make the trip, supplies are available in Saratoga. There is a day-use fee to park in the Castle Rock State Park parking lot. Parking along the highway is free.

Also nearby are Pomponio Falls, Tip Toe Falls, San Lorenzo River, Loch Lomond Reservoir, Berry Falls, Golden Cascade, Silver Falls and Sempervirens Falls.

Directions: *From the junction of the 101 and 17 Freeways in San Jose, drive south on the 17 Freeway past Campbell and exit Highway 9 (Saratoga Avenue). Follow Highway 9 through Saratoga to Highway 35 (Skyline Road). Turn left and drive 2.5 miles to Castle Rock State park on the right.*

The brink of Castle Rock Falls as seen from the wooden overlook.

Sempervirens Falls

Rating: 6

How Short? Drive-To

How Easy? 1

Best Time to View:
December to June

Need Information?
Contact: Big Basin
State Park
(831) 338-8860

It had been a long day. Taking the route from Waddle Beach in Big Basin State Park, a friend and I had already hiked to Berry, Silver and Cascade Falls, done a little fishing at Loch Lomond Reservoir and fished the San Lorenzo River. But the fun wasn't over yet. We had one more waterfall to visit.

Hiking to Berry Falls, we ran into a group of backpackers who told us there was another waterfall in Big Basin State Park. They told us they read about it in a book a few years ago, and although they didn't remember its name, they did recall that it could be reached via a trail near the visitor center. They said the trail was about four miles long.

Did I mention it was a cold rainy day and our clothes were already soaked? We weren't thrilled about another hike. Listening to my shoes slush with each step, I walked over to the visitor center and asked a park ranger if there was a waterfall nearby. Sure enough, he said there was.

"How long will it take us to get there?" I asked.

"About three minutes." He could tell that this answer had me a bit mystified. "You guys weren't planning on hiking there, were you?" He glanced at my trekking poles hanging from my backpack. "There's no reason to walk. You can drive."

That was precisely what I wanted to hear. We took off all our rain gear, put on dry clothes and drove to the falls.

Although many hikers think the only way to reach Sempervirens is by foot, that's just a myth. Actually, it's the easiest waterfall to reach in the park, only a short drive from the visitor center. After driving a half-mile from the visitor center (towards Boulder Creek), turn left at the second road on the left. The road goes to Huckleberry, Wastahi and Sky Meadow Campgrounds.

Sempervirens Falls

Follow the road 1.1 miles to a dirt pullout on the right. There is only enough room for two cars there, so if the pullout is full, continue about 100 yards to a pullout on the left. Sempervirens Creek Falls can be seen by looking down in the canyon that's to the right of the first pullout. There's a trail that takes you to a wooden platform at the base of the falls.

The waterfall plunges roughly 20 feet, landing in a deep clear pool, ideal for swimming. Most of the year, however, the water is too cold to swim in. Although the hillsides are covered with ferns, Sempervirens, which is another name for a coastal redwood, got its name because redwoods line most of Sempervirens Creek.

For those who prefer to hike to the falls, park near the visitor center and pick up the Sequoia Trail near the center. The trail passes through Jay and Wastahi Campgrounds. Soon after passing Wastahi, a signed trail breaks away from the Sequoia Trail and continues to the falls.

If you plan to make the trip, supplies are available in Boulder Creek.

Also nearby are Berry Falls, Golden Cascade, Silver Falls, San Lorenzo River and Loch Lomond Reservoir.

Directions: *From Santa Cruz, drive 23 miles east on Highway 9 to the city of Boulder Creek. In Boulder Creek, turn left on Highway 236 and drive approximately nine miles to the Big Basin State Park Visitor Center. At the visitor center, backtrack a half-mile to the second turnoff on the left. Turn left and drive 1.1 miles to a dirt pullout on the left.*

Silver Falls and Golden Cascade

Rating: 8

How Short? 13.5 Miles

How Easy? 3

Best Time to View:
December to July

Need Information?
Contact: Big Basin
State Park (831) 338-
8860, Backpacking
Reservations
(831) 338-8861

Don't get caught up in the assumption that Silver Falls and Golden Cascade are going to be as dramatic and heart pounding as Berry Creek Falls, because there are few waterfalls in the state that can successfully accomplish that feat. However, Silver Falls and Golden Cascade do have unique characteristics that Berry doesn't, namely, colorful rock formations that make even geologists salivate and fern filled canyon walls that draw botanist's from all over the state to see these plants in their native state.

Located shortly upstream from Berry, the first cataract you come to is Silver Falls. While Silver does not astonish you with colorful rocks, it does make a bold impression from the get go, stamping a "wow" into your emotions at first sight. From the onset, it's the 50-foot freefall that awes you, however, soon after, the array of ferns grab your attention in this cool, damp canyon. Banana slugs and newts can be seen crawling through the ferns and wading in the stream. The only setback here is a downed tree that fell across the face of the waterfall, obstructing a clear view.

Directly upstream along Berry Creek from Silver is Golden Cascade. While this waterfall itself isn't inspiring, its characteristics are. The cascade's orange and tan colors are addicting and will prompt you to return year after year. Park rangers gave me two explanations for this phenomenon. The first is that brown algae grows on the sandstone giving it an orange, tan color. The other was that the rock underlying West Fork of Berry Creek has a natural tanish color. No matter what explanation, the colors are intriguing, and coupled with the rain forest like environment felt at this gently sloped 50-foot cascade, many hikers feel like spending some time here. Day-dreaming is popular, as the hikers I saw appeared to be in "la-la" land.

Use the next write-up to get to Berry Creek Falls. Once you make it to Berry, reaching the other falls are a synch. Continue upstream along the Berry Creek Trail, climbing above Berry. In a tad more than one-tenth of a mile the stream splits, with Berry Creek breaking off to the right. Staying on the path, veer left, following the West Fork of Berry Creek. In six-tenths of a mile you'll arrive at Silver Falls. Golden Cascade is less than one-tenth of a mile upstream from Silver.

The trio can also be reached via a long, 12-mile trek from the Big Basin State Park Visitor Center. Take the Skyline to the Sea Trail to the Berry Creek Trail and then return on the Sunset Trail.

If you plan to make the trip, supplies are available in Santa Cruz and Boulder Creek.

Directions: *From Highway 1 in Santa Cruz, drive approximately 18 miles north to the* **Silver Falls**
Waddle Beach parking area on the left side of the highway.

Berry Creek Falls

Rating: 9

How Short? 12.0 Miles

How Easy? 3

Best Time to View:
December to July

Need Information?
Contact: Big Basin
State Park (831) 338-
8860, Backpacking
Reservations
(831) 338-8861

It was a cold rainy April morning along the scenic stretch of beach from Santa Cruz to Half Moon Bay. Taking advice from a few hikers we bumped into a couple days earlier, my friend Scott Wiessner and I were headed to Big Basin State Park to see Berry Creek Falls. Being from Southern California, I had never heard of the waterfall, but we were told it was the best waterfall along the Central Coast.

When we arrived at the trailhead, we weren't sure if we felt like going on a 12-mile hike in the rain and wind. At the trailhead we learned that bikes were allowed on the path for the first five miles, so we strapped on our raingear and began biking to the falls. The rain had chased away the crowds, but when we saw the falls, we were sure glad we battled the winter conditions.

Berry Creek Falls is the best waterfall along the Central Coast and better than any waterfall I've seen in Southern California. Just a notch down from the great waterfalls of Yosemite National Park, visiting Berry is a must for anybody living in the Bay Area or near Santa Cruz.

Relaxing on the wood platform directly in front of Berry, it feels like you're standing in a rain forest. This 65-foot waterfall is set under a canopy of redwoods and Douglas firs, spraying a cool mist throughout the canyon. Surrounded by moss and ferns, Berry Creek gushes off the dark rock face, creating a cool, damp, lush-green canyon below.

The journey to Berry is as a wonderful as the falls itself. On the west side of the Pacific Coast Highway, park in the dirt parking area at Waddle Beach. Checking for oncoming traffic, carefully cross the highway and walk around the locked gate on the paved service road. In a few hundred yards, the path passes by the Rancho del Oso Office on the right. Past the office, there are a horse camp and a parking area for those who have horses.

The trailhead for the Skyline to the Sea Trail is beyond the parking area. Here, the pavement turns to dirt. Shared by hikers, mountain bikers and horseback riders, the road is wide enough for two cars in most places. It angles to the right before crossing a bridge over Waddle Creek, and then cuts through farms. Once past the cultivated fields, the road begins to parallel the creek.

There are several points of interest to use as trail markers: the first is Alder Camp, a popular backpacking destination just one mile from the trailhead. Two-tenths of a mile further is Twin

Newts are common at Berry Creek Falls

Redwoods Campground. The trail is fairly level until Herbert Campground, 2.5 miles from the trailhead, where it begins to gradually ascend. Just past Herbert, a footbridge aids the crossing of the East Fork of Waddle Creek.

From just beyond the farms to the top of the falls, the scenery is remarkable. Redwoods, alders and Douglas firs shelter the path, which follows Waddle Creek the entire way. Under the canopy of trees, an undergrowth of ferns thrive in the canyon. Small tributaries pour into Waddle Creek along the way, but the most enjoyable things we encountered were the newts and banana slugs. The red brick-colored newts average four to six inches, mobbing the path on rainy days, while the yellow slugs, mostly three to four inches, can be seen clinging to the lush green hillsides.

At five miles from the outset, the dirt road ends and turns to a single track. If you rode your bike in, lock it up at the bike rack here and continue on foot. The path makes a quick stream crossing and then proceeds uphill on a narrow track, before descending back down to the creek, where it makes another stream crossing and arrives at a trail junction. The right fork is signed for the park headquarters. Stay left, following signs to Sunset Camp and Berry Falls.

In fewer than five minutes, you'll arrive at a wooden platform, which offers a fabulous view of the falls. With frothy water spilling off its brink, Berry reminds me of the artificial waterfalls at the Mirage Casino in Las Vegas, only the crowds are much lighter here.

If you plan to make the trip, supplies are available in Santa Cruz. Berry can also be reached from the park headquarters near Boulder Creek.

Also nearby are Cascade Falls, Golden Falls and Silver Falls.

Directions: From Highway 1 in Santa Cruz, drive approximately 18 miles north to the Waddle Beach parking area on the left side of the highway.

Maple Falls

Rating: 6

How Short? 6.4 Miles

How Easy? 2

Best Time to View:
December to June

Need Information?
Contact: Nisene Marks
State Park
(831) 763-7064

Hiking to Maple Falls it's hard to believe you are in California. To me, it felt like I was in the rain forest. Well, I can't be sure because I've never been to one before, but by comparing it to the footage I've seen on National Geographic Explorer, in the spring the trail to Maple Falls and the rain forest are a good match.

In Maple Fall's case, the waterfall is secondary to the feeling of being in the wilderness and a redwood forest, especially considering you are less than a mile away from the coastal urban setting of Santa Cruz.

Unfortunately, there used to be many more redwoods in Nisene Marks State Park, nevertheless, logging has been detrimental to the forest. Many of the redwoods still standing are referred to as second growth redwoods. Back in the mid 1800's the area was logged to attain wood to build houses and accommodate the population growth along the Central Coast. There is so much history in this park a college history course couldn't cover everything in a semester. Fortunately, many bridges, remnants of railroads and structures still remain for your viewing. Maple Falls just adds to the overall experience.

To help you better understand what has occurred here's a quick history lesson I learned from retired state parks ranger Jerry Wagner. Prior to the logging that occurred from the mid-1800's through 1912 redwoods thrived in Aptos Canyon, as well as several other smaller canyons nearby. The Loma Prieta Lumber Company was responsible for logging Aptos and Bridge Creeks, which both will be seen on your way to Maple Falls. In 1884, the lumber company constructed a mill where Aptos and Bridge Creeks meet. The mill spanned across Bridge Creek and allowed them to transport lumber downstream to cities along the coast via newly constructed railroad lines by the Southern Pacific Railroad. By the time the logging ended in the mid 1910's most of the redwoods had been wiped out. The majority of the lumber was sent to San Francisco to help rebuild from the devastating earthquake of 1906. The entire logging operation produced some 140 million board feet of redwood. Many artifacts from this operation can still be seen on the way to Maple Falls.

Aided by well signed trails locating the waterfall is easy. From the Porter Family Picnic Area walk around the locked gate and continue eight-tenths of a mile on the wide dirt access road to the sign for Mill Pond Road. Here a signed trail breaks off to the left. Follow the trail as it descends to and uses a wooden footbridge to cross Aptos Creek. The path then passes a wooden bench resting on the left and ascends up a few flights of wooden steps to the Porter House Site. Prior to the late Nineties many hikers took the Bridge Creek Trail at this junction; however, that route has been closed indefinitely.

The Bridge Creek Trail used to follow an old railroad track across the bottom of the valley. Unfortunately, a bridge on the path was washed out and it is not expected to be

The path to Maple Falls is clearly marked and easy to follow.

rebuilt so a detour exists. The new path climbs over the mountain, rather than around its base. Following the detour, take the Mill Pond Trail for roughly a half-mile to the junction of the Bridge Creek Trail and the Loma Prieta Grade Trail. The path ascends up and over the top of the mountain and then drops you back down to Bridge Creek, thus tying you back into the Bridge Creek Trail and the new footbridge. At the junction you can take either fork. Personally, I'd take the Bridge Creek Trail because it follows scenic Bridge Creek to the falls. If you take the Bridge Creek Trail it's 1.4 miles to the Bridge Creek Historic Site and then another half-mile upstream of the site to the falls.

If you choose to take the Loma Prieta Grade Trail: The Loma Trail continues one mile to the Hoffman Historic Site and then 1.2 miles to the Bridge Creek Historic Site before rejoining the Bridge Creek Trail. This route adds some distance to your trip.

Maple Falls isn't your stunning, heart throbbing California waterfall. It's situated in the back of a cool, damp, fern filled canyon plentiful with banana slugs and rich with overgrown plant life. The waterfall is an oozing 35-foot drop along Bridge Creek. In late winter and lasting through spring the waterfall displays some force allowing it to shoot over the sheer canyon walls. However, by June (in most years) the stream subsides, and if not going completely dry the flow turns to a trickle that sucks to the canyon walls pretty much destroying its splendor.

If you plan to make the trip, supplies are available in Santa Cruz. The road is closed from the winter gate to Porter Family Picnic Area from the first heavy rainfall in December to March 1. When the closure is in affect add 2.2 miles to your roundtrip. The closure varies depending on the severity of the winter. When the park is staffed a day-use fee is collected.

Also nearby is Five Finger Falls.

Directions: *From Highway 1 in Santa Cruz drive south and take the Aptos exit. Exiting the freeway, stay left and then turn right on Soquel Drive. Continue approximately one-half mile and turn left on Aptos Creek Road. Continue to the Porter Picnic Area.*

Maple Falls in March of 2001

Five Finger Falls

Rating: 5

How Short? 12.1 Miles

How Easy? 3

Best Time to View?
December to June

Need Information?
Contact: Nisene
Marks State Park
(831) 763-7064

How Five Finger Falls got is name is a mystery. Rather than telling you what we don't know, here's what we do know. Hence its name, Five Finger Falls doesn't have any fingers. The waterfall is located on an unnamed tributary to Aptos Creek, which is located in Nisene Marks State Park. The earliest record to the origin of the name Five Finger stems back to the late 1800's when the name was visible written in black and white on a photo of the waterfall.

Scott Wiessner poses near the origin of the Loma Prieta quake of 1989.

To set the record straight from the get go. Five Finger Falls isn't an awe inspiring waterfall with massive force and a river of water. Roll back your expectations. Five Finger Falls is a small, 20-foot tall sliver of water that compares more to a hose being used to drain a swimming pool. The best way to describe the flow is somewhere between an oversize garden hose and a fire hose. Also, the waterfall suffers from a lack of light. The falls sit in a small canyon, roughly 10 yards from Aptos Creek. The area is so thick with greenery that few solid rays of light ever peek through the canopy overhead.

The hike to the falls is far better than Five Finger itself. From the Porter Family Picnic Area walk through the locked gate and continue on Aptos Creek Fire Road for 1.6 miles to the Bottom of the Incline. Make sure your legs are stretched and continue on the fire road for another 1.2 miles to the Top of the Incline. Then trek another 2.0 miles from the Top of the Incline to the turnoff for White's Lagoon Trail on the right. Turn right and descend on the White's Lagoon Trail. In four-tenths of a mile a path to White's Lagoon breaks off to the left. Ignore it. White's Lagoon is an intermittent lagoon. It's used by mostly by migratory waterfowl.

Continue on the Big Slide Trail for 1.3 miles as it descends and ends at the Aptos Creek Trail where you'll get a great view of the canyon below. Turn left on the Aptos Creek Trail and follow the path as it drops down to Aptos Creek. Eventually you'll cross the stream and the route begins to fade in and out. It's eight-tenths of a mile from the Big Slide/Aptos Creek junction to Five Finger Falls. Don't worry about missing it.

Greenery is abundant on the path to Five Finger Falls

Keeping an eye out for a small canyon on the right continue rock-hopping upstream to the 20-foot waterfall. Keep in mind the waterfall is not on Aptos Creek. It's comes from a small tributary on your right.

To mix things up and avoid seeing the same scenery, take the Aptos Creek Trail back to your car. Fortunately, you know how to get back to the junction of the Aptos and Big Slide Trails. From this point, continue up a few switchbacks and then pass the Epicenter from the 1989, 7.1 Loma Prieta Earthquake. Keep on chugging. Soon, well 2.5 miles from the junction with the Big Slide and the Aptos Creek Trail, you'll be back on the Aptos Creek Fire Road at the Bottom of the Incline. Take a left and continue 1.6 miles to your car.

If you plan to make the trip, supplies are available in Santa Cruz. The road is closed from the winter gate to Porter Family Picnic Area from the first heavy rainfall in December to March 1. When the closure is in affect add 2.2 miles to your roundtrip. The closure varies depending on the severity of the winter. When the park is staffed a day-use fee is collected.

Also nearby is Maple Falls.

Directions: *From Highway 1 in Santa Cruz drive south and take the Aptos exit. Exiting the freeway, stay left and then turn right on Soquel Drive. Continue approximately one-half mile and turn left on Aptos Creek Road. Continue to the Porter Picnic Area.*

Region ③

Ansel Adams, John Muir and Golden Trout Wilderness

Gem Lake Falls
Garnet Lake Falls
Nydiver Falls
Shadow Creek Falls
Shadow Lake Falls
Purple Lake Falls
Minnow Creek Falls
Peter Pande Falls
Anne Lake Falls
Silver Pass Falls
Summit Lake Falls
Long Falls
N.F.of the M.F. of Tule River Falls
Volcano Falls
Grasshopper Creek Falls

Gem Lake Falls

Rating: 5

How Short? 9.0 Miles

How Easy? 4

Best Time to View:
June to July

Need Information?
Contact: Mammoth
Lakes Visitor Center
(760) 924-5500, Inyo
National Forest
Wilderness Permits
(760) 873-2483

Gem Lake's dam is the first thing most hikers notice when they hike from the Silver Lake Trailhead to Gem Lake. And it surely takes them by surprise. Who expects to see a dam built on a lake in a wilderness area? Without boring you with a long history lesson, here's the story in a nutshell:

First, Gem Lake is a real backcountry lake, as opposed to one that is totally man-made. The lake was simply enlarged back in the 1920s, when a dam was built that allowed the lake to retain more water. The added water was used to create hydroelectric power for the June Lake Loop. There were also dams built above Gem at Waugh Lake and below Gem at Agnew Lake.

Located at 9,050 feet in the Ansel Adams Wilderness, deep, emerald Gem Lake is a popular destination for day hikers, who often stumble upon Gem Lake Falls. As Rush Creek enters the lake on its west shoreline, it feeds this cascade. Viewing the falls, however, can be a little tricky.

Rush Creek gets its origins from water flowing out of Marie, Rodgers and Davis Lakes; it then enters Waugh Lake, where its releases are controlled by the Waugh Lake Dam. So, in order to experience the thundering roar of Gem Lake Falls as it empties into Gem Lake, crashing against granite boulders, you'll have to come when water is being released from Waugh Lake. Unfortunately, it's difficult to predict exactly when this is going to happen, however, it occurs fairly consistently from June through August.

You don't need to be an expert backcountry hiker to reach Gem Lake Falls, but you do need to be in shape, because the path gains nearly 2,000 feet over the 4.5 miles to the falls. Pick up the trail near Silver Lake, the path wastes no time before climbing uphill, offering breathtaking views of Silver. It then angles off to the right, climbing to Agnew Lake. The path bends around the north side of Agnew Lake above its dam, and then on to Gem's east shore. It then bends to the right, winding around Gem Lake.

After about four miles comes a trail junction. The right fork climbs over Gem Pass. Continue straight towards the Billy Lakes and Gem Lake Falls. You'll first come to Billy Lakes, then the falls, a mere half-mile from the junction. This 50-foot tall roaring cascade consists mostly of whitewater.

If you plan to make the trip, supplies are available at Silver Lake. A wilderness permit is required for overnight travel in the Ansel Adams Wilderness.

Also nearby are Agnew Lake, Waugh Lake, the Clark Lakes, Sullivan Lake, Weber Lake, Billy Lakes and the June Lake Loop.

Directions: *From Bishop, drive north on Highway 395 to the June Lakes Loop turnoff. Turn left and drive approximately seven miles to the trailhead, located across from Silver Lake.*

Gem Lake Falls can be seen as a white sliver of water feeding into the lake in the center of the picture. This photo was taken more than two miles away from the falls.

Garnet Lake Falls

Rating: 8

How Short? 14.2 Miles

How Easy? 4

Best Time to View:
June to July

Need Information?
Contact: Mammoth
Lakes Visitor Center
(760) 924-5500, Red's
Meadow Pack Station
(760) 934-2345 or
(800) 292-7758, Inyo
National Forest
Wilderness Permits
(760) 873-2483

Garnet Lake is one of the most popular backpacking and fishing destinations in the Ansel Adams Wilderness. Also offering to many families prized camping spots in the summer, this 212–acre backcountry playground is often pictured on postcards and calendars. Most hikers reach the lake by hiking the River Trail from the Agnew Meadow Trailhead to the Shadow Lake Trail. After passing Shadow Lake, they typically follow the John Muir Trail to Garnet Lake; however, by doing this, they miss out on seeing Garnet Lake Falls. Most hikers are unaware of the path to the falls.

Garnet Lake Falls

Garnet Lake Falls is worth a trip, even though it's not the main attraction in this section of the wilderness, which is best known for its glacier-carved lakes filled with hungry brook and rainbow trout, as well as snow capped mountains and vistas that make photographers salivate. Although the falls can be worked in as a day hike, due to the hike's 1,300-foot elevation gain, most would rather plan a backpacking trip through the region to see it.

Located about 50 yards east of Garnet Lake's outlet stream, Garnet Lake Falls is fed by runoff from the lake. Backpackers unable to find a camping spot around the lake often stumble upon the falls on the way to Altha Lake, where more camping sites can be found. The falls is a 50-foot cascade that tumbles out of Garnet's outlet pool and crashes against large granite boulders on its way to the San Joaquin River. The falls has a lot of force in June and July, but the roar it produces when pounding against the boulders often dissipates by mid-summer.

To get to Garnet Lake Falls from the Agnew Meadow Trailhead, follow 1.8 miles along the River Trail to a junction just past Olaine Lake. At this junction, leave the River Trail and take the left fork signed for the "Shadow Lake Trail." The path crosses the San Joaquin River ascends short switchbacks before passing Shadow Lake Falls and Shadow Lake.

In 1.9 miles the Shadow Lake Trail meets the JM Trail. Continue nine-tenths of a mile on the Shadow Lake/ JM Trail to another junction. The left fork leads to Ediza Lake; stay right, following the JM Trail 2.5 miles uphill to Garnet's outlet pool. Leaving the JM Trail, bear right towards Altha Lake and the River Trail. In fewer than 100 yards, Garnet Falls will be on the left.

If you plan to make the trip, supplies are available at Red's Meadow Resort and in Mammoth Lakes. Minaret Road usually doesn't open until late June. Call ahead for updated road conditions. No vehicular traffic is permitted from 7:30 a.m. to 5:30 p.m. Exceptions apply only to those who have campground reservations or reservations at Red's Meadow Resort. Those who arrive during the restricted hours must ride a shuttle into the valley. There is a fee to ride the shuttle and enter the park. Road restrictions run from late June through Labor Day. A Wilderness Permit is required for overnight travel in the Ansel Adams Wilderness.

Also nearby are Ruby Lake, Emerald Lake, Clarice Lake, Laura Lake, Altha Lake, Thousand Island Lake, Shadow Lake and Shadow Creek Falls.

Directions: From Highway 395 in Mammoth, exit west on Mammoth Lakes Road and drive three miles to Minaret Road. Turn right and drive approximately 7.9 miles on Highway 203/Minaret Rd. to the trailhead on your right.

Nydiver Falls

Rating: 7

How Short? 11.2 Miles

How Easy? 4

Best Time to View:
June to August

Need Information?
Contact: Mammoth
Lakes Visitors Center
(760) 924-5500,
Devil's Postpile
National Monument
(760) 872-4881
(Winter) or (760) 934-
2289, Red's Meadow
Pack Station
(760) 934-2345 or
(800) 292-7758, Inyo
National Forest
Wilderness Permits
(760) 873-2483

As the famous saying goes, "The journey is greater than the inn." At Nydiver Falls, this is the definitely case. Although the waterfalls aren't the greatest, the trip to them includes visits to two other waterfalls, spectacular panoramas of towering snow-capped peaks and deep, clear high-country lakes. Add to that the fresh mountain air, which can only be described as fantastic, and you have an unbeatable combination.

Fed by runoff from the three Nydiver Lakes and set in a basin below Banner Peak and Mt. Ritter, these glacier-carved lakes are some of the most magnificent in the Sierra. As stellar as the lakes may be, however, the view offered from the surrounding mountains actually surpasses their splendor. Walking to any of the peaks southwest of Lower Nydiver Lake, you can see Iceberg Lake, Ediza Lake, Cabin Lake, Shadow Creek, Shadow Lake and Mammoth Mountain in the distance. It's truly one of the best vistas in the Sierra.

Upper Nydiver Falls

There are three waterfalls along Nydiver Creek. Just below Lower Nydiver Lake, Upper Nydiver Falls is a 40-foot cascade that glides down smooth granite and plunges off a ledge into a four-foot deep pool with clear turquoise water. It would be an ideal swimming hole if the water weren't so cold.

Follow Nydiver Creek downstream, and in a few hundred yards you'll come to Middle Falls. Middle Nydiver is a 20-foot cascade. The creek washes over a boulder that splits it into two streams, which then cascade down a wall of granite protrusions.

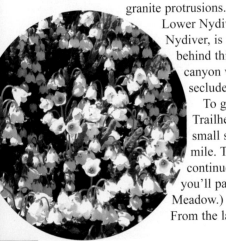

Lower Nydiver, a quarter-mile downstream from Middle Nydiver, is my favorite of the three falls. You can actually walk behind this 30-foot freefall, because it shoots out from the canyon walls. Behind the wall of water, you'll get the cool, secluded feeling of standing in a cave.

To get to the Nydiver Falls, from the Agnew Meadow Trailhead follow the Shadow Lake Trail, crossing two small streams. You'll reach a junction in four-tenths of a mile. The left fork goes to Red's Meadow. Stay right and continue 1.2 miles to Olaine Lake. (On the way to the lake you'll pass another trail junction that also takes you to Red's Meadow.)

From the lake, continue on the Shadow Lake Trail, crossing a small stream, until you come to another junction. Stay left, veering away from the River Trail. Use a footbridge to cross the San Joaquin River and begin to climb up some fairly easy switchbacks. Near the top of the switchbacks, is a glimpse of Shadow Lake Falls on your left. Continue on the trail past the falls to Shadow Lake.

Following the trail to the north end of Shadow, another junction will appear. The left fork breaks off to Rosalie Lake, Johnston Lake and Devil's Postpile National Monument. Stay right. Follow the Shadow Lake/John Muir Trail about a mile to another junction. This time veer left onto the Ediza Lake Trail. Parallel Shadow Creek, pass Shadow Creek Falls and climb over two small mountains, each with short switchbacks, before coming to the first stream crossing since there was a bridge allowing passage of the stream near Shadow Lake's inlet. This is Nydiver Creek.

A faint trail that often disappears leads to the lake. The easiest way to avoid getting lost is to follow the creek to the lakes. After 10 minutes, the stream forks. Take the left fork, which passes by the three falls and ends at Lower Nydiver Lake. Total distance from the Ediza Trail is about a half-mile. The Middle and Upper Nydiver Lakes are directly above Lower Nydiver.

If you plan to make the trip, supplies are available at Red's Meadow Resort and Mammoth Lakes. Trail and road restrictions for Garnet Lake Falls also apply to Nydiver Falls.

Also nearby are Ediza Lake, Olaine Lake, Cabin Lake, Devils Postpile National Monument and Starkweather Lake.

Directions: From Highway 395 in Mammoth, turn west on Mammoth Lakes Road and continue three miles to Minaret Road. Turn right and drive 7.9 miles on Highway 203/Minaret Rd to the trailhead on your right.

Lower Nydiver Falls

Middle Nydiver Falls

Shadow Creek Falls

Rating: 5

How Short? 10 Miles

How Easy? 3

Best Time to View:
June to August

Need Information?
Contact: Mammoth
Lakes Visitor Center
(760) 924-5500, Red's
Meadow Pack Station
(760) 934-2345 or
(800) 292-7758, Inyo
National Forest
Wilderness Permits
(760) 873-2483

If you've reached Shadow Creek above Shadow Lake, and you haven't yet figured out why it's so difficult to obtain wilderness permits to backpack in the Ansel Adams Wilderness, stop for a second and take a look around you. The first thing you might notice in the distance are the immaculate snow-capped mountain peaks that make up the border between the Ansel Adams Wilderness and Yosemite National Park. Then, directly in front of you, you'll experience the cool, untouched beauty of Shadow Creek as it meanders through lush green meadows bristling with hundreds of wildflowers. In the early mornings and late evenings, deer and the occasional bear can be seen sipping pure water from the cold mountain stream, under the tall pines that thrive on its shores. It's the kind of picture you'd expect to find on the cover of a nature magazine, but you're lucky enough to be in the center of it.

The Ansel Adams Wilderness is one of the state's most treasured lands, and to complement the natural beauty of the high country, there are two waterfalls along Shadow Creek. Between Shadow and Ediza Lakes, Upper and Lower Shadow Creek Falls aren't particularly remarkable, in themselves. As integral parts of the already superb surroundings they'll definitely make you stop and turn your attention to the beauty with which we've been graced.

Let's first work on getting to the falls. From the Agnew Meadow Trailhead, follow the River Trail 1.8 miles to a junction, just past the small, marshy Olaine Lake. At the junction, leave the River Trail, taking the left fork signed for the Shadow Lake Trail. The path crosses the San Joaquin River and ascends up short switchbacks, before passing Shadow Lake Falls and then Shadow Lake, both on the left side of the path.

After hiking 1.9 miles from the junction with the River Trail, which includes nearly a 500-foot gain in elevation, the Shadow Lake Trail meets the John Muir Trail. Continue north on the Shadow Lake/ JM Trail, and in fewer than 50 yards, Lower Shadow Creek Falls is on the left.

Shadow Creek Falls' 40-foot cascade is the culmination of a torrential flow of water, which plummets over granite to make its final decent into Shadow Lake. The way Shadow

Creek gushes forcefully over the boulders reminds me a lot of Glen Alpine Creek Falls near Fallen Leaf Lake in the Lake Tahoe Basin. The best way to get to the base of the falls is to walk along the trail until the path becomes perpendicular to the base of the waterfall. Here, there is a trail spur that guides you to its base.

   To get to the upper falls, continue on the JM Trail, paralleling Shadow Creek for eight-tenths of a mile to the junction with the Ediza Lake Trail. Veer left, leaving the JM Trail, and continue following Shadow Creek to a 30-foot cascade on the left. Here, Shadow Creek rages over a giant slab of granite creating a powerful cascade. From this point, the turnoff for Nydiver and Ediza Lakes is a short trek upstream.

If you plan to make the trip, supplies are available at Red's Meadow Resort and in Mammoth Lakes. Road restrictions to Garnet Lake Falls also apply to Shadow Creek Falls.

Also nearby are Ruby Lake, Emerald Lake, Clarice Lake, Laura Lake, Altha Lake, Thousand Island Lake, Shadow Lake, Garnet Lake Falls and Shadow Lake Falls.

Directions: From Highway 395 in Mammoth, exit west on Mammoth Lakes Road and drive three miles to Minaret Road. Turn right and drive approximately 7.9 miles on Highway 203/Minaret Rd. to the trailhead on the right.

A short distance upstream of Shadow Creek Falls, Ediza Lake (Pictured) is one of the most scenic lakes in the Sierra.

Shadow Lake Falls

Rating: 6

How Short? 6.0 Miles

How Easy? 3

Best Time to View:
June to August

Need Information?
Contact: Use Same
Phone Numbers as
Shadow Creek Falls

Devils Postpile National Monument has several waterfalls that are main attractions, however, they tend to get crowded even during the week. Nearby Shadow Lake Falls isn't as thrilling as these other waterfalls, but it can guarantee smaller crowds and an equally satisfying outdoor experience.

The hike to Shadow Lake Falls is a short one from the Agnew Meadow Trailhead. It passes little Olaine Lake, crosses the San Joaquin River and meanders through a pine forest dappled with wildflowers. The trip can be capped off with a picnic at Shadow Lake, located just above the falls.

Shadow Lake Falls is a series of drops fed by Shadow Lake's outlet stream, Shadow Creek, which is funneled through a narrow granite gorge between the Shadow Trail and a steep mountainside. There are seven drops, totaling about 70 feet. The first and the last are freefalls, while those in between are all cascades.

Even more memorable than the falls is the view seen from its base. Looking south, you can see Mammoth Mountain, the San Joaquin River Drainage and Red's Meadow. From this vantage point at 8,700 feet in the Ansel Adams Wilderness, however, you can't see any specific landmarks in the Postpile or at Red's Meadow, because they're all hidden beneath the pines.

Now that you've made the 500-foot climb from Agnew Meadow, it's time for a break. Shadow Lake is just a few yards past the falls. This emerald high-country lake is waiting to host your picnic.

To reach Shadow Lake Falls, begin at the Agnew Meadow Trailhead and follow the River Trail east, passing Olaine Lake on the left. After 1.8 miles, veer left onto the Shadow Lake Trail, which crosses a footbridge over the San Joaquin River. The trail then follows a series of short switchbacks to the falls, which is on the left just before Shadow Lake.

If you plan to make the trip, supplies are available at Red's Meadow Resort and in Mammoth Lakes. Road restrictions to Garnet Lake Falls also apply to Shadow Lake Falls.

Also nearby are Nydiver Falls, Garnet Lake Falls and Shadow Creek Falls.

Directions: *From Highway 395 in Mammoth, exit west on Mammoth Lakes Road and drive three miles to Minaret Road. Turn left and drive approximately 7.9 miles on Highway 203/Minaret Rd. to the trailhead on the right.*

Shadow Lake Falls

Purple Lake Falls

Rating: 9

How Short? 34 Miles

How Easy? 4

Best Time to View:
Mid-June to August

Need Information?
Contact: Vermilion
Resort (559) 259-4000
(Summer) or (559)
855-6558 (Winter),
Sierra National Forest
(559) 297-0706 or
(559) 855-5360, High
Sierra Ranger Station
(559) 877-7173

Even in the backcountry, crowds can be a problem, especially on the John Muir and Pacific Crest Trails in the Sierra high country. Once you leave these major trails, however, solitude can be attained. You can find out for yourself by traveling to Purple Lake Falls between Edison Lake and Red's Meadow in the John Muir Wilderness.

Located along the JM/PCT Trail, Purple Lake can get crowded with backpackers at night. Unfortunately, most of these backpackers stay the night at Purple Lake and never realize there is a waterfall just a short walk away. Hidden on a trail that descends from Purple Lake to Fish Creek, Purple Lake Falls is located just off the JM/PCT Trail.

Directly across from Minnow Creek Falls, at 9,400 feet in the John Muir Wilderness, Purple Lake Falls, formed by Purple Lake's outlet stream, stands roughly 700 feet tall; however, like Minnow, much of its drop is obscured by tall pines. Purple Lake Falls is a grand drop, creating a thunderous roar as it tumbles down a granite mountainside, surging from Purple Lake's basin into Cascade Valley. Closely resembling Horsetail Falls near the Desolation Wilderness and the Lake Tahoe Basin, the waterfall is best viewed from the mountainside west of Fish Creek, where it looks like a white sliver of light that stretches up to the pine line and races down a gigantic slab of granite.

Purple Lake Falls

No matter which way you approach the journey to the falls, it's going to take some time. As with Minnow Creek Falls, Purple can be reached from either Red's Meadow or Edison Lake. Because it is more scenic, I'd choose the path from Edison. Following the directions in the following write-up about Minnow Creek Falls, pass the junction to Ira Hot Springs and Beetle Bug Lake, and then slowly work your way down a series of steep switchbacks. Halfway down the mountain, the canopy of trees thins, opening to a flat clearing. Perch yourself on a rock, grab some water and look across the canyon at the stunning view of Purple Lake Falls.

If you plan to make the trip, supplies are available at Vermilion Resort. Road restrictions for Silver Pass Falls also apply to Purple Lake Falls.

Also nearby are Fish Creek, Purple Lake and Minnow Creek Falls.

***Directions** to Silver Pass Falls also apply to Purple Lake Falls.*

Minnow Creek Falls

Rating: 7

How Short? 40 Miles

How Easy? 5

Best Time to View:
June to August

Need Information?
Contact: Vermilion
Resort (559) 259-4000
(Summer) or (559)
855-6558 (Winter),
Sierra National Forest
(559) 297-0706 or
(559) 855-5360, High
Sierra Ranger Station
(559) 877-7173
(Summer Only)

There is no easy way to reach Minnow Creek Falls. From Edison Lake, the waterfall is a 20-mile one-way trip, or 16.5 miles from Red's Meadow. Because of far better scenery, I recommend hiking the route from Edison, rather than taking the shorter trip from Red's Meadow. While the trip from Red's Meadow is extremely easy to navigate, the route is much dryer, passing only one lake and a few small streams. From Edison, the path travels by five lakes that directly border the trail. There are another eight lakes within a mile of the trail, giving you the option of visiting up to 13 lakes on the trip.

Now ask yourself a question before deciding to head out on this long trip: Is hiking 20 miles to a waterfall worth it? I'm going to be honest with you, Minnow Creek Falls isn't an awe-inspiring waterfall. The scenery along the way, however, offers plenty of rewards for making the decision to set out into the John Muir Wilderness.

For those in good shape, it's possible to complete the hike in a weekend; however, you're cheating yourself if you choose to do it that way. Instead, set aside a long weekend or a weeklong trip so you can enjoy the surroundings without

having to walk all day. You won't really be able to enjoy this precious wilderness by rushing through it. If you can manage to get away from work for a few days, an unforgettable trip begins at Edison Lake on the western side of the Sierra and ends at Red's Meadow, near Mammoth Lakes. The hike passes five waterfalls, including Silver Pass Falls, Anne Lake Falls, Peter Pande Falls, Minnow Creek Falls and Purple Lake Falls.

Let's concentrate on reaching Minnow Creek Falls from Edison Lake. To save space and to avoid making you read the same instructions over and over again, we'll use two of the other write-ups in this chapter to get to Grassy Lake. The write-up for Silver Pass Falls will get you to the top of Silver Pass, and the

Minnow Creek Falls, photographed here from Fish Creek

Peter Pande Falls write-up brings you from Silver Pass to Grassy.

From Grassy, continue northeast on the Minnow Creek Trail, rock-hopping over Grassy's outlet stream and then over the larger Minnow Creek. After crossing Minnow, the path winds into Jackson Meadow, before meandering down a few switchbacks to a trail junction. A trail breaks off to the left, leading to Beetle Bug Lake and Ira Bell Hot Springs. Stay right.

Over the next mile, your knees will get tested as you descend nearly 700 feet into Cascade Valley, down dozens of short but steep switchbacks. About halfway down the mountain the pines that shade the route give way to a clearing, allowing you an unobstructed view of Purple Lake Falls across the canyon. At this point you can hear Minnow Creek Falls, but can't see it because it's located 100 yards or so to the right.

At the bottom of the descent, the path comes to Fish Creek. Up until at least late July, this stream crossing is waist deep. We took off our boots and socks and held our packs up over our heads to ensure our gear would stay dry. About 100 yards after crossing Fish Creek is a trail junction. The left fork goes to Second Crossing. Stay right, following signs to Tully Hole, and continue on the trail as it begins to gain elevation again.

Just before ascending up switchbacks to Purple Lake, you'll be forced to make

another decision. Veering away from Tully Hole, steer left, heading towards Purple Lake. Halfway up the switchbacks, the pine canopy yields to an open meadow. Look across the canyon for a bird's-eye view of Minnow Creek Falls.

Minnow Creek Falls is roughly a 400-foot drop that spills off the rugged granite mountainside and tumbles down into Cascade Valley. In spite of this long drop, you can only see about a 100-foot section of it. The rest of the waterfall is hidden behind the pines.

If you plan to make the trip, supplies are available at Vermilion Resort. Road restrictions to Silver Pass Falls also apply to Minnow Creek Falls.

Also nearby are Wilbur May Lake, Minnow Creek, Minnie Lake, Anne Lake, Grassy Lake, Olive Lake, Purple Lake Falls, Fish Creek and Silver Pass Drainage.

Directions *to Silver Pass Falls also apply to Minnow Creek Falls.*

Peter Pande Falls

Rating: 8

How Short? 34.6 Miles

How Easy? 5

Best Time to View:
June to August

Need Information?
Contact: Vermilion
Resort (559) 259-4000
(Summer) or (559)
855-6558 (Winter),
Sierra National Forest
(559) 297-0706 or
(559) 855-5360, High
Sierra Ranger Station
(559) 877-7173

Have you ever heard of Peter Pande Lake? Let me give you a hint: it's in Central California. Still doesn't ring a bell? Here's another hint: it's on the western side of the Sierra Nevada, in the John Muir Wilderness. To be even more specific, it's in the Minnow Creek Drainage. Still stumped? Don't feel bad.

Because of its remote location in the backcountry - a tough 17.3-mile hike from Edison Lake - few people visit Peter Pande. What surprises most hikers who do come to the lake is learning there is a waterfall nearby. Don't try to find the waterfall on a topo map; it's not there. The only way to locate Peter Pande Falls without stumbling upon it is by reading the following directions carefully.

First of all, Peter Pande Falls doesn't drop into Peter Pande Lake. Rather, the waterfall is formed by Peter Pande's outlet stream. This unnamed stream that begins at Peter Pande Lake drains into a small pond and picks up speed as it flows downhill, where it finally plummets off a rounded granite cliff 100 yards downstream from Olive Lake.

Reaching the waterfall is going to take a full day. First, follow the directions in the write-up later in this chapter to Silver Pass Lake, located 11.7 miles from the trailhead at Edison Lake. From Silver Pass Lake, continue on the JM/PCT Trail, gradually climbing about a mile uphill to the top of Silver Pass. (You'll pass a small pond on your left.) The top of the pass marks the Silver Divide and also offers a stunning panorama of the Yosemite backcountry looking north.

Snow usually remains a few feet deep on the pass until late July. Don't worry about getting lost when the trail's snowed over, however, because there will be other hikers' footprints to follow downhill. You'll know you're on the right track if you first pass Warrior Lake on the right and then Chief Lake on the left.

Peter Pande Falls is easy to spot from the Olive Lake Trail

At 1.5 miles from Silver Pass Lake, less than a quarter-mile past Chief, is a trail junction. The right fork breaks away from the JM/PCT Trail; stay left, following signs to Goodale Pass. Continue past Papoose Lake, which is three-tenths of a mile from the junction. One-tenth of a mile past Papoose, at the junction with the Goodale Pass Trail, head right. Lake of the Lone Indian is three-tenths of a mile ahead.

At the middle of the west shoreline of Lake of the Lone Indian, pick up the Minnow Lake Trail, which can be difficult to find because it's unsigned. The easiest landmark to use is a small stream that enters the lake. It's about three feet wide and less than a foot deep. Gradually climbing uphill for three-tenths of a mile, the trail follows this stream to a small open sandy area guarded by tall pines.

You'll get your first view of Grassy Lake on the right when the trail winds to the left and descends below the tree line. With the help of a few switchbacks, the path twists downhill and arrives at a stream crossing. This unnamed stream is Wilbur May Lake's outlet. Just after crossing it, there's a sign for Wilbur May Lake on a tree.

Staying to the right, ignore the sign and continue eight-tenths of a mile through the wooded forest to Grassy Lake. Along the way pass the turnoff for Peter Pande Lake. From Grassy Lake, the path descends down a small hill and crosses over the lake's outlet stream. Twenty yards after the stream crossing, veer left onto the Olive Lake Trail. With Minnow Creek off to the right, tall sheer-granite cliffs overshadow the trail.

In a tad more than three-fourths of a mile, Peter Pande Falls comes into view, tumbling down the cliff on the left. Powerful in late spring and early summer, the waterfall sends a roar down the canyon as it races through a narrow crevice in the rock and crashes against a Coke machine size boulder halfway down the 150-foot cascade. From the point where it hits this boulder, the falls' single drop gets divided into two drops.

Now that you've come all this way, continue two-tenths of a mile upstream to Olive Lake and set up camp. There should still be a bit of sunlight left to catch a few rainbow trout for dinner.

If you plan to make the trip, supplies are available at Vermilion Resort. Road restrictions for Silver Pass Falls also apply to Peter Pande Falls.

Also nearby are Minnow Creek, Minnie Lake, Anne Lake and Anne Lake Falls.

Directions *to Silver Pass Falls also apply to Peter Pande Falls.*

Slightly upstream of Peter Pande Falls, Olive Lake is known for its extrodinary reflections

Anne Lake Falls

Rating: 7

How Short? 36.4 Miles

How Easy? 5

Best Time to Visit:
June to August

Need Information?
Contact: Vermilion
Resort (559) 259-4000
(Summer) or (559)
855-6558 (Winter),
Sierra National Forest
(559) 297-0706 or
(559) 855-5360, High
Sierra Ranger Station
(559) 877-7173

When it comes to splendid backcountry scenery, the Minnow Lakes Basin offers some of the best. There are clear blue lakes, snowcapped mountain peaks, lush green meadows, wildflowers and large granite outcroppings. Anne Lake Falls also adds to the basin's beauty.

As enticing as this natural beauty may sound, none of it can be reached without enduring a long and difficult hike. Because of the 500-foot elevation gain required to reach Anne Lake Falls from Grassy Lake, the hike can make you huff and puff "just a little." Yet, the trip is worth the loss of breath.

Still interested? Here's how to get to the waterfall: First, follow the directions in the previous write-up to Grassy Lake. Then, from the Minnow Lake Trail, walk nearly five-tenths of a mile south towards Wilbur May Lake to the turnoff for Peter Pande Lake. The sign is easy to locate.

The trail leads to an unnamed stream. After crossing this stream, it can be difficult to find the trail again, because the path is not marked. To avoid veering off course and getting lost, look for horse tracks and horse droppings. Pack trips that make Peter Pande their destination know exactly where the trail is.

Shortly after crossing the stream, begin hiking up some switchbacks. Near the end of the climb, the switchbacks shorten, and the trail leaves the cover of pines and progresses into a large meadow, where you'll get your first view of the lake. Halfway across this lush green meadow, cross

Anne Lake Falls

over a small stream and shortly after trekking through a muddy area, the descent to Peter Pande begins. Now, prepare to get your feet wet. It's time to cross Minnow Creek, Peter Pande's outlet. In late July, the creek, which is about 10 yards wide, is typically low enough to expose small rocks that can be used as steppingstones, but these stones are submerged from June to mid-July. Continue on the path around Peter Pande's north shore to Anne Lake Falls on Peter Pande's west shore.

Anne is the largest of the lakes in the Minnow Creek Drainage, and because of its size, its outlet stream has a lot force in June and July, when snowmelt keeps Anne full and its outlet stream flowing fast. Anne Lake Falls is a 100-foot cascade that makes an "s" shape as it winds down a large slab of granite into Peter Pande, located just

downstream from Anne. Although Anne's outlet stream has a lot of force, its waterfall isn't as spectacular as you might expect.

With pines soaring above the shorelines, snowy peaks in the backdrop and a Tahoe-blue looking Peter Pande sparkling in the distance, the panorama seen from the top of Anne Lake Falls is much better than the view from its base. To reach the fall's brink, simply walk up the side of the waterfall. There is no trail, however, climbing up the granite is easy.

If you plan to make the trip, supplies are available at Vermilion Resort. Road restrictions to Silver Pass Falls also apply to Anne Lake Falls.

Also nearby are Wilbur May Lake, Minnie Lake, Grassy Lake, Olive Lake, Minnow Creek Falls, Fish Creek and the Silver Pass Drainage.

Directions *for Silver Pass Falls also apply to Anne Lake Falls.*

Peter Pande Lake is breathtaking from the top of Anne Lake Falls (pictured above)

Silver Pass Falls

Rating: 6

How Short? 19.4 Miles

How Easy? 4

Best Time to View:
June to August

Need Information?
Contact: Vermilion
Resort (559) 259-4000
(Summer) or (559)
855-6558 (Winter),
Sierra National Forest
(559) 297-0706 or
(559) 855-5360

Camping at Edison Lake is popular in the summer. Many families use the lake as a base, making day trips to nearby Florence Lake, Mono Creek, Ward Lake and the San Joaquin River. Few vacationers, however, plan any hiking trips into the John Muir Wilderness. They're making a big mistake, because just above the lake, the wilderness area is one of the best The Golden State has to offer.

Leaving the steep rocky shorelines of Edison Lake and entering the high country, there are unlimited options for hikers, including waterfalls, great fishing opportunities and clear, blue lakes. One of the closest and most rewarding hikes is the 11.7-mile trek to Silver Pass Lake, where you'll encounter Silver Pass Falls.

Getting to Silver Pass Falls is a tough, but satisfying trip, which can be done in a day if you do it right. First, in the morning you can catch the ferry that leaves from Vermilion Resort and drops hikers off near Mono Creek. Taking the ferry reduces the trip by 8.2 miles, leaving a 15.2-mile (instead of 23.4-mile) trip, providing you make it back in time to catch the evening ferry back. So, by taking the water taxi, the hike can be done in a day; otherwise, you'll have to stay overnight.

Silver Pass can be covered in snow through July

If you miss the boat, begin at the Mono Creek Trailhead. The path parallels the north shore of Edison, where a footbridge aids you in crossing Cold Creek, before a series of short switchbacks help you over a small hill. From the top of the hill descend down to the Mono Creek inlet, where the water taxi drops off hikers.

Leaving the shores of Edison, parallel Mono Creek for less than a mile before coming to Quail Meadow. Shaded by trees and surrounded by tall grass, this pretty meadow offers wooden footbridges that allow passage through it without getting covered in the mud.

Continuing on towards Pocket Meadow, cross the North Fork of Mono Creek. There's a trail junction after the crossing. One trail breaks off to the right. Stay left, heading towards Pocket Meadow. Now, on the Pacific Crest/John Muir Trail, the path embarks on a small climb, bringing you to Pocket Meadow. (It's 2.8 miles from the stream crossing to the end of Pocket Meadow.) This long, colorful meadow covered with wildflowers is best used as a brief resting spot. Take a look at the tall cliffs to the north and you'll see Silver Pass Falls. It looks like it's far away, but that's where you'll end up in about a half-hour.

At the end of Pocket Meadow cross the North Fork of Mono Creek for the last time, where another choice needs to be made. The right spur leads to Mott Lake. Crossing over the creek, take the left fork. Now begins the toughest part of the climb to Silver Pass Falls. (Except, the stream crossing can be difficult through July.) Enduring what seems like an infinite amount of switchbacks, the path takes you to the top of Silver

Pass Falls, where you actually walk across the middle portion of the falls. Don't forget to look over your left shoulder for stunning views of the Silver Pass and Mono Creek Drainages.

At the top of the waterfall, you'll be faced with your biggest decision: turn back to Edison Lake or continue on to Silver Pass Lake? It's two miles from the top of the falls to the lake. Turning back now is an option, however, Silver Pass Lake is worth the extra four miles of hiking. The views from Silver Pass Lake and Silver Pass Creek are indescribable. Looking south, the stellar views of snowcapped peaks in Kings Canyon National Park are second to none.

Silver Pass Creek Falls isn't a grand waterfall, but in this section of the wilderness where few waterfalls exist, it offers a satisfying destination. The falls is formed by Silver Pass Creek sliding off a series of smooth granite boulders. It then cascades some 600 feet, before emptying into the North Fork of Mono Creek. Although there is no established trail to its base, it can be reached by rock-hopping downstream from the Mott Lake junction to the confluence of Silver Pass Creek and the North Fork. Then, follow Silver Pass Creek to the falls' base.

If you plan to make the trip, supplies are available at Vermilion Resort. There is a fee to ride the water taxi, which makes one run in the morning and another in the evening. A wilderness permit is required for overnight travel in the John Muir Wilderness. If visiting in June or July, bring along lots of insect repellent. The mosquitoes are nearly unbearable. Kaiser Pass Road is closed from the first snowfall (usually in November) to Memorial Weekend, or as soon as the road can be cleared of snow. During long winters, the road may not open until early July. Call ahead for updated conditions. Trailers are not recommended.

Also nearby are Minnow Creek Falls, Anne Lake Falls and Peter Pande Falls.

Directions: *From the 99 Freeway in Fresno, drive 72 miles east on Highway 168 to the east end of Huntington Lake. Turn east on Kaiser Pass Road and continue approximately 5.5 miles until the road becomes one lane. Follow the road another 19 miles to Vermilion Resort, staying left at the fork. (The right fork leads to Florence Lake.) Continue a half-mile past the resort to the trailhead.*

The lower portion of Silver Pass Falls hides between the pines

Summit Lake Falls

Rating: 6

How Short? 14.0 Miles

How Easy? 4

Best Time to View:
May to July

Need Information?
Contact: Balch Park
Pack Station
(559) 539-2227
(Summer) or (559)
539-3908 (Winter),
Sequoia National
Forest (559) 784-1500

Few people have the chance to see Summit Lake Falls at peak flow. Located at 9,200 feet in the Golden Trout Wilderness, just below the southernmost boundary of Sequoia National Park, it's just too difficult to reach. Its life is also short, so its visitors only have a small window of opportunity to make the challenging seven-mile hike packed with a 3,000-foot elevation gain. Yet, the rewards that can be reaped along the way to Summit Lake Falls are hard to pass up.

To begin with, the hike takes you through a sequoia grove in Mountain Home State Forest. Then, following the Tule River, it offers majestic views of the North Fork of the Middle Fork of the Tule River Falls, Long Falls, the Golden Trout Wilderness and Summit Lake in Sequoia National Park. As a matter of fact, most people who visit the falls love the area so much, they end up camping at Maggie Lakes and fishing for golden trout.

A true outdoors lover would have trouble turning down a trip to Summit Lake Falls, which can be done as a long day trip. But to do it right and really enjoy yourself, it's best to make a backpacking trip out of it. Popular nearby backpacking destinations are Maggie Lakes, Twin Lakes, Summit Lake and Frog Lake.

To reach Summit Lake: from the Balch Park Trailhead, you'll waste no time before climbing a well-maintained trail above the North Fork of the Middle Fork of the Tule River. Then, briefly leave Mountain Home State Forest and enter the Sequoia National Forest. After reentering the state forest and descending down towards the river comes to the first stream crossing.

At this stream crossing, sequoias begin to dot the landscape along the trail. Be sure to look over your right shoulder for a stunning view of the Mt. Home Sequoia Grove. From this lofty perspective, you'll see just how much taller sequoias are than pines.

Summit Lake Falls is hidden between the pines.

At 1.8 miles in, just after the first stream crossing, you'll hear the North Fork of the Middle Tule River Falls, which is actually a series of cascades located downstream. A better view of these falls can be seen on the trip back. This crossing is called Redwood Crossing, named after a fallen redwood tree that extends over the stream. Immediately after crossing the river, you'll come to a trail junction. The right fork leads to Hidden Falls; stay left, following signs to Summit Lake.

On the left side of the trail just before Strawberry Meadow, you'll see the last sequoia, which is a unique one: unlike most other sequoias, it has branches from the top of the tree all the way down to its base. Also, when you come down the mountain, on the north side of the river just before Strawberry Meadow, keep an eye out for Long Falls. It runs year-round and can be striking at peak flow in the spring.

After passing through Strawberry and Long Meadows cross the stream again and walk

Tim Shew provides pack trips to Summit Lake and Summit Lake Falls.

through two more small meadows, before coming to another trail junction, 4.3 miles from where your car is parked. The left fork climbs over Tuohy Pass to the South Fork of the Kaweah River. Stay right, crossing the stream for the final time after 4.7 miles, and begin climbing to Summit Lake Falls.

Enduring a solid climb with more switchbacks than I care to count, you'll come to a clearing, which unfortunately has no pine trees to provide shade. Once again, you'll find yourself above the river, where spectacular views of Long Canyon below, and Moses Mountain can be seen in the distance.

In about five minutes, the path crosses the base of Summit Lake Falls, which is actually more of a long cascade fed by overflow water from Summit Lake. The route passes by the bottom of the falls, offering a great view of its entire length.

For those who prefer to continue on, Sequoia National Park and Summit Lake are a short distance ahead.

If you plan to make the trip, supplies are available in Springville. The trail to Summit Lake Falls is usually snowed in until sometime in June. Call ahead for trail conditions. A wilderness permit is required for overnight travel in the Golden Trout Wilderness and Sequoia National Park.

Also nearby are Twin Lakes and Maggie Lakes.

Directions: *From Bakersfield, drive north on the 99 Freeway to Highway 190 east. Continue on Highway 190 east past Porterville and Lake Success to Springville. In Springville, turn left on Road J-37 (Balch Park Road) and drive 2.4 miles to Road 220. Turn right and continue approximately 12 miles to Mountain Home State Forest. Follow signs to the Balch Park Pack Station. The trailhead is just past the pack station.*

Blake Lezak raises a brook trout caught at Summit Lake 61

Long Falls

Rating: 6

How Short? 4.0 Miles

How Easy? 2

Best Time to View:
May to August

Need Information?
Contact: Balch Park
Pack Station (559) 539-
2227 (Summer) or
(559) 539-3908
(Winter), Sequoia
National Forest
(559) 784-1500

Usually, Long Falls is inadvertently stumbled upon by those enjoying a stroll through the Mountain Home Sequoia Grove. Hikers are often surprised by the waterfall because it isn't shown on any maps, nor is it listed in guide books as an attraction. Because the falls is admittedly far from spectacular, visitors mostly come for the scenery along the way, which is unforgettable.

The grove is one of the largest young groves in the world, and in spite of the magnificent vistas seen throughout the grove and along the North Fork of the Middle Fork of the Tule River, the area isn't heavily visited by tourists. Ideally, the best way to visit the falls is on horseback.

Tim Shew, owner of Balch Park Pack Station, provides daily trips through the grove to Long Falls. These inexpensive, educational, family-oriented trips allow you to enjoy the wilderness without having to navigate or watch your footing along the trail. You will also learn about the sequoia grove, the flora and fauna in Mt. Home State Forest and the Golden Trout Wilderness.

The falls is named "Long Falls" because it's located above Long Canyon. Flowing year-round,

Long Falls

it is a small, narrow chute that cascades more than 1,000 feet before emptying into the river. If planning a hike to the falls, the roundtrip is a bit more than four miles. Allow more time than you would normally allot for a hike of this length, however, because there's great scenery you'll want to stop and enjoy along the way.

Begin the trek at the Hidden Falls parking lot and follow the trail on the south side of the Tule River, heading approximately two miles through the sequoia grove and Long and Strawberry Meadows. After the meadows, keep an eye fixed up in the canyons across the river. You can't miss the long column of water shimmering like a silver ribbon down the tall, vertical mountainside.

If you plan to make the trip, supplies are available in Springville. In winter and spring, call ahead for road conditions. The road into Mountain Home State Forest closes in the winter.

Also nearby are Summit Lake, Hidden Falls, North Fork of the Middle Tule River Falls, Redwood Lake and Balch Park Lakes.

Directions *to Summit Lake Falls also apply to Long Falls.*

North Fork of the Middle Fork of the Tule River Falls

Rating: 6

How Short? 1.5 Miles

How Easy? 1

Best Time to View:
April to August

Need Information?
Contact: Balch Park
Pack Station (559) 539-
2227 (Summer) or
(559) 539-3908
(Winter), Sequoia
National Forest
(559) 784-1500

The North Fork of the Middle Fork of the Tule River Falls is one of only a few waterfalls in California located in a sequoia grove. In this case, however, the waterfall, located in the Mountain Home Grove, has a lot more to offer than just stunning views of giant sequoia trees.

For starters, the waterfall is also located on one of the best wild trout fisheries in the Sequoia National Forest. In a land known for its sequoias, fishing often gets overlooked, but those who take time to fish here are rewarded with high catch rates of rainbow and brown trout. Although this section of the river is not stocked with fish, there are still plenty to go around.

To reach the falls, begin at the day-use parking area at Hidden Falls. If you are going to fish, it's best to walk to the river and fish your way up to the falls. One advantage to walking up the stream is that it allows you to see many other smaller cascades along the stream.

The falls is only three-fourths of a mile upstream, but the trip will take at least an hour if you allot time for fishing. If not fishing, simply pick up the trail on the south side of the stream and follow it upstreamto a trail junction, approximately eight-tenths of a mile upstream. At the junction, known as Redwood Crossing, begin walking downstream, and in five minutes you'll be at the top of the falls.

The falls is a series of cascades that total about 50 feet high. Sequoias are scattered all around the stream and on the hillsides.

If you plan to make the trip, supplies are available in Springville. In winter and spring, call ahead for road conditions. The road into Mountain Home State Forest is commonly closed due to snow. The North Fork of the Middle Tule River is closed to fishing from November 16 to the last Saturday in April. Only artificial lures and flies with barbless hooks are permitted.

Also nearby are Summit Lake, Long Falls and Balch Park Lakes.

Directions to Summit Lake Falls also apply to the North Fork of the Middle Fork of the Tule River Falls.

Scott Wiessner stands near the upper portion of the NF of the MF of the Tule River Falls

Volcano Falls

Rating: 6

How Short? 40.8 Miles

How Easy? 5

Best Time to View:
May to July

Need Information?
Contact: Sequoia
National Forest (661)
548-6503, Sequoia
National Park
Wilderness Permits
(559-565-3761) or
(559-565-3766),
Sequoia National Park
(559) 565-3134

"Volcano Falls" sounds like a colossal waterfall, perhaps located on one of the Hawaiian Islands or somewhere on the Pacific Rim. You'd think there would be a volcano close by or at least lava pits. Well, none of the above is true. So, what's Volcano Falls' relationship to volcanic activity? The same as Rainbow Falls in Devils Postpile National Monument: the rocks surrounding both are volcanic.

Tony Abel enters into the Golden Trout Wilderness

Partly because most its drop is hidden in a dark, narrow, inaccessible gorge, Volcano Falls doesn't create a sense of awe in its visitors. In fact, if you hike the 20.4 miles in from the Jerky Meadow Trailhead just to see the waterfall, you've gotta' be crazy. This waterfall isn't worth it. Yet, there are many other nearby places that do warrant the long trek.

Take Golden Trout Creek, for example, which feeds Volcano Falls. This is one of the best, seldom fished backcountry creeks in California. For those of you who aren't familiar with the creek, the California State fish, the golden trout, originated in Golden Trout Creek; and it's one of the last remaining waters in the country that still holds native golden trout.

Above Volcano Falls, which is located in the Golden Trout Wilderness just south of the boundary to Sequoia National Park, is Little Whitney Meadow, one of the Southern Sierra's most unspoiled places. Shaded by pines and filled with tall grass and colorful wildflowers, this meadow is graced by Golden Trout Creek, which meanders down its center. It's a true dream.

Because the trek in is a butt-kicker and only a small portion of the waterfall is visible when you arrive,

ENTERING
SEQUOIA NATIONAL PARK
PETS, WEAPONS, WHEELED
VEHICLES PROHIBITED.
WILDERNESS PERMITS
REQUIRED

Volcano doesn't receive many visitors. To be one of the few who has seen Volcano Falls, here's what to do: first, follow the directions in the write-up for Coyote Creek Falls.

At the Kern Canyon Ranger Station, 100 yards northeast of Coyote Creek is a trail junction. Continue straight on the path signed for Funston Meadow. Then, veer right, following a sign to Little Whitney Meadow. The trail leaves Sequoia National Park, enters the Golden Trout Wilderness, crosses the Kern River and begins to gradually climb up switchbacks over the steep mountain south of the gorge where Volcano is situated.

About halfway up the mountain, keep your eyes on the gorge to the north. There are no signs for Volcano, nor is there an overlook, so you'll have to find it on your own. In late spring and early summer, you'll hear the falls before seeing them. There's only about 100 yards where you can see the falls. When the trail nears the edge of the cliff, look carefully and you should be able to see Volcano spilling off the volcanic rock, falling out of view. As I said, the waterfall isn't great. At least not from this vantage point, nor any other that's easily accessible.

Volcano Falls can also be reached via a 37-mile roundtrip hike from the Horseshoe Meadow Trailhead near Lone Pine, as well as a 45-mile round tripper from Mineral King.

If you plan to make the trip, supplies are available in Kernville and Ponderosa. A wilderness permit is required for overnight travel in the Golden Trout Wilderness and Sequoia National Park. Depending on road conditions, Road 22S82 may not open until late May. Call the Forest Service for updated road conditions.

Also nearby are Grasshopper Creek Falls, Coyote Creek Falls and Kern River (Upper).

Directions: *From the 99 Freeway in Bakersfield, exit Highway 178 east and drive 45 miles to Lake Isabella. From Lake Isabella, drive 11 miles north on Highway 155 to Kernville and turn left on Mountain 99. Drive approximately 24 miles on Mountain 99 to a fork in the road and veer right onto Road 22S82, signed for Camp Whitsett and Lower Peppermint Creek. Continue approximately 21 miles to the trailhead at the end of the road.*

Volcano Falls is situated in this steep and narrow canyon near the Kern River and Sequoia National Park.

Grasshopper Creek Falls

Rating: 7

How Short? 27.4 Miles

How Easy? 5

Best Time to View:
May to July

Need Information?
Contact: Sequoia
National Forest
(661) 548-6503

Prior to the late Seventies, the Upper Kern River near the border of Sequoia National Park was easily accessible. Because motorcyclists were permitted on the trails that led into the drainage, this backcountry playground was a popular weekend hangout. When the 303,287-acre Golden Trout Wilderness was established in 1978, however, the roads into the wilderness area were closed to all vehicular traffic. The long trek to the Upper Kern, which once took an hour on a motorcycle, became at least a half-day journey on foot or horseback.

Although the road closure may have upset some visitors, it did wonders for the forest. Damaged meadows and trails were restored, the fishing got better and the backcountry once again offered solitude. The long walk kept away many visitors who preferred the short bike ride. Instead, the bikers flocked to the drive-to section of the Kern, such as the stretch from Kernville to the Johnsondale Bridge.

Ironically, most of the teenagers and young adults who rode motorcycles to the Upper Kern, prior to the creation of the wilderness area, are now in their late-forties and fifties, and the long hike has become too much for their legs. Some of them, however, still return to the wilderness on horseback.

Last time I hiked through the Upper Kern Drainage, I ran into a group of men in their fifties. "The trout bite's just too good up here for me to stop coming," said a bearded guy cooking hotdogs for an afternoon snack over a campfire. "I come back every year."

"So, you know this area pretty well, then?" I asked, adjusting the 70-pound pack on my back, while chewing on an energy-producing protein bar. "Does Grasshopper Creek Falls always have this much water in it?"

"You mean Grasshopper Creek just upstream? Yah, this time of year there's a lot of water in it," he told me. One of his buddies was eavesdropping, while reading a book on a hammock hanging near the riverbank.

"Not the stream, the waterfall," I replied, thinking the hot dog looked far more appealing than the health bar I was trying to swallow without chewing. I was into it for the protein, not the taste.

"There's no waterfall there. I'd know about it. I've been coming here for 30 years," he mumbled, munching on a mouth-watering charcoal-blackened hot dog. To prove him wrong, I had him follow me upstream and told him to look down a clearing through the trees. "Well, I'll be damned. How could I have missed that?" He walked

Little Kern River and footbridge

Resting in Willow Meadow

back to get his buddy to show him the waterfall.

I told him not to feel so bad. Thousands of hikers walk past this point each year and most don't see the falls. They're usually too tired, dragging their feet, looking for a camping spot. Who's got the energy to look for waterfalls? As a reward, he gave me one of his hotdogs, reminding me that they've got a lot of protein, too. I guess these older guys know a thing or two.

Next time you backpack through this region, it really doesn't take that much effort to look up and see the falls. Especially after completing the long journey that begins at the Jerky Meadow Trailhead and kicks your butt from the get-go, gaining more than 1,000 feet over the first 1.6 miles.

Beginning at the top of the peak, the path leaves the Sequoia National Forest and enters the Golden Trout Wilderness at Jerky Meadow. For the next mile and a half, the trail winds through a pine forest, dropping a few hundred feet on the way to Jug Spring. At Jug Spring, a small stream on the right of the path serves as a good place to fill your water bottles.

Over the next 1.2 miles, the path looses nearly 500 feet, coming to a bridge used to cross the wide and otherwise un-passable Little Kern River. After crossing the bridge, continue along the path, following signs for Trout Meadows. From the bridge, the meadow is 2.5 miles ahead, with another 400-foot elevation gain.

Trout Meadows isn't a lush green meadow like those seen in the high-country of Yosemite National Park. Although it's filled with tall grass, it's also surrounded by barbed wire fences, still intact from the days when ranchers grazed cattle and horses, before the wilderness area was created. In another half-mile is the Trout Meadows Ranger Station.

Now, 7.3 miles from your car, this is a good place to take a rest. There is a spring near a picnic table in front of the ranger station to refill water rations. Then, push on. In two-

Tony Abel in Trout Meadows 67

tenths of a mile, a trail signed for Kern Flat splits off to the right. Ignore it. The next 2.5 miles are fairly flat, as you continue through Trout Meadows and enter Willow Meadow.

There is another spring in Willow Meadow to refill water and give your knees a chance to rest before descending to the Kern River. The drop is gradual for the first 1.8 miles, taking you to an overlook of the drainage. The Kern looks powerful from here, and its whitewater can be clearly seen even this high above the river.

About 2.5 miles from Willow Meadow, cross Angora Creek and listen for the roar of the Kern. About 10 minutes after crossing Angora, a junction signed for Hole in the Ground veers off to the right. Continuing straight, 13 miles from the Jerky Meadow Trailhead and an 800-foot descent from Willow Meadow, you'll cross Leggett Creek and be along the shores of the 50- to 75-foot wide Kern River.

Take a deep breath. You're almost at Grasshopper Creek Falls. Paralleling the Kern for two-tenths of a mile upstream, you'll cross another stream. There's a tree here with a sign nailed to it that reads, "Grasshopper Creek." Continue another two-tenths of a mile into Grasshopper Flat and begin looking through the trees on the left for the waterfall.

Pat yourself on the back; you've come 13.7 miles, and mostly likely it will have taken almost the whole day. Pick out a campsite and rest. You earned it! Adding up all the peaks you've climbed, it totals almost 2,700 feet. That doesn't take into account the mountains whose switchbacks you've climbed down, descending some 2,600 feet. So, in one day your knees withstood a total of 5,300 feet of ascending and descending. Not bad for a day's work.

Grasshopper Creek Falls is a splinter of water that plunges 50 feet off a granite ledge. From the trail, only the top 30 feet of the drop can be seen. It is possible to scramble to the base of the falls; however, it's a tough hike that I don't recommend. Although you'll get a closer view of Grasshopper from the base, it's not necessarily better, and the short quarter-mile rock-hopping adventure could take at least 45-minutes each way.

Also, chances are your legs are going to be too tired to fight the thick brush, climbing without a trail down the steep cliffs and jumping over rocks to reach the bottom of the falls. If you want to try it, backtrack to where Grasshopper Creek crosses the trail and bushwhack upstream to the base of the falls.

If you plan to make the trip, supplies are available in Kernville and Ponderosa. A wilderness permit is required for overnight travel in the Golden Trout Wilderness. Depending on road conditions, the road to the trailhead may not open until late May. Call the Forest Service for updated road conditions.

Also nearby are Coyote Creek Falls, Volcano Falls, Golden Trout Creek and Kern River.

Directions *for Volcano Falls also apply to Grasshopper Creek Falls.*

The upper tier of Grasshopper Creek Falls

Inyo National Forest

Region ⓸

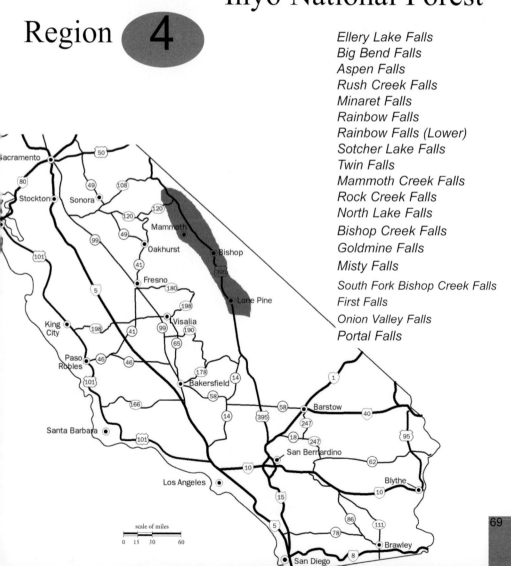

Ellery Lake Falls
Big Bend Falls
Aspen Falls
Rush Creek Falls
Minaret Falls
Rainbow Falls
Rainbow Falls (Lower)
Sotcher Lake Falls
Twin Falls
Mammoth Creek Falls
Rock Creek Falls
North Lake Falls
Bishop Creek Falls
Goldmine Falls
Misty Falls
South Fork Bishop Creek Falls
First Falls
Onion Valley Falls
Portal Falls

Ellery Lake Falls

Ellery Lake Falls is what I consider a warm-up waterfall. A few miles outside the eastern boundary of Yosemite National Park, near Tioga Pass, Ellery Lake Falls isn't going to make you "ooh" or "ah." It is, however, a sign of things to come: the land of great waterfalls lies just ahead!

With no trails to its brink or base, Ellery Lake Falls is a drive-to waterfall. Pull off Tioga Pass Road, look down the side of the mountain, and you'll see the waterfall cascading down Lee Vining Creek. The falls begins at Ellery Lake's outlet and tumbles down roughly 300 feet of rocky rubble. Made up of two drops, the second is a few-hundred yards downstream from the first, and a few-hundred feet longer. Both are best viewed in May and June when snow runoff is at its peak.

Both are hit-and-run waterfalls. Don't waste a lot of time here. Get out of your car, snap a few pictures and move on. Remember, many of the world's best waterfalls are just a short drive away.

If you plan to make the trip, supplies are available in Lee Vining. In winter, call ahead for road conditions. The road may be closed due to snow.

Also nearby are Tioga Lake, Ellery Lake, Lee Vining Creek, Saddlebag Creek, Saddlebag Lake, Gardisky Lake and Yosemite National Park.

Directions: *From Highway 395 in Mammoth, drive north past the June Lakes turnoff to Highway 120 and turn left. Drive 8.3 miles to a pullout on the left.*

Ellery Lake Falls is best viewed from Highway 120

Big Bend Falls

Rating: 7

How Short? Drive To

How Easy? 1

Best Time To View:
April to November

Need Information?
Contact: Inyo National
Forest (760) 647-3044

Lee Vining Creek is one of the most overlooked drive-to streams in the Sierra. Even its terrific fishing doesn't attract heaps of anglers. Unfortunately, or fortunately for those who enjoy solitude, Big Bend Falls on Lee Vining Creek gets the same lack of respect.

Of the three waterfalls on Lee Vining Creek, Big Bend is the best. This 35-foot cascade is powerful year-round, with whitewater crashing against boulders, before splish-splashing its way downstream. There's so much water in the stream during the spring and early summer, you can't see the splendid reddish-brown-colored rocks that become visible when the creek begins to subside.

What mostly attracts visitors to Big Bend is its accessibility. This waterfall requires no hiking. You don't even need to leave your car; it can all be seen through your window. For those who prefer a closer view than the one from their car, where the waterfall is 20 yards away, there's a trail that takes you to its base. This short 20-yard trek is fit for all ages.

At the base of the falls, there's an inviting handball court size boulder calling out to visitors to sit on it and eat lunch, although few do. Let's not forget the great fishing that can be had here as well. The California Department of Fish and Game plants the stream weekly during the fishing season above and below the waterfall.

If you plan to make the trip, supplies are available in Lee Vining. In winter call ahead for road conditions. Poole Power Plant Road may be closed due to snow. Lee Vining Creek is closed to fishing from November 16 to the last Saturday in April.

Big Bend Falls

Also nearby are Aspen Falls, Ellery Lake Falls, Tioga Lake, Lee Vining Creek (South Fork) and Saddlebag Creek.

Directions: *At the junction of Highways 395 and 120 in Lee Vining, drive 3.5 miles west on Highway 120 to Poole Power Plant Road and turn left. Continue 2.5 miles to Big Bend Campground and the waterfall on the left.*

Aspen Falls

Rating: 5

How Short? Drive To

How Easy? 1

Best Time To View:
April to November

Need Information?
Contact: Inyo National
Forest 760) 647-3044

Of all the waterfalls in this book, there's only one where you can set up a tent, cook dinner on a picnic table and roast marshmallows over a fire pit at the waterfalls' base. While there are several waterfalls listed in this book that can be viewed from a campsite, none are like Aspen, which, at 7,575 feet in the Inyo National Forest, near the town of Lee Vining, is a mere 10 yards from the campsites in Aspen Campground. Unfortunately, the waterfall itself isn't great, but the camping at Aspen Falls' base earns it a few extra points.

Just a warning: don't pump yourself up to see a spectacular freefall, because Aspen is an uneventful cascade. At only about 30 feet tall, its drop is much less vertical than most cataracts on the eastern slope of the Sierra. Nearly all sightseers come to Aspen Falls because of the splendid scenery that is exhibited along the shores of Lee Vining Creek. About a mile downstream from Big Bend Falls, Aspen is also blessed with an enchantment of aspen and pine that line the 20-foot wide stream.

As summer crowds taper off and the campgrounds become half-full, day use gets more popular. And in many ways, fall is the best time to visit. The aspens, which begin to change colors and shed their yellow, orange and gold leaves, make for fascinating photos. Most day users come here to fish the creek, which is stocked weekly by the California Department of Fish and Game. With the magnificently colored canopy of aspens, however, many anglers would rather enjoy the crisp air and unforgettable scenery than get their hands sticky with Power Bait and fish.

If you plan to make the trip, supplies are available in Lee Vining. In winter call ahead for road conditions. Poole Power Plant Road may be closed due to snow. Lee Vining Creek is closed to fishing from November 16 to the last Saturday in April.

Also nearby are Big Bend Falls, Ellery Lake Falls, Tioga Lake, Lee Vining Creek (South Fork) and Saddlebag Creek.

Directions: *At the junction of Highways 395 and 120 in Lee Vining, drive 3.5 miles west on Highway 120 to Poole Power Plant Road and turn left. Continue 1.5 miles to Aspen Campground. The waterfall is at the far end of the campground.*

Aspen Falls

Rush Creek Falls

Rating: 6

How Short? Drive-To

How Easy? 1

Best Time to View:
April to August

Need Information?
Contact: June Lake
Chamber of Commerce
(760) 648-7584

Because Rush Creek Falls has uncertain flows, it's extremely difficult to pinpoint the best season to visit. At one time, prior to the construction of dams on Agnew, Gem and Wahoo Lakes, when snowmelt from the Ansel Adams Wilderness swelled Rush Creek, Rush Creek Falls was a majestic sight as it plummeted off steep cliffs down into the June Lake Loop. Now, Rush Creek is controlled by releases from these three dams, and there's no telling when the waterfall will be running.

Agnew Lake, which is located directly above the waterfall, was once a natural lake, as were Gem and Waugh, both situated in basins above Agnew. Then dams were constructed to increase the amount of water the lakes could retain and to generate hydroelectric power for the June Lake Loop and Lee Vining.

So, when is the best time to visit Rush Creek Falls? Well, the waterfall runs consistently from late April through June, but on and off most of the summer. Towards the end of summer when the lakes are slowly drawn down for power generation, the waterfall again becomes attractive. If you're in the June Lake Loop, my best suggestion

Rush Creek Falls

is to take the time to make the short drive and see if the waterfall is running.

Rush Creek Falls is best viewed from Reversed Creek and Silver Lake. To find the waterfall, first locate the tall mountains west of Silver Lake. Then look about 500 feet up the mountain above the point where Rush Creek enters Silver Lake, and you'll be able to spot the waterfall plunging down the mountainside.

If you plan to make the trip, supplies are available in June Lake.

Also nearby are June Lake, Gull Lake, Reversed Creek, Silver Lake, Grant Lake and Ansel Adams Wilderness.

Directions: *From Bishop, drive about 60 miles north on Highway 395 to Highway 158 (signed for the June Lake Loop) and turn left. Drive 5.5 miles to an unsigned pullout with great views of the falls.*

Minaret Falls

Rating: 8

How Short? 2.2 Miles

How Easy? 1

Best Time to View:
June to August

Need Information?
Contact: Mammoth
Lakes Visitors Center
(760) 924-5500,
Devil's Postpile
National Monument
(760) 872-4881
(Winter) or
(760) 934-2289

If you've been to Red's Meadow or Devils Postpile National Monument, then you've surely heard the word "minaret." Located nearby are the Minarets, a group of mountain peaks in the Minarets Wilderness. Also using the name "minaret" are the Minaret Lakes, Minaret Creek and the "minaret" that is most known by visitors, Minaret Falls. Anything with the word "minaret" in this region has a great deal of natural beauty to it, however, to view most of the Minarets up close, long strenuous hikes are required. That's not the case with Minaret Falls.

Requiring a short drive from Mammoth Lakes and a short walk from Devils Postpile, Minaret Falls is one of the area's biggest tourist attractions. Located a tad outside the national monument's boundary, Minaret Falls is a 300-foot plus waterfall in the Ansel Adams Wilderness, which empties into the San Joaquin River. Like nearby Rainbow Falls, it is wide and powerful.

Minaret Creek tumbles down a gigantic sheet of smooth granite, creating more than a dozen drops, including two large drops and nearly a dozen smaller cascades. During peak flow in late June and early July, the waterfall can grow as wide as 50 feet where Minaret Creek breaks into as many as three smaller streams. It's a powerful sight that reminds me a lot of Peter Pande Falls in the John Muir Wilderness.

Getting to the falls is as easy as tying your shoes. No rock-hopping or bush whacking is required. From the Devils Postpile Visitor Center, follow the well-signed trail towards the Postpile. In about 300 yards, veer right at a sign for Minaret Falls. After the footbridge across the San Joaquin River, take a right on the Pacific Crest Trail. The PCT parallels the river for the next half-mile. At the junction with the John Muir Trail, stay right and continue on the PCT to the base of the falls. From there the entire waterfall can be viewed.

If you're camping in Minaret Falls Campground, there's no need for any hiking at all. Simply open up your tent, look across the San Joaquin River and the falls is directly in front of you. It can also be seen from Minaret Road between the Postpile and Pumice Flat.

If you plan to make the trip, supplies are available at Red's Meadow Resort. Road restrictions for Rainbow Falls (Lower) also apply to Minaret Falls.

Also nearby are Starkweather Lake, Devils Postpile, and Sotcher Lake Falls.

Directions *for Rainbow Falls (Lower) also apply to Minaret Falls.*

Minaret Falls

Rainbow Falls

Rating: 10

How Short? 2.0 Miles

How Easy? 1

Best Time to View:
June to October

Need Information?
Contact: Mammoth
Lakes Visitors Center
(760) 924-5500,
Devil's Postpile
National Monument
(760) 872-4881
(Winter) or
(760) 934-2289

Many waterfalls in the world continually change from year to year. Rocks on top, below, or in the body of the waterfall can be loosened by torrential flows, trees can get swept downstream and other natural phenomenon can alter a waterfall's complexion. Yet, aside from the amount of water that spills off its lip, Rainbow Falls in Devils Postpile National Monument remains unchanged. Rainbow Falls is made up of volcanic rock that erodes so slowly it will appear unchanged long after you and I pass.

Ranking up there with the great waterfalls of Yosemite National Park, Rainbow Falls is one of the state's most treasured waterfalls. Displaying both grace and an awesome amount of force, it maintains tremendous year-round volume. There are few waterfalls in California that can top the impressiveness of its 101-foot drop.

The San Joaquin River feeds Rainbow Falls, as it tumbles over a sheer cliff of volcanic rock. The waterfall empties into a cold pool of clear deep water that is almost always crowned by numerous bright rainbows. It's not uncommon to see three or more at one time, arching from the lush green hillside to the right of the falls out over the pool. The rushing water creates a drenching mist in the canyon below, keeping the fertile hill to the right of the falls bursting with lush green grass and sparkling with colorful wildflowers throughout spring and summer.

Rainbow Falls is a true tourist trap, one of the most popular in the entire Sierra. It's not uncommon to see hundreds of hikers on the trail to the falls. Although I've seen a few die-hard swimmers make feeble attempts at wading in the pool below the falls, not many can withstand its frigid water.

The trip to Rainbow Falls is a must for everyone. Even if you don't enjoy the outdoors, you'll love the falls. The wide, dirt path begins at the Rainbow Falls parking area. Following signs to the falls, walk downhill past the junction of the Pacific Crest and John Muir Trails. Then, cross over a small feeder stream, just before coming to a sign announcing your entrance in the Ansel Adams Wilderness.

Continue downhill, and after about 15 minutes of leisurely walking comes the first of two overlooks. The first, signed overlook provides an outstanding side view of the falls. Another short five-minute walk brings you to the second overlook. From this vantage point you'll get a fabulous view of the San Joaquin River on the left and Rainbow Falls on the right. It is also possible to view the falls from its base. Between the two overlooks there is a steep trail consisting of 101 stone and wooden steps, which is the same height as the falls and takes you to its base.

If you plan to make the trip, supplies are available at Red's Meadow Resort. Road restrictions for Rainbow Falls (Lower) also apply to Rainbow Falls.

Also nearby are Sotcher Lake Falls, Minaret Falls and Devils Postpile
.

Directions: From Mammoth, take Highway 203 3.7 miles west through the town of Mammoth. Turn right on Minaret Road and drive 13.1 miles to Rainbow Falls.

Rainbow Falls is the best waterfall in the Eastern Sierra

Rainbow Falls (Lower)

Rating: 5
How Short? 3.0 Miles
How Easy? 1
Best Time to View: May to October
Need Information? Contact: Mammoth Lakes Visitors Center (760) 924-5500, Devil's Postpile National Monument (760) 872-4881 (Winter) or (760) 934-2289

After visiting Rainbow Falls, Lower Rainbow Falls seems like a real letdown. Like winning $100 jackpot at a casino in Las Vegas just after cleaning up $100,000. Who cares... so what?

Lower Rainbow Falls just doesn't compare to Rainbow Falls, which is one of the most spectacular falls in the state. Needless to say, after a visit to Rainbow Falls, few even feel the need to see its smaller and less-visited counterpart. Those who do make the short trip for the most part find themselves unimpressed, especially after seeing Rainbow Falls, a perfect "10" on the scale.

Cascading some 30 feet into a deep swimmer-friendly pool, the lower falls is located just outside the western boundary of Devils Postpile National Monument. Because most tourists congregate at Rainbow Falls and don't take the time to visit here, chances are you'll have the falls all to yourself.

The lower falls is more popular with anglers, swimmers and cliff jumpers. Although the water remains cold even on the hottest summer days, teenagers can't resist jumping off the adjacent rocks. Fishing also tends to be good here. The stream isn't stocked, but there are many wild rainbows and brooks, as well as a few browns in the San Joaquin River. Try casting Panther Martins towards the falls, let your line sink for a few seconds and slowly retrieve. You should catch plenty of fish.

To reach Lower Rainbow Falls from Rainbow Falls, continue west, gradually descending just over a half-mile to the falls.

If you plan to make the trip, supplies are available at Red's Meadow Resort. Minaret Road usually doesn't open until late June. Call ahead for updated road conditions. No vehicular traffic is permitted from 7:30 a.m. to 5:30 p.m. Exceptions apply only to those who have campground reservations or reservations at Red's Meadow Resort. Those who arrive during the restricted hours must ride a shuttle into the valley. There is a fee to ride the shuttle and enter the park. Road restrictions run from late June through Labor Day.

Also nearby are Starkweather Lake, Sotcher Lake Falls, Minaret Falls, Devils Postpile, Minaret Creek and Sotcher Lake.

Directions: From Mammoth, take Highway 203 3.7 miles west through the town of Mammoth. Turn right at Minaret Road and drive 4.5 miles to the Devils Postpile entrance station. Depending on the time of day, you can either continue 9.1 miles to the sign for Rainbow Falls or take the shuttle to the falls.

Jason McLean at Lower Rainbow Falls in August of 1998

Sotcher Lake Falls

Rating: 4

How Short? 0.50 Miles

How Easy? 1

Best Time to View:
June to October

Need Information?
Contact: Mammoth
Lakes Visitors Center
(760) 924-5500

In the tourist-infested lands near Devil's Postpile National Monument and Red's Meadow, any place that isn't bombarded by visitors is difficult to find. Tucked away in the Inyo National Forest, however, there's a tiny spring-fed waterfall that can't be seen on any map. This special, peaceful place is called Sotcher Lake Falls.

This 25-foot cascade splits into two branches about halfway down, before emptying into Sotcher Lake's outlet stream. Greenery flourishes everywhere around the waterfall, which is a botanist's dream, surrounded by thousands of wildflowers that stay in bloom from May to October.

Sotcher Lake Falls

Located between Sotcher Lake and Red's Meadow Resort, tucked away in a corner of Red's Meadow, the falls doesn't compare in size or volume to nearby Rainbow or Minaret Falls, but it does offer the solitude the others can't. Because it's so close to Red's Meadow, the falls is a great place to take time to relax and enjoy the wilderness without having to battle the crowds that swamp the rest of the area.

To reach the falls locate the Sotcher Lake Nature Trail, which circles the lake. After walking up a small mountain, you'll get a priceless view of Sotcher Lake. Then, drop back down to the lake's shore and cross the outlet stream on the far west shore. At this point, you can see the falls on the right. Take the right fork, veering off the nature trail, and walk to the falls.

If you plan to make the trip, supplies are available at Red's Meadow Resort. Minaret Road usually doesn't open until late June. Road restrictions for Rainbow Falls (Lower) also apply to Sotcher Lake Falls.

Also nearby are Starkweather Lake, San Joaquin River, Minaret Falls, Rainbow Falls, Johnston Lake, Devils Postpile, Minaret Creek and Sotcher Lake.

Directions: *From Highway 395 in Mammoth, exit west on Mammoth Lakes Road and drive 3.7 miles to Minaret Road. Turn right and drive 11.8 miles to the junction for Red's Meadow and Devil's Postpile. Veer left and Sotcher Lake will be on your left just past this junction. The nature trail can be picked up from the parking lot.*

Twin Falls

Rating: 7

How Short? Drive To

How Easy? 1

Best Time to View:
May to September

Need Information?
Contact: Mammoth
Lakes Visitors Center
(760) 924-5500

Twin Falls provides an added incentive for anglers to fish Twin Lakes instead of the other lakes in the Mammoth Lakes Loop. The waterfall, actually more of a large cascade, is created by Lake Mamie's overflow, which travels under Highway 203 and then comes crashing for more than 250 feet on its way down into the first of the three Twin Lakes.

Yes, despite its name, Twin Lakes is actually composed of three small, shallow, connected lakes, which are all heavily used by recreationists from Memorial Day weekend through Labor Day. Twin Lakes is known for good fishing for rainbow trout, but it also offers the possibility of hooking a few browns and brooks.

As for the waterfall, it can be enjoyed by all: tourists, hikers and anglers. Ideally, the best way to view it is from a float-tube or canoe while fishing Upper Twin Lake. There, you can inhale the fresh high-country air filled with the scent of the surrounding pine-capped mountains, while listening to the stimulating roar of water crashing over boulders.

The falls is best from May through July, when snowmelt flows the strongest. Because the road to the waterfall commonly freezes over, it is closed in the winter, and the falls can't be reached without snowshoes, a snowmobile or cross-country skis.

There are two good spots to view the falls. Both offer great, but considerably different views. From the brink, all three Twin Lakes, as well as the two bridges that connect them, can be seen. There is also a picnic area up here, which offers a place to munch on a sandwich while staring at some spectacular scenery.

Although you can walk to the falls' base from Upper Twin Lake, the best view is from the bridge that connects Upper and Middle. From this vantage point, the entire cascade can been seen, unobstructed by the pine trees that line the south shore.

If you plan to make the trip, supplies are available in the general store at the lake. The road to Twin Lakes closes in the winter and usually opens by Memorial weekend. Call ahead for updated road conditions.

Also nearby are Lake Mamie, Lake Mary, Horseshoe Lake, Lake George, Mammoth Creek, Mammoth Mountain Ski Area and Devils Postpile National Monument.

Directions: From the junction of Highways 395 and 203 near Mammoth, take Highway 203 west 3.7 miles to Lake Mary Road. Veer left and drive 2.3 miles to the Twin Lake turnoff. For the falls overlook continue two miles to the Lake Mamie parking area.

Twin Falls at low flow in May

Mammoth Creek Falls

Rating: 7

How Short? 0.40 miles

How Easy? 2

Best Time to View:
May to October

Need Information?
Contact: Mammoth
Lakes Visitors Center
(760) 924-5500

And you thought there were no secret spots left in the Mammoth area? I'm not talking about some hidden backcountry lake. All of those have definitely been found and fished, and they're most likely shown on maps, anyway. Ski areas? Naw. Those are extremely publicized, along with every inch of Devils Postpile National Monument. Still searching for what I'm talking about? How about a waterfall?

Ironically, Mammoth Creek Falls is not hard to find at all; most tourists just don't seem to look in the right place. The waterfall lies in a canyon four-tenths of a mile downstream from Twin Lakes, and while hundreds of thousands of sightseers drive past it each year, few, if any, have ever seen the powerful 40-foot drop.

At 8,200 feet in the Inyo National Forest, Mammoth Creek Falls is a mere 1.4 miles downstream from Twin Falls, which flows out of Lake Mamie into Twin Lake. While few out-of-towners have seen the falls, a few locals have. I saw evidence of their rare visits when I found a partially beaten trail that guided me down to a perfect overlook. Most inspiring in May and June when snow runoff keeps Mammoth Creek racing fast, this waterfall has a tremendous amount of force as it plunges off its dark brown cliff.

Mammoth Creek Falls in June of 2001

To find Mammoth Creek Falls, from either unmarked dirt pullout (mentioned below), look for a small clearing in the trees. If you've located the correct clearing, there will be a trail that descends into the canyon. Don't continue down any clearings that don't have trails. After walking less than one-tenth of a mile through a pine-covered area, the path winds through hundreds of manzanita bushes before it nears the canyon and Mammoth Creek. At this point, you should be able to hear the waterfall. If you can't, continue towards the canyon, keeping an eye out for the drop on your right.

If you plan to make the trip, supplies are available in Mammoth.

Also nearby are Twin Lakes, Lake Mary, Lake Mamie, Twin Falls and Lake George.

Directions: *From the junction of Highways 395 and 203 near Mammoth, take Highway 203 west 3.7 miles to Lake Mary Road. Veer left and drive 1.9 miles to an unmarked dirt pullout on either side of the road.*

Rock Creek Falls

Rating: 3

How Short? 0.50 Miles

How Easy? 1

Best Time to View?
May to September

Need Information?
Contact: Rock Creek
Lakes Resort (760)
935-4311, Inyo
National Forest
(760) 873-2400

Rock Creek Lake is one of the most beautiful and heavily fished lakes in the Sierra. Downstream of the lake, Rock Creek offers the same magnificent scenery, quality fishing and wilderness atmosphere. But, the creek offers a bit more. Located a short distance downstream of the lake, Rock Creek Falls, may not be imposing, but at 9,600 feet in the Inyo National Forest it is situated in a heavily forested area and maintains a flow year-round.

The falls isn't imposing, but a relaxing hike and getaway from the crowds that form in the campgrounds, and at the lake. To find the waterfall pick up the trail across from Rock Creek Lakes Resort. It is unsigned. However, if you walk down to Rock Creek, which is only 20 yards from the road and head downstream you'll be headed in the right direction. You really don't need a trail to find the falls. This section of Rock Creek is relatively flat, but that's not an indication of what's ahead. You'll see a small, green Forest Service building on your left and then the path starts to lose elevation. Within two-tenths of a mile you'll be descending into Lower Rock Creek Canyon. As you near the bottom of the decline, keep your eyes peeled on the gorge where Rock Creek is located.

Rock Creek Falls is hidden in this gorge and in order for you to get a close view of it, you'll need to leave the path and scramble to the stream. Rock Creek Falls is only 25 feet high, but can be powerful in the spring and early summer when runoff hits peak flow. There are also several smaller drops in this gorge. Nonetheless, most people don't spend much time here. There are fish biting in the lake!

If you plan to make the trip, supplies are available in Bishop and Mammoth. In winter, call ahead for road conditions. Chains may be required.

Also nearby are the Little Lakes Valley, Crowley Lake and McGee Creek.

Directions: *From Highway 395 in Bishop, drive 30 miles north to the town of Tom's Place and turn left on Rock Creek Road. Continue approximately eight miles to Rock Creek Lakes Resort, just before Rock Creek Lake.*

Rock Creek Falls gets extremely low in October. This picture was snapped on October 20, 2002.

North Lake Falls

Rating: 4

How Short? Drive-To

How Easy? 1

Best Time to View?
May to August

Need Information?
Contact: Bishop Creek
Outfitters (760) 873-
4785, Inyo National
Forest (760) 873-2400

At 9,300 feet in the Inyo National Forest, North Lake Falls can only been seen from afar. To many hikers, that's enough. Especially with the high country setting offered at this elevation. If it weren't for the dogs barking and the smell of feces from horses at Bishop Creek Outfitters this place would be truly pristine. The air is crisp and clean, North Lake has sparkling clear water and the view of the jagged mountain peaks near Piute Pass can be breathtaking. The sunsets are particularly remarkable.

North Lake Falls owes its existence to Grassy Lake. Overflow from the lake, and ultimately Wishbone Lake, the Lamarck Lakes and the Wonder Lakes keeps the waterfall flowing year-round. Its peak time occurs from May through early July. The waterfall can't be viewed from its base. Your best bet is to park in the North Lake parking area and walk back to the intersection of North Lake Road and the turnoff for Bishop Creek Outfitters. No parking is permitted at or near the junction.

From this point North Lake Falls can be seen cutting through the trees behind the barbed wire fence and horses. Figure one thing. The horses are going to be wondering what you are doing standing there on the road looking at them, when in reality you are looking past them at the waterfall. To keep them at ease bring along a few apples. They'll let you admire the falls all day.

Let's face it: tourists come here to see North Lake, not the falls. North Lake serves two purposes; it's a local favorite to anglers and a staging area for backpackers headed to the John Muir Wilderness. If you arrive content that the waterfall isn't going to inspire you and consider it an added bonus to an already picturesque setting you'll be complacent.

North Lake Falls at low flow in September of 2002

If you plan to make the trip, supplies are available in Bishop. In winter and early spring call ahead for updated road conditions. The road may be closed due to snow.

Also nearby are the Goldmine Falls, North Lake, Intake II and Bishop Creek Falls.

Directions: From Highway 395 in Bishop drive west on Highway 168 (West LineStreet) for approximately 18 miles to North Lake Road. Turn right and continue 1.6 miles to the turnoff for Bishop Creek Outfitters. Turn right and continue to the North Lake parking area.

Bishop Creek Falls

Rating: 8

How Short? Drive-To
or 0.25 Miles

How Easy? 2

Best Time to View?
April to October

Need Information?
Contact: Inyo National
Forest (760) 873-2400

Bishop Creek Falls is the best, least know waterfall in the Eastern Sierra and is only outmatched by a few on the list: Rainbow Falls, Minaret Falls and Mammoth Creek Falls. Like its neighbor Goldmine Falls, Bishop Creek Fall's popularity suffers because of its close proximity to Lake Sabrina and other majestic and scenic high mountain lakes in the Bishop Creek Drainage.

Bishop Creek Falls is worthy of its own stop in this heavily visited section of the Inyo National Forest. At nearly 9,000 feet, roughly one-mile downstream of Lake Sabrina and a quarter-mile upstream of the North Fork of Bishop Creek and Goldmine Falls this 150-foot cascade can accompany a thunderous roar in the spring when snowmelt from the John Muir Wilderness keeps the Middle Fork of Bishop Creek raging forcefully.

While sightseers drive by Bishop Creek Falls on their way to Lake Sabrina they can't see the waterfall because the cascade is hidden beneath passenger's panorama on the north side of Highway 168. Bishop Creek Falls is most often first seen by passengers looking over their right shoulder on North Lake Road, on the way to North Lake. This, in fact, is one of your best vantage points.

Another exceptional viewing point is from the base. This view can be attained by parking at the intersection of Highway 168 and North Lake Road and locating the Middle Fork of Bishop Creek. Roughly 20 yards downstream of North Lake Road there's a wooden footbridge that crosses the creek. Carefully, cross the creek and make a right, heading downstream. There's a fairly steep path that zig-zags to the waterfall's base.

If you plan to make the trip, supplies are available in Bishop. In winter and early spring call ahead for updated road conditions. The road may be closed due to snow.

Also nearby are the Goldmine Falls, North Lake, Intake II and Misty Falls.

Directions: *From Highway 395 in Bishop drive west on Highway 168 (West Line Street) for 17.9 miles to a pullout on the right (at the junction of Highway 168 and North Lake Road.)*

Bishop Creek Falls in September of 2002

Goldmine Falls

Rating: 5

How Short? Drive-To

How Easy? 1

Best Time to View:
May through August

Need Information?
Contact: Inyo National
Forest (760) 873-2400

Goldmine Falls isn't your thrilling, overpowering California heart stopping waterfall. In fact, without a pair of decent binoculars you'll surely be disappointed. Your visual of Goldmine Falls comes from a distance. Standing on Highway 168, nearly a half-mile from the cascade the falls are all but imposing from this vantage point. Nevertheless, with binoculars Goldmine's true colors stand out. Goldmine is striking when see close up. That is, when its half dozen or so cascades and freefalls can be viewed tumbling down the rugged mountainside.

Goldmine Falls is a portion of the North Fork of Bishop Creek where the creek exits North Lake and makes its decent to the Middle Fork of Bishop Creek. The falls was given its name because it is located s near the old Cardinal Goldmine which was used heavily in 1906. The goldmine hasn't been active since the 1930's and is just a short walk from the town of Aspendell.

Most visitors, however, drive right past the waterfall on their way to scenic Lake Sabrina. The waterfall is best viewed in the spring when peak runoff occurs. There is a possibility of walking to its base. On the other hand, in this case the best view is rewarded to those who put forth the least effort; roadside waterfall seekers with binoculars.

If you plan to make the trip, supplies are available in Bishop. In winter and early spring call ahead for updated road conditions. The road may be closed due to snow.

Also nearby are Bishop Creek Falls, North Lake, Intake II and Misty Falls.

Directions: *From Highway 395 in Bishop turn west on West Line Street (Highway 168) and continue 17.2 miles to a unmarked pullout on the right.*

Goldmine Falls in September of 2002

Misty Falls

Rating: 6

How Short? Drive To

How Easy? 1

Best Time to View?
April to October

Need Information?
Contact: Bishop Creek
Lodge (760) 873-4844,
Inyo National Forest
(760) 873-2500

Misty Falls is mystical in its own way. While not the world's most powerful waterfall by any means, the way it was formed may be most intriguing. Misty Falls hasn't been around forever. The waterfall was created in the Twenties when the owner of the property decided to surprise his new wife by diverting water off a natural spring in the mountains, thus creating the waterfall for their honeymoon. What a great surprise!

As you've figured out the waterfall is surrounded by Inyo National Forest land, however, the drop itself is on private property so you can't hike to its base. In the summer of 2002 some of the woodsy allure of the falls was taken away when a house was recently constructed at its base. Fortunately, the best view is had from the road. Misty flows year-round; however, the road to the falls closes in the winter when an ice cap forms over the falls. It volume is always minimal so do expect to be awed.

Its beauty, on the other hand, may overtake you. The waterfall is best viewed in the fall when the aspen trees prepare to shed their leaves by changing over to magnificent gold, orange and yellow colors that bring a sense of Adirondack life. At 8,600 feet in the Inyo National Forest, Misty Falls borders the South Fork of Bishop Creek which is Sportsman's heaven. People come here for the fishing. The waterfalls are secondary. Keep that in mind and you wont be disappointed.

If you plan to make the trip, supplies are available at Bishop Creek Lodge and in Bishop. Call ahead for updated road conditions. The road is commonly closed from late fall through early spring.

Also nearby are the Tyee Lakes, South Lake, Misty Falls and Intake II.

Directions: *From Highway 395 in Bishop turn west on Highway 168 (West Line Street) and continue 14.9 miles to South Lake Road. Turn left and continue to Bishop Creek Lodge. From the lodge drive roughly a half-mile to a pullout across from the waterfall.*

South Fork Bishop Creek Falls

Rating: 6

How Short? 0.25 Miles

How Easy? 1

Best Time to View?
May to November

Need Information?
Contact: Bishop Creek
Lodge (760) 873-4844,
Inyo National Forest
(760) 873-2500

Gary Olsen has strong feelings on the value of the South Fork of Bishop Creek Drainage. "You don't have the pressure here that you have in Mammoth," he said. "We have 22 cabins. They have 5,000 hotel rooms. Mammoth is LA in the woods. What we sell here is solitude and peace and quiet. When you come here you are in the woods. It's peaceful."

Olsen, owner of Bishop Creek Lodge couldn't have put things better. At the South Fork Bishop Creek Falls that is exactly what you get. The waterfall isn't your towering Yosemite thriller or an overpowering and deafening cascade. It is, however, a small cascade in a picturesque setting that can only be outdone by a few others in this type of serene setting.

At 9,400 feet in the Inyo National Forest the waterfall combines a fast flowing high mountain stream, hundreds of pine and aspen trees, eager wild and stocked rainbow and brown trout coupled with an excellent picnic area set alongside the creek. The picnic area is a mere 50 yards downstream of the falls, which can be reached by following a well-established, but unmarked footpath.

The waterfall itself isn't grand. It's a 30-foot cascade that bends its way down a rugged rock face before settling into a 20-foot wide and calm stretch of water perfect for fishing. While the waterfall appears to be in a pristine setting things can be a bit deceiving. A short distance upstream the South Fork of Bishop Creek's flows are regulated by a dam on South Lake. No need to worry. To protect the fish, flows are always kept stable insuring the waterfall is sufficient year-round. The only draw back is the road is closed most years from December through April.

If you plan to make the trip, supplies are available at Bishop Creek Lodge and in Bishop. Call ahead for updated road conditions. The road is commonly closed from late fall through early spring.

Also nearby are the Tyee Lakes, South Lake, Misty Falls and Intake II.

Directions: From Highway 395 in Bishop turn west on Highway 168 (West Line Street) and continue 14.9 miles to South Lake Road. Turn left and drive six miles to a parking area on the left. (The parking area is one-tenth of a mile upstream from La Hupp Picnic Area.)

First Falls

Located at 8,100 feet, along Big Pine Creek, First Falls is nestled upstream from one of the region's most popular fishing areas. Hikers rather than anglers, however, usually take advantage of First Falls. You don't have to go on a long backpacking trip in the high-country to visit First Falls. It's just a short quarter-mile walk along a dirt road.

Backpacking is definitely an option, if that's more to your taste. Above First Falls is a walk-in campsite. It's far more peaceful to sleep here than sleeping in a tent next to generators and motor homes, which are all too common in Sage Flat Campground near the trailhead. At the walk-in camp, nature creates far more relaxing and soothing sounds.

The sound of First Falls, for example, is both soothing and exhilarating, at once. It's rushing water, which comes from high-country snow runoff, crashes against boulders, cascading 200 feet down a steep mountain. When you're above the falls, the sound of the water pounding against the boulders isn't so strong that it might keep you from sleeping. But the sound of any running water, whether plashing or pounding, always seems to put me to sleep at night.

The path to First Falls is easily navigated. From the day-use parking area, walk to the north side of the stream and continue up the dirt road. You'll see a few cabins on the right and Big Pine Creek on the left. Paralleling the creek, continue for a quarter-mile upstream to a wooden footbridge. That short 10-minute walk through a heavily pined forest brings you to the base of First Falls. The trail also continues into the John Muir Wilderness and to Big Pine Lakes.

There is no way to see the entire cascade from one vantage point. Too many overgrown trees and bushes obstruct a clear view. For me, however, listening to the thundering roar of the falls is more rewarding than viewing its physical beauty. Once you're at the base of the falls, you'll have a few choices: continue upstream to the walk-in camp; sit on the bridge and eat lunch; or do what I did and bring along a fishing pole. You can work your way back downstream, casting small Panther Martins into the pools along Big Pine Creek.

If you plan to make the trip, supplies are available in Big Pine. Call ahead for road conditions. Chains may be required into mid-May. Big Pine Creek is closed to fishing from November 1 to the last Saturday in April.

Also nearby are the Big Pine Lakes and Palisade Glacier.

Directions: *From Mojave, drive north on Highway 14 to Highway 395. At the Texaco gas station in Big Pine, turn left on Glacier Lodge Road. Continue approximately 10 miles, past Sage Flat Campground, to the end of the road, and park in the day-use area.*

First Falls

Onion Valley Falls

Rating: 6

How Short? Drive-To

How Easy? 1

Best Time to View:
May to July

Need Information?
Contact: Independence
Chamber of Commerce
(760) 878-0084, Inyo
National Forest
(760) 876-6200

Day users rarely visit Onion Valley, one of the many drive-to recreation areas in the Eastern Sierra. Located in the mountains above the town of Independence, a 13-mile drive up a winding road from Highway 395 is required to reach Onion Valley. The drive includes a few thousand feet change in elevation, with drastically changing scenery: the desert environment at the bottom in Independence becomes a pine forest by the time you reach the end of the road just below the 13,000-foot peaks. Here, you'll find clear, cold high-mountain streams and trails that ascend from the valley up into the John Muir Wilderness.

At 9,200 feet in the Inyo National Forest, pretty Onion Valley is a popular staging area for hikers and outdoor lovers, yet few stick around long enough to take advantage of it. Many hikers driving from Independence to Onion use the valley as a parking lot. Just as quickly as they can park their cars, they strap on their backpacks and hike to one of many popular backcountry destinations, such as Robinson Lake, Golden Trout Lake, Kearsarge Pass, Kings Canyon National Park and other lakes in the area.

When it comes to cars, Onion Valley looks like a used car lot. Yet, when you look around for all the people who belong to those cars, it looks more like a ghost town. It's too bad more people don't spend time here relaxing and enjoying the superb scenery and lovely waterfalls.

Of the three streams that merge in Onion Valley, two create appealing waterfalls that can be seen from the parking lot without any hiking at all. The largest stream, Independence Creek, ironically is the oddball that doesn't have a waterfall.

To the left of Independence, a small unnamed stream from Robinson Lake announces

itself on the mountainside as 200 feet of whitewater cascading down from Robinson's basin to Onion Valley. To the right of Independence, an unnamed stream from Golden Trout Lake presents a more spectacular drop, plunging off a 50-foot wall of granite into Onion. Both waterfalls can be seen from the parking area. Although there are no trails to their bases, you can bushwhack to them.

If you plan to make the trip, supplies are available in Independence. The road to Onion Valley closes in the winter. Call ahead for updated conditions.

Also nearby is Independence Creek.

Directions: *From Mojave, drive north on Highway 14 to Highway 395. Drive north on Highway 395 to the town of Independence. Turn left on Onion Valley Road, just north of the Independence Post Office, and continue approximately 13 miles to the end of the road.*

Onion Valley Falls

Portal Falls

Rating: 8

How Far? Drive-To

How Easy? 1

Need Information?
Contact: Whitney
Portal Store (760) 937-
2257, Inyo National
Forest (760) 876-6200

Whitney Portal is one of the most popular lift off destinations for backpackers and hikers in the United States. The last stop for a juicy burger and salty fries before ascending up to Mt. Whitney, the tallest point in the continental US, the Portal is a staging area coupled with hundreds of pine covered campsites along Lone Pine Creek. The Portal is one of the most heavily visited spots in the Eastern Sierra and has lots of amenities, including to food, beer and basic supplies. The area also offers great fishing, camping and hiking.

While its waterfall is one of its better attractions, Portal Falls suffers from poor location. In reality, Portal is situated in a perfect spot. It can be seen in full view from the parking area. Nevertheless, the spotlight goes to Mt. Whitney, some 6,000 feet overhead. Dwarfed by its 14,495-foot neighbor, Whitney gets the bulk of the attention and has sightseers eyes peeled on it, rather than Portal Falls.

Portal Falls is worthy of its own peek. To reach it you'll need to use Lone Pine Creek as a landmark. If your car is parked facing Whitney Portal Pond make a 180 degree turn and walk 20 yards to the stream. If your trunk is facing the pond the stream is five feet in front of you. Once you locate the stream, staying in the parking lot walk upstream to the end of the parking lot and through a break in the trees you'll get an unobstructed view of Portal Falls.

While its exact height isn't known, it's said to be in the range of 100-150 feet tall. The waterfall isn't a dazzling freefall, but as it is fed by runoff from Lone Pine and

Consultation Lake it does flow year-round and displays a great deal of force from May through July when the cascade is crashing against the granite boulders. At 8,300 feet in the Inyo National Forest you can either walk to the falls base or its brink. There is an unmarked trail that skirts up the right side of the waterfall. Nearing the brink the trail gets steep and difficult to navigate. Only skilled hikers and rock climbers should attempt to hike in this area.

If you plan to make the trip, supplies are available in Lone Pine or at Whitney Portal Store. Whitney Portal Road is closed due to snow from December through at least May. Call the Forest Service for updated conditions.

Also nearby are Upper and Lower Lone Pine Creek.

Directions: *From Highway 395 in Lone Pine turn west on Whitney Portal Road and continue 12 miles to the Whitney Portal day use area.*

Portal Falls

Region 5   *Yosemite National Park (North)*

Foresta Falls
Little Nellie Falls
Tueeulala Falls
Wapama Falls
South Fork Tuolumne River Falls
Tioga Pass Falls
Pywiack Cascade
Pywiack Dome Falls
Tuolumne and White Cascades
California Falls and Le Conte

scale of miles
0   15   30   60

For Tueeulala Falls see page 95

Foresta Falls

Rating: 7

How Short? Drive-To

How Easy? 1

Best Time to View:
March to July

Need Information?
Contact: Yosemite
National Park
(209) 372-0200

While most of Yosemite National Park is crowded with sightseers, Foresta Falls remains relatively untouched. Foresta is a local's waterfall, hidden in an overlooked area of California's most popular national park. Although Foresta isn't nearly as grand as many of the other waterfalls in the park, it gives visitors a chance to enjoy a waterfall without having to fight tour buses for parking spots, stand in line to use the bathroom or push through crowds to take a picture. No buses visit Foresta, nor do most tourists. They might if they knew it existed, but the waterfall isn't advertised on the park brochure handed out at the entrance kiosk.

There are two waterfalls along Crane Creek near the town of Foresta. Upper Foresta Falls, a small 20-foot cascade, is a bore. But the lower falls will make you "ooh" and "ah." Six-tenths of a mile downstream along a dirt road, Lower Foresta Falls is the top attention getter. There is no parking along the bridge, so you'll have to drive down the road to one of the dirt pullouts to see it.

In the spring, Crane Creek keeps Lower Foresta Falls gushing. The cascade is 40 feet tall, dashing over a dark granite face. There are pine trees scattered on top of the falls and several types of trees below the bridge, where the undergrowth thickens. If you are standing on the bridge in May and June, the mist from the falls will probably get you damp, but surely wont soak you like many other falls in the park.

One downfall here is that there is no good place to have a picnic. If you don't mind soggy food, I guess you could unwrap the Saran wrap off your turkey sandwich on the bridge. You might be able to stay out of the way of incoming traffic if you sit on the metal railing. Although there is no trail to the base of the upper falls, it's easily doable. Simply climb down the fire-scarred hill to the stream. The falls is on the left and can also be seen from the road.

If you plan to make the trip, supplies are available in Yosemite Village. There is a fee to enter Yosemite National Park.

Also nearby are Wildcat Falls, Cascade Falls and Little Nellie Falls.

Directions: *From the 99 Freeway in Fresno, exit north on Highway 41 and drive 41 miles to Yosemite National Park's entrance. Remaining on Highway 41, drive into the park and continue about 34 miles to the turnoff for Northside Drive. (Highway 41 becomes Southside Drive near Bridalveil Falls.) Turn left on Northside Drive, crossing over El Capitan Bridge, and continue 3.4 miles to a fork in the road. Veer right on Big Oak Flat Road and drive 3.5 miles to the turnoff for Foresta. Turn left and drive 1.7 miles to a fork in the road. Veer left onto Foresta Road, leaving Old Coulterville Road. In approximately six-tenths of a mile, the paved road becomes dirt. Continue three-tenths of a mile, pull over to the side of the road and walk down to the river. To get to the lower falls, continue six-tenths of a mile on the dirt road.*

Little Nellie Falls

Rating: 5

How Short? Drive-To

How Easy? 1

Best Time to View:
February to July

Need Information?
Contact: Stanislaus
National Forest
(209) 962-7825

Most people think that because Little Nellie Falls is only 23 miles from Highway 120 it will only take a half-hour or so to drive to it. What they don't take into account is that the roads to the falls require slow driving. Although maintained, these narrow dirt roads are full of large potholes that keep speeds below 15 mph for most of the drive. So, a drive anticipated to take 15 minutes, in reality, takes well over an hour. By the time visitors get back to Highway 120, half of their day is gone.

This means the crowds are scant at Little Nellie Falls. If visiting, you probably won't run into anyone else. I last visited on a Saturday in June and didn't see another car on the road to the falls. Most tourists were at the more popular areas nearby in Yosemite.

Little Nellie Falls is located at 4,600 feet in the Stanislaus National Forest, within walking distance of the national park's boundary. Fed by tiny Little Crane Creek, the falls is best viewed in the spring when the creek's flows are highest. As its name implies, Little Nellie is small, but it's still a great place to get away from the tourists that overwhelm most of the surrounding area.

Little Nellie is an ideal spot for a family picnic. Afterwards, you can do a little fishing, if you don't mind that the wild rainbow trout in the stream are small, rarely over six inches.

The 20-foot falls is located in a heavily shaded area surrounded by pines that keep you cool on even the hottest of days. You can walk to the falls' brink and base; both are easy, because they are only a few feet from the road. Now, it's time to endure the long, slow drive back to Highway 120. With the solitude found here, however, I think you'll agree that the trip was well worth it.

Little Nellie Falls

If you plan to make the trip, supplies are available in Groveland. Call ahead for road conditions. After storms, four-wheel drive vehicles may be needed to reach the falls.

Also nearby are Rainbow Pool Falls, South Fork of the Tuolumne River, Foresta Falls, Merced River, Cascade Falls, Diana Falls, Bull Creek and Bean Creek.

Directions: *From Groveland, drive approximately 20 miles east on Highway 120 to Haraden Flat Road. Turn right on Haraden Flat Road and drive three-tenths of a mile to Road 2S30. Veer left and follow signs for 5 Corners. Drive eight miles on Road 2S30 to Road 1S12 and veer left, following signs for Trumbull Peak. Drive 15 miles on Road 1S12 and make a hairpin left turn on an unsigned road just before the falls. Continue two-tenths of a mile to the falls on your left. Caution: There are many forks in the road. Always stay on the main road, and, if ever in doubt, take the left fork.*

Tueeulala Falls

Rating: 8

How Short? 3.0 Miles

How Easy? 1

Best Time to View:
March to June

Need Information?
Contact: Yosemite
National Park
 (209) 372-0200

Like many other reservoirs in California, Hetch Hetchy is man-made. Built to provide water to the city of San Francisco, it has unfortunately destroyed the natural flow of the Tuolumne River. Once, waterfalls poured profusely off sheer granite cliffs on the north rim of Hetch Hetchy Valley and the Tuolumne meandered across the valley floor. This valley was known as Yosemite Valley's twin. Because of the reservoir, however, the valley has been flooded, and its natural beauty will probably never be restored. Since Hetch Hetchy Reservoir has caused the kind of destruction that is both unwanted and unneeded in our national parks, things here will never again be the same.

While most of the valley's original features have been eradicated by the floods, a few landmarks do remain untouched: Tueeulala Falls, a 600-foot freefall that pours off the reservoir's north rim, is one of them. Although their backdrops and surroundings differ, in shape and form Tueeulala and Bridalveil Falls are nearly identical. One difference, whereas Bridalveil is likely to flow year-round, Tueeulala typically dries up by early July.

Like Bridalveil, Tueeulala's drop reminds me of a slender column of milk being poured from a carton's triangular spout. Because it is fed by an extremely small watershed, Tueeulala has less force than most waterfalls in the park, but that doesn't detract from its magnificence. As afternoon breezes pick up, Tueeulala wavers in the wind with the graceful rippling of a flag on top of a flagpole.

Although the best view is probably from the parking area at O'Shaughnessy Dam, the vantage from its base is worth the short walk. From the parking area, walk across the dam and through the tunnel on the north end of the reservoir. The trail angles off to the right and parallels Hetch Hetchy. The path gradually ascends before coming to a junction. The left fork is signed for Beehive, Laurel Lake and Vernon Lake. Take the right fork, signed for Wapama Falls. The route continues to Tueeulala's base and then on to Wapama Falls.

Tueeulala Falls

Directions *and trip info for Wapama Falls also apply to Tueeulala Falls*

Wapama Falls

Rating: 9

How Short? 4.8 Miles

How Easy? 2

Best Time to View:
March to July

Need Information?
Contact: Yosemite
National Park
(209) 372-0200

Looking east from the dam at Hetch Hetchy Reservoir, sightseers can get a glimpse of two waterfalls. The closest, Tueeulala, about a mile away, can be seen in its entirety. Many tourists think they can also see Wapama Falls, three-quarters of a mile further, in its entirety. Don't be fooled. Although Wapama looks magnificent from here, its true majesty can't be experienced without a trip to its base.

Only the base of Wapama can be viewed from the dam's distant overlook. From here, the waterfall looks fairly unimposing, like a channel of water pouring out from a crevice a few hundred yards east of Tueeulala Falls. A moderately level walk around Hetch Hetchy to the base of Wapama, however, reveals much more of the falls' true nature.

When you're looking up at it from its base, Wapama gets your heart racing. Its tremendous force and volume thundering through a narrow gorge are a combination that certainly isn't easy to forget. As far as I'm concerned, it's one of the most memorable falls in the park. Yet, most vacationers don't bother to see the waterfall up close. They're satisfied with the view from the dam and don't want to take time out of their busy sightseeing day to hike to it. Do yourself a favor and allot time for the 4.8-mile roundtrip to Wapama. It's worth the outing.

Getting to Wapama isn't that difficult a task. From the parking area next to O'Shaughnessy Dam, walk across the dam to a tunnel at its end. After walking through the tunnel, the trail twists to the right and gradually ascends, before coming to a junction one mile from the parking area. Veering away from signs to Beehive, Laurel Lake and Vernon Lake, stay right and follow the sign to Wapama Falls. The path continues to parallel the reservoir and reaches the base of Tueeulala Falls at seven-tenths of a mile

Tueeulala Falls (Left) and Wapama Falls (Right) from O'Shaughnessy Dam

from the junction. Crossing a few small feeder streams, the path stays roughly 50 feet above Hetch Hetchy for the last seven-tenths of a mile to Wapama.

Reaching Wapama is the easy part. Photographing it, or even viewing it up close, can be tricky without getting soaked. During peak flow (May and June), Wapama's thunderous waters crash against its granite floor, churning up a drenching mist. There's no way to avoid it.

Although there are several footbridges along the trail to aid hikers in crossing Falls Creek, which feeds the

The path to Wapama Falls can flood in the spring

waterfall, during peak flow these footbridges don't solve the mist problem. So much water is carried down Falls Creek that it flows over many of the footbridges. Where the water isn't high enough to spill onto the bridges, the mist takes over, waterlogging your clothes and anything else you might happen to be carrying, including your camera.

To photograph the waterfall, I had to use my two friends as shields. I asked them to stand on the bridge in front of me and then pulled out my camera from under my shirt. As soon as I was ready to snap the picture, they moved out of the way as fast as they could. Even though it only took a split second to snap the photo, the lens still got soaked. We had to dry it off and go through the whole process all over again.

Wapama is made up of a series of cascades, totaling roughly 1,700 feet. Not all the drops, however, can be seen from the base. Some are tucked back in the canyon. If you cross all the footbridges, you'll be able to capture both Wapama and Tueeulala Falls in one photo. One of the reasons for walking to the base is to view the tallest drop, which cascades a few-hundred feet down into the gorge and cannot be seen from the dam.

If you plan to make the trip, supplies are available in Groveland. There is a fee to enter Yosemite National Park.

Also nearby are Cherry Lake and Rainbow Pool Falls.

Directions: *From Modesto, drive approximately 50 miles east on Highway 120 to the junction with Highway 108. Veer right, staying on Highway 120, and continue through Groveland, driving another 25 miles east to Evergreen Road. Turn left on Evergreen Road and drive about seven miles to the town of Mather. Turn right on Hetch Hetchy Road and continue to the road's end at Hetch Hetchy Reservoir.*

Wapama Falls

South Fork Tuolumne River Falls

Rating: 7

How Short? Drive-To

How Easy? 1

Best Time to View:
May to June

Need Information?
Contact: Yosemite
National Park
(209) 372-0222

There are many small waterfalls along Tioga Pass Road, also known as Highway 120, however, none are more spectacular than the South Fork Tuolumne River Falls. And because it's located away from the popular areas of Yosemite Valley, it doesn't get attacked by camera happy sightseers. It's true that Tioga Pass Road does get some visitors, but nowhere near as many as Yosemite Valley, the Mariposa Grove and Hetch Hetchy Reservoir.

At 6,900 feet in Yosemite National Park, the South Fork Tuolumne River Falls is fed by snow runoff from the Yosemite Wilderness. One of many drive-to waterfalls in Yosemite National Park, there is no walking or hiking required to view this waterfall, so it's a great pit stop on the way to Tuolumne Meadows, Tenaya Lake, Olmsted Point or other popular drive-to destinations. You don't even need to get out of your car. (Please pull off the road though.) Simply roll down the window, look to the right and admire. The South Fork Tuolumne River rumbles hundreds of feet down granite slopes, before cascading under the highway.

For those who have enough energy to leave their car, the most noteworthy cascades are downstream from the highway. Although there is no maintained trail to the falls, they can be

South Fork Tuolumne River Falls in May of 2001

seen by standing on any of the boulders located off the north side of the highway or by bushwhacking down to the riverbank.

When planning a visit to the falls check to see if Highway 120 is opened. The road is closed seasonally in winter and spring. May 2, 1987 was the earliest the road has opened since 1980. It didn't open until July 1 during the El Nino season of 1998.

If you plan to make the trip, supplies are available in Tuolumne Meadows and Crane Flat. There is a fee to enter Yosemite National Park. Call ahead for road conditions. Due to snowfall, Tioga Pass Road closes in the winter and spring.

Also nearby are Wildcat Falls, Cascade Falls, Foresta Falls and Little Nellie Falls.

Directions: *From the Big Oak Flat Entrance Station of Yosemite National Park, drive approximately eight miles east on Highway 120 to Tioga Pass Road. Remaining on Highway 120, turn left on Tioga Pass Road and continue approximately eight miles to a small dirt pullout on the right, just after crossing over the South Fork of the Tuolumne River.*

Tioga Pass Falls

Rating: 6

How Short? Drive-To

How Easy? 1

Best Time to View:
May to June

Need Information?
Contact: Yosemite
National Park
 (209) 372-0263

To most tourists, anything with the name "Tioga Pass" in it sounds spectacular. And in most cases they're right. Although it isn't as dramatic as other more popular sites along Tioga Pass, such as Olmsted Point, Tenaya Lake and Tuolumne Meadows, Tioga Pass Falls is no exception.

If you call the national park and ask them about Tioga Pass Falls, they won't know what you're talking about. The falls isn't popular and doesn't accumulate crowds. The park rangers will most likely point you in the direction of Yosemite Falls, which you should certainly visit, but try not to pass up Tioga Pass Falls.

Sometimes, wonderful adventures happen when you get brave and do a little sightseeing at a place that isn't highlighted on your park map. Don't get me wrong, your jaw isn't going to drop when you see Tioga Pass Falls; but you will be overwhelmed, and you won't even have to leave your car. That's right: Tioga Pass Falls is a drive-to waterfall. Yes!

Coming from the west the waterfall is on the left side of Tioga Pass Road, three-tenths of a mile past the Yosemite Creek Picnic Area. Unlike most of the park's waterfalls, it isn't a huge freefall or a roaring cascade; yet, the 25-foot cascade is still worth visiting.

Tioga Pass Falls tumbles off granite boulders before being diverted under the road and then down into the Yosemite Creek Picnic Area. In May and June, when snow runoff from the high country is at its peak, it really catches visitors' eyes, as the swollen stream tumbles down the near-vertical mountainside.

Tioga Pass Falls

I know it's difficult in a place like Yosemite, but if you can forget about size comparisons, this relatively small waterfall offers a unique overall picture. Just above the small cascade, there's a congregation of pine trees, and at the edge of the pines, the falls' 10-foot-wide feeder stream unexpectedly crashes onto boulders often as large as dumpsters. When runoff is at its highest, it appears that the water is going to spill onto Tioga Pass Road, however, a stone wall was built to prevent this from occurring.

Normally, the season to view Tioga Pass Falls would begin in April and end in early July, but some years, deep snow can keep the road closed until July. If that's the case, the season to view the falls can extend out into August; however, during most years, the creek will dry up by July.

If you plan to make the trip, supplies are available in Tuolumne Meadows. There is fee to enter Yosemite National Park. Call ahead for road conditions over Tioga Pass. The road may be closed until July.

Also nearby are Olmsted Point, Tenaya Lake, Tuolumne Meadows, Dana Meadows, Waterwheel Falls, Le Conte Falls and California Falls.

Directions: From the Big Oak Flat Entrance Station at Yosemite National Park, drive approximately eight miles east on Highway 120 to Tioga Pass Road. Turn left on Tioga Pass Road and continue approximately 19.4 miles to the Yosemite Creek Picnic Area. Drive three-tenths of a mile past the picnic area to the falls on the left.

An unanmed pond near Dana Meadows

Pywiack Cascade

Rating: 9

How Short? 6.0 Miles or 11.5 Miles

How Easy? 2

Best Time to View? June to August

Need Information? Contact: Yosemite National Park (209) 372-0200, Tuolumne Meadows Visitor Center (209) 372-0263

A trip to the Pywiack Cascade can be looked at two ways: a chance to see one of Yosemite's lesser known and seldom viewed waterfalls or a chance to see the cascade and several vantage points of Yosemite National Park that most people never get the chance to see. The latter includes breathtaking vistas of the Pywiack Cascade, Tenaya Canyon, Three Chute Falls, Tenaya Creek, Half Dome, Illilouette Falls, Mirror Lake, Snow Creek, Basket Dome and the eastern end of Yosemite Valley.

There is a catch: the first is a roundtrip hike. The second is a one way trip and you need two cars or reservations on a shuttle to complete. To me, there is no need for a choice. You have to choose the one way trip. Do all you can; pay someone to drive you to Olmsted Point, book a shuttle, bring and extra person who doesn't enjoy hiking so they can serve as a chauffeur. This trip ranks among the best, offers some of the sweetest views in the park and should not be ignored. It consists of 11 miles, all downhill, with a 4,300 foot loss, most of which comes all at once when you descend the Snow Creek Trail. The trip is easily doable in a half day for anyone in descent shape.

The journey begins at Olmsted Point. Locating the trailhead is equally as difficult as pulling yourself away from the exceptional view of the backside of Half Dome and the Yosemite Backcountry as seen from this popular roadside vista. Once you are able to draw yourself away, start at the southwest end of the parking area. Look south and pick up the trailhead, which is unsigned, but can be found by locating rocks lined up on the granite to highlight the beginning of the trail. Known as the Cutoff Trail, the path swoops downhill for 100 yards, then ascends briefly before reaching a small granite peak. Shortly, the route abandons the granite and embarks on dirt. The path winds downhill briefly over the next half-mile. In three-quarters of a mile from the road a small pond is visible on the right.

This unnamed pond near Olmsted Point serves as a good landmarker while on the Cutoff Trail.

Take a few pictures of the delightful reflections in the shallow water, tighten your laces and push on. The journey has just begun.

If there is still snow on the ground this part can be tricky. We got lost several times before steering ourselves onto the right path. Most likely, through at least early June, and as late as the end of July in some years, the path will be hidden under a few feet of snow. Here's a tip: if you get lost follow the tracks of hikers with snowshoes. Try not to get sidetracked following footprints of the deer, bears and mountain lions. Your goal is to reach the Tenaya Lake/Tuolumne Meadows Trail which lies approximately four miles ahead. If the snow is thick at the pond you might want to consider turning around. Plan the hike another time when conditions are more favorable. If there is snow at this point things are definitely going to get worse. Without a pair of snow shoes, a good map and your own directional skills to go with it, you are putting yourself in danger. If the path is snow free or sports just patches of snow you're in good shape.

Scott Wiessner and Nicole Shaffer search for the Cutoff Trail. As shown above, during the spring the path may be covered by snow.

From this point until you near Snow Creek the route is fairly flat and easy to navigate, if not for the snow. After passing the pond, the trail makes a gradual shift to the right, heading back towards Tioga Pass over the next quarter-mile. At 1.3 miles, and a mere half-mile from the pond you'll be forced to make your first stream crossing. The crossing of this unnamed stream is simple. Don't get the stream confused with Snow Creek. You still have a long way to go.

Over the next 1.5 miles the path stays flat while you parallel, but stay above the creek, working your way towards Tenaya Canyon. The canyon widens and deepens with each step. At first glimpse of Tenaya Canyon, which is on the left, start looking for the Pywiack Cascade. While more than a mile away the drop is still imposing. A slender sliver of rushing white water the cascade is a result of Tenaya Creek exiting Tenaya Lake and embarking on its descent into Yosemite Valley where it later meets the Merced River. The cascade is a 600-foot drop in a remote, rugged and treacherous section of the park. The National Park Service urges hikers to stay away from Tenaya Canyon above Three Chute

Although located in the same panorama, don't mistake this seasonal waterfall for Pywiack Cascade.

Falls because of frequent rock slides and hazardous conditions.

This vantage point is one of the best, and although you can't see the entire drop, you are fortunate to see enough to realize the worth of this magnificent plunge that isn't seen by thousands of tourists a day like most of the parks waterfalls.

Luckily, this portion of the route is free of trees and other obstructions allowing you a clear view of the falls. The cascade can also be seen from the top of Half Dome, along the Sunrise Trail and from Glacier Point (if you have great eyes, a zoom lens or a pair of binoculars). The scene from here is heart throbbing, however, the best view may be from its base. Unfortunately, I've never been opportune enough to experience the view from that locale because repelling gear is necessary to surmount the steep cliffs.

Now it's decision time: either turn back and wrap up the six mile excursion or continue on your descent to Yosemite Valley. For those of you continuing on, the trail looks different for the next few miles. No longer are you adored by stunning vistas and

gigantic slabs of granite. The new setting is ruled by a canopy of pines. Continue through the shaded area as it gradually heads downhill for 1.5 miles to the first trail junction.

The right fork ascends to May Lake and the left fork, which is basically staying straight heads towards Yosemite Valley, 5.4 miles ahead. Stay left. Now on the Tenaya Lake/Tuolumne Meadows Trail, in one-tenth of a mile you'll cross a small, unnamed tributary to Snow Creek. Parallel the creek briefly as it drops down to Snow Creek. While you'll still be able to hear it, the path gradually switchbacks itself away from the stream and begins to parallel Snow Creek.

Roughly 1.75 miles from the junction is a footbridge over Snow Creek. Use the footbridge to cross the stream, which looks like a river in the spring. In fewer than 100 yards you'll come to another junction. Keep going straight and Yosemite Valley, via the Mirror Lake Loop is 3.7 miles ahead. Choosing to break off to the right requires a climb to North Dome, Yosemite Falls and Yosemite Point. Enjoy the next quarter-mile. Things get rough afterwards.

Pywiack Cascade

At 6.6 miles and a 1,800-foot loss in elevation from your locked car at Olmsted Point you embark on, but unfortunately can't see, the brink of Snow Creek Falls. At 6,700 feet it's all downhill from here. You'll descend 2,600 feet over the next 1.4 miles. Ouch. Take it slow. The well being of your knees depend on it.

Taking your time won't be an issue. The extraordinary views are continuous beginning with an eye level view Basket Dome, then Half Dome and shortly after an unhindered view of Illilouette Falls. The first section of the never ending switchbacks is narrow and steep. Take this portion carefully and slowly. Roughly halfway down the mountain the view switches levels, now showcasing Tenaya Canyon, Three Chute Falls and Mirror Lake. Soon after viewing these landmarks still some 1,000 feet below, you'll drop under the cover of trees and lose the outstanding views. At the base of the mountain take a right on the Mirror Lake Loop Trail and continue one-mile to Mirror Lake. Take a rest, enjoy the scenery and cherish the last three-quarters of a mile to the Tenaya Bridge where you can pick up the free shuttle. Congratulations! You've just completed one of Yosemite's best hikes.

If you plan to make the trip, supplies are available in Yosemite Village. In late spring and early summer call ahead for road conditions. Tioga Pass is common closed into July in some years due to snow and wintery conditions. There is a fee to enter Yosemite National Park.

Also nearby are Tenaya Lake, Pywiack Dome Falls and Tuolumne Meadows.

Directions: *From the Big Oak Flat Entrance Station at Yosemite National Park, drive approximately eight miles east on Highway 120 to Tioga Pass Road. Turn left on Tioga Pass Road and continue approximately 30 miles to Olmsted Point on the right.*

Pywiack Cascade from Glacier Point with a 300 mm zoom lens

Pywiack Dome Falls

Rating: 4

How Short? 0.50 Miles

How Easy? 1

Best Time to View:
May to July

Need Information?
Contact: Yosemite
National Park (209)
372-0200, Tuolumne
Meadows Visitor
Center (209) 372-0263

A secret little waterfall in Yosemite National Park? Do you have to hike dozens of miles to reach it? Are your legs going be exhausted when you finally get there? Are you actually going to be able to find this place? What if I told you the waterfall was one of the easiest to reach in the park (excluding the drive-to waterfalls, of course)?

While Pywiack Dome Falls is just a short walk from either Tioga Pass Road or the Tenaya Lake Picnic Area, it is definitely not one of the park's better waterfalls. The waterfall is just a small 30-foot cascade along Tenaya Creek.

So if the waterfall isn't grand, why should you visit it? For a few reasons: First off, it offers a chance to dodge the crowds that bombard nearby Olmsted Point, Tenaya Lake and Tuolumne Meadows. Such seclusion is a rarity in this park where clusters of sightseers mob most waterfalls. Also, it gives you an opportunity to have a picnic on the shoreline of a high mountain stream, in a heavily forested area next to a waterfall.

Because of its lack of grandeur, even if it were listed on park maps (which it isn't), most tourists would pass on the chance to visit Pywiack Dome Falls. Unlike most of the park's waterfalls, Pywiack Dome Falls isn't an awe-inspiring freefall or a deafening cascade. Mist doesn't drench you when nearing its base, and, most likely, you won't take more than a few pictures.

This simple waterfall is created by Tenaya Creek sliding unspectacularly down a giant slab of granite on the east side of Pywiack Dome. Although the cascade is visible from the top of the dome, the reason most people climb up there is for stunning views of Tenaya Lake, which is roughly a mile south.

There are two ways to reach the waterfall. The hike from Tioga Road is the shortest route, but it requires a brief off-trail trek. From the turnoff for Tioga Pass in Crane Flat, drive 33 miles to an unmarked pullout on the right side of the road. (The pullout is more of a shoulder.)

After parking, walk to the base of Pywiack Dome. Cross a small stream, which is easily doable with the help of fallen trees. Continue walking east to the far side of the dome, less than 200 yards away. At the edge of the dome, leave the granite path and begin walking on soil. Roughly 50 yards after reaching the soil, you'll come to Tenaya Creek.

Pywiack Dome Falls

From Tenaya Creek, the waterfall is noticeable on the left. Walking to its base is an option, and you can also walk to the brink. As with the walk in, there is no trail, and luckily one isn't needed. Simply walk on the smooth granite to the brink. This is a great place for a picnic.

If you opt to take the longer, but easier route from the picnic area, there is a trail that follows Tenaya Creek upstream for approximately one mile to the falls.

If you plan to make the trip, supplies are available in Tuolumne Meadows. There is a fee to enter Yosemite National Park. Call ahead for road conditions. In some years Tioga Pass can remain closed into July.

Also nearby are Tenaya Lake, Olmsted Point, Tuolumne Meadows and Tuolumne River.

Directions: *From Yosemite National Park's Big Oak Flat Entrance Station, drive approximately eight miles east on Highway 120 to Tioga Pass Road. Turn left on Tioga Pass Road and continue approximately 33 miles to an unsigned pullout alongside Tioga Road.*

Karen Becker with a set of genuine Yosemite pinecones

Tuolumne Falls and White Cascades

Rating: 8
How Short? 10.8 Miles
How Easy? 3
Need Information? Contact: Tuolumne Meadows Visitor Center (209) 372-0263, Yosemite National Park (209) 372-0200, High Sierra Camp (559) 253-5674

I've talked numerous times about trips where the journey is greater than the inn, and spots where the river or stream is more spectacular than the waterfall itself. We've also come across places where their memorable names have only set visitors up for disappointment. While this day-long excursion through the backcountry of Yosemite National Park does guide you to four waterfalls, these waterfalls aren't comparable to the more dramatic cataracts in Yosemite Valley and at Hetch Hetchy Reservoir. These waterfalls aren't the normal, awe-inspiring drops that are known worldwide in the state's busiest national park. Don't get me wrong, the trip through the Tuolumne River Drainage is a must do at some time for every avid hiker. At some point, however, if not for the waterfalls, the wildflowers, the solid fishing found in its many pools, the great vistas of Cathedral Peak seen along the way and the fantastic rock formations beside the wide and winding river warrant the exhausting hike that will leave cramps and soreness in your legs for a few days after the trip. (Providing you chose to walk all the way to

The Tuolumne River winds through Tuolumne Meadows above Tuolumne Falls

Waterwheel Falls and don't choose to turn back at Glen Aulin.)

Before I deter you from going on this hike, keep one thing in mind. In this comparison, these waterfalls are being measured against the other waterfalls in Yosemite, not the rest of the waterfalls in this book. Thus, I may be giving somewhat of a false impression. The point I'm trying to make is that if you first visit the waterfalls of Yosemite Valley and then Hetch Hetchy Reservoir, you will probably be disappointed with these waterfalls located off Tioga Pass Road. They don't compare to the 2,425-foot drop of Yosemite Falls, the 317-foot plunge of Vernal Falls, or the gentle grace and elegance Bridalveil Falls exuberates while leaping off the valley's south rim. Yet, they are impressive when shown next to most of the state's other waterfalls.

So you're ready to sign up? Park alongside the dirt road signed for Dog Lake and Lambert Dome. Beware that this route can be deceiving in the beginning. While it's fairly flat over the first few miles, the rest of it has a great deal of elevation loss, which means you should save some energy for the climb back out.

The trail begins in the grassy meadows of Tuolumne Meadows and stays flat in the beginning. Many hikers get a false perception of how the day is going to be from this grassy meadow dawned upon from the get go. With Lambert Dome at your back and the Tuolumne River to the left, walk through the locked gate and begin trotting down the dirt service road. In a roughly a half-mile the trail splits, with the road continuing to the left, towards a bridge across the calm, 30-foot wide Tuolumne. Stay left, passing many informational sign boards and keep to the right of Parson's Memorial Lodge, a small shelter still intact from when explorers used it to survive the harsh winters that occur at this elevation. Still a relaxing hike, continue through Soda Springs. Leaving the grassy meadows, you'll embark on a forested area.

In 1.3 miles a trail to Lambert Dome and Dog Lake breaks off to the right. Stay left, cross Delaney Creek and continue on the flat path for another four-tenths of a mile to another junction. Now 1.7 miles in, the right fork ascends to the Young Lakes. Staying on the Pacific Crest Trail, veer left and in one-mile hop over Dingley Creek and regain sight of the Tuolumne. For the next quarter-mile keep an eye out on the left for memorable views of Cathedral Peak with small cascades along the Tuolumne in the

Tuolumne Falls

White Cascades (GlenAulin)

foreground.

At 4.2 miles from the car-filled parking lots near Highway 120, you'll make your first stream crossing; by using a wooden footbridge to safely cross the Tuolumne. At this point the path has lost a mere 266 feet, however, prepare your knees, downhill is on the way. In a mere one-tenth of a mile the first series of cascades are on the right. Personally, this waterfall is pathetic and not worthy of its own name in  such spectacular waterfall country, and which is most likely the reason it hasn't been given one. Continue to descend and after another four-tenths of a mile of trekking on solid granite, another uneventful cascade can be seen on the right. Don't mistake these cascades for the named waterfalls. In a tad more than three-tenths of a mile, the first named waterfall, Tuolumne Falls can't be missed. This is what you've been waiting for and have descended nearly five miles and 550 feet to see.

Tuolumne Falls is a grand cascade nearly 100 feet tall, displaying a powerful personality while creating an influential roar as the river crashes against slabs of granite. Snap a few photos, catch your breath, and continue the descent. Two-tenths of a mile ahead is a junction hidden below a canopy of pines. Ignore signs pointing to the left for McGee Lake, Tenaya Lake, May Lake, Ten Lakes and Yosemite Valley. Stay right and push on the final two-tenths of a mile towards signs to Glen Aulin.

At 5.3 miles in you'll come to the second footbridge, this one marking your arrival to Glen Aulin, and more importantly White Cascades, referred to as Glen Aulin Falls to some. Because it falls at a less inclined slope than Tuolumne Falls, this 75-foot cascade is the end of the road for many hikers, and the start of a luxurious camping trip for others. Those who don't like to rough it can book a tent and a hot meal at High Sierra Camp, which is 100 yards away and offers hot showers, sack lunches and frame beds!

Now it's decision time unless you've made early reservations and reserved a tent at the camp. Either unlace your boots and rest over lunch before your 5.4-mile, 730-foot ascend back to Tuolumne Meadows, or continue downriver to California, Le Conte and Waterwheel Falls.

If you plan to make the trip, supplies are available in Tuolumne Meadows in the summer months. Highway 120 is closed during the winter and through most of spring. Call ahead for updated road conditions. Reservations at High Sierra Camp are done via a lottery system. Make reservations early.

Also nearby are Tenaya Lake, Ellery Lake and Pywiack Dome Falls.

Directions: *From the 99 Freeway in Merced, exit east on Highway 140 and drive past Mariposa to the entrance for Yosemite National Park. Drive through the Big Oak Flat Entrance Station and continue approximately eight miles east on Highway 120 to Tioga Pass Road. Turn left on Tioga Pass Road (also known as Highway 120) and continue approximately 39 miles to a dirt road signed for Dog Lake and Lambert Dome just after the river crosses under the road. Turn left and park as close to the locked gate as you can. The trailhead is beyond the gate.*

California and Le Conte Falls

Rating: 7

How Short? 16 Miles

How Easy? 3

Need Information?
Contact: Tuolumne
Meadows Visitor
Center (209) 372-0263,
Yosemite National Park
(209) 372-0200,
High Sierra Camp
(559) 253-5674

Those of you who have decided to continue past Glen Aulin and onto California and Le Conte Falls must be true die hards. These waterfalls are hardly impressive and force you to descend further and further, making the return trip longer and tougher. If you are in shape, the journey can be fit into one day. It took my partner and I about six hours; however, we didn't take the time to relax and cherish the wilderness. Unfortunately, we rushed because we had plans that night in Fresno.

Use the previous write-up to reach Glen Aulin, 5.4 miles from Tuolumne Meadows. At Glen Aulin, cross the footbridge over the Tuolumne River and walk fewer than 50 yards to a trail junction. Here you have three choices. With the aid of a footbridge, the right fork surmounts Conness Creek and guides you to hot meals and showers at High Sierra Camp. That's an option providing you made reservations months before reading this book. If you were to continue straight it's a long grueling climb on the Pacific Crest

Trail into Virginia Canyon (11 miles) and Mattehorn Canyon (14 miles). For our purposes, stay left following signs to Waterwheel Falls 3.3 miles ahead and Pate Valley, a whopping 14.3 miles downhill.

On my first trip in this section of the Tuolumne Drainage, locating waterfalls became more of a hassle than a pleasure. The problem is that there are so many cascades and smaller drops that it's difficult to discover the named waterfalls without confusing them with the unnamed ones. Even with topo maps I had to consult several other hikers, who aided me in locating California Falls, which is roughly 1.4 miles away. A quarter-mile downstream from Glen Aulin is an uneventful cascade. It's tempting to stop, cast a line

California Falls (pictured above)

in for some wild rainbow and brown trout, however, better opportunities await downstream. Continue along the fairly flat, now dirt path meandering through a pined forest, dappled with wildflowers.

The easiest way to locate California is to continue to descend. When the trail begins to steepen and wind down a few short switchbacks, you'll find yourself at the base of California Falls. California is not a freefall. It's an uneventful and poorly sloped cascade. The waterfall as a whole fails to impress, yet, bits and pieces of it can be intriguing.

Picture a skateboarder speeding downhill with a great deal of force. He's going so fast that it's impossible to stop when needed, and he crashes into a solid wall in the middle of the road. Now replace that sore feeling of the skateboarder with water, in this case the Tuolumne, which races downhill only to have its flows slowed by five-foot tall granite walls positioned in the middle of the river. Depending on the volume of the river and what month you arrive, the water can shoot up more than 20 feet in the air upon slamming into the wall. When the river begins to subside, the water pounds against the wall, slows, and is forced to the left where it begins to regain speed sliding down more cascades into a large, swimmable, but frigid pool downstream.

To reach Le Conte Falls, descend another 1.2 miles along the Tuolumne to the cascades. For those who have enough energy, I've been told the final group of cascades, known as Waterwheel Falls, is the best on the trip. If you turn around from Le Conte, an eight-mile trek including a 1,525-foot climb is all it takes to get back to Tuolumne Meadows. Take breaks and you'll have no problem. To Waterwheel, it's another mile with more than an 800-foot drop in elevation. Yikes!

Directions *and trip info to Tuolumne Falls and White Cascades also apply to California and Le Conte Falls.*

Small cascades are abundant along the Tuolumne River

Region 6 Yosemite National Park (South)

Snow Creek Falls
Three Chute Falls
Nevada Falls
Vernal Falls
Illilouette Falls
Staircase Falls
Royal Arch Cascades
Lehamite Falls
Yosemite Falls
Sentinel Falls
Ribbon Falls
Bridalveil Falls
Silver Strand Falls
Fissure Falls
Chilnualna Falls
Wildcat Falls
Cascade Falls

Snow Creek Falls

Rating: 10
How Short? 4.0 Miles
How Easy? 2
Best Time to View: February to July
Need Information? Contact: Yosemite National Park (209) 372-0200

You probably wouldn't be too surprised to know that if I ranked the top 10 waterfalls in California, at least five would be in Yosemite Valley. And others in the valley would also be close candidates. You might be surprised, however, if I told you that only one percent of the park's visitors know about one of the best waterfalls in the valley.

I asked 100 tourists at Yosemite Village if they'd ever heard of Snow Creek Falls. Not one answered "yes." Then, I surveyed hikers on the trail to Mirror Lake, and it wasn't until after the 33rd "no" that I ran into this guy with long hair, wearing a San Francisco Giants T-shirt, who seemed to have at least a vague idea what I was talking about.

"Well, I saw something on the map that said Snow Creek. Does that help you? The map said it's that way," he pointed east.

Informal as it may be, I believe my poll proves my point: although one of the most powerful and spectacular waterfalls in all of Yosemite (perhaps all of California!), Snow Creek Falls is not showcased in most of the park's publications, nor is it even listed on the free park map handed out at the entrance kiosks. Talk about getting no respect!

And the few who do know about the falls keep it to themselves, so it remains quiet and relatively untouched. When I last visited the falls on a Saturday at high noon in late May, there wasn't another person within a half-mile; yet, the rest of the trails in the valley were all packed.

What makes Snow Creek Falls so grand? It's height, for one thing. Although not all of it can be seen from any one vantage point, Snow Creek is taller than 2,000 feet. That would make it the second tallest in the park, only a few hundred feet shorter than Yosemite Falls.

Yosemite and Snow Creek may both be giants, but they are quite different in appearance. While Yosemite is a freefall, Snow Creek is a cascade. And Yosemite can be seen from many different vantage points, while Snow Creek only has a few from which it is visible.

Originating from May Lake at 9,329 feet in the Yosemite Wilderness, Snow Creek is one of the park's larger streams. This becomes apparent when you reach the falls and witness the force of the creek as it spills over the falls' lip and tumbles down a

This photo was taken atop Three Chute Falls. If you look across the picture in the backdrop you'll be able to see Snow Creek Falls.

narrow winding gorge, crashing loudly against large boulders the entire way.

Although Snow Creek is wide above the falls, as gravity forces it down the cascade and into the gorge, its waters narrow and pick up speed. Because of the tremendous volume of water crashing down several cascades, there's an earsplitting roar that can be heard within a half-mile of the falls.

With SUV-sized granite boulders in the water's path, the impact of torrential currents crashing into these huge boulders causes the water to shoot up nearly 20 feet into the air. So, Snow Creek Falls does in fact look like snow as the frothy white water crashes against boulders and ricochets high into the air.

Simply standing at the base of Snow Creek Falls is an experience not to be forgotten. With tall, granite cliffs towering up on each side, it reminds me of Kings Canyon National Park. From here, my favorite thing is to walk along the south side of the stream to where Snow Creek empties into Tenaya Creek, and then walk up the mountain. The easiest way to do this is to find a small dry creek bed and walk up. After 50 yards or so, I'm above the tree line.

Up here, you can perch yourself on a boulder, and directly across the valley you'll see the last 400 feet of Snow Creek Falls. To the right above the pine trees is Three Chute Falls. And Tenaya Creek is on the left, flowing towards Mirror Lake. From this vantage, 100-foot-tall pine trees look like Legos. You'll also be able to see clearly how the jagged tree line stops abruptly at the point where the fertile soil along the banks of Tenaya Creek gives way to granite.

A close up of Snow Creek Falls

The hike to Snow Creek Falls is as remarkable as the falls itself. If you don't take the shuttle to stop No. 17, add 1.5 miles to your trip. From Tenaya Creek Bridge, follow the trail for seven-tenths of a mile through the pine forest to Mirror Lake. Leaving behind the crowds at Mirror Lake, continue 1.2 miles to a footbridge. (This is also the turnoff for the Snow Creek Trail.)

While walking from Mirror to the bridge, keep an eye out for herds of deer grazing in the meadows along Tenaya Creek's banks. These delicate meadows are filled with dozens of species of wildflowers in the spring. At the bridge, make sure you stay on the south side of Tenaya Creek, because the waterfall is difficult to see from the north side.

Snow Creek meets Tenaya one-tenth of a mile past the bridge; this is an important marker. The falls is above this point, but can't be seen from here because of tall pines. Now it's time to walk up a creek bed to get to higher ground.

Snow Creek Falls can also be seen from a few other places. The best are the top of Half Dome and Three Chute Falls. Only about the last 500 feet of the waterfall can be seen from its base. The rest is tucked away back in the gorge. I tried to climb alongside the falls from the base of Snow Creek to get a better view of the falls, but the granite wall was too steep. Don't even try it!

If you plan to make the trip, supplies are available in Curry Village. There is a fee to enter Yosemite National Park.

Also nearby are Staircase Falls, Lehamite Falls, Sentinel Falls, Ribbon Falls, Three Chute Falls, the Royal Arch Cascades, Mirror Lake, Vernal Falls, Nevada Falls, Half Dome, Illilouette Falls and El Capitan.

Directions: *From the 99 Freeway in Fresno, exit north on Highway 41 and drive 41 miles to Yosemite National Park's entrance. Remaining on Highway 41, drive into the park and continue 30.6 miles to the day-use parking area at Curry Village. (Highway 41 becomes Southside Drive near Bridalveil Falls.) Pick up the shuttle to stop No. 17.*

Snow Creek Falls from the top of Half Dome

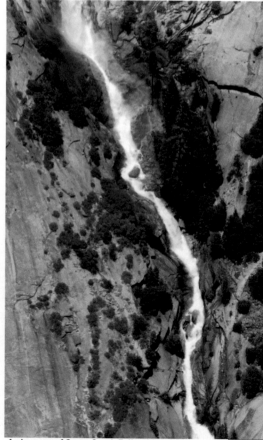

A close up of Snow Creek Falls with a 300mm zoom lens from near Quarter Dome

115

Three Chute Falls

Rating: 9

How Short? 4.5 Miles

How Easy? 2

Best Time to View:
February to July

Need Information?
Contact: Yosemite
National Park
(209) 372-0200

Yosemite National Park has hundreds of waterfalls, both named and unnamed. That's not to say that the unnamed waterfalls aren't worth visiting. Take Three Chute Falls, for example. You're saying, "But it has name." Maybe. At any rate, the waterfall is one of the most unique in the park, even though it's not listed on any park maps.

One sunny May morning, I went to the Yosemite Valley Visitor Center to try to unlock the mystery of why Three Chute Falls has been so rudely ignored.

"There's a waterfall there?" the woman at the counter said curiously. "Are you sure there's a waterfall there? I've never heard of it. Let me ask someone else." She asked everyone else. Not one person had ever heard of or been to Three Chute Falls.

One reason why they'd never heard of Three Chute Falls was that I had just named it that morning on my way to the visitor center. But named or unnamed, why they didn't know it existed boggled me. The waterfall is less than a mile-and-a-half past Mirror Lake, one of the park's most renowned tourist traps, and numerous people have obviously been there before. Many curious hikers have probably wandered past the lake and run into the falls. There's even a trail that ends at its base.

I did, however, glean one clue to this mystery from the woman at the visitor center: the National Park Service strongly discourages hikers from entering Tenaya Canyon, which begins directly above the falls. Because of rockslides and a treacherous river, the canyon has been deemed unsafe.

That same day, I went around the park talking to all the park rangers I could find. I wanted to see if any had heard of the waterfall on Tenaya Creek. As I guessed before I set out on this mission, not one had a clue.

I went back to the visitor center and notified the woman of my findings. "If nobody around here has ever heard of it, then I guess you're entitled to name it," she relented.

Mirror Lake at 8 a.m. on a late May morning in 2000

Brandi Koerner scrambles over a few granite rocks near the base of Three Chute Falls.

"Just tell us what you're going to call it, so we'll know where to send people when they ask."

So, why did I name it "Three Chute Falls"? Let me explain. Tenaya Creek is a large creek, more like a river, which averages 20 feet wide and four feet deep, until its form changes drastically at the waterfall. Just above the falls, Tenaya Creek meets up with a large, exposed, fairly flat layer of granite lying in the stream's path. As the stream cruises over this sheet of rock, it gets forced down three separate, narrow concave funnels that conduct its water into the three chutes.

The water doesn't just plunge off the rocks, it shoots out, crashing against the boulders below and generating a strong mist. My camera and I didn't even last a minute near the freefalling chutes of water. We were soaked. The base of the falls is interesting, too. Although there isn't a pool, there are hundreds of boulders, ranging in size from as large as a 7-Eleven to as small as a lunch box.

Sounds interesting? Well, it is. I still haven't found another place in California just like it. By now you probably want to know how to get there. Here's what you do:

Take the free shuttle to stop No. 17 (Mirror Lake/Tenaya Bridge) and start walking on either side of Tenaya Creek to Mirror Lake. At Mirror Lake, eight-tenths of a mile from Tenaya Bridge, the scenery begins to change. Along with fewer people, come green open meadows filled with wildflowers and perhaps deer, if you're lucky. The edges of the meadows are lined with tall pines.

Continue to parallel the creek, and in 1.2 miles you'll come to a footbridge. This bridge was washed away during the Yosemite Floods in January of 1997, however, the National Park Service finished rebuilding it in June of 2001. At this juncture, make sure you're on the south side of the stream. Surprise! You're standing almost directly below Half Dome.

Carry on 100 yards east, and Snow Creek Falls will be on the left. Continue past Snow Creek Falls, which can be viewed through the trees. Two-tenths of a mile upstream from the juncture below Half Dome, there is a fallen pine tree about 20 yards long, and also a small waterfall (in May and June) that comes down a large granite boulder on the right. Walk across the log and carefully continue upstream. The falls ("Three Chute Falls," that is) is just above this small waterfall. Use caution, the mist from the waterfall makes the rocks slippery. Note: Three Chute Falls is on the right. Don't be fooled by the group of small cascades that can also be seen on the left.

Although it can be extremely tricky to find, there is also a path that guides you to Three Chute's brink. This path is not on maps, nor is it maintained. Good route-finding skills are a necessity. Think you can find it? From the juncture, continue east and begin looking for a dry streambed on the right side of the trail. There are two dry streambeds from this point to the falls.

Abandon the path and start rock-hopping up the boulders. You'll need to walk about 100 yards up the streambed and then make a left, paralleling Tenaya Creek. Don't forget to look across the canyon for a great view of Snow Creek Falls. Continue another one-tenth of a mile east to the base of the falls. Caution! This stretch is only recommended for skilled hikers. Again, there is no maintained path. Off-trail hiking is required.

While the cataract runs year-round, the best time to see it is in May and June, when the chutes are running the fastest. Three Chute Falls becomes far less dramatic as the summer progresses. Remember when you get to Yosemite to ask for it by name.

If you plan to make the trip, supplies are available in Curry Village. There is a fee to enter Yosemite National Park.

Also nearby are Staircase Falls, Lehamite Falls, Sentinel Falls, Ribbon Falls, Snow Creek Falls, the Royal Arch Cascades, Mirror Lake, Vernal Falls and Nevada Falls.

Directions: *From the 99 Freeway in Fresno, exit north on Highway 41 and drive 41 miles to Yosemite National Park's entrance. Remaining on Highway 41, drive into the park and continue 30.6 miles to the day-use parking area at Curry Village. (Highway 41 becomes Southside Drive near Bridalveil Falls.) Pick up the shuttle to stop No. 17.*

Three Chute Falls

Nevada Falls

Rating: 10

How Short? 5.2 Miles

How Easy? 4

Best Time to View: Year-Round

Need Information? Contact: Yosemite National Park (209) 372-0200

There are few waterfalls in the United States that hikers, vacationers, nature lovers and families will travel thousands of miles to visit. Nevada Falls in Yosemite National Park is one of them. Yet, in spite of Nevada's popularity, not everyone can handle the vigorous and demanding hike required to reach it. It's a mere 2.6 miles to the top of the falls, however, with the falls' brink at 5,940 feet, the hike requires a 1,910-foot elevation gain.

Although the hike to the top of Nevada is a real butt-kicker, it's worth it. Witnessing the Merced River make its 594-foot plunge out of Little Yosemite Valley is an experience you'll never forget. With wildflowers scattered along the trail, sheer granite cliffs towering above on both sides and spectacular views of Yosemite Valley over your left shoulder, the hike to Nevada is unforgettable.

Many hikers who choose to continue on to the top of Half Dome use the brink at Nevada Falls as a resting spot. Depending on the time of day, the top can be packed with exhausted hikers resting on the banks of the Merced, before descending back into Yosemite Valley.

The falls is astonishing any time of the year, but most memorable in May and June when snow runoff is at its peak. At peak flow, Nevada looks like a giant fog machine. Although you can hear the water crashing onto the rocks at its base, the constant spray of mist is so thick, the roiling water below is invisible to the eye.

The falls loses force as summer progresses, and it slows dramatically by winter when it's often partially covered by ice and snow. Although there is no single best place to

The view from the brink of Nevada Falls

Mist from Nevada Falls

view the falls, the views from Clark Point, the bridge above Emerald Pool and from both the Mist and John Muir Trails are remarkable.

Even though Nevada Falls sounds perfect, there is one downfall: from Memorial Day to Labor Day weekend, the trail to the falls becomes terribly overcrowded. I can guarantee you there will always be too many other hikers around.

Ready to be awed, here's what to do: begin the climb at Happy Isles. The trail can be picked up on the north side of the Happy Isles Footbridge. Follow the trail that parallels the Merced River, eight-tenths of a mile to the Vernal Falls Footbridge. Get a glimpse of Vernal Falls, and don't pass on the last chance to fill up water bottles with piped water. Near the restrooms there is a water fountain that is fed by a spring. Unfortunately, the fountain is shut off in the winter.

After crossing over the Vernal Falls Footbridge, follow the signs to the JM Trail, less than 50 yards ahead. At this point, you are faced with two choices: the Mist and JM Trails offer much different views of both Vernal and Nevada Falls, as well as Yosemite Valley. Keep in mind, the only way to get the best views of both falls is to walk both trails.

At the junction of the JM and Mist Trails, follow the JM Trail. From this junction to Clark Point, is the toughest part of the hike, because the trail zigzags up both long and short switchbacks. Stoping to catch your breath, turn around for an awe-inspiring view of Yosemite Valley and Upper and Lower Yosemite Falls.

From Clark Point, it's a tad under a mile to the top of Nevada Falls;

David Savage, of New York, enjoys the granite formations near the brink of Nevada Falls.

Nevada Falls from the John Muir Trail

however, you are once again faced with two options: either continue on the JM Trail to the top of the falls or take a trail spur to the left that leads to the Mist Trail and the base of Nevada Falls. Stay on the JM Trail and take the Mist Trail on the way back.

Although the trip back offers stunning views, it is all downhill and not generally good on the knees. After the climb you've endured to get to the top of Nevada Falls, however, downhill seems a welcome sight. Take your time; your legs won't be at full strength. Ankle and knee injuries are easy to come by if you aren't careful.

If you plan to make the trip, supplies are available in Curry Village. In winter, call ahead for road conditions. Chains may be required. There is a fee to enter Yosemite National Park. If you don't ride the tram from Curry Village to Happy Isles, add an extra mile-and-a-half to the roundtrip.

Also nearby are Half Dome Illilouette Falls, Emerald Pool and Staircase Falls.

Directions: From the 99 Freeway in Fresno, exit north on Highway 41 and drive 41 miles to Yosemite National Park's entrance. Remaining on Highway 41, drive into the park and continue 30.6 miles to the day-use parking area at Curry Village. (Highway 41 becomes Southside Drive near Bridalveil Falls). Take the free shuttle at Curry Village to Happy Isles or walk to the trailhead.

Half Dome is a short distance from Nevada Falls

Just above Nevada Falls a footbridge across the Merced River allows hikers to access the Mist Trail from the JMT

Vernal Falls

Rating: 10	
How Short? 3.4 Miles	
How Easy? 3	
Best Time to View: Year-Round	
Need Information? Contact: Yosemite National Park (209) 372-0200	

Walking up the trail to Vernal Falls, I wondered if somebody was giving something away. There were more than 1,000 people on the trail, all tired, but with a certain look of anticipation on their faces. To intensify that anticipation, none of the hikers on their way back from the falls looked disappointed. All talked with the same sense of excitement one gets after the thrill of riding a roller coaster.

So, was there anything really being given away? There sure was, but it wasn't anything tangible. It was nature offering for free a priceless, breathtaking view of Vernal Falls. One of our most spectacular waterfalls, Vernal is known worldwide for its magnificent and powerful 317-foot drop. Even in the waterfall-rich Yosemite National Park, Vernal Falls stands out as one of its most popular attractions.

As wide as 75 feet during peak flow in the springtime, the falls serves as California's own little Niagara Falls, dousing its visitors in mist as far as a half-mile downstream at the Vernal Falls Bridge. The hike to Vernal Falls is an unforgettable experience, and a must for nature lovers, as well as families with children. It's an experience you can't get anywhere else in California.

After walking three-fourths of a mile from Curry Village (or taking the free shuttle to the Happy Isles stop), pick up the trail to Vernal Falls on the north side of the Merced River. Quickly entering the Yosemite Wilderness the path wastes no time climbing steadily uphill. Crossing the

NEVADA FALL	2.4
GLACIER POINT	7.2
HALF DOME	7.2
CLOUDS REST	
MERCED LAKE	12.2
TENAYA LAKE	15.4
TUOLUMNE MDWS	
JOHN MUIR TRAIL	

The trailhead sign at Happy Isles

Hiking the Mist Trail below Vernal Falls on a warm spring day

wilderness boundary, you'll be able to see remnants of a bridge that was washed out during the great floods that occurred in Yosemite in 1997. There is a marker at the gauging station where the bridge used to be; it shows how high the water rose in the flood.

As you ascend, start looking to the right for the Illilouette Gorge. At the top of the gorge is Illilouette Falls. Still paralleling the Merced River, the next landmark is the Vernal Falls Bridge, which is eight-tenths of a mile from Happy Isles Bridge. This is the first glimpse of the falls from the often-crowded bridge.

Just after crossing the bridge, take advantage of the last chance to suck down a little water from the only water fountain on the trail. There is no piped water beyond this point. Now you'll be posed with two options. The John Muir Trail breaks off and winds up a series of long switchbacks to the top of Nevada Falls, then on to Half Dome and

(Top) Vernal Falls from the Mist Trail   (Bottom) The Mist Trail as seen from the brink of Vernal Falls

other destinations in the Yosemite backcountry. The Mist Trail goes to the base of the falls.

You'll be doing yourself a great injustice if you don't choose the Mist Trail. Only a few-hundred yards upstream from the bridge, there is a signed lookout on the left side of the trail that provides one of the best views of the falls. The lookout is one of only a few locations where artists and photographers can set up for a clear and unobstructed view of the falls. From here, Vernal Falls is an exuberant display of both power and grace, as the massive Merced plummets off a granite shelf and freefalls more than the length of the Statue of Liberty into a clear pool below.

Vernal Falls in May of 2002. Those red and white dots on the right side of the photo are hikers on the Mist Trail.

Continuing upstream, it's time to get out the rain gear; although it probably won't be raining, it sure will feel like it. In the spring and early summer, there is no way around getting soaked. The power of the Merced making its final tumble into Yosemite Valley creates a constant flow of drenching mist, which forces you to put your cameras in protective cases, wrap them in plastic bags or risk damaging them.

The Mist Trail is lined with wildflowers and green moss that glisten with mist in the spring and summer. The granite steps you'll use to reach the top of the falls will also be

Half Dome, Vernal Falls and Nevada Falls from Glacier Point

wet and extremely slippery, so be sure to use caution not to slip and fall. Because these granite steps get blanketed with ice in the winter, the Mist Trail remains closed until early spring in most years.

At the top of Vernal Falls is the Vernal Falls overlook. There is a chain fence to protect you from falling over the brink. Be sure not to climb over this fence in search of a better view. I've seen people do it many times, but the danger is much greater than the rewards the view might offer. People have slipped off the rocks and died here.

There is still one more marvelous view of Vernal Falls left to see. Continue east, passing Emerald Pool just above the falls, and pick up a trail spur that bends to the right, up to Clark Point and the JM Trail. Halfway up the trail you'll come to an unsigned overlook that shows off the best view of Vernal Falls. It's the only spot above the falls where you get to see it in its entirety. From here the falls looks like a gigantic narrow tidal wave crashing against the beach, except it's pounding against granite rather than sand.

If you aren't planning to continue on to the top of Nevada Falls, the easiest way back into Yosemite Valley is via the John Muir Trail. Nevada Falls can be seen by looking east from the intersection of the JM and the trail that connects the JM to the Mist Trail. Head west on the JM, walking past Clark Point, and begin your descent back into Yosemite Valley. Eye-catching views of Upper and Lower Yosemite Falls can be seen in the distance. After enduring many long switchbacks, you'll end up back at the Vernal Falls Bridge.

Vernal Falls changes considerably with the seasons. From May to June, the falls is at peak flow, and it begins to gradually subside through fall, when it becomes a slow, gentle freefall. As winter approaches, Vernal's force becomes even more greatly reduced, its surroundings are generally covered in snow and the pool below is partially frozen. So, it's a good idea to plan your visit to Vernal in advance, choosing the month that would best suit your taste.

Crowds are something else you'll need to take into account. Anytime from Memorial Day to Labor Day, there will be more than

Vernal Falls in mid-October of 1998

1,000 people on the trail each day, and hordes of tourists can definitely detract from the wilderness experience. May and June also get pretty crowded, but from October to April, crowds tend to be light. Nevertheless, the falls is worth visiting any time of the year.

If you plan to make the trip, supplies are available in Curry Village. There is a fee to enter Yosemite National Park. In winter, call ahead for updated road conditions. Chains may be required.

Also nearby are Half Dome, Nevada Falls, Illilouette Falls, Staircase Falls, Merced River, Yosemite Falls, Ribbon Falls, Three Chute Falls, Snow Creek Falls, Lehamite Falls, Silver Strand Falls, Bridalveil Falls and Sentinel Falls.

Directions: From the 99 Freeway in Fresno, exit north on Highway 41 and drive 41 miles to the entrance of Yosemite National Park. Remaining on Highway 41, drive into the park and continue 30.6 miles to the day-use parking area at Curry Village. (Highway 41 becomes Southside Drive near Bridalveil Falls.)

Snowplant

Hikers begin the ascent to Half Dome's summit

Vernal Falls from the cutoff trail. For a sense of size, those dots to the right of the falls are hikers.

Vernal Falls in May of 2001

Illilouette Falls

Rating: 10

How Short? 4.0 Miles

How Easy? 3

Best Time to View:
May to August

Need Information?
Contact: Yosemite
National Park
(209) 372-0200

Illilouette is one of those waterfalls that leaves you speechless. Can a waterfall in California really be this good? In Yosemite National Park the answer is yes. Illilouette is a "wow!" waterfall that will inspire you to keep coming back to the park year after year. Reached via a short two-mile trek through a fire-scarred forest, Illilouette is a 370-foot wall of water that leaps off a sheer granite cliff into a dark, narrow gorge, before emptying into the Merced River near Happy Isles.

Although the hike to the falls is fairly easy, drawing yourself away from the spectacular view from the trailhead at Glacier Point is difficult. The Panorama Trail, which takes you to the falls, can be picked up at Glacier Point. This point offers one of the better panoramas of Yosemite Valley and beyond, with a birds-eye view of Upper and Lower Yosemite Falls, North Dome, Half Dome, Royal Arch Cascades, Vernal Falls, Nevada Falls, and Yosemite Valley, not to mention the Yosemite high-country in the backdrop. It's a view you'll definitely never foget.

Once you manage to pull away from the breathtaking view from Glacier Point, pick up the trailhead for the Panorama Trail, which begins at Glacier Point and continues to the John Muir Trail above Vernal Falls. From this trailhead, the path immediately descends, traversing the fire-scarred mountainside.

In one mile, the trail passes just below Washburn Point. Paralleling the Illilouette Gorge, it gradually continues downhill for the next eight-tenths of a mile before coming to a trail junction. The right fork leads to Edson Lake, Hart Lakes, Buena Vista Lake, Chilnualna Lakes, Buena Vista Pass, Mono Meadow, Upper and Lower Merced Pass Lakes; however, you'll want to stay left.

From this trail junction, Illilouette Creek can be heard cascading through the gorge below. The trail's switchbacks, then descends a few-hundred feet over the next half-mile, before arriving

Illilouette Falls

at a side view of Illilouette. This view is actually much better than from above. The trail passes by the falls, before continuing upstream to a footbridge over Illilouette. There's no trail to Illilouette's base.

Perch yourself on one of the many huge granite boulders, re-hydrate and admire Illilouette. The gush off the brink of the falls looks like a fire hydrant's been opened. A flood of water shoots out and plunges off the cliff, fanning out on its way down into the gorge. When you're ready to return to Glacier Point, take a good stretch first; it's more

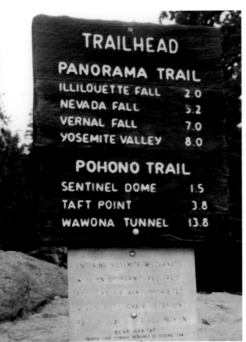

TRAILHEAD
PANORAMA TRAIL

ILLILOUETTE FALL	2.0
NEVADA FALL	5.2
VERNAL FALL	7.0
YOSEMITE VALLEY	8.0

POHONO TRAIL

SENTINEL DOME	1.5
TAFT POINT	3.8
WAWONA TUNNEL	13.8

than a 1,200-foot climb back out.

Illilouette Creek is the Merced's largest tributary, supplied by a large area of runoff that keeps Illilouette's volume of water sufficient to awe-inspire tourists year-round. Since Glacier Point Road is closed seasonally (usually from late November to Memorial weekend - sometimes even into late June), the Panorama Trail is generally best traveled from June to September.

Glacier Point can be reached with snowshoes when the road is closed, but there is also an alternative option. Illilouette can be seen from the John Muir Trail near Happy Isles, which remains opened all year. About a half-mile upstream from the Happy Isles Bridge, begin looking up the canyon wall on the right. Illilouette Falls looks tiny from here unless you have a pair of binoculars. The view from the Panorama Trail can't be matched.

If you plan to make the trip, supplies are available in Wawona. There is a fee to enter Yosemite National Park. In winter call ahead for road conditions. Chains may be required. Glacier Point Road is closed beyond Badger Pass from November until at least mid-May.

Also nearby are Chilnualna Falls, Washburn Point, Taft Point, Sentinel Rock, Nevada Falls, Vernal Falls and Yosemite Valley.

Directions: From the 99 Freeway in Fresno, exit north on Highway 41 and drive 41 miles to Yosemite National Park's entrance. Remaining on Highway 41, drive into the park. Continue 16.5 miles to Glacier Point Road and turn right. Drive 15.3 miles to Glacier Point.

As shown above, Illilouette Falls can be seen in its entirety from the Snow Creek Trail

Staircase Falls

Rating: 6

How Short? Drive-To

How Easy? 1

Best Time to View:
February to May

Need Information?
Contact: Yosemite
National Park
(209) 372-0200

Everywhere I go, I'm always spouting information like a tour guide. Often my peers only half listen, giving most of their attention to women in short shorts and what song is playing on the radio. One day, however, driving into Yosemite Valley on Highway 41, I found something to say that got their complete attention.

I'd pulled off the road and parked in the Tunnel View parking lot to show them how beautiful Yosemite Valley was. Ribbon Falls' was on the left, Bridalveil Falls on the right; Merced River meandered down the middle and El Capitan and Half Dome filled the backdrop. These friends from Los Angeles had to admit it was a lot different than seeing smog, freeways and gutters filled with trash. In fact, they were overwhelmed.

What I told them next really seized their interest. I described a waterfall that skips from rock to rock to rock for 1,700 feet before tumbling down into Yosemite Valley.

"What do you mean skips?" said Todd McLean, one of my hiking buddies. "No way. Waterfalls don't do that. I've heard of a cascade and a freefall, but they don't skip. I think you're nuts."

To prove I wasn't "nuts," I drove them to Curry Village and stopped in the parking

lot. Todd stepped out of the car and looked up the mountain. "No way. That's awesome!" Then, he said in an apologetic tone, "I've never seen anything like that before"

From February to May, Staircase Falls skips from one horizontal granite slab to the next. The waterfall is one of the narrowest you'll ever see, no more than a foot wide at peak flow. Its string-like form is stirring, but even more eye-catching is the 3,000-foot-high vertical granite cliff with outcroppings that the falls skips down. The cliff is about 2,900 feet high. That's 10 Statues of Liberty!

Staircase begins near Glacier Point. For the first 1,200 feet it cascades through a dark, narrow canyon and is difficult to see. The last 1,700 feet of the waterfall, however, can be easily spotted on Yosemite Valley's south wall, directly behind Curry Village.

Some opt to walk to its base, but the best view is from a distance. Any of the

Staircase Falls nearly dry in June 2001

meadows near Curry are great viewing areas. If you have trouble locating the falls, look for the Royal Arch Cascades, directly across the valley on the north canyon wall. Get here before the end of June. Come any later, and Staircase Falls will mostly likely have dried up.

If you plan to make the trip, supplies are available in Curry Village. There is a fee to enter Yosemite National Park.

Coyote

Also nearby are Royal Arch Cascades, Lehamite Falls, Sentinel Falls, Ribbon Falls, Three Chute Falls, Snow Creek Falls, Mirror Lake, Vernal Falls, Nevada Falls, Half Dome, Illilouette Falls and El Capitan.

Directions: *From the 99 Freeway in Fresno, exit north on Highway 41 and drive 41 miles to Yosemite National Park's entrance. Remaining on Highway 41, drive into the park and continue 30.6 miles to the day-use parking area at Curry Village. (Highway 41 becomes Southside Drive near Bridalveil Falls.)*

Mule Deer

Half Dome can be overwhelming from Curry Village

Royal Arch Cascades

Rating: 4

How Short? Drive-To

How Easy? 1

Best Time to View:
February to June

Need Information?
Contact: Yosemite
National Park
(209) 372-0200

Because there are so many waterfalls in Yosemite Valley, the chances of not viewing any particular one are high; and if you're planning on overlooking a waterfall, the Royal Arch Cascades is probably a good candidate. Unlike the more popular waterfalls in the valley, Royal Arch doesn't have a lot of volume, and it doesn't create a thunderous roar when it crashes against granite boulders. Yet, even though Royal Arch is a gentle cataract, it does have certain qualities that the deafening and awe-inspiring waterfalls don't.

Just as its name suggests, its cascades gently arch down a vertical granite face. Flowing over a pine-capped peak, these cascades begin their descent by breaking up into several drops, and by the time they've completed half of the 1,250-foot fall, these drops have broken into nearly a dozen smaller ones. Fed by a tiny watershed, the cascade doesn't usually flow past June; however, if a storm hits the park after June, the falls will reappear until shortly after it passes.

Just opposite Staircase Falls, Royal Arch is located on Yosemite Valley's northern wall, due west of North Dome and east of Lehamite Falls. The cascades can be seen up close from Ahwahnee and Stoneman Meadows. Or, if you prefer viewing them from afar, you can do so atop Half Dome and Glacier Point.

If you plan to make the trip, supplies are available in Curry Village. There is a fee to enter Yosemite National Park.

Also nearby are Lehamite Falls, Sentinel Falls, Ribbon Falls, Three Chute Falls, Snow Creek Falls, Mirror Lake, Vernal Falls, Nevada Falls, Illilouette Falls and El Capitan.

Directions: *From the 99 Freeway in Fresno, exit north on Highway 41 and drive 41 miles to Yosemite National Park's entrance. Remaining on Highway 41, drive into the park and continue 30.6 miles to the day-use parking area at Curry Village. (Highway 41 becomes Southside Drive near Bridalveil Falls.) Just before the day-use parking area at Curry Village, park next to Stoneman Meadow.*

Royal Arch Cascades

Lehamite Falls

Rating: 5

How Short? Drive-To

How Easy? 1

Best Time to View:
March to July

Need Information?
Contact: Yosemite
National Park (209)
372-0200, Yosemite
Visitor Center
(209) 372-0299

All but a few waterfalls in the world would suffer from the comparison to Yosemite Falls. Lehamite Falls is no different. A tall, but lackluster waterfall tucked into a small crevice in the gorge northeast of Yosemite Village, partly because of Lehamite's proximity to Yosemite Falls, it gets little to no attention.

Two creeks, Indian Canyon and Lehamite, merge, creating Lehamite Falls. Because these creeks are fed by an extremely small amount of runoff, Lehamite's volume is minuscule compared to other waterfalls in Yosemite National Park, and its possibilities of grandeur are limited.

Most of the park's visitors have never heard of Lehamite, and that situation is not likely to change. Unlike most waterfalls in the park, Lehamite has no outstanding characteristics that the National Park Service can use to attract visitors. Also, there is no trail to the falls.

The falls can be best seen from the parking lot in Yosemite Village. If you are facing the village store, turn your head 90 degrees to the right and look up the sheer granite cliff. Then, look up the mountain directly in front of you. The falls is tucked back in the canyon.

If you plan to make the trip, supplies are available in Yosemite National Park. There is a fee to enter the park. In winter call ahead for road conditions. Chains may be required.

Also nearby are Merced River, Upper and Lower Yosemite Falls, Ribbon Falls, Mirror Lake, Royal Arch Cascades, Staircase Falls, Vernal Falls, Nevada Falls, Snow Creek Falls, Three Chute Falls, Bridalveil Falls and Illilouette Falls.

Directions: From Highway 99 in Fresno, exit north on Highway 41 to Oakhurst. Continue 33 miles through Oakhurst to Wawona. Continue east on Highway 41 to Yosemite Valley. Just past the Bridalveil Falls turnoff, Highway 41 becomes Southside Drive. Continue approximately 4.5 miles east and turn left at Sentinel Bridge. Follow signs to Yosemite Village.

Lehamite Falls

Yosemite Falls

Rating: 10

How Short? Drive-To
or 7.2 Miles
(Upper Yosemite
Falls) or 0.50 Miles
(Lower Yosemite Falls)

How Easy? 1 or 5

Best Time to View:
January to June

Need Information?
Contact: Yosemite
National Park (209)
372-0200, Yosemite
Valley Visitor Center
(209) 372-0299

It was a clear May evening. Just a few stratus clouds could be seen in the blue sky. The view from Glacier Point was breathtaking as the setting sun cast a golden hue over the tip of Half Dome. Photographers were snapping shots as quickly as their fingers could click their shutters. The insect-like sound of camera clicks was overwhelmed by this huge, pervading silence. Everyone was in awe. The beauty of the Yosemite National Park had overcome us all.

Upper Yosemite Falls and the Merced River

Then, as quickly as dusk's caramel light descended on Half Dome, the silence was broken. "Is that Yosemite Falls?" came an Irish accent from a man who was pointing at Vernal Falls. "Wait! What about that one? Is that Yosemite Falls?" He was still way off, pointing this time at Nevada Falls.

"This must be your first time here," a woman said to him. "You're looking in the wrong direction. Yosemite Falls is over there." When the man turned to it, he was stunned. "I wish the boys back at the pub could see this. It's one hell of a sight!"

I overheard the man say he was visiting with his family from Dublin. He said he saw the waterfall years ago in a National Geographic and had been eager to visit it ever since. He clearly wasn't disappointed, his expectations having been more than exceeded.

So, what makes Yosemite Falls so great that people from all over the world want to visit it? Its size, for starters. At 2,425 feet, the waterfall is the tallest in North America and the fifth tallest in the world.

Yosemite Falls is hands down the best waterfall in California, and perhaps the best-known waterfall in the world. The poster child for Yosemite National Park, when most people think of Yosemite, the first thing that comes to mind is Yosemite Falls.

Vacationers fly thousands of miles to get a glimpse of the falls; and, providing it hasn't dried up, I can't imagine anyone leaving disappointed. Millions of sightseers use up hundreds of thousands of rolls of film at Yosemite Falls each year. If you could only choose one landmark in California to visit, Yosemite Falls should be it.

There are dozens of places to view the falls, but it's hard to beat the view from its brink. Overlooking Yosemite Valley at more than 6,300 feet, this tremendous view isn't, however, achieved without sacrifice.

Gaining 2,700 feet over 3.6 miles, the hike makes your legs feel like Jell-O when you're finished; that is, if you do finish. Many hikers don't have the stamina.

Pick up the trailhead to Upper Yosemite Falls at the east end of parking lot, near Sunnyside Campground off Northside Drive. Meandering through a mostly oak-filled forest, the path immediately begins to ascend, gaining 1,000 feet in the first mile, before coming to Columbia Point. Tired out from the short but exhausting climb, many hikers choose to turn back here.

Although the falls can't be seen from Columbia Rock, you do get fabulous views of the valley below, the Merced River, Sentinel Falls, Half Dome, Yosemite Point, Sentinel Rock and North Dome.

If your legs are up to it, Yosemite Falls is just around the corner. From Columbia, the path zigzags up a few sandy switchbacks and crosses a small

Lower Yosemite Falls in October of 1998

seasonal stream in roughly 100 yards, then another seasonal stream about 50 yards further. By now, you'll have noticed that the path has taken a downward slope. About 150 yards past the second stream crossing, the path bends to the left and levels out… Yes! Finally flat ground!

When the flat ground finally arrives, however, you'll notice that no one seems to care; not when Upper Yosemite Falls towers in front of you. Standing about 200 yards from the 1,430-foot drop, the awe-inspiring plunge stops visitors in their tracks as they admire the grandeur of the freefall.

Once you're able to pull yourself away from this spectacular view, continue along the trail, following this rare stretch of straight path for the next few minutes, before the switchbacks resume. At the end of the level path, the rock-bottomed trail winds under a canopy of trees, guiding you up even more short switchbacks. At the end of each switchback, don't forget to look over your shoulder for a terrific view of the falls.

The views are most intriguing in the winter when a snow cone forms at the base of the falls. On cold nights, the water from the falls freezes at the base, accumulating up to 200 feet high. The snow cone usually exists from January through March.

If you come in the winter, use caution on this stretch of the path. Ice commonly forms on the trail, and icicles often fall off the trees during the daytime. The combination of snow and ice on the path can become so dangerous, it sometimes forces the National Park Service to close the trail beyond this point.

Had enough? I hope not. The best is yet to come. But again, it can't be attained without a little effort. As the path leaves the cover of trees, although you'll be exposed directly to the sun, the heat won't be your main concern. With even the slightest breeze, mist from the falls lands on the trail, making the granite path extremely slippery. Even though the mist might seem refreshing, remember it makes trail conditions dangerous.

The brink of Yosemite Falls

Many of the other trails in the park are also granite, but most were built with granite steps, making them easier to walk on than this section of the trail to the brink of Yosemite Falls, which has no steps. All the rocks are laid down seamlessly so you can't step up from one rock to another. It might sound easier to hike without steps, however, we found it to be more difficult. You're much more likely to slip, so you have to walk considerably slower to avoid losing your footing.

For the next few hundred feet, you'll get a different view with each step you take, before continuing up the canyon west of the waterfall and losing sight of it. The most fascinating thing about the drop is the various shapes the water takes as it falls. Take a minute and look closely as it plummets off the lip. You'll see isolated strands of water, no two dropping in exactly the same way.

Sentinel Dome

It's like watching smoke twist and twirl in millions of different shapes and forms out of a pipe. Some strands of water look like mist sprayed out of a mist machine, while others swirl in a corkscrew fashion. Several strands even reminded me of fireworks; others looked like shooting stars.

Continuing up, the switchbacks get shorter as you near the end of the climb to the brink. At the end of the switchbacks, just after passing through a gate, you'll enter a pine forest and come to a trail junction. The path continues on to Eagle Point, Yosemite Creek Campground and Tioga Road; however, you'll want to take the right fork, signed for Yosemite Falls, Yosemite Point and North Dome.

Smile! You're done climbing. The brink is only two-tenths of a mile away. Sticking to the path, you'll reach Yosemite Creek in less than five minutes; then make a right turn, moving carefully towards the overlook. Roughly 100 feet before reaching the stream, the footpath narrows. Metal rails are bolted into the granite to assist hikers down to the overlook.

If you're afraid of heights, chances are you won't enjoy the overlook. The only thing between you and a sheer 1,500-foot drop is a small bar two feet from the edge, which stands four feet tall. Whether you photograph it or not, standing beside the bar and looking off the brink of one of the world's best waterfalls is a moment that will stay with you forever. Watching frothy water freefall nearly 1,500 feet is an indescribable sight, especially when several rainbows are almost always visible below. After 10 a.m., this platform can get crowded. Best get here early and avoid the crowds.

Taft Point

Since you've come this far, you'd be silly not to walk another eight-tenths of a mile to

138

Yosemite Falls and its snowcone in March of 1999.

The view from the brink of Upper Yosemite Falls

Yosemite Point. I personally think the view from the point is better than the view from Half Dome. At 6,935 feet, the point presents awe-inspiring views of Half Dome, North Dome, the Merced River, Staircase Falls, the Yosemite backcountry, the eastern end of Yosemite Valley and Sentinel Rock. Here, just a few-hundred feet above and east of Yosemite Falls, Yosemite Village, almost directly below, looks like a miniature.

To reach Yosemite Point, backtrack one-tenth of a mile from the overlook to the signed junction for Yosemite Point. The route descends to Yosemite Creek, crosses a wooden footbridge over the creek and ascends to the point.

For those of you not inclined to endure the brutal hike to the top of the falls, don't fret; there are several other places in the valley to view the falls. Here are a few of the best: the Yosemite Falls parking lot, Yosemite Village, Sentinel Bridge, Glacier Point, Taft Point, Sentinel Rock, Southside Drive, Northside Drive, the Merced River, the trail to Vernal Falls, the John Muir Trail, Cooks Meadow, Stoneman Meadow and Ahwahnee Meadows. There are a lot of incredible places to view the falls, and all are close by and worthy of their own trip.

With all this attention given to Upper Yosemite Falls, we can't forget about Lower Yosemite Falls. The Lower Falls is more heavily visited and is the destination of hundreds of tour buses each day. Partly because the walk to its base is a mere quarter-mile, and also because the trail to it is paved, the base of Lower Yosemite Falls is one of the most heavily visited tourist spots in the park. The path is also wheelchair accessible.

Park in the Yosemite Falls parking area and begin down the paved path. Wait! Don't forget to look up. From this vantage point, you'll get a view of Upper and Lower Yosemite Falls, as well as the cascades between them. Although they can't be seen in their entirety, the cascades total 815 feet.

Once you reach the Yosemite Falls Bridge, which should take five to 10 minutes, prepare yourself to get doused with mist. The force of 320-foot Lower Yosemite Falls leaping to the Yosemite Valley Floor churns up a drenching mist that forces tourists to wear trash bags or some other form of raingear, or risk getting soaked. Getting waterlogged might sound refreshing, but you'll at least need to be concerned about your camera. If not protected, the mist can ruin cameras in a short time. Plastic bags are the best way to go.

When visiting Yosemite Falls, there are a few things to consider. The most important is season. Depending on snowmelt, Yosemite Falls can dry up as early as July. Yosemite Creek, which feeds the falls, originates at Grant Lakes, 9,462 feet up in the Yosemite backcountry, and flows four miles before crossing under Tioga Pass Road near Yosemite Creek Campground. Fed by dozens of smaller tributaries, the creek meanders through the wilderness for the next eight miles before reaching the brink of Upper Yosemite Falls.

As the first storms begin to roll into the park in late September and early October, Yosemite Falls comes to life again after drying up in the heart of summer (most years). At minimal flow, Yosemite isn't a spectacular sight. It can best be described as a ribbon dangling in the wind, with the same power as Ribbon Falls at peak flow. As winter approaches and snow begins to fall in the high country and melt, the waterfall slowly increases in size and force.

The best time to visit is from mid-March through June, when snowmelt is at its highest, giving Yosemite a tremendous force and power. At peak flow, the sound of Yosemite Falls crashing against the granite floor can be heard all along the eastern end of Yosemite Valley.

To me, the most fascinating time to view the falls is on full moon nights. Light from the moon reflects off the waterfall and creates "moonbows," which can be seen in the meadows near Southside Drive. Similar to rainbows, these moonbows glow iridescently at night under strong moonlight.

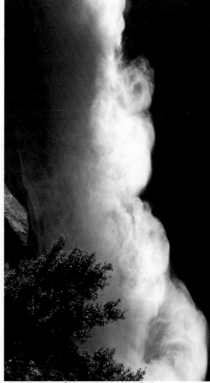

The use of guardrails are needed to reach the brink of Upper Yosemite Falls

A side view of Upper Yosemite Falls from the Yosemite Falls trail

My favorite time to hike to the brink of Upper Yosemite Falls is also when there's a full moon. The view of Yosemite Valley is incredible at night when these moonbows form. Similar fabulous views with moonbows can be observed from Glacier and Taft Points on full moon nights.

If you plan to make the trip, supplies are available in Yosemite Village. There is a fee to enter Yosemite National Park. If visiting from July through October, call ahead to make sure the waterfall isn't dry. In winter, sometimes sections of the trail to Upper Yosemite Falls are closed because of dangerous icy conditions.

Upper and Lower Yosemite Falls from the John Muir Trail

Also nearby are Lehamite Falls, Royal Arch Cascades, Sentinel Falls, Ribbon Falls, El Capitan, Mirror Lake, Bridalveil Falls and Snow Creek Falls.

Directions: *From the 99 Freeway in Fresno, take Highway 41 north to Oakhurst. Continue through Oakhurst 33 miles to Wawona. Continue north on Highway 41 to Yosemite Valley. Just past the Bridalveil Falls turnoff, Highway 41 becomes Southside Drive. Continue approximately 4.5 miles east and turn left at Sentinel Bridge. Follow signs to Yosemite Falls.*

Upper and Lower Yosemite Falls from Glacier Point

Yosemite Falls from Sentinel Dome

Sentinel Falls

Rating: 8

How Short? Drive-To

How Easy? 1

Best Time to View:
March to June

Need Information?
Contact: Yosemite
National Park
(209) 372-0200

I picked up a pictorial guide printed in 1998 by the Yosemite Association, called "The Waterfalls of Yosemite." The pamphlet listed the world's 10 tallest waterfalls. At 2,425 feet, Yosemite Falls was the fifth tallest, and 2,000-foot Sentinel Falls came in a close seventh.

I was confused. Where was Snow Creek Falls? Snow Creek is taller than 2,000 feet and should have taken over the seventh spot, right behind Norway's 2,307-foot Espelandfoss Falls. I called the Yosemite Association for an explanation, unfortunately never received a call back.

Whether Sentinel is the world's seventh or eighth tallest waterfall really doesn't matter. What does matter is that you visit Sentinel before July, because if you don't, you won't be able to see it at all. It dries up!

Sentinel is on Yosemite Valley's south wall, across from Yosemite Falls, just west of Sentinel Rock. It's a wonderful waterfall, but quite different than Yosemite Falls. While Yosemite carries a powerful force and a great deal of volume in the spring, Sentinel is narrow and lacks power, but it does have characteristics that should amaze you.

Sentinel's form, for instance, is quite unique. Sentinel is made up of dozens of drops, some cascades, others freefalls, with no two alike. These drops, ranging from 10 to 200 feet, tumble down an unusual serrated granite face.

The waterfall begins near Glacier Point Road, just below the Pohono Trail, between Taft and Morgan Points. Sentinel Creek has carved a long, thin groove into an enormous slab of granite, forming Sentinel Falls, and although the waterfall is seldom wider than a few feet, it can be seen from various points in Yosemite Valley.

The one problem with Sentinel is that its life can be short. Dependant upon the snowmelt from Pothole Meadows and the Illilouette Ridge, it usually dries up by late July or early August.

There are a few good spots for viewing Sentinel. The best is from the pullouts along Southside Drive, a few hundred yards west of the trailhead for the Four-Mile Trial. Along Northside Drive, on the other side of the Merced River, the best spots are between Three Brothers and El Capitan Bridge.

If you plan to make the trip, supplies are available in Yosemite Village. There is a fee to enter Yosemite National Park.

Also nearby are Wildcat Falls, The Cascades, Merced River, Little Nellie Falls, Bridalveil Falls, Ribbon Falls, Silver Strand Falls and Valley View.

A Yosemite Valley coyote

Directions: *From the 99 Freeway in Fresno, exit north on Highway 41 and drive 41 miles to Yosemite National Park's entrance. Remaining on Highway 41, drive into the park and continue 34 miles to the turnoff for Northside Drive. (Highway 41 becomes Southside Drive near Bridalveil Falls.) Drive three-tenths of a mile past the turnoff to the Cathedral Beach Picnic Area. The waterfall is on the right, west of Sentinel Rock.*

The Merced River and Sentinel Falls

Ribbon Falls

Rating: 8

How Short? Drive To

How Easy? 1

Best Time to View:
April to June

Facilities: None

Need Information?
Contact: Yosemite
National Park
(209) 372-0200

Ribbon Falls is situated against a giant slab of granite just west of El Capitan. Waving back and forth like a ribbon (thus its name) with even the slightest breeze, it flutters down to the valley floor below. Unlike most of Yosemite's spectacular waterfalls, Ribbon doesn't have a lot of force to it. This gentle giant quietly drops some 1,612 feet (Yosemite's tallest free-falling waterfall) before smacking onto the Yosemite Valley floor and eventually flowing into the Merced River.

Because the falls is fed exclusively by runoff from an area of approximately four square miles, it often dries up by early summer. So, despite its respectable size, most of the park's visitors have never seen Ribbon Falls. If fortunate enough to be in the park while Ribbon is active, however, don't miss it.

As soon as the snow starts to melt in the Yosemite Wilderness (usually by March), the waterfall begins to take shape. Rarely does it last into July. It's a shame Ribbon Falls is only visible for a few months of the year. People who come to look for it seldom find it.

There is no trail that guides you to either the base or the brink of the falls, but it is easily visible from the Bridalveil Falls parking lot and from Southside Drive near Bridalveil Falls.

If you plan to make the trip, supplies are available in Yosemite and Curry Villages. There is a fee to enter Yosemite National Park.

Also nearby are El Capitan, Merced River, Cascade Falls, Wildcat Falls and Bridalveil Falls.

Directions: *From the 99 Freeway in Fresno, exit north on Highway 41 and drive 41 miles to Yosemite National Park's entrance. Remaining on Highway 41, drive into the park and continue 25.7 miles to a pullout on the left side of the road. From here Ribbon can be seen on the north wall. (Highway 41 becomes Southside Drive near Bridalveil Falls.)*

Ribbon Falls

Bridalveil Falls

Rating: 10
How Short? Drive-To or Hike 0.25 Miles
How Easy? 1
Best Time to View: Year-Round
Need Information? Contact: Yosemite National Park (209) 372-0200

While Yosemite, Vernal, Nevada and Snow Creek Falls are known for awing visitors with tremendous height and force, Bridalveil Falls displays a different a kind of grandeur, one more associated with grace than power. Those other falls attract crowds with the thundering sound of millions of gallons of water crashing down from their brinks onto enormous granite boulders. They exhibit flows as wide as 75 feet, whereas Bridalveil's width rarely spans more than 10 feet. Yet, Bridalveil is still a first-class waterfall, and its free-leaping vertical drop is just as imposing.

In fact, the first "wow" most visitors experience when entering Yosemite Valley is Bridalveil plummeting 620 feet off the valley's south wall. Positioned between Lower Cathedral Rock on its left and Leaning Tower on the right, and almost always crowned with arching rainbows, Bridalveil acts like a welcoming committee, letting Yosemite National Park's visitors know just how special this park really is.

There are several great places to get stellar views of the falls. The most popular is from its base, which is an easy 100-yard stroll from the Bridalveil Falls parking area through a pine forest. The signed paved path begins in the lot and cuts through the forest, before crossing a footbridge over Bridalveil Creek and arriving at a platform near the base of the falls. If getting soaked bothers you, this isn't a good place to be. From May through July, the mist can saturate your clothes in seconds.

With no trail leading to the brink of the falls, I think the vista point at Tunnel View offers the best observation of Bridalveil. The spectacle is unforgettable. Standing nearly 500 feet above the valley floor, the landscape of the glacier-carved valley is awe-inspiring. Pine trees on the valley floor obscure the view of the wide, fast-flowing Merced River; however, it's not the trees that capture your attention.

Bridalveil Falls

Your eye is immediately drawn to El Capitan, an enormous sheet of sheer granite that makes up the valley's north wall. On the right, just east of Leaning Tower, Bridalveil Falls pours off the v-shaped mountain below

Cathedral Rocks. Looking deeper into the valley, you'll see Half Dome. And, if you're lucky enough to come here towards the end of the day, sunsets are remarkable.

The Valley View Lookout, which includes a scene of Cathedral Rocks towering above the falls, is especially inspiring after a dusting of snow. Standing along the snow-covered sandy shore of the 50-foot wide Merced River, the white waters of Bridalveil, streaming off a nearly symmetrical dish shaped lip of rock, look as pure and silky as a thin ribbon of milk twisting out of a carton. The stream leaps off the granite cliff, before disappearing beneath a congregation of tall pines.

Pullouts along Southside and Northside Drive also offer numerous access points for outlooks, offering outstanding views of the falls all over the valley floor west of El Capitan and east of Tunnel View. The best of these outlooks is from the Bridalveil Falls parking area.

Because Bridalveil benefits from a large area of runoff, when many of the other waterfalls in the valley have dried up, Bridalveil's flows remain. With its origins at Ostrander Lake, Bridalveil Creek is kept alive year-round by snow runoff from Westfall, Peregoy, Summit and McGurk Meadows. Its force, however, does change with the seasons. It flows fast from late winter through early summer; most of the rest of the year, it is reduced to a thin sliver of water dangling in the wind.

If you plan to make the trip, supplies are available in Yosemite and Curry Villages. In winter call ahead for road conditions. Chains may be required. There is a fee to enter Yosemite National Park.

Also nearby are Ribbon Falls, Sentinel Falls, Silver Strand Falls, Merced River, Yosemite Falls, El Capitan, Staircase Falls, Royal Arch Cascades, Lehamite Falls and Cascade Falls.

Directions: From the 99 Freeway in Fresno, exit north on Highway 41 and drive 41 miles to Yosemite National Park's entrance. Remaining on Highway 41, drive into the park and continue 25.4 miles to the turnoff for Bridalveil Falls. Turn right into the parking area.

El Capitan and Bridalveil Falls from Valley View in March of 2000

Silver Strand Falls

Rating: 8

How Short? Drive-To

How Easy? 1

Best Time to View:
March to June

Need Information?
Contact: Yosemite
National Park
(209) 372-0200

To many visitors, the Wawona Tunnel is known as the gateway to Yosemite Valley. After passing through the tunnel, magnificent rock formations, waterfalls and lush meadows can be seen everywhere. The parking area just past the tunnel, known as Tunnel View, offers one of the best views of Yosemite Valley, including Bridalveil Falls and El Capitan. One landmark that can be seen from this parking area, however, is often overlooked, and understandably so.

Similar to the way Lehamite Falls is overshadowed by Yosemite Falls, Silver Strand Falls disappears into the spectacular surroundings seen from Tunnel View. With sightseers' eyes fixed on Yosemite Valley, few think to look up the sheer granite cliffs on the right, where 1,170-foot Silver Strand Falls leaps out into Yosemite Valley.

Silver Strand's height makes it sound like a spectacular sight. Yet, height isn't always

indicative of how spectacular a waterfall is going to be. And it definitely isn't in this case. Because Silver Strand is a victim of a small watershed, it generally dries up by early summer. Meadow Brook, the stream that feeds Silver Strand, is just a tad more than a mile long and also dries up fast. Therefore, you must arrive between March and June to view the waterfall.

Don't get the impression Silver Strand isn't worth your time, because it is. Particularly in the evening about an hour before sunset, when the setting sun casts shadows on half of the waterfall, leaving the other half lit with a golden brown color, it can be quiet inspiring.

If you plan to make the trip, supplies are available in Curry and Yosemite Villages. There is a fee to enter Yosemite National Park.

Also nearby are Bridalveil Falls, El Capitan and Ribbon Falls..

Silver Strand Falls

Directions: *From the 99 Freeway in Fresno, exit north on Highway 41 and drive 41 miles to Yosemite National Park's entrance. Remaining on Highway 41, drive into the park and continue 24 miles to the Tunnel View parking area.*

Fissure Falls

Rating: 5

How Short? 2.4 Miles

How Easy? 1

Best Time to View:
Mid-May to June

Need Information?
Contact: Yosemite
National Park
(209) 372-0200

What is a fissure? The first definition given in Webster's New World Dictionary reads: "A long, narrow, deep cleft or crack." For our purposes, we can stop right there, because this definition is right on. Near Taft Point, on Yosemite Valley's south wall, the Fissures is an area where there are thin crevices in the granite. Only a few feet wide, but up to 1,000 feet deep, these crevices are among Yosemite National Park's most intriguing features.

While definitely fascinating, the Fissures isn't one of the park's more popular landmarks. Sightseers stumble upon the Fissures on their way to Taft Point. Offering eye-level views of El Capitan and Yosemite Falls, Taft Point is one of Yosemite's top sight-seeing spots. The trail to the point passes by the Fissures, one-tenth of a mile before reaching Taft.

Getting a closer view of Fissure Falls

To really appreciate the Fissures, you have to have some guts. Standing on the edge above one of the fissures will set butterflies stirring in your stomach. There are no rails between you and a 1,000-foot sheer drop. It can make your bones tingle. The first time I viewed the Fissures, I crawled on my stomach to the edge to take a look. What an experience!

Directly across the canyon from the Fissures is Fissure Falls. Don't go looking for the waterfall on your map; I made up the name. The waterfall comes from an unnamed stream near Pothole Meadows, which only drains an area of about four square miles. That's why its force and width are always kept to a minimum and the stream often dries up by July.

Fissure Falls, within sight of Profile Cliff, cascades more than 1,000 feet before dropping out of plain view and emptying into the Merced River. Because most tourists won't creep out to the edge, few have seen Fissure Falls. If you do brave a look, don't expect to be awed. Yet, if you are near Taft Point, it is worth the brief side trip to view the falls. Just make sure to be careful near the edge. One slip would mean certain death. People have died here before. Be safe and keep at least three feet back from the edge.

Reaching Fissure Falls requires only a short, fairly flat walk though a heavily forested area. From the parking area, walking away from Sentinel Dome, follow signs pointing to Taft Point and the Fissures. Shortly, you'll cross Sentinel Creek and then many other small feeder streams. In a tad more than a half-mile, the Pohono Trail veers off to the right and leads below Sentinel Dome. Ignore that and continue straight, where the route descends to the Fissures and Taft Point.

If you plan to make the trip, supplies are available in Wawona. There is a fee to enter Yosemite National Park. In winter and early spring, call ahead for updated road conditions. Glacier Point Road is closed in the colder months. When Glacier Point Road is closed, Fissure Falls can be accessed via cross county skiing.

Also nearby are Sentinel Dome, Washburn Point, Illilouette Falls and Glacier Point.

Directions: *From the 99 Freeway in Fresno, exit north on Highway 41 and drive 41 miles to Yosemite National Park's entrance. Remaining on Highway 41, continue 16.5 miles into the park to Glacier Point Road and turn right. Drive approximately 13 miles to the sign for Taft Point and Sentinel Dome. Park in the parking area on the left.*

Fissure Falls   *Karen Becker admires Fissure Falls*

Chilnualna Falls

Rating: 10	
How Short? 8.2 Miles	
How Easy? 5	
Best Time to View: April to July	
Need Information? Contact: Yosemite National Park (209) 372-0200	

Most of California's best waterfalls are located in Yosemite Valley, Tuolumne Meadows or at Hetch Hetchy Reservoir, all situated in Yosemite National Park. Also in Yosemite, Chilnualna Falls isn't found in any of these three better-known areas; however, it's still one of the state's premier waterfalls. A few minutes drive from Wawona, Chilnualna is a grand display of power; best of all, it can be enjoyed without the crowds that gather at the park's more publicized areas.

To reap Chilnualna's rewards, some hard work is required. The 8.2-mile hike, which includes a 2,500-foot elevation gain, isn't an easy one. Yet, if you take it slow, stopping to smell the flowers along the way, it's doable, even for those who aren't in tip-top shape. Remember to stretch properly before leaving the trailhead, bring a lot of water and take frequent breaks along the way. My friend and I completed the hike in two-and-a-half hours, but we ran into hikers who told us it took them six.

From the dirt parking area, walk across Chilnualna Falls Road and begin the uphill trek, which parallels Chilnualna Creek the first one-tenth of a mile. There are many cascades along this section of the creek, but none compare to what lies ahead. After the trail bends to the left, leaving the stream, it takes on what seems like a never-ending climb.

The panorama from Chilnualna Falls

At a little more than three-tenths of a mile, now well above the stream, the path angles to the right and parallels the creek for the next 2.5 miles. This section of the hike winds up switchbacks, meanders through pine forests, crosses small feeder streams and opens up into meadows, flourishing with deer clover and snow plants.

One thing is certain, the trail never stops climbing. Bring along suntan lotion; where the pines don't shade the trail, the sun will beat down on your head. On this portion of the hike, extraordinary vistas of the steep, dark mist-filled gorge below fade in and out of view, regularly obstructed by tall pines and small hills with each new turn of the path. Also, across the canyon on the right, you'll see Wawona Dome, a giant granite boulder roughly the size of the upper level at Dodger Stadium.

At mile number three, the path begins to level out, hugging the granite walls adjacent to

Chilnualna Falls

the lower section of Chilnualna Falls; the dirt trail also ends here and becomes granite. Chilnualna Creek plummets off a granite shelf on the right, but you can only see the top of the drop. The rest of the freefall is hidden in the gorge below. What you can't see, however, can certainly be heard: the water creates a loud roar as it pounds against the canyon bottom.

Continuing along the trail, 3.6 miles from your air-conditioned car, just below the most visible section of the falls, you'll arrive at a trail junction. The left fork leads to Alder and Bridalveil Creeks, Glacier Point Road and the Chilnualna Lakes. Veer right and walk the last three-tenths of a mile to the base of the falls.

Chilnualna looks like a liquid avalanche. The runoff from the Chilnualna Lakes, Grouse Lake and Turner Meadow creates a torrent that is funneled through a narrow granite channel, forming a fast flowing, deafening 300-foot cascade.

Take your time descending the 2,500 feet back to your car. On the left, you'll see a magnificent panorama of Wawona below and the Chowchilla Mountains in the distance. Where Chilnualna Creek meets the South Fork of the Merced River, there are some great swimming holes. And once July arrives, the thundering cascades seen near the parking lot during the spring have since turned to a normal stream and no longer deter you from swimming in these fabulous pools.

If you plan to make the trip, supplies are available in Wawona. There is a fee to enter Yosemite National Park. In early spring call ahead for trail conditions. At times the trail isn't snow free until mid-May.

Also nearby are Glacier Point, Illilouette Falls, Big Creek Falls and Fish Camp Falls.

Directions: From the 99 Freeway in Fresno, exit north on Highway 41 and drive 41 miles to Yosemite National Park's entrance. Staying on Highway 41, drive into the park and continue five miles to Chilnualna Falls Road. Turn right and drive 1.8 miles to a parking area on the right.

California Tree   50 yards
Upper Mariposa Grove   0.9 mi.
Mariposa Grove Museum   1.0 mi.
Fallen Tunnel Tree   1.3 mi.

Brett Ross with a fallen sequoia at the Mariposa Grove

Scott Wiessner (left), Karen Becker and Brett Ross in the Mariposa Grove

Mariposa Grove

Wildcat Falls

Rating: 7

How Short? Drive-To or Hike-In 0.25 Miles

How Easy? 1

Best Time to View: February to June

Need Information? Contact: Yosemite National Park (209) 372-0200

When it comes to world-class waterfalls, Yosemite Valley is the top spot in the United States; there are more fabulous waterfalls here than anywhere else in the lower 48. Just outside the western edge of Yosemite Valley, however, Wildcat is certainly not one of the more popular falls. It's not even well known within the park. In the land of giant waterfalls that pour off sheer granite cliffs, Wildcat Falls gets overlooked.

Located in the Merced River gorge a few hundred yards west of Cascade Falls, every now and then a driver will give Wildcat a passing glance on his or her way to Yosemite Valley; and that's about as much attention as Wildcat typically gets. Yet, those who make plans to see the waterfall can do so without taking a lot of time out of their day.

Across from the Cascades Picnic Area, Wildcat Falls is a series of gentle freefalls along Wildcat Creek. A lot like Staircase Falls, where the narrow stream spills in stair-step fashion from granite ledge to granite ledge down the mountain, Wildcat Falls is most striking in the spring when snowmelt pushes the creek at full force.

Wildcat's drops, however, are much taller than Staircase's. Wildcat has two 40-foot high freefalls, both dropping off sheer granite ledges. Across from the picnic area, the cataract ducks behind the cover of tall pines, where it cascades down another 30-foot drop. Wildcat Creek then flows under Highway 140 and into the Merced River.

The lower cascade can't be seen from the road. From the picnic area, walk across Highway 140 and pick up Wildcat Creek to view it. Follow the creek upstream roughly 50 yards to the cascade.

If you plan to make the trip, supplies are available in Yosemite Village. There is a fee to enter Yosemite National Park.

Also nearby are Cascade Falls, Merced River, Little Nellie Falls, Bridalveil Falls, Ribbon Falls, Sentinel Falls and Valley View.

Directions: From the 99 Freeway in Fresno, exit north on Highway 41 and drive 41 miles to Yosemite National Park's entrance. Remaining on Highway 41, drive into the park and continue about 34 miles to the Northside Drive turnoff. (Highway 41 becomes Southside Drive near Bridalveil Falls.) Turn left on Northside Drive, crossing over El Capitan Bridge, and continue 3.4 miles to a fork in the road. Veer left on Highway 140 and continue 1.75 miles to an unsigned dirt pullout on the right.

Wildcat Falls

Cascade Falls

Rating: 9

How Short? Drive-To
or Hike-In 0.25 Miles

How Easy: 1

Best Time to View:
February to July

Need Information?
Contact: Yosemite
National Park
(209) 372-0200

Did I hear you say you want visit a thrilling drive-to waterfall without crowds in Yosemite? Cascade would be the place. In this often-traveled section of Yosemite National Park, the waterfall gets ignored.

Just a few miles from Yosemite Valley, the park's most popular destination, visitors who enter the park through the Arch Rock Entrance Station usually see Cascade Falls on the scenic drive along the Merced River. Few, however, stop to get a closer look. Most tourists would rather spend their time at the more advertised waterfalls in the valley.

An odd thing about Cascade Falls is that its most awing section isn't really a cascade. It's a free-fall along Cascade Creek. Fed by a large watershed that carries a remarkable amount of volume in May and June, Cascade displays a tremendous force during these months.

Just above the falls, Tamarack Creek joins with Cascade Creek, and these commingled streams feed Cascade Creek Falls, which tumbles down a dark granite gorge and then shoots off the rocks, freefalling down into the Merced Gorge. The water freefalls in a massive, frothy chute, crashing against the granite boulders below. It churns up a constant wind, while creating a drenching blanket of mist. Standing at the overlook will surely soak you in minutes.

Although Cascade Falls is taller than 500 feet, standing across from the lower falls, you can only see the bottom tier. Don't feel bad; this drop is by far the most impressive. Big Oak Flat Road is a good place to view the upper tier. The road is

Cascade Falls

about 100 feet above the point, where Tamarack and Cascade Creeks converge. Another good spot to view the falls is about 100 yards west of the Wawona Tunnel. Here you can see both tiers.

The absolute best way to view the falls is from its base. From the pullout along Highway 140, walk about 30 yards east. There is a trail that leads up the mountain on the left. Follow the trail uphill as it gains a hundred or so feet, curving to the left. Once you're perpendicular with Cascade Creek, the trail bends to the right. In 100 yards, the path ends at a perfect overlook. I've seen people try to walk down to the waterfall's base, but it's not smart. The rocks are extremely slippery and dangerous to walk on.

Cascade Creek may cease flowing late in the fall or as early as mid-summer in some years, but as the snow begins to melt in the mountains above, the creek springs to life again. This occurs no later than early March, with the stream reaching its peak by the first week of June.

If you plan to make the trip, supplies are available in Yosemite Village. There is a fee to enter Yosemite National Park.

Also nearby are Wildcat Falls, Merced River, Little Nellie Falls, Bridalveil Falls, Ribbon Falls, Sentinel Falls, Valley View and Yosemite Valley.

Directions: From the 99 Freeway in Fresno, exit north on Highway 41 and drive 41 miles to Yosemite National Park's entrance. Remaining on Highway 41, drive into the park and continue about 34 miles, until Southside Drive meets the Northside Drive turnoff. (Highway 41 becomes Southside Drive near Bridalveil Falls.) Turn left on Northside Drive, crossing over El Capitan Bridge, and continue 3.4 miles to a fork in the road. Veer left at the fork onto Highway 140 and continue 1.75 miles to an unsigned dirt pullout on the right.

Cascade Falls from Highway 41

Nevada Falls

Region ⑦   Sierra National Forest

Fish Camp Falls

Rating: 7

How Short? 1.0 Mile

How Easy? 1

Best Time to View:
April to September

Need Information?
Contact: Sierra
National Forest
(559) 297-0706

While eating lunch in Oakhurst, I was flipping through the "Yosemite Sierra Visitors Guide 2000" and saw a picture of this dazzling waterfall in Fish Camp. Although the waterfall didn't compare to the waterfalls in Yosemite National Park, it rivaled nearly all of the others I'd seen in the Sierra National Forest.

I walked into the visitor center and asked the receptionist how to get to the waterfall. She said she didn't know. Neither did anyone else in the office. "All I can tell you is it's somewhere near Fish Camp," a retired volunteer told me. That didn't help. It said that in the photo caption. I drove to the Forest Service office near Fish Camp, and it was closed due to budget cuts. Next stop was Fish Camp General Store.

"Yes, that waterfall is around here," said the lady behind the counter. She looked like she was in her fifties and said she'd lived in Fish Camp her whole life, but never seen the waterfall. "I can't tell you where it is. All I know is it's off Big Sandy Road, near a diversion channel." Well, now at least I was pointed in the right direction. Big Sandy Road was only four-tenths of a mile away. I figured I could find a diversion channel.

Things are never that easy when people give you directions. I found the diversion channel, but the waterfall was nowhere in sight. This waterfall that was showcased in the visitor's guide was becoming a pain to find.

I was ready to give up when I ran into a young tour guide from the nearby Tenaya Lodge. "Dude, do you know where this waterfall is?" I asked, showing him the picture

Lower Fish Camp Falls

in the brochure.

"Yah, it's right over there." He pointed near the diversion channel I had walked past at least 10 times. The problem was I'd been walking in wrong direction.

At 5,400 feet in the Sierra National Forest, Fish Camp Falls was just a 10-minute walk away, and it was worth all the hassle I went through to find it. The waterfall in the picture is one of three freefalls along a quarter-mile section of the stream. All are easy to reach and have swimmer-friendly pools.

So, you want to find these waterfalls without getting lost? Park at the small, green building near the diversion channel (flume). There is a dirt parking area, which will probably have a few cars in it. Walk across the dirt road, past the locked gate and stay right, continuing past the wooden picnic table and cabin to the trail. Follow along the trail, which will shortly parallel Big Creek, and you'll come first to a 20-foot freefall. It has a nice swimming hole at its base; however, a giant log that has fallen into the pool can make swimming somewhat difficult.

A few yards upstream, the second freefall, another 20-footer, awaits. There is no log to obstruct swimming here, but the third waterfall is even better. Cross the stream above the second freefall (this is where the flume starts) and rock-hop a few hundred yards upstream.

This 25-foot freefall that's pictured in the visitor's guide is the granddaddy of them all. It's not striking because of its height or power. What's fascinating is the way the sun hits the smooth granite boulders that surround the falls, reflecting light that sparkles off the cataract's clear deep pool below.

This pool makes a great swimming hole and most of the time remains free of crowds. There are many wild rainbow trout in the stream, particularly in the pools below the falls. Try a little fishing, swimming; then, relax, lie down on a towel, open up a drink and eat a snack. You've earned it!

If you plan to make the trip, supplies are available in Fish Camp. Big Creek is closed to fishing from November 16 to the last Saturday in April.

Also nearby are Big Creek Falls, Nelder Creek, North Fork Willow Creek, Bass Lake, Yosemite National Park, Merced River and Nelder Grove.

Directions: *From the 99 Freeway in Fresno, exit north on Highway 41 and drive to Oakhurst. Continue on Highway 41 through Oakhurst, driving 14.5 miles east to Big Sandy Road, which is 9.4 miles past the Bass Lake turnoff. Turn right on Big Sandy Road and drive approximately 2.6 miles to a dirt pullout on the left.*

Fish Camp Falls

Big Creek Falls

Rating: 5

How Short? 0.25 Miles

How Easy? 1

Best Time to View:
April to August

Need Information?
Contact: Sierra
National Forest
(559) 297-0706

Because it's located near the border of Yosemite National Park, Big Creek Falls gets little-to-no attention, and understandably so. Big Creek Falls doesn't compare to Yosemite's sights, such as Half Dome, El Capitan, Yosemite Falls and Mirror Lake.

At 6,300 feet in the Sierra National Forest, near Fish Camp, unlike most of the popular sights in Yosemite, Big Creek doesn't get inundated by hundreds of thousands of visitors each year. It stays quiet and free from traffic and tour buses. That's why people enjoy coming here. It's all about serenity, which can be experienced here most of the time, except for holiday weekends.

Big Creek Falls isn't breathtaking or remarkable. Big Creek emerges from a pine forest, feeding the falls, which cascades down a chiseled sheet of granite, 50 feet tall and 10 feet wide. Because the rock face isn't vertical, the waterfall drops down the slope at an uneventful angle.

Big Creek is fairly large, about 10 feet wide and two feet deep in most places, and it's stocked weekly with rainbow trout in the spring and summer by the California Department of Fish and Game. The creek originates in the mountains above Fresno Dome, flows through Fresno Dome Campground and then cascades down into Little Sandy Campground.

Getting to the cascade requires a long, slow drive on a dirt road, beginning at Highway 41 in Fish Camp. From Highway 41, turn left on Big Sandy Road (if coming from Fish Camp) and drive 5.5 miles to Big Sandy Campground. Drive through the stream and continue 1.5 miles to Little Sandy Campground. The waterfall is on the right side of the road, a half-mile past Little Sandy. If you hit Fresno Dome Campground, you've gone a half-mile too far. There is a dirt pullout four-tenths of a mile from Little Sandy. Park here and walk to the falls.

If you plan to make the trip, supplies are available in Fish Camp. Big Creek is closed to fishing from November 16 to the last Saturday in April. The dirt road to the waterfall may be difficult to navigate in the late spring when Big Creek is running at full force. There is one stream crossing required. High clearance vehicles are recommended.

Also nearby are Big Creek (Fish Camp), Fish Camp Falls, Nelder Creek, North Fork Willow Creek, Bass Lake, Merced River (South Fork) and the Nelder Grove.

Directions: From the 99 Freeway in Fresno, exit north on Highway 41 and drive to Oakhurst. Continue on Highway 41 through Oakhurst, driving 14.5 miles east past Oakhurst to Big Sandy Road. Turn right and drive 7.8 miles to Big Creek Falls.

Big Creek Falls

Red Rock Falls

Rating: 5

How Short? 3.0 Miles

How Easy? 2

Best Time To View:
January to August

Need Information?
Contact: Sierra
National Forest
(559) 297-0706

To learn how Red Rock Falls earned its name you need to visit the cataract after the 4th of July, when Lewis Creek begins to subside. At that time, parts of its rock bed becomes exposed, and you'll be able to see the mid-day sun sparkling off these colorful reddish-brown rocks: hence its name.

Because Lewis Creek covers this 50-foot-long slab of rock during the spring and early summer, hikers don't get to enjoy its inspiring colors. The waterfall's pretty boring then, just a dull 15-foot drop into a large, shallow pool. So, don't expect to remember Red Rock as one of the state's great waterfalls.

The walk to the falls is as easy as an evening walk around your block. The trail is well packed (suitable for tennis shoes), easy to follow and nearly flat. Beginning at the signed parking area for Lewis Creek, follow the path as it descends and crosses Lewis Creek. After crossing the stream, make a left onto the Lewis Creek Trail.

The route stays on the south side of Lewis Creek, paralleling it the entire way to the falls. Although at times it climbs small hills, it constantly remains under the canopy of the forest. Arriving at a junction, locating the waterfall is made easy by a sign on the right side of the trail. The sign reads "Red Rock Falls" and points to the left off the Lewis Creek Trail. The cataract is only about 50 yards from this junction.

If you plan to make the trip, supplies are available in Oakhurst.

Also nearby are Corlieu Falls, Angel Falls, Devil's Slide Falls, Big Falls, Big Creek, Fish Camp Falls, Bass Lake and Yosemite National Park.

Directions: *From the 99 Freeway in Fresno, exit north on Highway 41 to Oakhurst. Continue through Oakhurst, driving 7.5 miles to the sign for Lewis Creek at a dirt parking area on the right.*

Red Rock Falls

Corlieu Falls

Rating: 7

How Short? 0.50 Miles

How Easy? 1

Best Time To View:
December to
September

Need Information?
Contact: Sierra
National Forest
(559) 297-0706

There are two waterfalls along a mile and a half stretch of Lewis Creek between Yosemite National Park and Oakhurst. One requires a three-mile roundtrip stroll through a dense forest, the other a short and sweet skip from your padded car seats and powered windows. Luckily for you, the better waterfall is the latter, which means your car will still be cool when you get back from the trip to the falls.

Corlieu is one of those "in between" waterfalls. It's not grand enough to be compared to the big boys, found an hour away in Yosemite Valley, but it's better than the average cataracts near Bass Lake and Fish Camp. Corlieu is worth a peek for sure, especially with the brief walk needed to reach it.

Corlieu is just a hop, skip and a jump from Highway 41, yet somehow crowds are kept to a bare minimum. To reach the cataract, follow the path roughly 100 yards from the parking lot to Lewis Creek. There is a footbridge to aid the stream crossing here, but wait, don't cross the stream. Instead, make a right on the dirt path that parallels the creek. It only took us about five minutes to reach a point on the trail where the falls could been seen, however, to really appreciate Corlieu you have to scramble down the narrow and steep route to its base.

If you plan to make the trip, supplies are available in Oakhurst.

Also nearby are Red Rock Falls, Angel Falls, Devil's Slide Falls, Big Falls, Big Creek, Fish Camp Falls, Bass Lake and Yosemite National Park.

Directions: From the 99 Freeway in Fresno, exit north on Highway 41 to Oakhurst. Continue through Oakhurst, driving 7.5 miles to the sign for Lewis Creek at a dirt parking area on the right.

Corlieu Falls

Devils Slide Falls

Rating: 7

How Short? 3.0 Miles

How Easy? 2

Best Time to View:
April to August

Need Information?
Contact: Sierra
National Forest
(559) 877-2218

It was a hot afternoon in late June. My hiking partner Brett Ross and I had driven to one of Bass Lake's inlets in search of what we were told were some of the state's best swimming holes at Angel Falls. Finding the North Fork of Willow Creek on the north shore was simple. Unfortunately, finding a swimming hole wasn't going to happen. Well, at least not one we could swim in.

Swimming holes we did find. By the dozens actually. Many of them complete with butt-sliding rocks and waterfalls. The problem: crowds. Angel Falls sure wasn't a secret. I walked several times up and down the quarter-mile section of the stream that is known for its great swimming holes and small waterfalls. No luck. It was packed.

I was discouraged. Then out of the corner of my eye, I got a glimpse of two hikers coming down a trail that lead upstream from the falls. "I'm glad we walked up there," a guy carrying a fishing pole and wearing a vest filled with fishing tackle said to his buddy as they passed me by. "I can't stand all these kids around here." Hmm, this guy knew something I didn't.

"Excuse me," I hollered. "What's up there?" He didn't seem to have a problem sharing his secret with me, because he could see I didn't look like an angler (at least not on that particular day). So, he figured the fish in his secret holes were in no danger.

Devils Slide Falls is an excellent swimming hole and stays relatively quiet compared to the crowds at Angel

Before answering, his head gave a kind of Austin Powers' swivel, making sure no other anglers were listening. Then he edged back toward me. "Walk about 20 minutes that way," he kept his tone just above a whisper. "There's a big waterfall. None of these damn teenagers go up there and there are tons of fish. Great swimming hole too."

I was game. So Brett and I wasted no time. Within 15 minutes we were standing at the base of what we later found out was Devils Slide Falls. What a change of scenery! There was no one around. No drunken teenagers, broken beer bottles, empty soda cans, Taco Bell wrappers or cigarette butts. On the other hand, there were no women in bikinis either. I guess you have to sacrifice a few things for serenity.

Even though it's not nearly as popular as Angel Falls, Devils Slide Falls stamped a much stronger impression on my mind. In addition to several smaller cascades, the final drop was about 50 feet high and had a great deal of force to it. It's formed as the North Fork of Willow Creek plummets down a near-vertical slab of granite into one of the grandest swimming holes I've ever seen. It's roughly 20 yards long, 10 yards wide, and I can't even tell you how deep it is, because I failed to touch bottom.

Is the waterfall as easy to find as the guy with the fishing rod said? Yes. From the dirt parking area follow the path upstream past Angel Falls. (Stay on the left side of the stream.) In a half-mile (at the top of Angel Falls), you'll need to cross the stream. Because of high water this crossing can be a little tough in the spring. There is a steel cable that hangs over the stream, which can be used to help you get across.

Once you're on the other side of the creek, make a left on the trail and begin walking upstream. In a quarter-mile the path bends to the right and enters a canopy of trees with a tremendous undergrowth of ferns and smaller flora. Here the path parallels the creek. Then it gradually leads uphill for the next three-quarters of a mile, slowly leaving the streambed and climbing about 100 feet above it.

Just before you near the waterfall, a trail breaks off to the right. Stay left. Shortly, you'll see a fence on the left above the waterfall, which protects you from falling down the cliff into the cataract. To reach the waterfall's base, backtrack a few yards to a few trail spurs that lead down the mountain to the stream. Be careful. The rocks are slippery here.

If you plan to make the trip, supplies are available at Bass Lake.

Also nearby are Angel Falls, Bass Lake, Willow Creek Falls, Nelder Creek, Whiskey Falls, Manzanita Lake, Willow Creek, Lewis Creek, Big Creek and Fish Camp Falls.

Directions: *From the 99 Freeway in Fresno, exit north on Highway 41 and continue to Oakhurst. Drive 3.5 miles past Oakhurst to Road 222 and turn right. Drive another 3.5 miles and bear left on Road 274. Continue nine-tenths of a mile to a dirt road on the left side of the highway, just before the bridge. Turn left and park wherever you can find a spot.*

Devils Slide Falls

Angel Falls

Rating: 5

How Short? 1.0 Mile

How Easy? 1

Best Time To View:
March to August

Need Information?
Contact: Sierra
National Forest
(559) 877-2218

Remember back when you were in high school? It was a Saturday night, when there was no party, and you and your crew struggled to find something to do? The new movie theaters were not yet an option, and unfortunately the local restaurants closed by 10 p.m. The last resort was always that barren parking lot behind the gas station, and even though no one wanted to go there, that's where you usually ended up. When the ghetto blasters were turned up, crowds developed quickly and the cigarettes came out. And let's not forget about the alcohol, which a few of your sneaky friends managed to bring with them.

If I was beginning to forget, my first glimpse of Angel Falls brought it all back as if it were yesterday. It was a weekday in late-June. Although many schools were still in session, the parking area was full. I counted more than 20 cars, and I was forced to make my own spot by putting my car into four-wheel drive and driving up a hill. I could tell most of these cars belonged to teenagers. Bumper stickers read "Fresno Union High School," "Clovis West High School," "Go Bulldogs" and "Backstreet Boys."

As I headed toward the stream, I saw two guys wearing board shorts carrying a cooler. They had three girls with them, all in bikinis. I counted at least a dozen waterfalls along this quarter-mile stretch of the North Fork of Willow Creek on Bass Lake's north shore. And every waterfall was surrounded by groups of teenagers.

This stretch of the creek is known as Angel Falls. There's a small dam above Angel Falls that forces some of NF Willow Creek into pipelines, but there always seems to be a flow in the stream. And although none of the dozen or more cascades are too impressive (most are smaller than 20 feet), it doesn't seem to deter the crowds.

When I got to the falls, the kids were having a blast, catching the rays on house-sized granite slabs, swimming, fishing, eating lunch, butt sliding, jumping off rocks, drinking, smoking, listening to radios and of course making out. This place was the supreme local hangout zone!

Angel Falls

At 3,700 feet in the Sierra National Forest, this is nature's idea of a Raging Waters Theme Park, and it's sure no secret. When the water is warm enough for swimming, typically from May through summer, the kids mob the superb swimming holes at the bases of these falls. You'll see them sliding off slippery granite slopes and jumping off granite ledges into clear, deep holes.

Reaching Angel is easy. There's a sign for the Willow Creek Trail at the parking area. Although there are several trails that lead upstream, my advice would be to ignore all of them. Following the streambed is more rewarding. Then you won't miss any of the cascades along the way. Don't forget to wear a bathing suit. If you can find a spot, a dip is refreshing.

If you plan to make the trip, supplies are available at Bass Lake. Arrive early! As the day progresses, parking can become as impossible as finding an open spot at a swimming hole.

Also nearby are Devils Slide Falls, Bass Lake, Nelder Creek, Whiskey Falls, Manzanita Lake, Lewis Creek, Big Creek and Fish Camp Falls.

Directions: *From the 99 Freeway in Fresno, exit north on Highway 41 and continue to Oakhurst. Drive 3.5 miles past Oakhurst to Road 222 and turn right. Continue 3.5 miles and bear left on Road 274. Drive nine-tenths of a mile to a dirt road on the left side of the highway, just before the bridge. Turn left and look for a place to park.*

Teenagers make a day out of jumping, sliding and swimming in Angel's many pools

Bass Lake Falls

Rating: 4

How Short? Drive-To or Boat-To

How Easy? 1

Best Time to View: March to September

Need Information? Contact: Sierra National Forest (559) 877-2218, alifornia Land Management (559) 642-3213

Because Bass Lake Falls is small and doesn't have any unique characteristics, we've given it a "four" rating. If it were given a fun rating, however, there is no doubt it would be a "10." Anyone can have a blast at Bass Lake Falls, and most people do. On the lake's north shore in the back of one of the coves, the falls is the lake's most visited site. It's not uncommon to see hundreds of people in the cove, crowding around the falls. Sounds like a lot of people? It is.

Picture this: about 30 yards away from the falls on a sandy beach, there are 30 to 40 people with video cameras, digital cameras, 35-mm cameras and drugstore disposables. Most are parents waiting for their children to slide down the waterfall into the lake. Another 100 people are tanning themselves on the beach in the cove. Some read newspapers or sit on lounge chairs, listening to the radio; others cast fishing lines, basking in the hot sun. Then, there's another few dozen people playing on tubes and rafts or swimming near the back of their boats, which are either anchored in the cove or beached on shore.

But the main attraction is Bass Lake Falls, with a line of people waiting to slide down it. Smooth and perfectly rounded, the granite is just right for sliding. With all the people on rafts, tubes and boogie boards, not to mention those sliding down the 20-foot granite face, many on their butts, it reminds me of a water park.

The North Fork of Willow Creek, which creates Bass Lake Falls and empties into Bass Lake, flows year-round. The waterfall, however, is only warm enough from May through October to slide down. The slide is located a few feet below North Shore Road and can be accessed by day users, as well as those camping or living on the lake. Those with boats drive into the cove, while day users park in The Falls parking area and walk down to the beach. There is no parking permitted directly above the falls.

Upstream from the road, there are more waterfalls on Willow Creek, but most visitors tend to stay near the lake. Located in the Bass Lake Recreation Area, Bass Lake Falls gets extremely crowded on weekends and during the week in the summer. Get there early for a good spot on the beach.

If you plan to make the trip, supplies are available at Bass Lake.

Also nearby are Nelder Creek, Manzanita Lake and Fish Camp Falls.

Directions: *From the 99 Freeway in Fresno, exit north on Highway 41 and drive to Oakhurst. Continue through Oakhurst to Road 222 and turn right. Drive approximately four miles to the intersection of Road 222 and Road 432 (North Shore Road). Veer left onto Road 432 and drive eight-tenths of a mile to The Falls parking area.*

Bass Lake Falls on a typical summer day

Jackass Falls

Rating: 9

How Short? 0.25 Miles

How Easy? 1

Best Time to View:
May to August

Need Information?
Contact: Sierra
National Forest
(559) 877-2218

While driving to Granite Creek from Mammoth Pool Reservoir, I pulled off to the side of the road to check my GPS and make sure I was headed in the right direction. I had a few kids with me, and one of them asked me if he could go play in the waterfall.

I didn't know there was a waterfall around here. What was this kid talking about? The GPS wouldn't give me a reading, so I stepped out of the car to get a better signal. The kid was right! On the other side of the road, less than 30 yards away, was a small 20-foot cascade, with what looked like a nice swimming hole at its base.

Now I really wanted my GPS to work. Where was I, and why didn't I see it on the map? I finally got a reading, typed the coordinates into the computer and pressed enter. It read "Jackass Creek." I grabbed all the literature I had in the car and looked in the indexes. Not a single book or brochure had anything about it.

Curious, I put down the GPS and decided to do some exploring. The portion of the waterfall I could see from the car was minuscule compared to what I was about to discover. After a little rock-hopping, we found two other waterfalls, a 50-foot cascade and a 175-foot whopper.

Wow! How come these falls weren't written up? Hadn't any writers taken the time to enjoy these dazzling waterfalls? You'd think in this heavily used national forest someone would have stumbled upon them. If they had, I guess they hadn't bothered to mention them.

At 6,150 feet in the Sierra National Forest, about a two-and-a-half hour drive from Fresno, Jackass Creek offers one of the best waterfalls in California, yet few people know about it. Jackass Falls is striking from May through July, when snow runoff from the Jackass Lakes and Jackass Meadow keeps Jackass Creek flowing fiercely. Jackass is a perfect destination to bring the family to see one stunning waterfall, as well as two other impressive falls. An added incentive is that there are small wild rainbows and browns in the stream.

Here's what to do: To reach the

Upper Jackass Falls

upper two waterfalls, walk across the road to the 20-foot cascade. There is no trail, however, you can see the waterfall from the car. For the 50-foot cascade, rock-hop fewer than 50 yards upstream to the waterfall. Although both waterfalls have nice swimming holes at their bases, the water is extremely cold.

Lower Jackass is the best of the three. It can be viewed both from its brink and base. Walk back across the road to the bridge and look over the side railing. It might remind you of the view from atop the Nevada Falls Bridge in Yosemite National Park. In the spring the water crashes against granite boulders near the base and fills the dark canyon below with a heavy mist.

The view is better from its base. Take a right and walk about 80 yards down the road to a dirt trail that breaks off to the left. Follow this well-graded sandy trail for about three minutes to the unmarked falls overlook. From this vantage, you'll get an unobstructed view of the entire drop. Although it's possible to continue to the base, the

view is best from here. The way the water skips and crashes off the boulders is reminiscent of Peppermint Creek Falls in Sequoia National Forest, only better.

If you plan to make the trip, supplies are available in North Fork and at Wagner General Store near Mammoth Pool Reservoir. The road to Jackass Falls is commonly closed from mid-November until May. Call ahead for updated road conditions.

Also nearby are Mammoth Pool Reservoir, Chiquito Creek, West Fork of Chiquito Creek, Granite Creek, West Fork Chiquito Creek Slides, Chiquito Creek Falls, Rock Creek, Rock Creek Falls and Fish Creek.

Directions: *From the 99 Freeway in Fresno, exit north on Highway 41 and drive 28 miles to Road 200 (signed for North Fork). Turn right and drive 19 miles to North Fork. From North Fork, continue east, heading through the town of South Fork, and drive 40 miles to the junction with Road 6S25. Bear left and drive 7.5 miles to the bridge over Jackass Creek.*

Dan Sulitzer (Left) and Nick Haraden pose at Jackass Falls

Chiquito Creek Falls

Rating: 6

How Short? 0.25 Miles

How Easy? 2

Best Time to View:
May to August

Need Information?
Contact: Sierra
National Forest
(559) 877-2218

In a word, Chiquito Creek Falls is "powerful." Located on a stream that is popular with campers, anglers, swimmers and rafters, Chiquito Creek Falls is unknown to most of the creek's visitors. A few miles upstream from Mammoth Pool Reservoir, a cataract is formed where Chiquito Creek is forced through a narrow portion of the canyon, causing its water to pound against granite boulders. This white water terminates in Chiquito Creek Falls' 70-foot cascade, which tumbles into a giant pool, ideal for swimming and fishing.

The pool below the falls is deep. A friend and I dove down with masks and snorkels but failed to touch bottom. In June and early July, swimming can be difficult because of the force of the falls, but as summer progresses, conditions improve. Unless you walk out to the middle of Chiquito Creek, you won't be able to get a view of the entire falls, because the first section of the cascade is hidden off to the right behind the lower section of the falls which can be seen from the shore.

Most Chiquito Creek visitors don't come for the waterfalls; rather, they accidentally stumble upon them while fishing. The stream is stocked with rainbow trout by the California Department of Fish and Game in Wagner Camp, below the falls, and at Sweetwater Campground, just above the falls. However, most of the fish caught here are wild rainbows and browns.

There is another waterfall about 100 yards up from the Chiquito Creek Falls. This one is a 20-foot freefall that can be seen from the road. Both falls have unmarked dirt trails leading to them.

If you plan to make the trip, supplies and gas are available at Wagner's General Store across from Wagner Campground. The road to Chiquito Creek closes in winter, so call ahead for updated conditions. Chiquito Creek is closed to fishing from November 16 to the last Saturday in April.

Also nearby are Mammoth Pool Reservoir, West Fork of Chiquito Creek, West Fork Chiquito Creek Slides, Jackass Creek Falls, Granite Creek and Mile High Vista.

Directions: From the 99 Freeway in Fresno, exit north on Highway 41 and drive 28 miles to Road 200 (signed for North Fork). Continue east and drive 19 miles to North Fork. Continue another 40 miles on Road 200, through the town of South Fork to Road 6S25. Turn right and drive to a dirt pullout on the left side of the road, just past Sweetwater Campground.

Chiquito Creek Falls

West Fork Chiquito Creek Slides

Rating: 5

How Short? 0.25 Miles

How Easy? 2

Best Time to View:
May to August

Need Information?
Contact: Sierra
National Forest
(559) 877-2218

Leaving the West Fork Chiquito Creek Slides, one of the kids I brought on the trip said, "Chris, How much does is cost to come to this place? Is it cheaper than Disneyland? What's the name of it? I want my mom to bring me back."

I knew my answer before he'd finished. "This is nature," I told him. "It's free, but we don't want to tell everyone about it. Right now this is a special place, and we only want special people to know about it. People who won't treat it like Disneyland, where they can afford to hire a lot of workers to clean up the trash that everybody throws around. This place wouldn't be nearly as beautiful if everybody starting leaving trash by the water." I got the feeling the little guy knew what I was talking about, the same way I understood my Uncle Ron Shaffer many years ago when he told me how precious the wilderness is and how we should protect it.

The West Fork Chiquito Creek Slides is just one of many free "water parks" in the Sierra National Forest, all of which can create memories that will last a lifetime. About a quarter-mile upstream from Soda Springs Campground, across Minarets Road, the slides are a series of small cascades that fun seekers slide down on their butts, landing in the large pools below. It's a unique area with slick granite boulders that allow for smooth sliding. The creek that flows over these slides is a tributary to Chiquito Creek and carries a consistent flow of water throughout the summer months.

The walk to the falls is easy. Park at the end of the dirt access road and follow the trail about 100 yards along the stream to a large pool fed by two tall cascades. This, however, is only the bottom of the slides, not where fun starts. Climb over the granite slabs, and above the cascades to reach the fun park.

From this point you'll be able to see all the cascades. The first group of cascades runs over the "Six Craters," six trashcan-sized (like the ones you put out for the garbage truck) holes that were naturally carved into the granite by tumbling water. It's refreshing to sit in one of these craters, which are used as wading pools, with the falls flowing over you.

Below Six Craters is a small pool deep enough for swimming. There are also two more large swimming holes a few yards downstream that precede another five feet of

Swimming is extremely popular at West Fork Chiquito Creek Falls

cascades, before the stream forms one small, but deep pool that overflows into the final two cascades.

Phil Freed leaps into a 10-foot deep pool at West Fork Chiquito Creek Slides

Remember boys and girls, you aren't just coming here for the waterfalls: it's time to have fun and swim. And the water is warm enough that you won't have to jump out as soon as you jump in.

Another added attraction is the wild rainbow and brown trout in the stream. The section of the stream below the cascades is also stocked by the California Department of Fish and Game with rainbow trout. Don't forget to bring your pole.

If you plan to make the trip, supplies are available in North Fork. West Fork Chiquito Creek is closed to fishing from November 16 to the last Saturday in April. The road to the creek closes in winter, so call ahead for updated conditions.

Also nearby are Bass Lake, Whiskey Falls, Rock Creek, Rock Creek Falls, Mile High Vista, Mammoth Pool Reservoir, Chiquito Creek Falls, Chiquito Creek, Fish Creek, Redinger Lake and San Joaquin River.

Directions: *From the 99 Freeway in Fresno, exit north on Highway 41 and continue 28 miles to Road 200 (signed for North Fork). Turn right and drive 19 miles to North Fork. Continue east, heading through the town of South Fork, and continue 36 miles to Soda Springs Campground. From the campground, backtrack about 100 yards to a small dirt road on the right side of the highway. Turn right and drive to the end of the dirt road.*

Stephen Wiessner slides down one of West Fork Chiquito Creek's slides

Rock Creek Falls

Rating: 5

How Short? Drive-To

How Easy? 2

Best Time to View:
April to August

Need Information?
Contact: Sierra
National Forest
(559) 877-2218

Phil Freed (Left) and Blake Lezak cool off at Rock Creek Falls

Although Rock Creek Falls is not striking, it provides as much fun as a day at your favorite amusement park. A little more than an hour's drive from Fresno, the cascades are loaded with swimming pools, small waterfalls and natural granite waterslides. Best of all, there's no fee and no large crowds.

Rock Creek Falls is a secret place to have a blast. There are a total of six cascades to keep you busy all day. The top cascade is about 20 feet tall and is noteworthy because it's where Rock Creek morphs from a slow-moving stream to a series of waterfalls that tumble over a steep granite formation. Kids often zip down this granite waterslide on their butts into a three-foot deep pool.

The most popular butt-sliding hole, however, is the second cascade. It's 30 feet tall, and the smooth-granite moss-covered rocks are just perfect for sliding down into the four-foot deep pool below. Adjacent to the pool, but not part of Rock Creek, there is a giant hole in the granite that can be used as a platform for jumping.

Although these waterslides are a lot of fun, they can also be dangerous. You can slip, walking over the water-slick granite. It's like trying to keep your footing while walking over ice in tennis shoes. Serious injury can occur to those who aren't careful. Please use extreme caution approaching the slide.

Don't slide down cascades three and four, but they serve an important function. Only about five feet in total height, they empty into the pool that

Nick Haraden watches as Dan Sulitzer leaps into a deep crater hole at Rock Creek Falls

Stephen Wiessner slides down Rock Creek Falls

begins the fifth falls, which becomes a freefall when the creek is cresting in late May and June. It's about 20 feet tall and far too risky to slide down.

At the bottom of the third and fourth cascades, cross over to the left side of the stream and walk down the granite past the freefall to the final cascade. It's too dangerous to walk the right side. Just past the freefall is the final cascade, about 15 feet tall, which empties into a beautiful 10-foot deep swimming pool that marks the end of Rock Creek Falls.

But wait, there's more to do. Downstream from this point to Rock Creek Campground, and also for about an eighth of a mile upstream from the falls, the California Department of Fish and Game stocks rainbow trout from late April through July. There are also wild trout in the stream. Get out your poles!

If you plan to make the trip, supplies are available in North Fork. Rock Creek is closed to fishing from November 16 to the last Saturday in April. The road to Rock Creek closes in winter, so call ahead for updated conditions.

Also nearby are Bass Lake, Whiskey Falls, Fish Creek, Mile High Vista, Mammoth Pool Reservoir, Chiquito Creek Falls, Chiquito Creek, West Fork Chiquito Creek, West Fork Chiquito Creek Slides, Redinger Lake and San Joaquin River.

Directions: From the 99 Freeway in Fresno, exit north on Highway 41 and drive 28 miles to Road 200 (signed for North Fork). Turn right and continue 19 miles to North Fork. Continue east, heading through the town of South Fork, and drive 23 miles to the sign for Rock Creek Campground. Drive approximately a half-mile past the sign to a dirt pullout on the right side of the road.

Phil Freed launches into a pool at Rock Creek Falls

Whiskey Falls

Rating: 6

How Short? Drive-To

How Easy? 1

Best Time to View:
May to August

Need Information?
Contact: Sierra
National Forest
(559) 877-2218

There are three ways to drive to Whiskey Falls in the Sierra National Forest, all via dirt roads. The first is from the town of North Fork off Road 200. Then, there are two separate roads off Minarets Road, one near Fish Creek and the other near Rock Creek. All routes require a long, slow drive on twisting mountain roads. This grueling drive keeps Whiskey from becoming one of the region's main tourist traps.

Whiskey is the ideal place for campers to stay and have a diminutive waterfall all to themselves, free from the crowds and tour buses that storm other waterfalls that are only a short drive north in Yosemite National Park. We made the drive to Whiskey during the first week of July, and there wasn't one other sole staying in the campground.

At 5,800 feet in a secluded area of the forest between Bass Lake and Mammoth Pool Reservoir, Whiskey Falls is a small cascade 100 yards upstream from Whiskey Falls Campground. Because of its diminutive height, the waterfall isn't as inspiring as many others in the region, but it does get some brownie points for the cave-like area behind its 30-foot drop.

The falls formed as Whiskey Creek spills off a smooth granite ledge, freefalling 10 feet before striking a granite boulder nearly the size of a Suburban. The impact from the water hitting the boulder causes Whiskey to spray outwards, covering a width of about 20 feet. As the water bounces off the rock, it spreads out like water coming out of a garden hose when you put your thumb over its end. The umbrella of water creates a cave behind the final 20-foot drop.

Children enjoy playing in the water below the falls. After spraying out from the boulder at the base of the falls the stream continues over slabs of smooth granite, most of which are coated with moss, creating a great slippery slide. Also eye catching is the foliage around Whiskey Falls. Throughout the summer, the face of the falls is kept green by various ferns. Whiskey's peak flow occurs around June and slowly begins to subside by early August.

If you plan to make the trip, supplies are available in North Fork. In early spring call ahead for road conditions.

Also nearby are Bass Lakeand Rock Creek.

Whiskey Falls

Directions: *From the 99 Freeway in Fresno, exit north on Highway 41 and continue 28 miles to Road 200 .Turn right on Road 200 and drive 19 miles to North Fork. In North Fork, turn left on Road 225. Drive one mile on Road 225 and turn left on Cascadel Road (Road 233). Continue approximately two miles and veer left on Road 8S09. Drive approximately seven miles on Road 8S09. Turn right on Road 8S70 and drive two miles to Whiskey Falls Campground.*

Smalls Falls

Rating: 5

How Short? 8.2 Miles

How Easy? 3

Best Time to View:
May to July

Need Information?
Contact: Eastwood
Visitor Center (559)
893-6611 (Summer
Only), Sierra National
Forest (559) 855-5360
or (559) 297-0706

A waterfall's volume and force is limited by the watershed that feeds it. Most of the waterfalls in Yosemite, Sequoia and Kings Canyon National Parks are situated at 3,000 to 7,000 feet. With peaks up to 14,000 feet towering above them, these waterfalls have an extremely large drainage that provides them with a tremendous amount of volume and force during spring runoff.

Unfortunately, Smalls Falls in the Kaiser Wilderness isn't blessed with the same extensive watershed. Just below George Lake, it's located high up at 9,100 feet, just a little more than 1,000 feet below 10,310-foot Kaiser Peak, the wilderness's tallest mountain. Thus, Smalls' size and force are restricted by a pretty limited watershed.

So, before you continue reading, keep in mind that Smalls is not going to inspire you to become a waterfall lover. If you visit it, you're not going to need to wear bright-yellow rain jackets to protect you from a powerful pervading mist; nor be forced to wait in line just to snap a picture. As my hiking pal Brett "Smalls" Ross said, "This is a nice, little waterfall." He's right: "nice" is exactly the right word. Not spectacular or eye-catching, just… nice.

Tucked away in a dense pine forest 50 yards off the George Lake Trail, Smalls is part of the headwaters of Kaiser Creek. Forced through a crevice in the granite, this

uneventful 20-foot splash of water can, however, be a great resting spot for anglers who come to fish the Kaiser Wilderness, or a fabulous picnic area for hikers strolling by.

The biggest problem many hikers have when they come to Smalls is deciding which trail to take. Any of five paths access it: Potter Pass, Sample Meadows, California Hiking and Riding, Sample Cutoff and the Idaho Lake Trail. My favorite, which I also consider to be the easiest, is the Sample Cutoff Trail that begins on Forest Road 5, roughly two miles north of Kaiser Pass Road.

The route starts in the Sierra National Forest and within 100 yards crosses into the Kaiser Wilderness. Quickly the path descends, crossing Kaiser Creek a half-mile before bending to the left, where fallen trees can be used to re-cross Kaiser. The trail then climbs gently to another stream crossing of an unnamed stream, 1.7 miles from the trailhead.

Smalls Falls

Time to sweat a little: Over the next four-tenths of a mile, your knees endure a 350-foot climb before the path levels out in Round Meadow, where a trail signed for Badger Flat breaks off to the left. Stay right, continuing through the meadow, before briefly reentering the forest. Then, make an easy stream crossing, and roughly three miles from the steaks and burgers sitting in the cooler in your car, you'll arrive at the outlet of Upper Twin Lake.

From Upper Twin Lake to Smalls it's an easy 1.1-mile uphill stroll through the forest. At the outlet of Upper Twin, follow the George Lake Trail around Upper Twin. After the first three-tenths of a mile, the trail bends to the left, and George Lake's outlet stream can be seen down in the gorge on the left.

Pushing forward, a small pond is visible down in the canyon. Now it's time to start paying attention. Look carefully through the trees, the upper end of 20-foot Smalls Falls will appear. There is no trail to its base; you'll have to make your own. For those who enjoy fishing, rainbow and brook trout-filled George Lake is a measly one-tenth of a mile ahead. It's darn pretty too.

If you plan to make the trip, supplies are available at Huntington Lake. A wilderness permit is required for overnight travel into the Kaiser Wilderness. In heavy snow years, the trail may not be snow free until sometime in July. Call for up-to-the-minute conditions.

Also nearby are Upper and Lower Twin Lake, College Lake, George Lake, Campfire Lake and Jewel Lake.

Directions: *From the 99 Freeway in Fresno, drive 72 miles east on Highway 168 to the east end of Huntington Lake. Turn east on Kaiser Pass Road and continue approximately 5.5 miles. After the road becomes one lane, continue approximately 4.5 miles to Forest Road 5. Turn left onto the dirt road and drive about two miles to the trailhead and parking area.*

George Lake rests a short distance upstream of Smalls Falls

Rancheria Falls

Rating: 7

How Short? Drive-To

How Easy? 1

Best Time to View:
May to July

Need Information?
Contact: Eastwood
Visitor Center (559)
893-6611 (Summer
Only), Sierra National
Forest (559) 855-5360
or (559) 297-0706

In most cases Rancheria Falls isn't a destination for sightseers or tourists exploring the Huntington Lake Recreation area. Rancheria is often stumbled upon by passengers scanning the mountainside after making the right from Highway 168 onto Kaiser Pass Road. Within a mile of ascending towards Kaiser Pass, Rancheria appears about a quarter-mile across the canyon on the south side of the road.

Unfortunately, Rancheria is fed by a scant amount of snow runoff, and at 7,600 feet in the Sierra National Forest, this waterfall, fed by Rancheria Creek, can quickly turn to a trickle by the end of July in most years. However, it can be noteworthy from May through June. Although best viewed with a pair of binoculars, this 130-foot cascade is clearly visible to the plain eye as well, just don't count on being awed standing so far away.

There is a possibility to walk to the fall's base via a short trek on the Rancheria National Recreation Trail. However, I think the view from afar is equally rewarding. Trails to access the base can be picked up near the pack station and the Rancheria Falls Campground.

If you plan to make the trip, supplies are available at Huntington Lake. Snow closes Kaiser Pass Road in the winter and early spring.

Also nearby are Huntington Lake, Kaiser Wilderness, Portal Forebay, Mono Creek, Edison Lake and Florence Lake.

Directions: *From the 99 Freeway in Fresno, drive 72 miles east on Highway 168 to the east end of Huntington Lake. Turn east on Kaiser Pass Road and continue approximately one mile to a dirt pullout on the left.*

Rainbow trout, like this one caught by Brandi Koerner are stocked bi-monthly during the summer at Rancheria Creek.

Bear Creek Falls

Rating: 5

How Short? Drive-To

How Easy? 1

Best Time to View:
March to July

Need Information?
Contact: Sequoia
National Forest (559)
855-5360 or (559) 297-
0706, Dinkey Ranger
Station (559) 841-3404

On the scenic drive from Shaver Lake to Courtright and Wishon Reservoirs, there are many lovely places to stop, take a few pictures and cherish the forest. Bear Creek Falls is one that is often overlooked. Although the falls isn't designated on topo maps, it can be seen from the road just after the highway crosses Bear Creek.

There is a large dirt pullout on the right side of the road about 50 yards past the falls, from which it can be viewed. You can also walk to the fall's base, but there's no trail. The streambed leading to the falls is made up of large rocks, many of which are wobbly, so use caution not to twist an ankle.

The view from the road is as satisfying as a walk to its base. There are also more falls above, yet they can't be seen from the road, because they are hidden back in the canyon. All the falls in this area are best viewed in the spring when snowmelt makes them most impressive. By the time August arrives, their feeder streams are reduced to trickles.

There are heaps of tiny wild rainbow trout in the stream, but you'll have to hike downstream from the falls to find pools to catch them in. A better idea, however, is nearby McKinley Sequoia Grove, about 1.5 miles from the falls. It's a pretty sequoia grove that doesn't attract the kinds of large crowds that visit the sequoias in Sequoia and Kings Canyon National Parks.

If you plan to make the trip, supplies are available at the Dinkey Creek Inn and at Shaver Lake. Bear Creek is closed to fishing from November 16 to the last Saturday in April. In winter call ahead for road conditions. Chains may be required.

Bear Creek Falls

Also nearby are Courtright Reservoir, Wishon Reservoir, Big Creek (Kings), the McKinley Grove, Dinkey Creek, Dinkey Wilderness and Shaver Lake.

Directions: *From the 99 Freeway in Fresno, take Highway 168 east 51 miles to Dinkey Creek Road. Turn right and drive 12 miles to a bridge over Dinkey Creek. Continue three miles past the creek to a large dirt pullout on the right side of the road.*

Dinkey Falls

Rating: 5

How Far? 0.25 miles

How Easy? 1

Best Time to View:
April to June

Need Information?
Contact: Sequoia
National Forest (559)
855-5360 or (559) 297-
0706, Dinkey Ranger
Station (559) 841-3404

Dinkey Falls couldn't have been given a better name. For all but a few short months each year, Dinkey Falls is in fact very "dinkey." By the time late August rolls around, Dinkey's dribble turns dry. Why should you visit the falls if its going to be dry? Well, it isn't always dry. After becoming dry by late summer, it again regains full form in late winter, when snow runoff brings Dinkey Creek back to life. Arrive between late April and late June, and Dinkey Falls can be a powerful cascade.

A short five-minute walk brings you to the waterfall's base. Beginning at the trailhead sign for the Dinkey Lakes, the path leads downhill to Dinkey Creek, crosses the stream and then climbs 30 yards uphill. The trail winds downhill, and when it crosses Dinkey Creek again, the waterfall is on the right.

Dinkey is a mere 20-foot waterfall set in a cluster of granite. It freefalls for the first five feet, smacks into a granite ledge, then expands its width over the last 15-foot fall, terminating with a splash into the shallow pool below.

Unfortunately for Dinkey Falls, people drive to the trailhead mostly to go fishing at Dinkey Lakes, a few miles beyond the falls. Located in the Dinkey Lakes Wilderness, the lakes are popular with both day-hikers and backpackers. Unlike most backcountry destinations, the Dinkey Lakes are easy to reach and don't require a long, exhausting hike. An added bonus is that they are stocked by the California Department of Fish and Game.

The biggest problem with Dinkey Falls is driving to it. Rock Creek Road, which leads to the falls, usually doesn't open until sometime in June. In poor snow years, the road might open in May, but that's not likely. Other options are to walk the road to the falls or use snowshoes; however, most hikers don't consider the falls worth a 14-mile roundtrip walk from Dinkey Creek Road. Neither do I.

If you plan to make the trip, supplies are available at Dinkey Creek Inn. In late spring call ahead for road conditions. The road may be closed until late June.

Also nearby are Courtright Reservoir, Wishon Reservoir and Big Creek (Kings).

A dry Dinkey Falls in August of 2000

Directions: *From the 99 Freeway in Fresno, take Highway 168 east 51 miles to Dinkey Creek Road. Turn right and drive nine miles to the turnoff for Rock Creek Road. Turn left on Rock Creek Road and drive six miles to Road 9S10. Turn right on Road 9S10 and drive 4.7 miles to Road 9S62. Turn right on Road 9S62 and drive 2.2 miles to the Dinkey Wilderness Trailhead. (A high-clearance vehicle is recommended for the final 1.5 miles.)*

Road 9S10 Falls

Rating: 3

How Short? Drive-To

How Easy? 1

Best Time to View:
May to September

Need Information?
Contact: Sequoia
National Forest (559)
855-5360 or (559) 297-
0706, Dinkey Ranger
Station (559) 841-3404

I'm sure many hikers who drive to Dinkey Falls and find it dry in late summer think it would be nice to have another waterfall close by to go to as a way to salvage the day. Road 9S10 Falls is just such a place. Even when the much larger Dinkey Falls is dry, Road 9S10 Falls still flows.

The waterfall is a lot like Sotcher Lake Falls near Devils Postpile National Monument in the Inyo National Forest: fed by an unnamed stream, it's not listed on maps and mostly ignored. The difference between the two is that Road 9S10 is a drive-to waterfall where no hiking is required.

The falls has upper and lower sections. Driving towards the Dinkey Lakes Wilderness, the lower portion is on the driver's side, 2.4 miles from the turnoff for Rock Creek Road. Two-tenths of a mile up from where the road begins to curve along the mountain, the upper section is visible on the passenger's side.

Road 9S10 Falls isn't awe-inspiring; it's simply filler for days when Dinkey Falls is dry in late summer. Each section of the falls cascades down hillsides composed of dirt and rock. We found a group of wildflowers at the base of the upper section. Since there isn't a lot of traffic on the road, it's possible to park your car next to the waterfall. Get out and take a few photos before moving on.

If you plan to make the trip, supplies are available at Dinkey Creek Inn. In late spring call ahead for road conditions. The road may be closed until late June.

Also nearby are Courtright Reservoir, Wishon Reservoir, Big Creek (Kings), McKinley Grove, Bear Creek Falls, Dinkey Wilderness and Shaver Lake.

A close up of Road 9S10 Falls

Directions: *From the 99 Freeway in Fresno, take Highway 168 east 51 miles to Dinkey Creek Road. Turn right and drive nine miles to the turnoff for Rock Creek Road. Turn left on Rock Creek Road and drive six miles to Road 9S10. Turn right on Road 9S10 and drive 2.4 miles to the waterfall on the left.*

Big Creek Falls

Rating: 3

How Short? Drive-To

How Easy? 1

Best Time To View:
February to July

Need Information?
Contact: Sierra
National Forest
(559) 855-5630

Big Creek Falls is far from "big". In reality, it's one of the smallest and most pitiful waterfalls in this book. Yet, in this dry section of the Sierra National Forest, any modest cascade is appreciated. In this case, Big Creek Falls, which is an eight-foot tall cascade along Big Creek, fails to impress waterfall enthusiasts. Rather than spending time wading in the small pool below the cascade, it's more popular to drive three miles downstream and swim in Pine Flat Reservoir.

A tributary to Pine Flat, Big Creek is rarely visited by waterfall lovers. Mostly anglers come here to cash in on the pan-sized rainbow trout planted in the spring and early summer. Fishing can also be uneventful, however, it beats spending time trying to awe at such a boring cascade. In fact, few people plan trips to Big Creek Falls at all. Looking out their passenger window on their way (for the few lost soles who take these dirt back roads) to Shaver Lake, Wishon and Courtright Reservoirs, sightseers stumble on the falls. Although few people use this back route to those lakes because it's a winding, and slow moving dirt road, those who do are often impressed by the pretty foothill landscape and lack of traffic.

If you plan to make the trip supplies are available at Pine Flat Reservoir.

Also nearby are the Kings River below Pine Flat, Avocado Lake and Pine Flat Reservoir.

Directions: From the 99 Freeway in Fresno, take the Belmont Avenue exit east and drive 20 miles to Trimmer Springs Road. Turn northeast and drive 21 miles to Trimmer. In Trimmer, turn left on USFS Road 9, and continue 3.2 miles to a pullout on the right.

Big Creek Falls in August of 2000

Region

Sequoia/Kings Canyon National Parks

Mist Falls
Roaring River Falls
Sky Blue Falls
Rock Creek Falls
Tokopah Valley Falls
Marble Fork Falls
Cascade Creek Falls
Middle Fork Kaweah Falls
Middle Fork Falls
East Fork Falls
Mineral King Falls
Black Wolf Falls
Tufa Falls
Crystal Creek Falls
Franklin Falls
Coyote Creek Falls

scale of miles

0   15   30   60

Mist Falls

Rating: 8

How Short? 8.0 Miles

How Easy? 3

Best Time to View:
May to July

Need Information?
Contact: Kings Canyon
National Park
(559) 565-4307

Mist Falls in Kings Canyon National Park brings only good thoughts to mind. The trail to the falls is easy, attractive and, for the most part, flat. More importantly, the waterfall is beautiful. Located just above 5,600 feet, Mist Falls is only about 50 feet tall, but it has a great deal of power.

Begin the at the wilderness permit station at the end of the road. With the exception of the last mile, the trail is easy. It took us only two hours to complete the entire trip, hiking at four miles an hour.

The hike begins on a well-graded, soft dirt path that parallels the South Fork of the Kings River, crossing small feeder streams in the spring and early summer. The first two miles of the trail are flat. The first mile is partially covered by trees, but you won't get any consistent cover until coming to a wooded area surrounded by ferns and lush green meadows.

By this time, it's apparent that you're in a deep canyon, surrounded by tall, sheer granite cliffs. Keep an eye out for deer that commonly stroll though the meadows in the early morning and evenings. Before you know it, you'll be leaving the ferns.

Shortly, you'll come to a trail junction and a bridge that extends across the South Fork of the Kings River. Stay left, veering away from where Bubbs Creek pours into the Kings River, and proceed on the last two miles to the falls. The South Fork remains on the right, with trees and ferns blanketing its banks. Until the last mile, the trail stays cool, even on the most sweltering days.

Now, as the climb steepens the trip gets a little rough. After a few switchbacks, is a drop that many people mistake for Mist Falls. Although it's moving, don't be fooled by this cascade. Continue on the trail for a quarter-mile, and you'll be directly in front of the real Mist Falls, a large cascade along the South Fork.

At this point, there are two options. Either walk to the falls' base and be drenched with mist, or climb up to the brink. If you hike to the top of the falls, be sure to follow the signs. One warns you to stay on the trail because of slippery rocks. That sign is there for a reason. I almost found out the hard way, nearly slipping into the river, where I would have been carried down over the falls.

If you plan to make the trip, supplies are available in Cedar Grove. There is a fee to enter Kings Canyon National Park. The road to Mist Falls closes in winter.

Also nearby are Roaring River Falls, Boyden Cave and Grizzly Falls.

Directions: *From the 99 Freeway in Fresno, drive 55 miles east on Highway 180 to Kings Canyon National Park. Enter the park and after 1.7 miles veer left at a fork in the road. Drive 38 miles to the end of the road. The trailhead is near the wilderness permit station.*

Lower Portion of Mist Falls

Roaring River Falls

Rating: 6

How Short? 0.40 Miles

How Easy? 1

Best Time to View:
April to August

Need Information?
Contact: Kings Canyon
National Park
(559) 565-4307

While the summer traffic jams and crowds in Yosemite National Park can frustrate even the most patient visitors, Kings Canyon National Park is just the opposite: its visitors don't have to suffer clogged roads and crowded trails. The problem with Kings Canyon, however, is most of the park is located in the backcountry, far off roads and inaccessible without a long backwoods hike. So, even though it's only a four-hour drive from Los Angeles, King's Canyon has remained relatively unspoiled.

The good news is that Roaring River Falls is one of the few destinations in Kings Canyon that requires no hiking or off-trail scrambles. Roaring River is a powerful waterfall that can be reached via a brisk walk on a paved trail. As its name implies, Roaring River does in fact "roar." Its force can be ear-piercing in late spring when Roaring River is channeled through a narrow granite furrow. The rush of frothy water races like a flood and creates a thunderous roar as it smashes against granite, cascading 40 feet into a large, deep pool.

The pool is an ideal swimming hole, providing you swim to the left of the waterfall. It's not safe to swim on the other side of the pool, because the current from the river could sweep you downstream. The water is clear, sparkling and in many spots too deep to stand. Although refreshing on summer days when temperatures creep into the hundreds, most people don't take the time to swim here. These visitors are usually in a hurry to head up to Cedar Grove, a large sequoia grove a few miles up the road, so they take a few pictures of the falls and move on.

We opted to spend more time here. I brought along a mask and swam in the pool looking for rainbow trout. I found a few, too. Roaring River Falls empties into the Kings River, a half-mile downstream, and although many of the river's fish swim up here, the pool below the falls is as far as they get.

To reach the waterfall, pick up the paved trail at the signed parking lot on the right side of Highway 180 and take the easy five-minute walk to the base of the falls. There is no trail to its brink.

If you plan to make the trip, supplies are available at Cedar Grove. The road to the falls closes in the winter. There is a fee to enter Kings Canyon National Park.

Also nearby are Mist Falls and Boyden Cave.

Roaring River Falls

Directions: *From the 99 Freeway in Fresno, drive 52 miles east on Highway 180 to Sequoia/Kings Canyon National Park entrance. Continue 1.7 miles to a fork in the road. Veer left, heading north, and continue 27 miles on Highway 180 to Grizzly Falls. Follow the road eight miles past Grizzly Falls to a turnoff on the right for Roaring River Falls.*

Sky Blue Falls

Rating: 7

How Short? 28 Miles

How Easy? 5

Best Time to View:
June and July

Need Information?
Contact: Sequoia
National Park
Wilderness Permits
(559) 565-3761,
Sequoia National Park
(559) 565-3134, Inyo
National Forest
(760) 876-6200

Although Sequoia National Park is world-renowned for being rich with giant sequoia trees, sequoia groves are only located in some areas of the park. The Miter Basin, in the Sequoia Backcountry, is not one of them. Because of its remoteness, the Miter Basin, near New Army Pass, is one of the few areas of the park that isn't barraged by hikers and backpackers. But these people are missing out. With crystal-clear streams winding through lush green meadows, scenic lakes set in granite bowls, golden trout lurking in the streams and marmots chewing on the grassy shorelines, the basin is one of California's best natural wonders.

Sky Blue Lake sits at the back of the basin. At 11,550 feet, 14 miles from the trailhead, the lake is set above the tree line, near Crabtree Pass. It's surrounded by towering peaks and holds many golden trout. The falls adds to the lake's natural beauty.

Sky Blue is a 50-foot freefall at the back of Sky Blue Lake. It's not the kind of waterfall that's worth hiking the 28-mile roundtrip to see, however, if you are anywhere

The top of New Army Pass

Snow covers New Army Pass through July

in or near the Miter Basin, it's worth a visit. If not for the waterfall, come for the fishing. Although the lake was last planted in 1962 with 2,000 golden trout, fishing still remains good. Try using Thomas Buoyants or Kastmasters.

To get to the lake, begin at the Horseshoe Meadow Trailhead, walking through Horseshoe Meadow and over Cottonwood Pass. At the pass, there is a three-way fork in the trail. The middle fork leads to Big Whitney Meadow. The left climbs over Trail and Mulkey Passes. Follow the right fork towards Chicken Springs Lake, which is a pretty place to take a break and regain energy for the rest of the trip.

Leaving the lake, continue 3.2 miles on the Pacific Crest Trail to the boundary of Sequoia National Park. Approximately seven-tenths of a mile from the boundary, you'll come to a fork in the trail. The left fork leads to Siberian Pass, the right towards New

Army Pass and the Miter Basin. Take the right fork and walk one-mile to another fork. Stay left, crossing a small stream, and follow signs to Rock Creek.

In a half-mile another junction awaits. Turn right, you'll arrive at Lower Soldier Lake. Instead, take a left, and in seven-tenths of a mile you'll run into Rock Creek Lake. Walk towards Rock Creek Lake. From the lake, hike 2.4 miles on the trail that parallels Rock Creek to a fork in the creek, located at the end of the meadow and the back of the basin. If you veer right, you'll be headed towards Iridescent Lake. Stay left, towards Rock Creek Falls. Follow the trail past the falls to the lake. The trail begins to disappear halfway above the falls.

Directions *and trip info to Rock Creek Falls also apply to Sky Blue Falls.*

Downstream of Sky Blue Lake, Rock Creek
meanders through the Miter Basin (pictured above)

Rock Creek Falls

Rating: 7

How Short? 27 Miles

How Easy? 5

Best Time to View:
June to August

Need Information?
Contact: Sequoia
National Park
Wilderness Permits
(559) 565-3761,
Sequoia National Park
(559) 565-3134, Inyo
National Forest
(760) 876-6200

When it comes to finding serenity, it's hard to beat Rock Creek Falls. Located in the Miter Basin inside the eastern boundary of Sequoia National Park, Rock Creek Falls has it all: small crowds, great fishing, golden trout, lush green meadows, colorful wildflowers, jagged snowcapped peaks and a chance to see marmots and a pretty waterfall. These rewards, however, don't come without a price. It's a 13.5-mile hike from the Horseshoe Meadow Trailhead, only doable for the weekend backpacker.

Yet, I think of the trip to Rock Creek Falls as a perfect first backpacking experience. The trails are well signed, the scenery is exceptional and the total experience, which includes walking through the Inyo National Forest, Golden Trout Wilderness and Sequoia National Park, will surely hook you on backpacking. Don't get me wrong, there's a lot of elevation gain on the trip, but Cottonwood Pass is a much easier climb than most other passes in the Sierra.

Rock Creek Falls isn't the main attraction in the Miter Basin: fishing is. Beginning at the mouth of the basin, Upper and Lower Soldier Lakes offer great golden trout fishing; then, there's the fishing at Sky Blue Lake, which feeds Rock Creek and creates Rock Creek Falls.

The falls is situated directly below Sky Blue Lake, southwest of Iridescent Lake. After Rock Creek rushes out of Sky Blue Lake, it feeds Rock Creek Falls' 100-foot cascade, where cold, clear water tumbles down the mountain into the unnamed meadow below.

There are a few things to consider when

Rock Creek Falls

planning a trip to the falls. First, the Miter Basin may remain covered with snow until late June. Also, sometimes Horseshoe Meadow Road doesn't open until late June, leaving the trailhead inaccessible. To play it safe, check on snow conditions a few weeks before planning your trip.

The only problem with visiting the high country in late June and early July is the mosquitoes. Even the best repellant doesn't seem to work on these suckers, but the problem exists throughout the entire Sierra, so planning a trip elsewhere won't do you any good. At 11,500 feet, the falls is best from late June through July, when snow runoff from Mt. Newcomb, Mt. McAdie, and Mt. Mallory is at its peak. Although the falls still flows in August, it is much less spectacular.

To reach the falls, follow the directions in the write-up for Sky Blue Falls. The last leg of the trek, just before reaching Sky Blue Lake, passes by the falls. You can't miss it. The trail parallels Rock Creek from the end of the unnamed meadow to Sky Blue Lake.

If you plan to make the trip, a wilderness permit is required for overnight travel in Sequoia National Park. The road to the trailhead closes in the winter and spring. Call ahead for updated conditions.

Also nearby are Rock Creek, Rock Creek Lake, Iridescent Lake, Sky Blue Falls, Chicken Springs Lake, South Fork Lakes and Cottonwood Lakes.

Directions: *From Mojave, drive north on Highway 14 to Highway 395. Drive north on Highway 395 to the town of Lone Pine. In Lone Pine, turn left on Whitney Portal Road and drive three miles to Horseshoe Meadow Road. Turn south and drive approximately 16 miles to the Horseshoe Meadow Trailhead.*

The lower tier of Rock Creek Falls

Tokopah Valley Falls

Rating: 8

How Short? 3.6 Miles

How Easy? 2

Best Time to View:
May to July

Need Information?
Contact: Sequoia
National Park (559)
565-3134, Lodgepole
Visitor Center (559-
565-3782) Lodgepole
Campground
(559-565-3774)

The El Nino season of 1998 created problems for hikers in Sequoia National Park. It was mid-June of that year when I drove to Lodgepole to see the General Sherman Tree for the first time. When a few friends and I arrived, we were shocked at all the snow still on the ground. We were only at 6,850 feet, but there was still a few feet of snow almost everywhere. Snow also blanketed the bottom of the Sherman Tree, which is the world's largest living organism.

All the snow worried me. We had planned on hiking a few miles to Tokopah Valley Falls, but would we even be

able to see the trail through the deep snow? We drove to the kiosk at Lodgepole Campground, where I asked the park ranger if the hike was doable.

"Well, that depends," he responded, checking our car to see if we were prepared. "Do you men have any snowshoes with you? I heard some guy did it with snowshoes earlier in the week, but I haven't heard of anyone doing it on foot yet. It may be possible. Some of the snow has probably melted since then."

Whether the trail was suitable for hikers or not didn't matter to me at this point. I'd driven five hours to see this waterfall. My buddies and I were going regardless. Summer was almost here. There wasn't supposed to be snow at this elevation.

As we started out over the bridge across the Marble Fork of the Kaweah River, things looked good. There were footprints in the snow showing us where the trail was. After the first quarter-mile, however, the trail disappeared. I figured if we followed the river we'd have no problem finding the falls. I was correct, but things took a lot longer than we expected.

It's only a 1.7-mile hike to the falls, but the lack of a trail prolonged our trip, which normally takes less than 45 minutes. Although I was having a blast, my friends weren't so thrilled. They were wearing tennis shoes, and their shoes, socks and pants were soaked. We were all exhausted, but that should be expected when you're trekking through three feet of snow without snowshoes.

As we neared the waterfall, the conditions improved a little. Once

Tokopah Valley Falls in June of 1998

It's not safe to drink the water from the Kaweah River. Bring water on the trail with you.

we left the canopy of pines, the sun melted some of the snow. After two hours of hiking, we finally reached the falls. The trip was worth it. I also learned a precious lesson about hiking through deep snow: as I walked closer to the 1,200-foot Tokopah Valley Falls, I fell through the snow into the river. Little did I know I'd been standing on the river the whole time, but the snow blanket was so thick we couldn't see it.

Walking to the waterfall is much easier and more rewarding without the snow. The trail begins at the east end of Lodgepole Campground and parallels the Marble Fork the entire way. The path runs along the north side of the river, mostly through a pine forest, but sometimes passes through small meadows and over seasonal tributaries. We saw two bears on the trail, but unless you hike early in the morning or in the late evening your chances of seeing one are slim.

As you near the falls, gigantic vertical slabs of granite tower overhead. The waterfall is a cascade that tumbles and crashes against enormous slabs of granite the entire way down the canyon. Tokopah Valley is fed by runoff from the Tableland Divide and Pear, Aster, Heather and Emerald Lakes.

Keep in mind that this hike is one of the most popular in the park, and the trail gets crowded. High noon is the wrong time to come. Try early in the morning or in the late evening, unless you don't mind crowds.

If you plan to make the trip, supplies are available in Three Rivers and Lodgepole. Call ahead for trail conditions. The trail may not be snow free until June.

Also nearby are Moro Rock, Middle Fork Kaweah River Falls, Kings Canyon National Park, Woodward Creek Falls and Stoney Creek Falls.

Directions: *From Fresno, drive 55 miles east on Highway 180 to the Kings Canyon National Park entrance and continue 1.7 miles to Generals Highway. Turn right and drive 25 miles to Lodgepole Campground. Turn left and drive to the day-use parking lot near the Kaweah River. Walk across the bridge to the trailhead.*

(Pictured above)Tokopah Valley Falls was dry in September of 2002

Marble Fork Falls

Rating: 4

How Short? 0.50 Miles

How Easy? 1

Best Time to View?
July to September

Need Information?
Contact: Sequoia
National Park (559)
565-3134, Lodgepole
Visitor Center (559-
565-3782), Lodgepole
Campground
(559-565-3774)

Few, if any, will disagree that Tokopah Valley Falls is the best waterfall in Sequoia National Park. It's the tallest, carries the most water and is fed by a large drainage of lakes and streams in the backcountry. However, because Tokopah's drainage consists of granite, not soil, the waterfall's life is limited. Without soil in the surrounding area the aquifer is quickly depleted. Tokopah often dries up by August. On the upside, the granite base allows the waterfall to flow fast and furious in the spring when runoff begins. Unfortunately, without a soil bottom the water can't seep into the ground, therefore there isn't water left to permit year round existence. When all the snow melts Tokopah and portions of the Marble Fork of the Kaweah River, which feeds the waterfall dry up.

On the other hand, below Tokopah several sections of the streambed and surrounding topography are rich with soil. This allows the stream to maintain a year-round groundwater supply and permits the lower section of the Marble Fork of the Kaweah River to flow year-round.

This is where Marble Fork Falls come into play. When Tokopah is dry Marble Fork Falls are in good shape. At 6,850 feet in Sequoia National Park, Marble Fork Falls are two small waterfalls along the Marble Fork of the Kaweah River.

The lower waterfall is a small freefall only a short walk from Lodgepole Campground. To reach it, pick up the trailhead for Tokopah Valley Falls on the north side of the river. If you are 5-foot, 9 inches count out 940 steps to the waterfall on your right. To better aid your search look for these two landmarks. The falls is situated at the end of Lodgepole Campground located on the south side of the river,

Upper Marble Fork Falls in September of 2002

and also is the site of the first major congregation of granite since leaving the trailhead. An excellent wading hole awaits below the falls, not to mention wild rainbow and brown trout in the stream. The waterfall is a mere 20-foot freefall, but provides a cool alternative to the late summer heat.

The second falls is 400 steps further and the site of the second major congregation of granite. This drop is better described as a narrow 15-foot high chute of water that sneaks its way through a gathering of granite. Both falls are best viewed in August, September and October. Come any sooner and they'll be covered in raging water. These falls are late season bloomers.

If you plan to make the trip, supplies are available in Three Rivers and Lodgepole. Call ahead for trail conditions. The trail may not be snow free until June. There is a fee to enter Sequoia National Park.

Also nearby are Moro Rock, Middle Fork Kaweah River Falls, Kings Canyon National Park, Woodward Creek Falls and Stoney Creek Falls.

Directions: *From the Arch Rock entrance to Sequoia National Park continue 20.5 miles to the turnoff on the right for Lodgepole. Turn right and continue to the day use parking area.*

Lower Marble Fork Falls in September of 2002

Cascade Creek Falls

Rating: 6

How Short? 1.0 Mile

How Easy? 1

Best Time to View:
May to August

Need Information?
Contact: Sequoia
National Park (559)
565-3134, Lodgepole
Visitor Center
(559-565-3782)

Sequoia National Park offers so many activities, you'll have trouble deciding what to do. Make sure to include Crystal Cave in your plans. Discovered in 1918, Crystal is the only cave in the park that offers guided tours. The tours begin in mid-May and last through early September, focusing on hundreds of stalagmites and stalactites that remain at a constant 48 degrees.

On the way to Crystal Cave, it's impossible not to see Cascade Creek Falls as you hike along the half-mile trail to the cave. This 25-foot cascade along Cascade Creek can be quite imposing in the spring and early summer when snow runoff is high.

It requires a long, slow drive to reach the cave from anywhere in the park. Keep in mind there are no tickets sold at the cave for the tours; all tickets must be purchased either at the Foothill or Lodgepole Visitor Centers. After obtaining your tickets, driving the one and a half hours (from either visitor center) to the cave and taking the tour, half of the day will be gone. Make the best of it by bringing along a sack lunch and enjoying the waterfall. There are many other smaller cascades along the creek; however, none are as popular as Cascade.

There are also small wild trout in the creek, but to find them you'll have to scramble downstream to locate larger pools. To tell you the truth, the fishing isn't good enough to warrant the effort. People come to the park for the giant sequoias, and of course the waterfalls, not the fishing.

If you plan to make the trip, supplies are available in Lodgepole. Tickets are not available at the cave. They must be purchased at the Lodgepole or Foothill Visitor Centers. The cave and the access road to it are only opened seasonally. Call ahead for availability. The road to the cave is narrow and winding. Drive slowly, and use caution. There is a fee to enter Sequoia National Park.

Also nearby are the General Sherman Tree, Moro Rock, Marble Falls and Twin Lakes.

Directions: *From Bakersfield, drive north on the 99 Freeway to Highway 198. Exit east and continue to the city of Visalia. From Visalia, continue approximately 35 miles on Highway 198 to Sequoia National Park's entrance. Drive 15 miles into the park on a slow, winding road to the Crystal Cave turnoff. Turn left at the turnoff and drive approximately seven miles to the parking area.*

Cascade Creek Falls

Middle Fork Kaweah Falls

Rating: 5
How Short? 0.50 Miles
How Easy? 1
Best Time to View: March to August
Need Information? Contact: Sequoia National Park (559) 565-3134, Foothills Visitor Center (559-565-4212)

Under certain conditions, almost every outdoorsman wants to see a bear in the wild. For most, the desirable way would be from inside their car while driving down a mountain road, but the chances of that happening are slim. If you're willing to chance meeting a bear outside the protection of your car, at Buckeye Flat Campground in Sequoia National Park, black bears visit the campground just about every afternoon and evening from late spring through mid-summer. It's almost guaranteed. There are posted bear warnings in the campground, and a park ranger is generally stationed here to ease campers' worries.

So, what is the connection between bears, Buckeye Campground and the Middle Fork Kaweah Falls? Let me tell you a quick story to explain. Each year I come to Buckeye in late June, as the river begins to recede. From the campground, I walk up the Kaweah to one of my favorite swimming holes. Located at the base of the Middle Fork Kaweah Falls, this pool is about 20 yards long and just as wide, ranging from two to eight feet deep. It's the ideal swimming hole. With its location still in the foothills at 2,950 feet, the temperature reaches 100 nearly every day from June through August. The water's warm enough to bask in for hours. A few years back, a couple friends named it "Grand Tub."

Back to my story. After I get tired of swimming in the "Grand Tub," I'll usually walk back to Buckhorn, where I almost always find at least one bear in the campground. The first year I visited, the bear was in the campsite across from mine, playing with a shoe that was left to dry out on a rock. Another time, a bear was tearing apart a log looking for some grubs to munch on. Last time, I saw a bear sniffing around the backside of my tent. I don't mind the bears. I realize I'm invading their home; they aren't invading mine.

Despite the bears, Buckeye is a popular spring and summer campsite that fills up nightly. The campsites are situated along the Kaweah, and the trailhead for the Middle Fork Kaweah Falls is in also the campground. To reach the waterfall, walk to the east end of the campground, pick up the Paradise Trail and begin following the Kaweah. Shortly, you'll come to a bridge over the Kaweah. Cross the bridge and abandon the

The Grand Tub is one of California's best swimming holes

Black bears are common at Buckeye Flat Campground

trail, heading upstream along the creek for fewer than 10 minutes.

The short walk brings you to the base of the falls. The falls isn't the real attraction, though, the "Grand Tub" is. The waterfall is a 25-foot cascade, tumbling down a smooth granite face punctuated with outcroppings of jagged rocks. Most impressive is the water's clarity. This emerald blue pool, which is surrounded by slabs of granite, is a great place to snorkel.

Don't stop here. Both up and downstream, dozens of less-crowded swimming holes await. One thing to take into consideration, however, is timing. Before late June the river flows so rapidly it's too swift to swim in. By July, the river slows down enough to allow for swimming.

If you plan to make the trip, supplies are available in Three Rivers. There is a fee to enter Sequoia National Park. If not staying at Buckeye Campground, park along the road outside the campground and walk in.

Also nearby are Lake Kaweah, Lower Kaweah River, North Fork of the Kaweah River, Sierra View Catfish Farms, Cascade Creek Falls, Moro Rock and Tokopah Valley Falls.

Directions: *From Bakersfield, drive north on the 99 Freeway to Highway 198. Exit east and drive to the city of Visalia. From Visalia, continue approximately 35 miles on Highway 198 to Sequoia National Park's entrance. Drive approximately six miles past the entrance kiosk to a campground on the right.*

Middle Fork Kaweah Falls

Middle Fork Falls

Rating: 4

How Short? Drive To

How Easy? 1

Best Time to View:
July to February

Need Information?
Contact: Sequoia
National Park (559)
565-3134, Foothills
Visitor Center
(559-565-4212)

Middle Fork Falls isn't your typical tourist trap in Sequoia National Park. It's for sightseers who aren't concerned with being overwhelmed. Middle Fork Falls won't lure you into visiting the rest of the waterfalls in this book. However, it does offer a sense of outdoor allure. Unfortunately, the waterfall is located within rock throwing distance of Highway 198 so you don't get too withdrawn from civilization. On the other hand, the roar of the Middle Fork of the Kaweah River overshadows most of the passing by cars.

Middle Fork Falls isn't a grand display of falling water. It's a small drop on the Kaweah where the river is channeled through a large dip in the granite. The drop is best in the summer and fall when less water in the river exposes the 15-foot drop better. To reach the waterfall, exit your car and scramble down to the river. The 15-foot drop is 20 yards upstream. There is also a smaller six-foot drop 10 yards downstream.

Don't come here for the waterfall. Middle Fork Falls is best known for fabulous

swimming holes and fishing for small, wild rainbow trout. Visitation times make a big difference in your experience here. Avoid coming from March through June when the Kaweah is running fast and dangerously. I visit when runoff subsides, the water warms and the decreased volume allows for safe swimming.

This section of the Kaweah harbors some of the best swimming holes in the state. They may not be the warmest and deepest, but the clean, clear water makes for excellent swimming conditions. And, the granite banks pose exceptional tanning rocks.

If you plan to make the trip, supplies are available in Three Rivers. There is a fee to enter Sequoia National Park.

Also nearby are the Tunnel Tree, Middle Fork Kaweah Falls and Crystal Cave.

Directions: *From Bakersfield, drive north on the 99 Freeway to Highway 198. Exit east and drive to the city of Visalia. From Visalia, continue approximately 35 miles on Highway 198 to Sequoia National Park's entrance. Drive 5.6 miles past the Arch Rock entrance kiosk to a pullout on the right.*

East Fork Falls

Rating: 5

How Short? 2.4 Miles

How Easy? 2

Best Time to View:
May to November

Need Information?
Contact: Sequoia
National Park
(559) 565-3768

When planning a trip to most of California's mountain communities, national parks and national forests, there are a few rules of thumb to follow regarding the best time of year to visit. First, try to avoid Memorial and Labor Day weekends. Second, if you're visiting in the summer, try to avoid weekends altogether. Third, even if you've followed numbers one and two, just in case, always be prepared for crowds.

Regarding the East Fork Kaweah River Drainage, none of the above rules apply. Probably because the one-lane winding road that leads to this section of Sequoia National Park scares so many people off, crowds rarely develop here. So, when most campers are struggling to find a campsite elsewhere, those who arrive at this section of the park will most likely be able to score their own fire pit, picnic table and quiet campsite shaded by pines.

There is another bonus for sightseers who come here to beat the crowds: East Fork Falls. Although there is a 496-foot descent over the 1.2 miles to the waterfall, the trail is easily manageable for young children and those who aren't in great physical condition. The path's descent is gradual to the river and East Fork Falls.

Although 15-foot high East Fork Falls is just so-so, its surroundings are superb. The East Fork comes crashing against granite boulders through a canyon before feeding the falls. Above the falls, sequoias line the stream's clear, deep, cool pools. Although some are too shallow for wading, you'll probably hear others calling out your name.

At the end of Atwill Mill Campground, pick up the well-signed Hockett Trail. The path threads through a series of old sequoia stumps, passing the site of Atwill Mill before beginning its descent down to the East Fork. You'll see rusted machinery and other remnants of the old mill at this site. Pines, sequoias and cedars shelter the route the entire trip to the falls. After three-fourths of a mile cross Deadwood Creek, and soon be able to hear the roar of East Fork Falls. It's almost time to take a dip!

If you plan to make the trip, supplies are available in Mineral King. The road to Mineral King closes in the winter. Call ahead for updated conditions. There is a fee to enter Sequoia National Park.

Also nearby are Tufa Falls and Mineral King Falls.

Directions: *From the 99 Freeway in Fresno, drive south to the turnoff for Highway 198 east and Visalia. Drive approximately 39 miles to Mineral King Road and turn right. Continue 19.5 miles on the slow winding road to the turnoff on the right for Atwill Mill Campground.*

East Fork Falls

Mineral King Falls

Rating: 7

How Short? Drive-To

How Far? 1

Best Time to View:
May to November

Need Information?
Contact: Sequoia
National Park
(559) 565-3768

Some drivers are awfully impatient. But when you're driving to Mineral King you'd better be a patient driver. While many drivers are accustomed to traveling 35 mph on mountain roads, they need to ease their foot off the pedal when driving Mineral King Road. In other words, take the 15 mph speed limit here seriously. Any faster and you're definitely in danger of driving recklessly on this one-lane winding road.

Actually, at times slow driving can be good for passengers, giving them time to view points of interest that would otherwise go unnoticed. (You drivers keep your eyes on the road, now.) By going slow and giving our eyes time to wander the hillsides and canyons below, my friend Brett Ross and I discovered Mineral King Falls.

Although Mineral King Falls is a powerful cascade, the viewing area is small and if you don't look from the right spot, you'll miss it. Down in the canyon on the right, the waterfall is visible for three-tenths of a mile, between 22.8 and 23.1 miles from the turnoff at Highway 198. There is a slight problem, however, because there are only a few pullouts along this section of the one-lane road. Use caution where you stop. We took a chance and stopped in the middle of the road with cars behind us, hoping nobody would throw a fit. Luckily, they were thrilled we stopped, because they got to see a waterfall they otherwise would have missed.

Located on the East Fork Kaweah River, Mineral King Falls is the best waterfall in the Mineral King area of Sequoia National Park. Fortunately for tourists, because of the size of the river that feeds it, the cataract remains striking enough for visitors to enjoy from late spring through fall.

The National Park Service couldn't give me a specific height, so a rough guesstimate is that Mineral King Falls is somewhere between 100 and 200 feet tall. Situated in a narrow gorge, this waterfall is made up of a series of 50-foot cascades. When you park your car and look down the side of the canyon, they are best seen with a pair of binoculars, but can also be viewed just fine with the naked eye.

If you plan to make the trip, supplies are available in Mineral King. The road to Mineral King closes in the winter. Call ahead for updated conditions. There is a fee to enter Sequoia National Park.

Also nearby are Tufa Falls and Black Wolf Falls .

Directions: *From the 99 Freeway in Fresno, drive south to the turnoff for Highway 198 east and Visalia. Drive approximately 39 miles to Mineral King Road and turn right. Continue 22.8 miles on the slow winding road to a small pullout on the right.*

Mineral King Falls

Black Wolf Falls

Rating: 6

How Short? Drive-To

How Easy? 1

Best Time To View:
May to July

Need Information?
Contact: Sequoia
National Park
(559) 565-3768

There are still a few places in the Golden State where you can drive to a waterfall and have it all to yourself. Although tourists mob most of the state's waterfalls from sunrise to sunset during the spring and summer, Black Rock Falls in Sequoia National Park can provide a rare freedom from the crowds and sightseers that inundate these other natural wonders.

You ask how a waterfall in one of the country's most popular national parks can remain so untouched? It all has to do with Mineral King Road. Many travelers just don't want to deal with it. While most of the road is paved, it certainly isn't easy to drive. This slow, narrow, winding road is crammed with so many blind turns, if you drive faster than 10 mph it becomes extremely dangerous. There are also steep cliffs on the side of the road that overhangs the East Fork Kaweah River, causing even experienced mountain drivers to become jittery.

Don't get too revved-up about seeing Black Wolf Falls. While it will allow you a chance for a little relaxation, it's not an experience you'll call "awesome." Situated about a half-mile from the end of Mineral King Road, this 40-foot cascade along Monarch Creek is only about 50 yards from the road. Runoff from the Monarch Lakes keeps it flowing powerfully until mid-summer, when the stream subsides and the waterfall begins to lack merit as a tourist attraction.

If you plan to make the trip, supplies are available in Mineral King. The road to Mineral King closes in the winter. Call ahead for updated conditions. There is a fee to enter Sequoia National Park.

Also nearby are Crystal Creek Falls, Mineral King Falls, East Fork Falls, Tufa Falls and the Sequoia National Park backcountry.

Directions: From the 99 Freeway in Fresno, drive south to the turnoff for Highway 198 east and Visalia. Drive approximately 39 miles to Mineral King Road and turn right. Continue approximately 24.8 miles on the slow, winding road to the parking next to the falls.

Black Wolf Falls

Tufa Falls

Rating: 5

How Short? 0.50 Miles

How Easy? 1

Best Time to View:
May to September

Need Information?
Contact: Sequoia
National Park
(559) 565-3768

A healthy buck

Most Californians have never seen a marmot. In fact, they've probably never even heard of one. What exactly is a marmot? While there are several species of marmots, only the yellow-bellied marmot is found in California. A member of the squirrel family, marmots are typically found in rocky areas and meadows at high elevations, usually from 6,500 to 13,000 feet. These rodents that look like giant squirrels weigh anywhere from 15 to 25 pounds.

Marmots are plentiful in the Mineral King area of Sequoia National Park, and while they might look like cute furry little critters, they pose a major problem to visitors. I was at the trailhead for the Farewell Gap when I first caught wind of the problems they cause. I noticed that most of the cars in the parking area had their hoods up. What the heck was going on? This many people couldn't be experiencing car problems. Then I saw small metal and wire fences surrounding many of the vehicles. When I chatted with a few other hikers, I learned that these mischievous little buggers get a kick out of climbing under cars and chewing up hoses and wires near their engines.

Marmots caused a lot of damage to cars before the National Park Service began warning motorists of the dangers these rodents pose. Now there are signs warning tourists of the destruction they can cause to unprotected vehicles. Although fences keep marmots away from cars, many hikers don't think to bring wire or fences with them. The next best thing is to open your hood, which deters the munching varmints. "They are shy little guys that don't like to work in the light," a park ranger explained to me.

Deer are abundant near Tufa Falls

Even if you take these precautions, the marmots still might damage your vehicle. So many of them are now used to humans and cars that they aren't as easy to scare off as they once were. The only way to assure that your vehicle won't be harmed is not to leave it unsupervised. Fortunately, a visit to Tufa Falls will allow you time to enjoy the wilderness and get back before the marmots can do too much damage.

There's a trail from the parking lot that guides you to the base of Tufa. If you take it, however, you won't get a good view of the waterfall. Because the tall cascade is hidden behind a congregation of pines, it's almost impossible to see from this side of the canyon. To pick up the trail that leads to the best view, you'll need to backtrack a little. So, even though Tufa Falls is only about 100 yards from the parking area, you'll need to walk about a quarter-mile each way.

Backtrack roughly 50 yards from the parking area to where the East Fork of the Kaweah River crosses under the road. Just after the bridge, a road breaks off to the right towards a pack station. Follow this road past the pack station as it becomes a single-track dirt trail. Fewer than 50 yards after passing the pack station, look across the canyon for the waterfall cascading down a mountainside. Although it cascades hundreds of feet, even from this vantage only small sections can be seen through the pines and thick foliage, greatly reducing its scenic value.

If you plan to make the trip, supplies are available in Mineral King. The road to Mineral King closes in the winter. Call ahead for updated conditions. There is a fee to enter Sequoia National Park.

Also nearby are Crystal Creek Falls, Mineral King Falls, East Fork Falls, Black Wolf Falls and the Sequoia National Park backcountry.

Directions: *From the 99 Freeway in Fresno, drive south to the turnoff for Highway 198 east and Visalia. Drive approximately 39 miles to Mineral King Road and turn right. Continue 25.1 miles on the slow, winding road to the parking area at its end.*

A yellow bellied marmot

Crystal Creek Falls

Rating: 6

How Short? 2.0 Miles

How Easy? 1

Best Time to View:
May to September

Need Information?
Contact: Sequoia
National Park
(559) 565-3768

Disappointing Tufa Falls discourages many nature lovers from visiting other waterfalls in the Mineral King area of Sequoia National Park. These sightseers want to be able to view a whole waterfall from head to foot. With Tufa they only get to hear it, while straining for sketchy glimpses through a dense covering of pines. Don't be disheartened by Tufa, though, because those who are willing to walk just a little further up the trail are rewarded with a waterfall that's more than simply a tease.

A minuscule seven-tenths of a mile from Tufa, with only a 46-foot elevation gain, Crystal Creek Falls is the real deal. Fed by runoff from 10,800-foot-high Crystal Lake, Crystal Creek stays alive year-round and can be a stunning site from late spring through summer when runoff is at its peak.

Although not a rousing freefall or commanding cascade, this picturesque waterfall tumbles down a mountainside teeming with pine trees and a variety of smaller foliage. Here you can relax and enjoy the sight of a waterfall in its full splendor, while also immersing yourself in the entrancing sound of water splashing down into the East Fork Kaweah River Drainage.

Getting to Crystal Creek Falls takes little effort. From the parking area, backtrack to where the East Fork Kaweah River crosses under the road. Just after the bridge crossing, a road breaks off to the right. Following this unmarked road, take a right and walk past the pack station, where you'll pass stables and parallel the river.

A few-hundred yards after the pack station, you'll get glimpses of Tufa Falls across the canyon. As you continue through meadows rich with wildflowers, don't worry about passing by the waterfall without seeing it; Crystal Creek is the first stream you'll come to and the cascade is on the left.

If you plan to make the trip, supplies are available in Mineral King. The road to Mineral King closes in the winter. Call ahead for updated conditions.

Also nearby are Tufa Falls, Mineral King Falls, East Fork Falls and Black Wolf Falls.

Directions *for Tufa Falls also apply to Crystal Creek Falls.*

Crystal Creek Falls

Franklin Falls

Rating: 6

How Short? 4.0 Miles

How Easy? 1

Best Time to View:
May to August

Need Information?
Contact: Sequoia
National Park
(559) 565-3768

When families take a vacation in the mountains, it's not always towering mountain peaks, awe-inspiring waterfalls, wide fast-flowing rivers and marshmallows smoking over campfires that make their children want to return to the forest year after year. City kids often get excited at the mere sight of wildlife that's different from the squirrels and birds they see at home.

Even in the mountains you have to get a little lucky to see raccoons, bears and coyotes, which are the most common animals found in the wilderness. Yet, there are many places in the wilderness where it's quite common to see deer. As a matter of fact, there are a few areas in California where deer can almost always be seen. For example, you're nearly assured of a deer sighting at the Wawona golf course in Yosemite National Park, Yosemite Valley, in the meadows off Highway 89 near Mt. Lassen, Franklin Falls in the Mineral King area of Sequoia National Park, and at night along Highway 36 near Lake Almanor.

Of all the places to come face to face with a deer, Franklin Falls is the least known, but it's still worth a visit. Located between Mineral King and Farewell Gap, Franklin Falls is a long cascade with a few small freefalls near its base. It's certainly not a grand waterfall, if that's all you're interested in seeing. But you aren't coming here just for a waterfall: it's time to see some deer! And this is deer country, with a perfect grassy landscape for grazing deer to flourish.

The East Fork Kaweah River runs down the center of Mineral King Valley, twisting through pristine meadows with thousands of wildflowers and tall grass growing among pines. Fed by the four Franklin Lakes, Franklin Creek, the largest tributary in this part of the Kaweah Drainage, keeps Franklin Falls flowing forcefully from mid-spring through August.

Getting to this deer country is simple. It's only a two-mile hike with a gradual 600-foot elevation gain from the parking area to the falls. Franklin is one of three waterfalls along the route. Preceding it are Tufa and Crystal Creek Falls, in that order. From Crystal Creek Falls, continue nine-tenths of a mile up the path to the base of Franklin Falls. Franklin is the first stream on the left after passing Crystal Creek.

Directions *and trip info for Tufa Falls also apply to Franklin Falls.*

Franklin Falls

Coyote Creek Falls

Rating: 7

How Short? 37.8 Miles

How Easy? 5

Best Time to View:
May to August

Need Information?
Contact: Sequoia
National Forest (661)
548-6503, Sequoia
National Park
Wilderness Permits
(559-565-3761) or
(559-565-3766),
Sequoia National Park
(559) 565-3134

Most of the western boundary of Sequoia National Park can be reached by car, via long winding roads on narrow mountain highways; however, the eastern boundary can only be reached by foot or horseback on trailheads along the Eastern Sierra Nevada or the Kern River Drainage. While the western side of the park near Lodgepole and Mineral King is heavily visited by tourists, backpackers try to avoid the crowds that accumulate in the more accessible areas by heading for the eastern side.

Crowds are definitely not a problem at Coyote Creek Falls along the Upper Kern River, near the border of the Golden Trout

Wilderness and Sequoia National Park. When I last arrived in May of 2000, there were more bears than people in the region. Although Coyote Creek Falls isn't one of the park's more popular destinations, it might be if more hikers knew about it. Unlike Tokopah Valley Falls near Lodgepole, it isn't heavily publicized. I can almost guarantee that nobody but a park ranger who's worked the Kern Canyon Ranger Station (which is only a few hundred yards from the falls) will know what you're talking about if you mention Coyote Creek Falls.

Nearly 10,000 feet up in the park, Coyote Creek is fed by runoff from Coyote Pass. The creek twists and turns through the backcountry for about five miles, before tumbling off a jagged granite face, creating a loud roar as it crashes against boulders on its way into the Kern Drainage. In order to get to the falls, you'll need to follow the trail signed for Coyote Pass, Coyote Lake and Mineral King, from the Kern Ranger Station to the stream and falls.

To get to the Kern Ranger Station, follow the instructions to Grasshopper Flat in the write-up for Grasshopper Creek Falls, which is 13.7 miles north of the Jerky Meadow Trailhead. From Grasshopper Flat, continue two miles up the Kern River to Little Kern Lake. The trail then ascends, following switchbacks for a mile to Kern Lake. Both Kern and Little Kern are good fishing lakes for rainbow and brown trout.

From Kern Lake, continue north on the flat

trail as it parallels the river for a tad more than a mile-and-a-half to the boundary of Sequoia National Park. Less than a tenth of a mile after entering the park, use a fallen tree to cross over Coyote Creek. After the stream crossing is a trail junction. The right fork leads to the ranger station, Little Whitney Meadow and Funston Meadow. Stay left, following the sign to Coyote Pass, and continue to the falls. Nearing the falls, leave the trail and follow the stream to its base. The path ascends above the falls. The waterfall can also be reached via a 42-mile (roundtrip) hike from Mineral King.

If you plan to make the trip, supplies are available in Kernville and Ponderosa. A wilderness permit is required for overnight travel in Sequoia National Park. Depending on road conditions, Road 22S82 may not open until late May. Call the Forest Service for updated road conditions.

Also nearby are Grasshopper Creek Falls, Volcano Falls, Golden Trout Creek, the Kern River and Sequoia National Park.

Directions: From the 99 Freeway in Bakersfield, exit Highway 178 east and drive 45 miles to Lake Isabella. From Lake Isabella, drive 11 miles north on Highway 155 to Kernville and turn left on Mountain 99. Drive approximately 24 miles on Mountain 99 to a fork in the road and veer right onto Road 22S82, signed for Camp Whitsett and Lower Peppermint Creek. Continue approximately 21 miles to the trailhead at the end of the road.

Coyote Creek Falls

Region (9) Sequoia National Forest

Deer Cove Creek Falls
Grizzly Falls
Tenmile Creek Falls
Tenmile Creek Falls (Upper)
Stoney Creek Falls
Woodward Creek Falls
Bear Creek Falls
Hidden Falls
Tule River Falls
Poso Creek Falls
Boulder Creek Falls
Horse Canyon Falls
Nobe Young Falls (Upper)
Nobe Young Falls (Lower)
Freeman Creek Falls
Peppermint Creek Falls
Long Meadow Creek Falls
South Creek Falls
Brush Creek Falls
Salmon Creek Falls (Lower)

Deer Cove Creek Falls

Rating: 4

How Short? Drive-To

How Easy? 1

Best Time to View?
May to September

Need Information?
Contact: Kings Canyon
National Park (559)
565-4307, Sierra
National Forest
(559) 338-2251

Deer Cove Creek Falls is a pitiful waterfall. Its size is minuscule. Its charisma is plain and boring. And, its impression leaves a bland taste in your mouth. If this waterfall's qualities are so weak then you ask why I included it in this book. Good question. Here's my take. Deer Cove Creek Falls compensates for its lack of grandeur by providing a feeling of self worth. The falls is close to the road, yet so hidden it revives a childhood sense of curiosity in you. A sense of youthfulness set in, like you are an explorer who found a secret waterfall that no one has seen before. I'm sure others have, however, with so many nearby publicized attractions few sightseers, if any, would ever stop here. For one, it's not listed on the park map.

Don't expect anyone else to be at the waterfall. Situated in a small canyon off Highway 180 several landmarks help sway your view away from the falls. Kings Canyon itself is the biggest deterrent, not to mention Grizzly Falls a half-mile back, the South Fork of Kings River and dozens of species of wildflowers dappled along the roadside.

While nearly a mile outside the border of Kings Canyon National Park the 20-foot waterfall is situated at 4,400 feet in the Sequoia National Forest, just beneath the Monarch Wilderness border. Located a quarter-mile west of the Deer Creek Trailhead the waterfall is fed by Deer Cove Creek, an extremely small creek that is fed by an even smaller watershed. The Deer Creek Trailhead is used by hikers and backpackers heading into the Monarch Wilderness. Grizzly Lakes are a popular destination.

Reaching the waterfall is easier than you might expect. From the pullout walk back to the bridge, carefully cross the highway and within seconds you'll see the falls on the right side of the canyon. There are more cascades upstream, but none worth the rugged scrambling required to reach them.

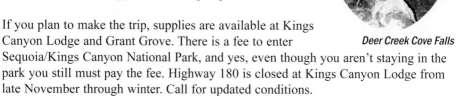

Deer Creek Cove Falls

If you plan to make the trip, supplies are available at Kings Canyon Lodge and Grant Grove. There is a fee to enter Sequoia/Kings Canyon National Park, and yes, even though you aren't staying in the park you still must pay the fee. Highway 180 is closed at Kings Canyon Lodge from late November through winter. Call for updated conditions.

Also nearby are Tenmile Creek Falls, Boyden Cave and Grizzly Falls.

Directions: *From the 99 Freeway in Fresno, drive 52 miles east on Highway 180 to the entrance to Sequoia/Kings Canyon National Parks. Continue 1.7 miles to a fork in the road. Veer left and continue 27.3 miles on Highway 180 to a pullout on the right, just after crossing a bridge with white fences on it.*

Grizzly Falls

Rating: 7

How Short? Drive-To

How Easy? 1

Best Time to View:
May to June

Need Information?
Contact: Sequoia
National Forest
(559) 338-2251

No matter where you're coming from, it's a long and winding road into the Cedar Grove section of Kings Canyon National Park. But the drive can seem a lot shorter if you make a brief stop at Grizzly Falls. Located at 4,300 feet in the Sequoia National Forest, the falls is a great place to stretch your legs. Without having to leave the main road, you can let your brakes cool while enjoying a pretty waterfall.

The falls is just 2.5 miles west of the national park. The top of the falls marks the boundary of the Monarch Wilderness, while the base is located in the Sequoia National Forest. You don't need to spend much time at the falls. Actually, you don't even need to leave the car. Yet, even though the falls can be seen through your car windows, you're only cheating yourself if you don't walk to its base.

At 70 feet tall, and as wide as 30 feet at peak flow, the falls can be quite spectacular in the spring, as Grizzly Creek cascades off its granite face. If you plan on visiting here, take a small piece of advice: do it before the 4th of July, because it is far less dramatic as snow runoff decreases.

The falls is fed by a small watershed, which receives its water from tiny Wren Creek, Choke Creek, the East Fork of Grizzly Creek and Grizzly Creek near Grizzly Lake. I've seen pictures of the falls in both May and July, and it looked like two completely different waterfalls. In May, I couldn't tell that its substructure was granite, there was so much water gushing over its brink. In July, however, the cascade had subsided to such a degree that I could make out the colors of the underlying rock.

Now, before you lose track of time, get back in the car and continue on into Kings Canyon National Park. There are plenty more waterfalls to visit.

If you plan to make the trip, supplies are available in nearby Cedar Grove. There is a fee to enter Kings/Canyon Sequoia National Parks; and, yes, even though you aren't visiting them, you still have to pay the fee. The road to the falls closes in winter.

Also nearby are South Fork of the Kings River, Boyden Cave, Roaring River Falls, Tenmile Creek, Mist Falls and Sequoia National Park.

Directions: *From the 99 Freeway in Fresno, take Highway 180 east 52 miles to the Sequoia/Kings Canyon National Parks' entrance and continue 1.7 miles to a fork in the road. Veer left, heading towards Cedar Grove, and drive 27 miles to the sign for Grizzly Falls on the left.*

Grizzly Falls

For Yosemite National Park's Ribbon Falls see page 146

213

Tenmile Creek Falls

Rating: 8
How Short? 3.5 Miles
How Easy? 2
Best Time to View? May to September
Need Information? Contact: Kings Canyon National Park (559) 565-4307

The Yucca Point Trailhead serves several purposes. The bulk of the traffic on the trail is anglers who follow the path down to the Kings River to fish for wild rainbow and brown trout. Others use the path as a gateway to a remote portion of the river ideal for swimming in summer and fall. For waterfall enthusiasts, the trail uncovers an exceptional drop in Sequoia National Monument. One that would remain a secret if it wasn't for the trail passing by the waterfall.

When water is running high through the system, Tenmile Creek Falls is the best waterfall in the northern section of the Sequoia National Monument. Runner up to only Freeman Creek Falls and Peppermint Creek Falls in the southern end of Sequoia National Monument, the 200-foot cascade is hard to beat in this neck of the forest. The other waterfalls nearby, Roaring River Falls, Grizzly and Deer Cove Creek Falls don't compare in size. They do however, come close if not succeed in outdoing Tenmile when it comes to volume. Unfortunately, this section of Tenmile is at the mercy of Hume Lake, which Tenmile flows into and out of. Hume's dam controls Tenmile's flows.

In the spring, when snowmelt is at its peak, expect the flows to be prosperous and the waterfall to be in great shape. In the heart of summer flows are diminished to provide recreation opportunities at Hume, however, beginning in September and lasting through October discharges are again increased to draw Hume down and prepare for wintry conditions. Any time of the year the waterfall is worth seeing.

The Yucca Point Trail isn't a stroll in the park. Over 1.5 miles the route loses more than 900 feet before meeting up with a trail spur that takes you to Tenmile Creek Falls. The descent is gradual. You won't notice it till the climb back out.

Trout caught in Tenmile Creek

The path is made up of two very long switchbacks that offer great views of the canyon below. The path loses more than 1,200 feet by the time it reaches the point where the South and Middle Forks of the Kings River join to

create the main stem of the Kings. Lucky for you, a trail spur breaks off to the left before the path reaches the river. This spur leads you to Tenmile Creek Falls, which is clearly visible from this vantage point.

The spur quickly drops you down to the creek where you'll need to do some rock hopping upstream to reach the falls. The waterfall is made up of three sections. The upper portion is a freefall, followed by two longer cascades over one gigantic slab of granite. The pool at the base of the falls is inviting, both for anglers and swimmers.

Hundreds of wild rainbow trout reside in the creek, which is catch & release only. Unpack a sandwich, drink some liquids and enjoy. This is paradise.

Directions: From the 99 Freeway in Fresno, drive 52 miles east on Highway 180 to the entrance to Sequoia/Kings Canyon National Parks. Continue 1.7 miles to a fork in the road. Veer left and continue 15.5 miles on Highway 180 to the Yucca Point Trailhead on the left.

If you plan to make the trip, supplies are available at Kings Canyon Lodge and Grant Grove. There is a fee to enter Sequoia/Kings Canyon National Park, and yes, even though you aren't staying in the park you still must pay the fee. Highway 180 is closed at Kings Canyon Lodge from late November through winter. Call for updated conditions.

Also nearby are Boyden Cave, Hume Lake, Roaring River Falls and Grizzly Falls.

The tip of Tenmile Creek Falls   *Tenmile Creek Falls*

Tenmile Creek Falls (Upper)

Rating: 6

How Short? 0.50 Miles

How Easy? 3

Best Time to View?
March through
September

Need Information?
Contact: Kings Canyon
National Park
(559) 565-4307

You want seclusion? Giant slabs of granite? Great swimming holes? Privacy? And all of it within close proximity to Sequoia and Kings Canyon National Park? What if I told you only a short hike was required? At Upper Tenmile Creek Falls it's all possible and attained with little effort.

This isn't, however, a place for families. While the trek to the falls is short, it is a bit demanding, requiring some rock hopping, rock climbing or wading to get to the better holes. The scrambling isn't tough, but it's not meant for children. Also, keep your eyes open. Skinny dippers call this hidden gem home.

Locating the stream is easy. Just before you reach Kings Canyon Lodge you'll cross a bridge over Tenmile Creek. Just after the bridge park in the dirt pullout on the right. There is no trailhead or maintained path. Dodging overgrown brush and trees work your way down to the creek, which lies a mere 20 yards away.

At 3,800 feet in the Sequoia National Monument this section of the stream is loaded with swimming holes. However, by mid-summer the water near the bridge gets a bit mossy and stagnant. For the better holes and waterfalls scramble upstream. It doesn't take long to locate some clear, deep, inviting swimming holes and small waterfalls.

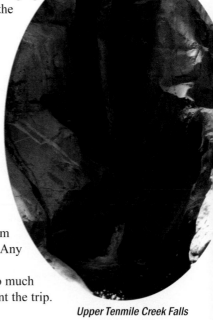

After a bit of rock hopping the first waterfall is a small freefall hindered by a sole granite boulder in its path. Just above this fall, however, is a much better drop. Located above a 50 yard section of smooth and flat granite along the streambed this waterfall is a 30-foot cascade that is best viewed from Noon to 2 p.m. when the sun is striking down on it. Any other time of the day shadows hurt its appearance. Upstream are several more drops. Unfortunately, too much bushwhacking and scrambling are required to warrant the trip.

Upper Tenmile Creek Falls

If you plan to make the trip, supplies are available at Kings Canyon Lodge and Grant Grove. There is a fee to enter Sequoia/Kings Canyon National Park, and yes, even though you aren't staying in the park you still must pay the fee.

Also nearby are Boyden Cave, Hume Lake, Roaring River Falls and Grizzly Falls.

Directions: *From the 99 Freeway in Fresno, drive 52 miles east on Highway 180 to the entrance to Sequoia/Kings Canyon National Parks. Continue 1.7 miles to a fork in the road. Veer left and continue 14.3 miles on Highway 180 to a small pullout on the right just after crossing a bridge. (If you reach Kings Canyon Lodge you've gone one-tenth of a mile too far.)*

Stoney Creek Falls

Rating: 5

How Short? 0.75 Miles

How Easy? 1

Best Time to View:
May to August

Need Information?
Contact: Sequoia
National Forest
(559) 338-2251,
Stoney Creek Lodge
(559) 565-3909

Nestled between Kings Canyon and Sequoia National Parks, at 6,000 feet in the Sequoia National Monument, Stoney Creek is a popular camping and fishing area for families who are trying to beat the crowds that swarm these national parks each summer. A small, but pretty stream, Stoney Creek is shaded by lofty pines and fed by snowmelt from the Sequoia Wilderness. From late spring through early summer, this popular camping area is also stocked with more than 3,000 rainbow trout by the California Department of Fish and Game.

By early August, the trout plants cease and the fishing slows, so visitors are forced to find other activities. One of the best local attractions is the short side trip to Stoney Creek Falls, a series of small drops along Stoney Creek. The falls is located downstream from the camping area, and although none of its drops are taller than 15 feet, they offer great swimming holes on hot summer days. And their granite boulders are prefect for butt-sliding down into the pools. Just be careful not to slip on the rocks; they can be extremely slippery.

Locating the trailhead requires no effort. From the Stoney Creek Lodge parking lot, walk to the southwest end and pick up the trail in a clearing surrounded by trees. The path gradually descends, and in fewer than 100 yards, Stoney Creek comes into view. From this point, it's less than a 10-minute walk to the falls. Once you see a swimming hole that's appealing to you, leave the trail and walk along the slabs of granite down to the stream.

For those who choose to continue, Woodman Creek meets up with Stoney Creek two-tenths of a mile downstream. Walk another half-mile and Stoney Creek enters Kings Canyon National Park, emptying into the headwaters of the North Fork of the Kaweah River. Although there is good fishing for wild rainbow trout in this area, casting can be difficult because the banks are steep.

If you plan to make the trip, supplies are available in Stoney Creek Village. There is a $10 fee to enter the national park. And yes, even though you aren't staying in the park, you must pay the fee. Stoney Creek is closed to fishing from November 16 to the last Saturday in April.

Also nearby are Big Meadow Creek, Jennie Lake, Hume Lake, Tenmile Creek and Bearskin Creek.

Directions: *From the 99 Freeway in Fresno, drive 52 miles east on Highway 180 to the Kings Canyon National Park entrance and continue 1.7 miles to a fork in the road. Veer right onto Generals Highway and drive 11 miles to Stoney Creek Lodge.*

Stoney Creek Falls

Woodward Creek Falls

Rating: 5

How Short? 3.0 Miles

How Easy? 3

Best Time to View: May to August

Need Information?
Contact: Sequoia National Forest (559) 338-2251,
Stoney Creek Lodge (559) 565-3909

On the small parcel of Forest Service land along Highway 198 between Sequoia and Kings Canyon National Parks, there are a few waterfalls that most visitors don't know about. At 6,450 feet up in the Sequoia National Monument, Woodward Creek Falls is one of them. Yet, even with its close proximity to the popular Stoney Creek Lodge, Woodward is rarely visited.

I last visited on a Saturday in late August. Although Stoney Creek Falls was packed, I didn't see one person at Woodward. There is a good reason for Woodward's anonymity. The falls is nowhere near as astonishing as other waterfalls nearby, such as Roaring River Falls, Mist Falls, Grizzly Falls and Tokapah Valley Falls. Woodward's small, gentle cascades compare best to its better-known neighbor Stoney Creek Falls, which is popular because Stoney Creek gets trout plants from the California Department of Fish and Game.

Simply because Woodward Creek Falls lacks size, doesn't mean you should scratch it off your list of sites to visit. Woodward offers something that the larger and more popular waterfalls don't: a chance to enjoy the serene sound of splashing water without having to watch where you step to avoid broken glass left from parties teenagers had.

To get to Woodward Creek Falls, park in the lot at Stoney Creek Lodge and pick up the path through a clearing in the trees at the southwest corner. Walk down the trail that

begins to parallel Stoney Creek. Continue seven-tenths of a mile from the trailhead to a feeder stream (Woodward Creek) that empties into Stoney.

Make a right and walk upstream. There will no longer be a trail. You'll come upon several cascades over the next mile, ending where the stream begins to parallel Highway 198. None are taller than 20 feet, but many empty into great swimming holes formed by granite bowls.

My favorite thing to do here is butt-sliding. Because the granite slopes are so slippery, it's easy to slide down the cascades into the pools. If you get a chance, bring along a mask and snorkel. The pools might be small, but they hold many wild rainbow and brook trout, which are much prettier than the stockers.

Directions *and trip into for Stoney Creek Falls also apply to Woodward Creek Falls.*

Woodward Creek Falls

Hidden Falls

Rating: 7

How Short? 0.20 Miles

How Easy? 1

Best Time To Visit:
May to September

Need Information?
Contact: Sequoia
National Forest (559)
784-1500, Mountain
Home State Forest
(559) 539-2321
(Summer) or (559)
539-2855 (Winter)

Hidden Falls is far from hidden. It's certainly no big secret. Rather, it's the most popular destination in the Mountain Home State Forest. Created in 1946, it was the first state forest established in California. According to a park brochure, the state of California purchased the land from a logging company to preserve more than 5,200 redwood trees in the Mountain Home Sequoia Grove.

Although the park consists of 4,807 acres, which contain numerous waterfalls, lush green meadows and three fishing lakes, many sightseers come specifically to see Hidden Falls. The falls is an easy-to-reach, ideal place to bring the family for a day trip. There are picnic areas nearby and the crowds tend to remain light, except for holiday weekends.

The falls are quite dramatic and noteworthy. Actually two sets of falls, both are segmented into two drops. The upper portion can be seen from the day-use parking area, where the North Fork of the Middle Fork of the Tule River races downhill. Here, the river slams into a giant boulder that divides it into two streams, creating two 30-foot high cascades.

Less than 50 yards downstream, the lower segment is smaller and far gentler. With its free flow obstructed by a much smaller rock than the giant boulder mentioned above, the river is also split into two drops, but the entire height of the falls is less than 10 feet. The lower drop empties into a small pool, ideal for wading.

To reach the falls, from the day-use parking area follow the well-marked dirt trail on the north side of the river. It is less than 100 yards downstream to the falls.

If you plan to make the trip, supplies are available in Springville. In winter and spring, call ahead for road conditions. The road into Mountain Home State Forest is commonly closed due to snow.

Also nearby are Bear Creek Falls, North Fork of the Long Falls, Redwood Lake and Balch Park Lakes.

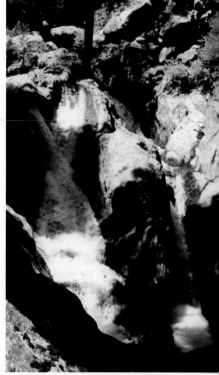

Upper Hidden Falls

Directions: *From Bakersfield, drive north on the 99 Freeway to Highway 190. Take Highway 190 east past Porterville and Lake Success to Springville. In Springville, turn left on Road J-37 (Balch Park Road) and drive 2.4 miles to Road 220. Turn right and continue approximately 12 miles to Mountain Home State Forest. Follow signs to the Balch Park Pack Station, and just before the pack station, veer right on a road signed for Hidden Falls. Park in the day-use parking area signed for Hidden Falls.*

Bear Creek Falls

Rating: 4

How Short? Drive-To

How Easy? 1

Best Time to View:
May to July

Need Information?
Contact: Balch Park
Pack Station (559) 539-
2227 (Summer) or
(559) 539-3908
(Winter), Sequoia
National Forest
(559) 784-1500

The Mountain Home State Forest is plentiful with activities for the whole family. On the contrary, few of these activities offer serenity or quiet time away from the crowds. Tiny Bear Creek Falls offers both.

Bear Creek Falls is the smallest waterfall in the state forest; so small, in fact, most visitors ignore it. The base of the falls is ideal for picnics. Situated so close to the road it's easy to bring a blanket, picnic basket and bottle of wine.

At 6,500 feet, Bear Creek is a charming little stream. It's banks sparkle with colorful wildflowers, which grow under the shade of soaring pines. Its 30-foot cascade is impressive in spring, even though it doesn't compare in size to nearby waterfalls, such as Hidden Falls and the North Fork of the Middle Fork of the Tule River Falls.

Although the falls can't be seen from the road, they are easy to find if you follow directions carefully. The easiest marker to use is Hedrick Pond, also called Redwood Lake. From the day-use parking area at the pond, drive 1.3 miles to a small dirt pullout on the right side of the road. If you roll your windows down, you should be able to hear the stream. Now, walk through the bushes on a narrow trail to the base. It takes less than one minute. If you end up at the turnoff for Frazier Mill Campground, you've driven two-tenths of mile too far.

If you plan to make the trip, supplies are available in Springville. In winter and early spring, the road into Mountain Home State Forest is commonly closed due to snow. Call ahead for road conditions.

Also nearby are the Mountain Home Sequoia Grove and Golden Trout Wilderness.

Directions: *From Bakersfield, drive north on the 99 Freeway to Highway 190 east. Continue on Highway 190 east past Porterville and Lake Success to Springville. In Springville, turn left on Road J-37 (Balch Park Road) and drive 2.4 miles to Road 220. Turn right and continue approximately 12 miles to Mountain Home State Forest. Once in the state forest, continue on Road 220 for 3.8 miles, going past Balch Park Lakes and Redwood Pond, to a small dirt pullout on the right side of the road. The pullout is just past Sunset Point Campground.*

This drop on the North Fork of the Middle Fork of the Tule River has much more volume than Bear Creek Falls

Tule River Falls

Rating: 8

How Short? 0.50 Miles

How Easy? 1

Best Time to View:
Year-Round

Need Information?
Contact: Sequoia
National Forest
(559) 539-2607

Although Californians have a fear of forest fires, in reality those fires are a normal and necessary process required for our forests to remain healthy. In many cases, fires are needed to keep the land fertile. This is true of the Edison Fire that was sparked by an unattended campfire and burned through parts of the Tule River Drainage during late spring of 2000.

The fire had another added benefit for hikers. Prior to the blaze, this section of the Middle Fork of the Tule River was extremely overgrown, and serious bushwhacking was required to reach its banks. But the fire served as a massive weed eater, not to mention clearing away dead brush and overgrown trees. Now

Tule River Falls is a piece of cake to reach.

Located in the Sequoia National Forest, this waterfall became part of the Giant Sequoia National Monument in April of 2000. Although not situated in a sequoia grove, there are several groves nearby. The monument was created to protect giant sequoia groves and to conserve the habitat for animals. Becoming a national monument has only added a few restrictions to the area: Motorcycles are now prohibited on trails, and unless visitors have a special permit, they are no longer permitted to remove anything from the forest, including firewood (with the exception of fish,

Jason Fractor poses next to Tule River Falls in fall of 2001

221

which are stocked in the Tule River).

Because the waterfall is located at the relatively low elevation of 2,900 feet, and the Tule River flows year-round, it remains an attraction long after many other cataracts in the region at higher elevations have dried up. In fact, as early as May, the water becomes warm enough to swim in, and with a large, deep pool at its base, Tule River Falls offers one of the more popular swimming holes in Central California.

While the surrounding scenery is the pits because the fire left the hillsides bare, the waterfall is something to brag about. Roughly 40 feet tall, the Tule plunges off a granite lip, making a grand display as it plummets into a crystal-clear pool.

To get to the waterfall, pick up the trailhead behind the Forest Service signboard. Travel upstream along the path, which begins by paralleling the river, before coming to a junction after 50 yards. Then head downstream, taking the right fork, and continue two-tenths of a mile to the waterfall.

If you plan to make the trip, supplies are available in Springville.

Also nearby are the Middle Fork of the South Fork of the Tule River at Camp Nelson and at Cedar Slope, Boulder Creek Falls and the North Fork of the Middle Fork of the Tule River (Wishon Camp).

Directions: *From Bakersfield, drive north on the 99 Freeway to Highway 190 east. Take Highway 190 past Porterville and Lake Success to Springville. Continue approximately seven miles on Highway 190 to the Camp Wishon turnoff (Road M-208). Drive 1.6 miles past the turnoff to a dirt pullout on the right. The unsigned trailhead can be picked up behind a wooden Forest Service sign.*

222   *Brown trout are not stocked in the Tule River, but wild brown trout can be found throughout the river*

Poso Creek Falls

Rating: 6

How Short? 0.25 Miles

How Easy? 1

Best Time to View:
February to May

Need Information?
Contact: Sequoia
National Forest
(661) 548-6503

Some call it pretty. Others say it's easy to visit, but remote. I call it one of the best places to see bobcats. On a cool and overcast weekend in March of 2000, I saw four bobcats on the short scenic drive from Posey to Posey Park.

Baffled by how many bobcats I'd come across in such a short period of time, I contacted the Forest Service. They told me that after struggling for quite some time, the bobcats have made a remarkable comeback in the area and have begun to build up their population. Although I spend my life in the wilderness, over the pervious three years I'd seen only one bobcat, at Lion Canyon Creek in the Los Padres National Forest. Seeing four was a real treat.

The falls made my day even better. Rarely visited by tourists, Poso Creek Falls is a series of four waterfalls on Poso Creek in the Sequoia National Monument. Because only a few locals visit the falls regularly, it's a place to come and contact your inner sense of serenity.

The first waterfall is the most astonishing. Although it's only a 20-foot drop, it offers the mystery and beauty often glimpsed in a Japanese brush-stoke painting. It must be viewed through the branches of trees, which block an unobstructed view. These branches perfectly frame the sparkling water, which freefalls half-way down, and then becomes a glistening cascade reflecting sunlight off the dark, mottled rock face. After the freefall, there is a short 10-foot cascade. Moving on downstream, the next drop is a 25-foot cascade that for a brief period splits the stream into two branches. The third drop is the tallest of these waterfalls along Poso Creek. It's a 40-foot cascade that precedes the fourth cascade, which stretches out over 20 feet.

To reach the falls, park alongside the road before entering Posey Park, which begins just after the creek crosses under the road. Walk downstream, and in about 10 minutes you'll come to the first of the four falls. The rest are just a short distance downstream.

Wait! Could that have been a rainbow trout I saw? Yes. Don't forget your fishing pole. Each spring the stream is stocked by the California Department of Fish and Game with rainbow trout. Get here before July. Come any later, and not only will all the fish have been caught, the stream will be a mere trickle.

If you plan to make the trip, supplies are available in Glenville.

Also nearby are the White River, White River Falls, Cedar Creek and Alder Creek.

Directions: *From the 99 Freeway in Bakersfield, drive north to Highway 65. Continue north on Highway 65 to Highway 155 east. On Highway 155, turn left on Jack Ranch Road, just before Glennville. Drive 5.5 miles on Jack Ranch Road to Road M-109 (signed for Posey). Turn right on Road M-109 and drive 3.5 miles through Posey, to Posey Park. You'll cross the stream just before entering the cabin area.*

Boulder Creek Falls

Rating: 8

How Short? Drive-To

How Easy? 1

Best Time to View:
February to June

Need Information?
Contact: Sequoia
National Forest (559)
539-2607, Ponderosa
Lodge (559) 542-2579

Boulder Creek Falls reminds me of the flood demonstration on Universal Studio's tram ride. In this attraction, reclaimed water is used to reveal how flood scenes are created in movies. The raging white water appears to be headed for the tram, but just before it strikes the railings on the cars, it empties into a drain.

A similar situation exists at Boulder Creek Falls in the Sequoia National Monument. The falls is fed by Boulder Creek, which flows through a steep, narrow canyon. The creek appears to be headed directly for Highway 190, but just before it hits the road, washing your car away, too, it is funneled through a storm drain under the road... most of the time, that is. In 1983, the creek got so high, it washed out Highway 190.

Boulder Creek Falls, also called Ponderosa Falls, because of its close proximity to the Ponderosa Lodge, can be quite exciting in the spring. The rumbling of the falls through the gorge reminds me a lot of Chilnualna Falls and the South Fork of the Tuolumne River Falls in Yosemite National Park, although there is no hiking required to reach Boulder Creek Falls.

At 6,500 feet, Boulder Creek Falls isn't the type of waterfall you'll want to spend a lot of time at. Most people never leave their cars. It cascades over a quarter-mile in its entirety, but only the last 100 yards are visible from the road. The rest of its waters are hidden in the canyon above.

About a mile downstream, the falls empties into the South Fork of the Middle Fork of the Tule River, where good fishing for rainbow trout is found. The falls is located just past a hairpin turn in the road. Pull off onto the dirt pullout that is only large enough for two cars; it is dangerous to stay in the middle of the road to view it.

If you plan to make the trip, supplies are available in Springville and at the Ponderosa Lodge. In winter call ahead for road conditions. Chains may be required.

Also nearby are Upper Peppermint Creek, Horse Canyon Falls, Tule River Falls.

Directions: *From Bakersfield, drive north on the 99 Freeway to Highway 190 east. Take Highway 190 past Porterville and Lake Success to Springville. Drive 14.3 miles east past Springville on Highway 190 to Camp Nelson. Continue another 5.6 miles to Cedar Slope. Drive 2.0 more miles on Highway 190 past Cedar Slope to the falls on your left. If coming from the south, the falls are 4.2 miles from the Ponderosa Lodge.*

Boulder Creek Falls in the spring

Horse Canyon Falls

Rating: 7

How Short? Drive-To or 0.50 Miles

How Easy? 1 or 4

Best Time to View: February to June

Need Information? Contact: Sequoia National Forest (661) 548-6503

A visit to Horse Canyon Falls can be remembered as a short trip to an average drive-to waterfall or a spectacular adventure to a rarely visited freefall. The choice is entirely up to you; however, before making it, you'll need to take a few facts into account.

The hike-to portion of the falls is short, but demanding and at times difficult, not to mention dangerous; whereas, the drive-to section can be seen from the road. There are no trails to the falls, and the hike is not recommended for those who aren't both adventurous and in top physical condition.

Horse Canyon Falls is situated 7,000 feet up in the Sequoia National Monument, near Peppermint Camp and Dome Rock. Although they're visible from Highway 190, few people know they exist. If visiting them as a drive-to waterfall, simply walk to the right side of the road (if you are coming from Springville) and listen for Boulder Creek. Fed by snow runoff from Freezeout Meadow, the creek flows quite rapidly in the spring. Once you find it, look up in the canyon to see two cascades. Both are about 75 feet high and powerful.

The few hikers who decide to continue on to the freefalls are the most satisfied. Above the cascades lie two freefalls that aren't visible from the road. Each freefall is about 20 feet, and both are hidden in Horse Canyon. To reach the freefalls, start on the north side of Boulder Creek and begin working your way upstream. Just before

Lower Horse Canyon Falls

reaching the first cascade, leave the stream and begin climbing uphill.

Here's where it starts to get dangerous. You'll be climbing over loose rocks, and many will roll out from under your feet, tumbling down the hillside. Make sure if anyone else is in your hiking party they don't walk below you. Getting hit with one of these boulders can mean serious injury.

After scrambling up the hillside, look upstream and you'll be able to see the freefalls. They can be reached a number of different ways. None of them are easy. Remember, there are no trails.

Either continue along the mountainside to the brink of the lower freefall, or work your way back down to the stream and follow it to the base. Although the upper freefall is just above the lower one, because of unstable hillsides and steep cliffs, it can't be reached on foot. There are many more falls upstream, unfortunately they are hidden in the canyon where hiking is not advised.

If you plan to make the trip, supplies are available at the Ponderosa Lodge. The road to the falls closes in the winter and early spring.

Also nearby are Peppermint Creek, Boulder Creek Falls, Trail of 100 Giants, Long Meadow Sequoia Grove and Middle Fork of the South Fork of the Tule River.

Directions: *From Bakersfield, drive north on the 99 Freeway to Highway 190 east. Take Highway 190 past Porterville and Lake Success to Springville. In Springville, continue 28 miles east on Highway 190 to Peppermint Creek Campground. Continue two miles past the turnoff for Peppermint Creek to an unsigned dirt pullout.*

Upper Horse Canyon Falls

Nobe Young Falls (Upper)

Rating: 7

How Short? 0.80 Miles

How Easy? 1

Best Time to View:
May to August

Need Information?
Contact: Sequoia
National Forest (661)
548-6503, Ponderosa
Lodge (559) 542-2579

There are so many waterfalls in the Sequoia National Monument, it's easy to overlook some of them. Don't overlook Upper Nobe Young Falls; it's definitely worth seeing. So, what makes it more worth seeing than dozens of other waterfalls in the region? A few things.

Unlike many of the other waterfalls, tourists don't mob Nobe Young Falls. Most travelers don't even know it exists, partly because there are no signs to alert them to its location. Aside from the lack of visitors, Nobe Young is a lot like its competitors, Peppermint Creek Falls, South Creek Falls and Freeman Falls. It's a granite waterfall, fed by a year-round stream that has small wild trout in its waters.

Nobe Young Creek originates in Round, Mule and Onion Meadows, works its way down through Nobe Young Meadow, crosses under Highway 190, and three-tenths of a mile downstream makes its way down the face of a large slab of rounded granite. Above the falls, the stream is a mere three yards wide; however, it widens as it fans out over the slab of granite and freefalls some 30 feet before crashing onto smaller granite boulders. Then, it cascades the rest of the way.

At 6,150 feet, 80-foot Nobe Young is in a dense pine forest. The foliage stays green throughout the summer and into the fall, so if you aren't particularly thrilled with waterfalls, come to see the lovely forest surrounding its fern-filled base and to smell fresh mountain air. Another plus: a small cave located behind the freefall provides a kind of makeshift covering, where you can sit on a granite ledge and remain protected from the waterfalls' raining mist.

If you don't follow directions carefully, finding the trailhead can be tricky, because it isn't signed.

Nobe Young Falls

But, the trail itself is pretty simple to follow. From the dirt pullout, begin walking to the left, towards Nobe Young Creek. In roughly 100 yards there is a clearing filled with a lot of dead trees (providing they haven't been cleared away yet).

At this point, the trail begins to angle off to the right. In another two-tenths of a mile, even though the thick foliage hides Nobe Young Falls, begin listening for the stream on your left. When you hear it, pick one of the many trails that lead to the base of the falls. Careful, they're steep.

Although Nobe Young is best in May and early June, it may not be accessible to vehicular traffic until late May. Because of snowfall, the road to the falls is closed from the Ponderosa Lodge to Johnsondale in the winter. Some years the road opens in April; other years, not until Memorial Weekend. Call the Forest Service for updated road conditions.

If you plan to make the trip, supplies are available at the Ponderosa Lodge.

Also nearby are Middle Fork of the South Fork of the Tule River at Camp Nelson and Cedar Slope, Middle Fork of the Tule River, Middle Fork Falls, Boulder Creek Falls, Trail of 100 Giants, Peppermint Creek (Upper) and North Fork of the Middle Fork of the Tule River.

Directions: *From Bakersfield, drive north on the 99 Freeway to Highway 190. Drive east on Highway 190 past Porterville and Lake Success to Springville. Continue 28 miles east on Highway 190 past Springville to the turnoff for Peppermint Creek Campground. Reset your odometer and continue approximately 5.5 miles to a sign for Nobe Young Creek, where the creek crosses under the highway (not where the trailhead is). From the sign, continue two-tenths of a mile to a dirt pullout on the left.*

A sideview of Nobe Young Falls

Nobe Young Falls (Lower)

Rating: 6

How Short? Drive-To

How Easy? 1

Best Time to View:
May to July

Contact: Sequoia
National Forest
(661) 548-6503

Many tourists like to do most of their traveling in their car. They aren't interested in long hikes, difficult stream crossings, dirt and bugs. They'd rather be able to drive up, roll down the window, take some pictures and move on to the next place. At Lower Nobe Young Falls, this is all possible.

North of Camp Whitsett, the falls is a series of small cascades that can be seen from the road. There is no hiking required, however, for those who don't mind a little rock-hopping, just upstream there are more impressive cascades that cannot be seen from your car. Reaching these cascades requires what many hikers would consider difficult hiking, because nearly all of this short hike is done on slippery granite and the use of extreme caution is needed to avoid injury.

For those looking from the car, simply look upstream at the cascades, which are most thrilling in late May and early June. There is no comparison between Upper and Lower Nobe Young Falls. The lower falls is much smaller, offer no awe-inspiring freefalls and really don't get your blood pumping. But any waterfall in the Sequoia National Monument is well worth the trip.

If you plan to make the trip, supplies are available in Kernville and Springville. The road to the falls usually closes in November and doesn't reopen until sometime in May. Call the Forest Service for updated road conditions.

Also nearby are Peppermint Creek Falls, Peppermint Creek, Freeman Creek, Freeman Creek Falls, Kern River, Nobe Young Creek, Long Meadow Creek Falls, Bone Creek, Golden Trout Wilderness and Dry Meadow Creek.

Directions: *From the 99 Freeway in Bakersfield, exit Highway 178 east and drive 45 miles to Lake Isabella. From Lake Isabella, drive 11 miles north on Highway 155 to Kernville. In Kernville, turn left on Mountain 99. Drive approximately 24 miles on Mountain 99 to a split in the road and veer right onto Road 22S82, signed for Camp Whitsett and Lower Peppermint Creek. Continue approximately 2.5 miles to the signed turnoff for the Western Divide Highway. Turn left and continue 1.4 miles to a bridge over the stream.*

Lower Nobe Young Falls in November of 2002

Freeman Creek Falls

Rating: 8

How Short? 2.0 Miles

How Easy? 4

Best Time to View:
May to July

Need Information?
Contact: Sequoia
National Forest
(661) 548-6503

Attempting a trip to Freeman Creek Falls? Plan on coming back dirty, exhausted and full of battle scars. The scramble to the waterfall makes you ask yourself if all the bushwhacking, rock-hopping and dangerous rock climbing was worth it. My answer is "yes," but unless you are in great physical shape and have good directional skills, please don't try the hike. I can almost guarantee the search and rescue team will need to be dispatched to bring you out of the canyon.

There's no question that Freeman Creek Falls is tough to reach, but for those with the proper skills, I think it's well worth it. It's an extraordinary cascade that not too many people have seen. Although it's nearly identical to Peppermint Creek Falls and also located in the Giant Sequoia National Monument, Freeman Creek Falls differs in that it has no trail to it. The Freeman Trail ends a few miles upstream, just below where Freeman Creek crosses under the Road 22S82.

Before setting out, it is a good idea to take along a compass, lots of water, snacks and a good topo map. It's not that the stream itself is hard to find, but finding your way back can be a real challenge.

Here's what to do: at the unofficial, unsigned trailhead, begin walking down the mountainside. Remember, there is no trail. It should take 15 minutes to a half-hour to reach Freeman Creek. You can't miss it, because the stream flows from the road near Freeman Creek Campground for 2.5 miles to the Kern River, and as long as you keep walking down the mountain you'll run into it.

You'll pass through areas where the brush grows above your head, but there are also many clearings. We found a small canyon and walked down it to the stream. It was much faster than bushwhacking and kept us on a fairly direct course. Don't forget, if you ever feel lost keep walking down the mountain. Once you find the stream, things get easier. Leave some kind of marker before exploring further downstream, so you can locate a familiar point of departure for your way back up the hill.

There is also fabulous fishing for tiny, wild rainbow trout in the stream. We spent a lot of time fishing before working our way down to the falls.

Continuing the journey downstream, you'll pass many small cascades; don't confuse them with Freeman Creek Falls. Standing on the top of Freeman Creek Falls is similar to the top of Peppermint Creek Falls; you'll find yourself overlooking the Kern River Drainage from this giant, round slab of granite.

The view is great from the brink of the falls, but it's even better from the base. Before climbing to the base, however, make sure you are on the right side of the stream. It is much too difficult to navigate down to the bottom on the left side.

Carefully climb down the right side of the stream to the base, to a large, fairly deep pool loaded with small wild trout. But it's hard to concentrate on the fishing, with a 150-foot cascade above. The cascade tumbles and crashes onto multiple levels of polished granite, which break the waterfall up into dozens of drops.

Okay, now it's time to see what kind of shape you're in. Ready to climb back up the mountain? Walk back upstream, and when you find your marker, begin the uphill climb.

It can take twice as long to hike up to your car as it did to reach the river, and this is the part where it's easy to get lost. Be sure to take the same path up that you did to get down. Use rocks, pinecones, sticks or whatever you can find as trail markers. If you think you are truly lost, return to the river and walk upstream until it crosses under the highway. Make a left on the highway and walk to your car.

From those who prefer, the cascades can also be viewed from afar. To do so, drive towards Johnsondale, continuing six-tenths of a mile from the cattle guard to a sign that reads, "Falling Rock." Walk to the Kern River side of the road and look down into the canyon. You'll be able to see a portion of the cascades, but it's not nearly as rewarding as the view from the falls' base.

If you plan to make the trip, from November through April (depending on snowfall and road conditions), the road to the creek is closed a few miles past Johnsondale. Call the Forest Service for updated conditions. Supplies are available in Springville and Kernville. Freeman Creek is closed to fishing from November 16 to the last Saturday in April.

Also nearby are Peppermint Creek Falls, Lower Nobe Young Falls and Long Meadow Creek Falls.

Directions: *From the 99 Freeway in Bakersfield, exit Highway 178 east and drive 45 miles to Lake Isabella. From Lake Isabella, drive 11 miles north to Kernville and turn left on Mountain 99. Continue approximately 24 miles on Mountain 99 to a fork and veer right onto Road 22S82, signed for Camp Whitsett and Lower Peppermint Creek. Continue 17.4 miles to Pyles Camp on your right. From Pyles Camp, backtrack 1.9 miles to a cattle guard, due south of a sign that reads, "Off-road vehicle travel prohibited."*

Freeman Creek Falls

Peppermint Creek Falls

Rating: 9

How Short? 0.50 Miles

How Easy? 2

Best Time to View:
May to July

Need Information?
Contact: Sequoia
National Forest
(661) 548-6503

Fall ended, and winter began to cast a cold spell over the Kern River Drainage. Although most campers had packed away their sleeping bags and tents for the year, I knew it was the perfect time to avoid the crowds and enjoy some beautiful scenery. So Rick Spadaro, and I made the trip from Los Angeles on a Friday night and set up camp on the North Fork of the Kern River, just below the Johnsondale Bridge.

When we awoke, neither of us wanted to get out of our sleeping bags. It was freezing outside! The thermometer read 22 degrees, and there was frost on the wool snow hat I'd been wearing all night. We both somehow found enough courage to leave the tent, and headed towards Peppermint Creek Falls, were it was obviously going to be colder, since it was another 1,500 feet up the mountain.

A few miles past Johnsondale, we ran into our first big problem. The road was closed for the winter. I figured the falls were only a few miles from the closure, so we decide to get out of the car and walk. The ground was covered with snow and the road slicked with black ice. Walking for more than an hour now we were just about to turn around and head back to the car, when a truck pulled up along side of us.

"How did you get past the gate?" I asked the driver.

"Never mind that; we own land back here. The real question is where are you two going?"

"Some place called Peppermint Creek Falls," I said.

The upper tier of Peppermint Creek Falls

"Oh," the man chuckled to his friend. "You'd better hop in the back on the truck. It's another five miles from here. I'll take you there, but you're going to have to walk back."

Whoops! I guess my calculations were a bit off.

In spite of it being winter, Peppermint Creek Falls still had a lot of water rushing down its face, and, sure enough, we had the falls all to ourselves. At 5,200 feet in the Sequoia National Monument, located downstream from Camping Area No. 6, the falls is fed by Peppermint Creek and is broken into two tiers.

The upper tier is a freefall, plunging 25 feet; and the lower is a 130-foot cascade. It's most unique characteristic is that it's one of only a few waterfalls in California that drops over a granite brink with a rounded edge. The best time to visit the falls is from

May through July, when snowmelt keeps Peppermint Creek flowing fast.

Peppermint Creek Falls has more to offer than just a waterfall. The California Department of Fish and Game stocks rainbow trout from spring through early summer. Also, the pools below both falls become ideal for swimming when the water begins to warm in the summer.

The trail to the falls is short, but steep. Begin at the dirt parking area in Camping Area No. 6 and follow the creek downstream for about 50 yards, to the top of the upper tier. Because of steep cliffs, the only way you can go is to the left. There are a number of steep trails, all of which lead to the base. Two more falls exist downstream, however, they are located on private property, so you can't enjoy them.

If you plan to make the trip, supplies are available in Kernville and Springville. The road to the falls usually closes in November and doesn't reopen until sometime in May. Call the Forest Service for updated road conditions.

Also nearby are Lower Nobe Young Falls, Freeman Creek, Freeman Creek Falls, Kern River, Nobe Young Creek, Long Meadow Creek Falls, Golden Trout Wilderness and Dry Meadow Creek.

Directions: From the 99 Freeway in Bakersfield, exit Highway 178 east and drive 45 miles to Lake Isabella. From Lake Isabella, drive 11 miles north to Kernville and turn left on Mountain 99. Continue on Mountain 99 approximately 24 miles to a split in the road and veer right onto Road 22S82, signed for Camp Whitsett and Lower Peppermint Creek. Continue approximately 12 miles to Lower Peppermint Campground. Drive past the campground to Camp Area #6.

Peppermint Creek Falls in December of 1998. For a meter of how big the waterfall is that's a person standing to the right of the waterfall. (Right)

Long Meadow Creek Falls

Rating: 5

How Short? 0.25 Miles

How Easy? 1

Best Time to View:
January to July

Need Information?
Contact: Sequoia
National Forest
(661) 548-6503

Partly because few people know it exists, Long Meadow Creek Falls is rarely visited by anyone other than a few locals. The falls isn't shown on topo maps, nor is it talked about in many books.

Long Meadow Creek Falls is a series of small cascades near Johnsondale in the Sequoia National Monument. Last time I was there, I ran into an interesting visitor.

"Is the road opened ahead?" asked the German tourist driving a rental caravan. "Can I make it through the snow?"

I was bent over on the side of the road tying my shoes. "Where are you trying to go?" I asked him.

"San Francisco," he replied.

I struggled to hold back my laughter. "San Francisco...Well, I think you're a little out of the way. San Fran is about 300 miles in the other direction."

"I know," he said in a thick German accent. "I'm taking the scenic route." The tall, blond-haired, blue-eyed man continued up the road. I saw him a few hours later, driving on Highway 178 towards Walker Pass. I guess he still didn't realize he was lost.

Aside perhaps from a few wacky tourists, Long Meadow Creek Falls is a place to go to get away from it all, especially tourists. The waterfall is fed by Long Meadow Creek, whose origin can be found in Redwood Meadow, directly across from the Trail of 100 Giants and the Long Meadow Sequoia Grove.

The falls consists of three cascades. The largest cascade is on the south side of Road 22S82 and is visible from a small pullout on the road's south side. In summer, youngsters often slide down this 50 foot long cascade on their butts into a tiny, shallow pool.

The best cascade, however, is found on the north side of the road. After parking in the pullout on the south side of Road 22S82, cross the road and pick up the stream. Walk upstream, whacking through overgrown trees and brush (there is no trail) for about 50 yards, where you'll come to a small cascade. Just past this cascade, you'll see Crater Holes, a granite rock formation with holes roughly three feet deep that were naturally carved by glaciers. They become mini-spas in the summer, when the sun heats up the small pools. Just past here is the finest of the cascades, a 25-foot drop that is most notable in the spring when Long Meadow Creek is at peak flow.

If you plan to make the trip, supplies are available in Kernville and Springville.

Also nearby is Peppermint Creek Falls.

Directions: *From the 99 Freeway in Bakersfield, exit Highway 178 east and drive 45 miles to Lake Isabella. From Lake Isabella, drive 11 miles north to Kernville and turn left on Mountain 99. Take Mountain 99 approximately 24 miles to a fork in the road and veer right onto Road 22S82, signed for Camp Whitsett and Lower Peppermint Creek. Drive approximately nine-tenths of a mile to a pullout on the right side of the road, just after the sign for Long Meadow Creek.*

Upper Long Meadow Creek Falls

South Creek Falls

Rating: 7

How Short? Drive-To

How Easy? 1

Best Time to View:
November to July

Need Information?
Contact: Sequoia
National Forest
(661) 548-6503

South Creek Falls is ideal for people who don't enjoy hiking. At 3,800 feet in the Sequoia National Monument, about 15 minutes north of Kernville and a half-mile from the Kern River, it's an easy-to-reach drive-to waterfall. You can get out of your car, walk a few yards, take a few pictures, get back in your car and drive away. There's no reason to hang here too long; there's not much to see or do. There are no restrooms, picnic areas or campgrounds.

While viewing the falls can be fulfilling in the winter months, a full view of the drop from the pullout can't be seen. Also, because of unstable hillsides, it's too dangerous to hike to the falls' base. So, your best bet is to walk from the parking lot about 30 yards downstream along Mountain 99, where you can get a view of the entire falls from the brink. South Creek Falls' 125-foot drop flows year-round down a slope that prevents it from being a freefall.

Prior to 1994, South Creek was also stocked by the California Department of Fish and Game with rainbow trout. Now, the only fish left in the stream are those that swim up the Kern River into the pools below the base of the falls. There are few fish in the stream above the falls, but not enough to warrant a fishing trip.

If you plan to make the trip, supplies are available in Kernville and Springville.

Also nearby are Peppermint Creek Falls and the Trail of 100 Giants.

Directions: *From the 99 Freeway in Bakersfield, exit Highway 178 east and drive 45 miles to Lake Isabella. From Lake Isabella, drive 11 miles north to Kernville and turn left on Mountain 99. Continue approximately 19.5 miles on Mountain 99 to the falls on your left, a half-mile past the Johnsondale Bridge.*

South Creek Falls

Brush Creek Falls

Rating: 5

How Short? 1.5 Miles

How Easy: 2

Best Time to Visit:
January to August

Need Information?
Contact: Sequoia
National Forest
(661) 548-6503

It was the week before New Years, when a few friends and I drove up to see if we could beat the winter storms that were bearing down on the Kern River Drainage. Our destination was Peppermint Creek Falls. It was already snowing as we passed through Lake Isabella, heading north along the Kern River.

Snow blanketed the road by the time we reached the Johnsondale Bridge, and my Ford Explorer, which didn't have four-wheel drive, was beginning to slide all over the place. With a winter storm warning in effect and the snow getting heavier, I became worried that I was going to get stuck in the snow, so I turned around and drove back to the fire station in Kernville to see if they had received the latest weather report.

At the fire station, they told me there was no way I was going to make it near the falls, especially without chains. "Why don't you go to Brush Creek Falls," one of the firemen suggested. "It's not a big as Peppermint, but it's awful pretty, and you won't have to worry about getting stuck. Snow wont stick to the ground there." When he showed me where it was located, I was shocked; I had fished Brush Creek many times, but never knew there was a waterfall only minutes away from where I used to catch rainbow trout.

At 4,200 feet in the Sequoia National Forest, Brush Creek is a tributary to the Kern River. It provides fair rainbow trout fishing and displays a series of small cascades, which can be reached by a short hike. Anybody who has fished the Kern River near the Johnsondale Bridge has driven over Brush Creek, but few know of the falls. And after a

Brush Creek Falls as seen from Sherman Pass Road in January of 2002

long day of fishing the Kern River, the falls is the perfect place to get away from the crowds for a while.

About three-fourths of a mile from the confluence of Brush Creek and the Kern River, Brush Creek Falls is a series of three larger and numerous smaller cascades. To reach the falls, begin at the dirt pullout where Brush Creek crosses under Mountain 99. Walk east, following the trail on the north side of the creek for a half-mile, until you come to a convergence of two canyons. The canyon on the left was formed by a tiny stream that is usually dry. You'll want to follow the canyon on your right, that's where Brush Creek is.

First is the smallest of the three large cascades at the mouth of the canyon. This drop is only about five feet high, but it empties into an inviting swimming pool. Another 20 yards upstream are the other two large cascades. Both are much taller, but their swimming holes aren't as deep. In the winter, the creek can freeze over after a cold storm. Don't fret, natural "ice bridges" allow you to cross over the stream.

For those who prefer, the falls can also be viewed from the road. Drive one mile past Brush Creek to the Sherman Pass turnoff. Turn right and drive approximately one mile to a dirt pullout on the right. The falls is on your right, down in the canyon.

If you plan to make the trip, supplies are available in Kernville.

Also nearby are the Kern River, South Creek Falls, Lower Salmon Creek Falls and Long Meadow Creek Falls.

Directions: *From the 99 Freeway in Bakersfield, exit Highway 178 east and drive 45 miles to Lake Isabella. Exit Highway 155 and drive 11 miles north to Kernville. Turn left on Mountain 99 and continue approximately 18.3 miles to a large dirt pullout on the left. Park, and walk across the highway to the stream.*

Upper Brush Creek Falls

Salmon Creek Falls (Lower)

Rating: 8

How Short? 1.0 Mile

How Easy? 2

Best Time to View:
January to August

Need Information?
Contact: Sequoia
National Forest
(760) 379-5646

On Mountain 99, where it parallels the North Fork of the Kern River, there's a sign on the side of the road that points east and says "Salmon Creek Falls." Being a waterfall freak, I pulled my car over at the sign, thinking I was going to get to see a waterfall. Boy, can that sign be deceiving! I ran into a number of hikers in that dirt pullout, all with conflicting stories about where the waterfall was. One thing was for sure, it wasn't anywhere near the sign.

The first guy I ran across told me Salmon Creek Falls was easy to see. But whether or not the faintly visible thin sliver of water he pointed to (cascading about 3,000 feet above where we were standing) was Salmon Creek Falls was anybody's guess. Another hiker, who was lacing up a pair of old muddy boots and putting a leash on his dog, told me he'd heard the waterfall was about a mile upstream from where we were standing, but admitted he had no idea where it was exactly. In other words, all I was getting was hearsay. Then I ran into two hikers who told me they too had seen the sign, yet had searched for two hours and never found the cataract.

I was now more determined than ever to get to the bottom of this mystery. So I grabbed my laptop and opened up my topo program. I did see some contour lines that ran close together at a place that seemed just upstream from where we stood. I figured these lines most likely indicated a waterfall. Although I thought I might have located Salmon Creek Falls on the map, it was nowhere near the sign.

Instead of setting out on a wild goose chase, I drove back into Kernville and visited the local ranger station. What a waste of time that was! The woman at the counter told me she'd located Salmon Creek Falls on the map (after I pointed it out to her), but had no idea how to get there. She sent me to the James Store on the east side of Mountain 99 to make inquiries of the men in the fishing section. If anyone knew how to get there, she said they would.

I walked up with map in hand, bundled up in my winter hiking attire and well-seasoned muddy boots, and asked one of the men at the counter about the waterfall.

"One sec," he said, as if the question had set off an alarm in his head. "I'll be right back." He walked over to a much older looking pal who was putting line on a fishing reel and whispered something in

Brandi Koerner (Left) and Nicole Shaffer at Lower Salmon Creek Falls

his ear. The other man stopped what he was doing and came over to chat with me. Although I was wondering just how much these locals knew, the real question was how much they were going to tell me.

Tony Abel caught this golden at Salmon Creek Falls

Salmon Creek Falls… what do you want to know about it? Let me think now… I've heard of Salmon Creek, but … no, never been to Salmon Creek Falls. Are you positive there's a waterfall there?" I chuckled a bit at the obvious deception, bought a jar of Power Bait to appear like a normal tourist who was fishing the Kern River, said thank you and walked back to the car.

Okay, now that was weird. I'm no detective, but I was smart enough to know those two were hiding something. It was time to do some research. I got back in the car, rolled up the windows so my paper maps wouldn't get blown around and started carefully studying them. Aside from locating a few dirt roads that led much further upstream than that parking area, I spotted a section of the creek where the contour lines on the maps narrowed. This was the most likely site for a waterfall. I plugged my printer into an inverter to get power and printed out several maps of the area so I wouldn't get lost. It looked to me like reaching the waterfall (if in fact there was one) was as simple as following the stream.

Scott Wiessner with a catch from Salmon Creek

Eager to see if this waterfall was worth all the headaches I'd gone through to try to find it, I headed back up Mountain 99. I was barely able to maneuver over the dirt roads, however, because they forked every which way all the way up to a flume that flowed above Salmon Creek. Reaching that flume had saved me roughly a half-mile of hiking.

I couldn't find a trail, and fighting my way through overgrown trees, it took me about a half-hour to walk the first 100 yards upstream. I started looking for alternate routes. This damn battle wasn't over yet. Sure I was frustrated with the length of time it took me to get about a football field's length upstream. And the fact that after a half-hour I'd ended up back at my car didn't help much.

But now I was determined to find this waterfall. Looking over the maps again I realized there was a four-wheel drive road just above where I'd parked. I scrambled up the mountain on foot, located the road and began following it uphill as it paralleled Salmon Creek on the left. Walking the road for about 200 yards, it suddenly narrowed into a trail and descended down toward the stream.

The more I followed the trail, the narrower the canyon walls became. I could tell by the topography I was getting close to my waterfall. I'd passed several smaller cascades and guessed the one I was seeking was probably about 50 yards upstream.

For a change, I was right on the ball and didn't even get lost on the way. It didn't take a genius to figure out why those two guys in the market didn't want me to know about Lower Salmon Creek Falls. (I later discovered that the sliver I was told about earlier

Upper Salmon Creek Falls from Mountain 99

was in fact Salmon Creek Falls.) This waterfall is a true gem. Nestled in a small gorge at 6,700 feet in the Sequoia National Forest, it has all the right characteristics to make it the quintessential waterfall.

The tall canyon walls were graffiti free, the stream was clear and clean, the gorge was cool, the air was crisp, and a few alder trees provided a canopy of shade over a perfect wading pool at the waterfall's base. To top things off, wild trout splashed in the pool below the gorgeous freefall. The trouble I'd gone through to reach this place was certainly worth it. This 60-foot freefall along Salmon Creek had me in awe as it plummeted the first 20 feet, before crashing against an Andy Gump-sized boulder, plunging its final 40 feet.

Now that I've figured it out for you, getting to the waterfall won't be as difficult as you'd think. The walk to its base is roughly a half-mile and includes a 400-foot gain in elevation. From the dirt parking area near the flume, you'll need to scramble up the steep hillside. Although this is tricky, because there is no trail and loose rocks make footing unstable, it's doable.

Just over the top of the hill you'll come to a dirt road. Make a left and follow the road a few-hundred yards uphill. At times, it will appear as if other trails break off to the right. Stay left. The road eventually turns into a single-track trail and works its way down to Salmon Creek. For the next quarter-mile continue on the path upstream. Sometimes the trail gets faint as it winds up and over rocks. No fear. Just follow the stream and you'll come to the base of the waterfall. Remember to pick up your trash. We want this waterfall to look like a secret!

If you plan to make the trip, supplies are available in Kernville.

Also nearby are the North Fork of the Kern River, Lake Isabella and South Creek Falls.

Directions: *From the 99 Freeway in Bakersfield, take the Rosedale Highway/Downtown exit (Highway 178 east) and continue 41 miles to Lake Isabella. From Lake Isabella, exit Highway 155 and drive 11 miles north to Kernville. In Kernville, turn left on Mountain 99 and drive 11.3 miles to an unsigned dirt road on the right. Turn right, drive two-tenths of a mile and veer left at a split in the road. Continue seven-tenths of a mile to a dead end and a flume. (The road comes to a three-way split before the flume; take the middle road signed for Salmon 8.)*

Small cascades on the way to Lower Salmon Creek Falls

Lower Salmon Creek Falls

Region 10 Central Coast (South)

Garland Ranch Falls
Pine Falls
Pheiffer Falls
McWay Falls
McWay Creek Falls
Canyon Trail Falls
Salmon Creek Falls
Limekiln Falls
Redwood Gulch Falls
Condor Gulch Cascades
Bear Gulch Cascades
Naciemento Falls
Santa Margarita Falls
Big Falls
Little Falls
Nojoqui Falls

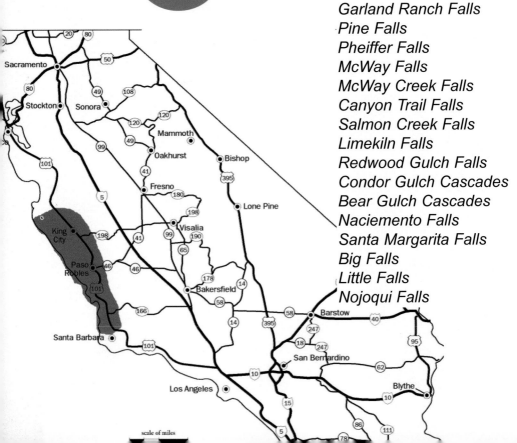

Garland Ranch Falls

Rating: 6

How Short? 1.5 Miles

How Easy? 1

Best Time to View:
January to May

Need Information?
Contact: Monterey
Peninsula Regional
Park District
(831) 659-4488

Garland Ranch Regional Park is one of the best spots in the Central Coast for families to walk their dogs. The trails are flat, well groomed and easy to navigate. Because of the easy access and their close proximity to nearby cities, these trails can get crowded, too.

The park is also a good place to bring your kids to learn about wildlife. There is a visitor center and a ranger station where most questions can be answered. Capping off your visit with a trip to Garland Ranch Falls can also be worth it, providing a good rainstorm has occurred in the past week or so.

The falls receives its water in an unusual way: no stream feeds it. A stock pond was built roughly 35 years ago on the Garland Ranch to collect runoff from an upland terrace that overlooks the Carmel River. Only when this pond overflows does the waterfall come to life. This means that the 60-foot high Garland Ranch Falls flows only in the rainy season. It also means that runoff is almost never sufficient enough to make it spectacular. After a rainfall, it looks like a thin ribbon of mist.

Reaching the falls is easy. From the dirt parking lot alongside Carmel Valley Road, walk across the footbridge over the Carmel River. Veer left on the dirt access road and follow signs to the visitor center. Don't take the right fork signed for the ranger station.

In about two hundred yards, you'll see the visitor center on the left, with signs pointing to the Waterfall Trail. After walking about 10 minutes comes a fork in the trail. Veer right and the Lupine Trail continues to the Mesa Trail. Instead, stay left, following signs to the Waterfall Trail. Ten yards beyond the sign, the trail splits again. Stay right, because the left fork descends to the river.

Now, the trail breaks away from open grass fields and becomes shaded by oak trees and other foliage. In 25 yards, the trail forks again. The right fork leads to the Cliff Trail. For the waterfall, stay left. Although the falls is fewer than 100 yards ahead, small trail spurs tempt many to leave the main trail. Don't be fooled.

Only a bit more climbing; a footbridge over the falls' stream awaits. This footbridge offers the best view, providing there is enough water in the stream to make the falls worth seeing. There is also a great vista of Garland Ranch and the Carmel River from here. The trail continues on, but no waterfalls exist upstream.

Horseback riders and anglers also use the ranch. Fishing tends to be poor in this portion of the Carmel River that cuts through the park. Check fishing regulations. The river is often closed to fishing to protect native steelhead runs.

If you plan to make the trip, supplies are available in Carmel Village. Call the park ahead of time to make sure the waterfall is running.

Also nearby are Carmel By the Sea, Pine Falls, 17 Mile Drive and Pebble Beach.

Directions: *From Highway 1 in Carmel, turn south on Carmel Valley Road and continue 8.6 miles to Garland Ranch Regional Park on the right.*

Pine Falls

Rating: 7

How Short? 10.8 Miles

How Easy? 4

Best Time to Visit:
December to May

Need Information?
Contact: Los Padres
National Forest
(831) 385-5434

Along California's Central Coast, the Ventana Wilderness offers hiking trails that will constantly remind you of you're close proximity to the ocean, as well as those that seem to have no maritime influence. Pine Creek Falls lies somewhere in the middle. Comfortably removed from the heavily visited beach tourist traps of Big and Little Sur, it offers some of the same beauty that attracts visitors to the wilderness's westernmost boundaries, including breathtaking ocean vistas, waterfalls, cool coastal breezes and redwood groves. The hike to Pine Falls in the Ventana Wilderness offers all of the above except the redwoods and cool coastal breezes.

Before making the trip to Pine, however, ask yourself one question: is the 11-mile roundtrip with a 1,500-foot descent (and an equally butt-kicking walk back to the car) really worth it? There are pros and cons. On the positive side, the trip offers great views of Monterey Bay and the Pacific Ocean, as well as a pretty, well-hidden waterfall with virtually no crowds. On the negative side, Pine Falls requires much more work than the easily accessed waterfalls located near the Ventana Wilderness off Highway 101. Because of the long and seemingly never-ending route, for many hikers, getting to Pine Falls can be a real drag.

Beginning at the trailhead, less than one-tenth of a mile past the sign for China Camp, the first six-tenths of a mile overlooks the valley below, while gradually winding uphill. But the most inspiring views are seen further in the distance. On clear days the Pacific Ocean and Monterey Bay are visible by looking north.

As the route descends a few small switchbacks and leaves behind the vistas of the ocean, Church Creek Canyon comes into view on the left. The descent, which parallels the canyon below, is under a half-mile. Then, for the next seven-tenths of a mile, the trail steadily climbs to its highest point at approximately 4,700 feet.

From this peak, the next 1.25 miles will test your knees, as the trail loses more than 1,000 feet before coming to the Church Divide Trail junction. There is a nice camping spot here and a few fallen logs serve as benches, allowing you to get a rest before gradually descending further to Pine Valley Campground. A point of interest: If you look at the mileage sign that points to China Camp, it reads 3.5 miles. In reality, the trip is just under three.

At the Church Divide Trail junction, there are four choices. Continue on the Pine Ridge Trail to Big Sur, 18 miles away. Turn left on the Church Creek Trail, Tassajara Road will be only seven miles away and Arroyo Seco will be 12. For Pine

Pine Creek Falls

Falls, turn right, following the Carmel River Trail for 1.65 miles to Pine Valley Campground. Of course, you could make the fourth choice and turn back, but it will be much too beautiful to do that.

Poison Oak

Don't expect to see any water near the trail until you cross Pine Creek in nine-tenths of a mile. (If there has recently been a lot of rain, the dry streambed on the left might offer a trickle of water.) From this point on, the creek picks up speed and parallels the trail to Pine Valley Campground. Although the campground is unsigned, its fire pits and picnic table will let you know you've reached it. Also, just before the stream crossing, there is a fence on the right side of the trail with a sign that reads "Pine Valley." Use this as a trail marker.

Now it's time to cross the stream. This is also a good place to fill water bottles. Coming out of a metal pipe, there is spring about 50 yards uphill from the stream crossing.

Pine Falls lies less than seven-tenths of a mile downstream. There is a trail, but be careful to avoid touching poison oak. In many places it grows on both sides of the trail and often creeps onto the trail itself. From here to the falls, the trail is sketchy in many places, prompting hikers to follow the streambed instead.

Whether following the stream or the trail, you can't miss the falls. It slides down a 55-foot cliff that inhibits further travel downstream. A little rock-hopping is required to reach the falls' base. Carefully working your way along the right side of the stream, keep a good grip on the rocks, using caution not to slip and fall.

At 2,850 feet, Pine Falls serves as the headwaters for the Carmel River. The pool below the falls is swimmer friendly, providing you show up in the wet months. The only problem during the warmer months here is the bugs. When I last visited the falls in mid-December, a few hunters told me that as soon as the temperature begins to warm, black flies flourish and can make life miserable. As far as I'm concerned, the best time to visit is in the winter, anyway. The crowds are light and the creek is almost sure to be flowing.

Along the top portion of the waterfall's drop, water is channeled through a narrow chute before it launches into a 20-foot freefall. At the base, the water splashes onto a rock ledge and cascades the last five feet into the wide pool below. There are also small wild rainbow trout in the stream, giving anglers a reason to bring along a small rod.

If you plan to make the trip, supplies are available in Carmel Village. A Forest Service Adventure Pass is required to park in the Los Padres National Forest. In winter call ahead for road conditions. After severe storms, the USFS sometimes closes the access road to the falls.

Also nearby are Garland Ranch Falls, Arroyo Seco River and Abbott Lakes.

Directions: *From the 101 Freeway in Greenfield, exit G-16/Monterey County Road and drive approximately 30 miles west to Tassajara Road. Turn left on Tassajara Road and continue to Cachagua Road. Turn left and drive nine miles to the trailhead, just past the sign for China Camp on the right. In 1.6 miles from Tassajara Road the road becomes dirt and then enters the Los Padres National Forest, five miles from Tassajara Road.*

Pfeiffer Falls

Rating: 7

How Short? 0.75 Miles

How Easy? 1

Best Time to View:
December to May

Need Information?
Contact: Big Sur
Station (831) 667-2315,
California State Park
Office (831) 649-2836

The hike to Pfeiffer Falls is much better than the waterfall itself. Located in Pfeiffer State Park along California's Central Coast in Big Sur, although Pfeiffer Falls is a popular waterfall, it's not what attracts all the visitors: the redwoods do.

The hike to Pfeiffer is short, easy and, best of all, something the whole family can enjoy. For some people, driving through the redwood forest to the trailhead is enough of an adventure. From my point of view, walking the trail to the falls can't be beat.

Pick up the trail 20 yards east of the dirt parking area. There is an information stand at the trailhead. To the left of the stand, a redwood's trunk has been turned on its side. An illustration on the trunk shows how to identify its age by counting the rings.

The well-groomed dirt path meanders through a thick forest, threading its way between redwoods and keeping you out of Pfeiffer Creek by crossing numerous wooden bridges. Even on the hottest summer days, the canopy of redwoods overhanging the path keeps you cool.

The first bridge you'll come to breaks off to the left and heads to Valley View. Don't cross over it; stay on the waterfall trail. The path then crosses four more footbridges, before a fifth tempts you off the path to the left. Again, stay right. Walk up two flights of wooden stairs to a platform. You've made it to the falls overlook.

Pfeiffer is a 60-foot waterfall that flows year-round. On the other hand, its volume is only powerful in the winter and spring. Most of the year, the waterfall dribbles down the granite face. If you arrive during (or shortly after) a good rain, however, the water gushes off its lip.

There is an overlook with wooden benches for you to enjoy the view of the waterfall. From here, ferns that have made a home on the canyon walls are easily visible. The best views of the entire drop, however, can be seen from the dirt landing between flights of stairs.

Before heading back to the car,

a brief side trip to Valley View is a must. At the bridge, just before the stairs, cross the creek, following the path to Valley View. Soon, you'll leave the shade of the redwoods and enter the dry coastal foothills covered with manzanita, shrubs and other coastal foliage.

In a half-mile comes a stunning overlook. In the distance you'll see the Pacific Ocean and Point Sur. Between you and the ocean, Pacific Coast Highway can be seen weaving through the redwood forest, and the Big Sur River cutting through the trees. Go ahead, scream it: "I'm on top of the world."

When coming to Pfeiffer Falls, keep one thing in mind, this place is popular and gets crowded. If you want to make the best out of the trip, plan an early morning or late evening hike, or come during the week.

If you plan to make the trip, there is a day-use fee to enter the state park. Supplies are available at the park's lodge.

Also nearby are Little Sur, Salmon Creek Falls, Hearst Castle, Morro Bay, Monterey, Carmel, Canyon Falls, Mc Way Falls, Mc Way Creek Falls and Limekiln Falls.

Directions: *From Highway 1 in Monterey, drive south through Carmel to Big Sur. In Big Sur, turn left at the entrance for Pfeiffer State Park.*

Pheiffer Falls at low flow

Mc Way Falls

Rating: 9

How Short? 0.25 Miles

How Easy? 1

Best Time to View:
December to June

Need Information?
Contact: Big Sur
Station (831) 667-2315,
California State Park
Office (831) 649-2836

Lets have a little fun… close your eyes and imagine the ideal waterfall along California's Central Coast. Okay, open them again, and I'll help paint the picture:

From the parking area, you walk down towards the ocean, sniffing the moist salty air. A breeze sifts through your hair. You come to a cold, clear mountain stream that meanders through a grove of redwood trees. The calm cool stream then descends to the Pacific Ocean between canyon walls that are lined with ferns. From time to time, the water stirs, as the stream is about to tumble over rocks into small waterfalls.

You walk to the right, following a sturdy wooden platform to an overlook heavily shaded by tall trees. From here, you are graced with a remarkable view of a calm cove, with an aquamarine ocean rolling onto its shore. It reminds you of a cove along the shores of a remote island in the Caribbean, and you can't help but hear the sounds of seals playing on the rocks near the water.

Tall cliffs cast deep shadows on the sandy beach, and the white crests of curling waves thin out to glistening foam, where a stunning 75-foot waterfall plunges off a cliff directly across from you. The narrow chute of water from the falls gracefully tamps the sand, and before it can form a stream that disappears into the ocean, its flows become smothered by the curling fingers of waves.

Now, stop daydreaming and get moving. The picture we've just painted is real and seen by thousands of tourists each year. It's a description of Mc Way Falls in Julia Pfeiffer Burns State Park,

Mc Way Falls

located between Gorda and Little Sur, along a scenic stretch of Highway 1. The waterfall is one of many along the coast that keep visitors coming back each year. It's reached via a short path and is accessible even by wheelchair. The one downfall is that crowds develop daily, so arrive early.

The trail to the falls overlook is so easy you can walk it in sandals. It begins at a trailhead in the parking area signed for Mc Way Falls and descends approximately 50 yards, before leading through a tunnel and making a sharp right. From here to the end of the wooden path, Mc Way Falls can be seen plunging off the cliff across the way. Many people try to think of ways to climb down the steep cliffs to reach the waterfall's base; however, no off-trail hiking is permitted. Only the seals get to enjoy the beach beneath the falls.

If you plan to make the trip, supplies are available in Little Sur. A day-use fee is charged.

Also nearby are Canyon Trail Falls, Mc Way Creek Falls, Limekiln Falls, Pfeiffer Falls and Salmon Creek Falls.

Directions: *From Highway 1 in Monterey, drive south through Carmel, Big Sur and Little Sur to Mc Way Canyon in Julia Pfeiffer Burns State Park. Turn left and park in the day-use parking area.*

An array of wildflowers can be seen along the path to Mc Way Falls

Mc Way Creek Falls

Rating: 6

How Short? 0.75 Miles

How Easy? 1

Best Time to View:
December to June

Need Information?
Contact: Big Sur
Station (831) 667-2315,
California State Park
Office (831) 649-2836

There are two trails that lead to waterfalls in this section of Julia Pfeiffer State Park. Both are well maintained, easy to follow and offer short walks to three considerably different waterfalls. Mc Way Falls is a tall freefall that spills onto a sandy beach on the shores of the Pacific Ocean. Canyon Trail Falls is a small cascade, which can be reached via a stroll through a dense redwood forest. Mc Way Creek Falls is a small freefall.

The three waterfalls are less than a mile apart, but they differ greatly in the number of visitors they receive, Mc Way Falls receives 90 percent of the visitors. Mc Way Creek Falls is also located in this section of the state park, but isn't known to most of the park's visitors, because there is no trail leading directly to it, nor any signs making tourists aware of its existence.

Mc Way Creek Falls brings together aspects of both Canyon Trail Falls and Mc Way Falls. Like Mc Way, it's a pretty freefall; and like Canyon Trail, it's reached via a stroll through a dense redwood forest. Because there is no signed trail, you'd never know it, but it's fewer than five minutes from Canyon Trail Falls.

To get to Mc Way Creek Falls, follow the same trail that goes to Canyon Trail Falls. The trailhead is found at the east end of the day-use parking area, behind a sign for the Picnic Area, Canyon Trail and Ewoldsen Trail. Cross the stream, walk past the picnic area and stay left at the junction signed for the Ewoldsen Trail. Shortly, you'll notice two streams coming together on the left.

From this confluence, Canyon Trail Falls is on the right and can be viewed by following the path as it angles off to the right. To get to Mc Way Creek Falls, abandon the trail and walk down to the stream on the left. Scramble upstream along Mc Way Creek for about five minutes, and you'll end up at the bottom of a 10-foot high freefall.

Make your way to the right side of the stream. Climb up the slippery boulders, making sure to keep hold of the trees on the right. At the top of the rocks, Mc Way Creek Falls will be directly in front of you. The waterfall is a 20-foot freefall surrounded by an array of ferns growing out of fertile soil along the streambed and in crevices above and to the side of the waterfall.

If you plan to make the trip, there is a day-use fee to enter the state park.

Also nearby are Hearst Castle, Pfeiffer Falls, Mc Way Falls, Canyon Trail Falls and Limekiln Falls.

Directions: *From Highway 1 in Monterey, drive south through Carmel, Big Sur and Little Sur to Mc Way Canyon in Julia Pfeiffer Burns State Park. Turn left and park in the day-use parking area.*

Mc Way Creek Falls

Canyon Trail Falls

Rating: 6

How Shorts? 0.70 Miles

How Easy: 1

Best Time to View: December to June

Need Information? Contact: Big Sur Station (831) 667-2315, California State Park Office (831) 649-2836

Canyon Trail Falls isn't your normally superlative Central California Coast waterfall. It is far less appealing than other waterfalls, such as Salmon Creek Falls, Mc Way Falls, Pfeiffer Falls and Limekiln Falls, also located along the same stretch of Highway 1 from Hearst Castle to Big Sur.

Canyon Trail Falls does, however, possess certain strengths, privacy being one of its most important. Other waterfalls, which are located in more popular sections of the many California State Parks along the coast, are overrun daily by tourists; whereas, Canyon Trail Falls usually remains quiet and peaceful. This is partially because Canyon Trail Falls is far less striking than the others, but also because nearly all the visitors to Mc Way Canyon in Julia Pfeiffer State Park are at Mc Way Falls, which can be reached from a trailhead at the west end of the parking lot.

Reaching Canyon Trail Falls is a synch. Instead of taking the route towards the ocean that goes to Mc Way Falls (not Mc Way Creek Falls), simply pick up the trail behind a sign for the Picnic Area, Canyon Trail and Ewoldsen Trail on the east end of the parking lot, which leads up the canyon. After crossing the stream, follow the path past the picnic area to the junction of Canyon and Ewoldsen Trails.

Ewoldsen Trail splits off to the right; however, you'll want to stay on Canyon Trail, which continues through a redwood forest to the convergence of two streams. The trail angles off to the right and ends shortly at the base of a small 30-foot cascade. For those who would prefer to continue hiking, it's possible to climb over the falls into steeper and narrower parts of the canyon. There is a faint trail leading past the many small cascades upstream.

If you aren't into off-trail scrambles, join the rest of the park's visitors at Mc Way Falls. Or, better yet, break for lunch at the picnic area sheltered by tall redwoods. After lunch, why not take the short trip to Mc Way Creek Falls? It's only a 10-minute walk on the same trail that leads to Canyon Trail Falls, requiring just another short five-minute scramble near Canyon Trail Falls to the 20-foot freefall.

If you plan to make the trip, supplies are available in Big Sur. There is a day-use fee to enter the state park.

Also nearby are Big Sur, Little Sur, Salmon Creek Falls, Hearst Castle, Morro Bay, Monterey, Carmel, Pfeiffer Falls and Limekiln Falls.

Directions: *From Highway 1 in Monterey, drive south through Carmel, Big Sur and Little Sur to Mc Way Canyon, Julia Pfeiffer Burns State Park. Turn left and park in the day-use parking area.*

Canyon Trail Falls

Limekiln Falls

Rating: 9

How Short? 1.0 Mile

How Easy? 2

Best Time to View:
December to July

Need Information?
Contact: Big Sur
Station (831) 667-2315,
California State Park
Office (831) 649-2836,
Limekiln State Park
(831) 677-2403

Would you be interested if I told you there was a way to see six great hike-to waterfalls all in a half-day trip? I'm not talking about Yosemite National Park, either. Do you have any idea where I'm talking about? Are you stumped? Try California's Central Coast, along the precious stretch of the Pacific Ocean between Hearst Castle and Big Sur. The total 5.2-mile roundtrip to all the falls' bases, including a hike to Salmon Creek, Limekiln, Mc Way, Canyon Trail, Mc Way Creek and Pfeiffer Falls, can be completed in less than a half-day.

Where do you sign up? Begin at either Salmon Creek Falls at the south end of the trip, or at Pfeiffer Falls at the north end, to complete an enjoyable hike to these fabulous coastal waterfalls. In this write-up we are going to discuss Limekiln Falls. To learn about the other falls consult the rest of this chapter.

Located in Limekiln State Park (established in 1995) and fed by Limekiln Creek, Limekiln Falls cascades nearly 90 feet down a jagged limestone face. The drop is practically identical to Lower Rose Valley Falls in the Los Padres National Forest, and also to Lower Escondido Falls in the Santa Monica Mountains National Recreation Area. Above the falls, Limekiln Creek is fairly narrow, about three to four feet wide, however, when it makes its descent over the falls, it fans out, becoming as wide as 20 feet, and its frothy water hugs the moss-covered rock.

If you haven't visited the state park in the last few years, you won't recognize the path to the falls. Prior to the summer of 2000, the trail didn't lead all the way to its base, and visitors were forced to rock-hop the last quarter-mile. Now, a path equipped with wooden footbridges completed in spring of 2000 makes the hike much easier.

The trail begins at the dirt parking area just past the entrance kiosk, and gradually ascends through a campground along the shore of Limekiln Creek. After the campground, the path angles off to the left and crosses over a footbridge. In about 100 yards, just after crossing a second footbridge, the trail comes to a junction at the convergence of the West Fork and Limekiln Creeks. Veer right, crossing the stream, and follow the path as it winds through the narrow canyon to the base of the falls.

If you plan to make the trip, supplies are available in Gorda and Little Sur. There is a day-use fee to enter the state park.

Also nearby are Salmon Creek Falls and Hearst Castle.

Directions: *From Highway 1 in Monterey, drive south through Carmel, Big Sur and Little Sur to the turnoff for Limekiln State Park. Turn left into the parking area.*

Limekiln Falls

Salmon Creek Falls

Rating: 9

How Short? Drive To
or 0.50 Miles

How Easy? 1

Best Time to View:
December to June

Need Information?
Contact: Los Padres
National Forest
(831) 385-5434

Salmon Creek Falls can be viewed by a simple drive or an easy quarter-mile hike. The decision is entirely up to you. However, if you don't take the short walk to its base, you're doing yourself a great injustice. Situated in a canyon between Hearst Castle and Limekiln State Park, Salmon Creek Falls is one of the best waterfalls along California's Central Coast.

Many people discover the waterfall by accident while driving south on Highway 1. Awed by the stellar view of the Pacific Ocean, they come to the hairpin turn and screech their cars to a halt.

Catching a glimpse of the falls out of the corner of their eyes most people just pull off the road onto the dirt pullout, look at the waterfall to make sure it's real and move on. Big mistake. Salmon Creek Falls deserves more attention than that.

In the parking lot of Pfeiffer State Park in Big Sur nearly 50 miles away from the falls, I fell in love with Salmon Creek Falls at first sight when I saw a photo of it while reading a free newspaper called El Sur Grande. I was equally impressed when I saw it from the dirt pullout along the road; however, nothing compares to the view from its base.

More than 110 feet tall, Salmon Creek Falls in the Los Padres National Forest is one of Central California's best. There is a giant boulder resting on top of the falls that diverts Salmon Creek into three branches that plunge off the lip. It crashes onto other boulders and fans out into the large pool at its base. The waterfall is truly striking, even long after a rain.

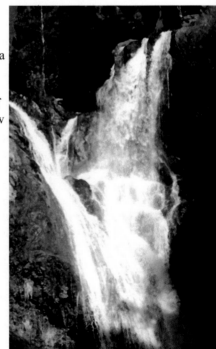

Getting to the base of the falls requires little effort. From the dirt pullout, pick up the trail in the parking area. The narrow path signed for Spruce Camp, Estrella Camp and Coastridge Road, quickly climbs steadily uphill, however, the climb is short. In fewer than 50 yards is a gate where you'll need to veer left on any of the trail spurs that head down into the canyon. (We saw a sign on the trail that said, "Falls That Way," which helped us decide which spur to follow.) The trails all merge at Salmon Creek. Continue rock-hopping upstream to the base of the falls.

If you plan to make the trip, supplies are available in Gorda.

Also nearby are Hearst Castle and Limekiln Falls.

Directions: *From on Highway 1 in San Simeon, drive about 19 miles north to a hairpin turn and a large parking pullout on the right.*

Salmon Creek Falls

Redwood Creek Falls

Rating: 4

How Short? 0.25 Miles

How Easy? 1

Best Time to View?
December to June

Need Information?
Contact: Los Padres
National Forest
(805) 925-9538

Redwood Creek Falls is one of the smallest and least known waterfalls along the Central Coast. Keeping that in mind, don't expect anyone to recognize its name. Nor will you find it listed on maps. Prior to the production of this book it had no name. My brother in law and I stumbled across it after we spotted a sign for the Nathaniel Owings Memorial Redwood Grove and decided to do a little investigating. Curious, we opted to do a bit of snooping around. We didn't find the redwood grove, but we did find a trickle of waterfalls in this seldom visited canyon of which Redwood Gulch Creek runs through the Los Padres National Forest.

Redwood Creek Falls isn't going to inspire you to cheer after viewing it. On the other hand, it's a rare opportunity to have a small cascade all to yourself, and adds to the already tremendous scenic environment found along the Central Coast.

To reach the waterfall, pick up the trail on the east side of Highway 1. The sign for the redwood grove tells you that you're in the right place. Just after passing the sign a stone drinking fountain can be spotted on the right. Walk past it and in 10 yards; you'll come to a streambed. Depending on the amount of rainfall that has fallen recently it will either be dry or hold a scarce amount of water. This section of the stream runs underground most time of year. Either way, the waterfall will have life.

From the stream continue up the canyon where two streams merge. Take the left fork and within 20 yards you'll be able to see the lower cascade. It's roughly 20 feet high. Unfortunately, a fallen tree down the center on the cascade inhibits a clear view of the drop. For those who enjoy a little rock-hopping several more cascades

Redwood Creek Falls

are located upstream. However, the trek is a little tricky. The rocks are extremely slippery and with a maritime influence the rocks are almost always damp. Use caution.

If you plan to make the trip, supplies are available in San Simeon.

Also nearby are Salmon Creek Falls and Limekiln Falls.

Directions: *From on Highway 1 in San Simeon, drive about 22.5 miles north to a hairpin turn and a large parking pullout on the right.*

Condor Gulch Cascades

Rating: 5

How Short? 1.8 Miles

How Easy? 3

Best Time to View:
February to March

Need Information?
Contact: Pinnacles
National Monument
(831) 389-4485

What the heck is a pinnacle? A pinnacle is the reason why Pinnacles National Monument was created in 1908. Here, a "pinnacle" refers to the tall rock formations that made this national monument famous. There are hundreds of rocky peaks that glisten with sienna and rust colors on sunny days. So, why are we talking about pinnacles when we're supposed to be discussing Condor Gulch Cascades? Simple, the waterfall, located inside of the monument, is overshadowed by the pinnacles.

Partly because the season to view the falls is brief, few visitors come to see it. Most hikers accidentally stumble upon the falls while walking the Condor Gulch Trail on their way to the High Peaks Trail. For these hikers, the falls is just a sideshow, far from the main attraction.

To reach the falls, begin at the trailhead for the Condor Gulch Trail. The well-signed trail can be picked up across the road from the visitor center. You won't waste much time ascending along a short but demanding walk to the Condor Gulch Overlook. The trip to the overlook is nine-tenths of a mile and requires a 550-foot elevation gain. From here, you'll get a great view of the falls.

For those who choose to do some more hiking, continue on the trail for eight-tenths of a mile to the junction of the Condor Gulch and High Peaks Trails. Turn left where the trail leads to the pinnacles you were admiring from below. The trail actually cuts through the middle of the pinnacles. There are steps carved into the rocks, and metal handrails assure a safe climb through the pinnacles.

Continue 1.7 miles on the High Peaks Trail to the turnoff for the Rim Trail. If you take the right fork, it's a half-mile trip to Bear Gulch Reservoir. Stay on the main trial, and in eight-tenths of a mile you'll end up back at the visitor center.

If you plan to make the trip, supplies are available in Soledad and Kings City. There is a fee to enter Pinnacles National Monument. Call ahead for waterfall conditions. Condor Gulch Creek may not run in poor rain years.

Also nearby are Bear Gulch Cascades, Bear Gulch Reservoir, Bear Gulch Cave and Balconies Caves.

Directions: From Gilroy, drive south on the 101 Freeway to Highway 25. Drive south on Highway 25 to Highway 146. Turn right on Highway 146 and continue approximately five miles to the park visitor center. (It may look easier to access the park through Soledad on the west side, but the reservoir can only be accessed from the east, because no roads traverse the park.)

The path to Condor Gulch Cascades

Bear Gulch Cascades

Rating: 5

How Short? 1.0 Mile

How Easy? 1

Be Time to View:
February to March

Need Information?
Contact: Pinnacles
National Monument
(831) 389-4485

Pinnacles National Monument is a popular place for hikers and rock climbers; however, it's not known by many waterfall lovers. Partially because the rainy season is short, and also because the park's few waterfalls are far from memorable, not many outdoor enthusiasts know that any waterfalls exist here.

There are only three named streams within the park boundaries (Chalone, Bear and Condor Gulch) and none hold water for more than six months of the year. Yet, when the rainy season begins and the streams start to flow, two waterfalls come to life: Bear Gulch and Condor Gulch Cascades. Although they are the only two falls in the park, neither is a popular tourist attraction.

Bear Gulch Cascades, located a half-mile downstream from the visitor center, only runs in February and March. In poor rain years, these cascades may not run at all. It is fewer than 30 feet in total height, but can be somewhat impressive in wet years.

The falls can be reached by following the Bear Gulch Trail downstream from the visitor center for a half-mile, where the canyon begins to narrow and gets steeper. The cascades can also be accessed by walking 2.5 miles upstream from Pinnacles Campground.

Bear Gulch Reservoir was built for fire protection purposes in 1937. The cascade is fed by water that spills over its dam. Although no water is released from the dam, some seeps through its cracks. It was once a popular fishing spot, plentiful with catfish. After determining the catfish were not native to the park, officials chose to poison the lake in the early Nineties. The lake is now barren of fish. Water is also fed into Bear Gulch Creek from Moses Spring.

Another nearby attraction is the Bear Gulch Caves, but be sure to call ahead to see if it's opened to visitors. Most of the year it is closed to protect bat populations.

If you plan to make the trip, supplies are available in Soledad and King City. There is a fee to enter Pinnacles National Monument. Call ahead for waterfall conditions. Bear Gulch Creek may not run in poor rain years.

Also nearby are Bear Gulch Reservoir, Bear Gulch Cave and Balconies Caves.

Directions: *From Gilroy, drive south on the 101 Freeway to Highway 25. Exit south on Highway 25 to Highway 146. Turn right on Highway 146 and continue approximately five miles to the park visitor center. (It may look easier to access the park through Soledad on the west side, but, because no roads traverse the park, the waterfall can only be accessed from the east.)*

Pinnacles tower above Bear Gulch Reservoir

Naciemento Falls

Rating: 5

How Short? Boat-To

How Easy? 1

Best Time to View:
January to April

Need Information?
Contact: Lake
Naciemento Resort
(800) 323-3839

Lake Naciemento is one of the largest lakes in San Luis Obispo, Santa Barbara and Monterey Counties. This family-friendly body of water is one of the most popular boating, fishing and camping lakes in all of California.

With more than 5,000 acres of water surrounded by both rolling and rocky hills, the lake has 160 miles of shoreline, numerous marinas and hundreds of coves. Dominated most of the year by the whining engines of water-skiers and jet skiers, or the hot-dogging antics of wake boarders, the lake also offers the possibility of peace and quiet. To reach its tranquil recesses, however, a long, but rewarding boat ride into the Narrows is required.

From the Lake Naciemento Resort, it's a good 20-minute boat ride (assuming you're going 30 mph) to the Narrows. When you reach the Narrows and its 5 mph speed limit takes effect, it requires another 20 to 30 minutes of slow driving to the waterfall.

The waterfall is located all the way at the back of the lake, in its northwestern-most arm, just north of the Gould Creek inlet. It's a good idea to pick up a map before heading into the Narrows, so that you won't be enticed by the dozens of enchanting coves into making a wrong turn. With a map, the waterfall is easy to find; simply steer towards the Naciemento River inlet. The waterfall is on the right, near the inlet.

Visitors swarm the area around the inlet for more than just the waterfall. They come here, as well as to the lake's other major inlets, to catch white bass during the March spawn. It's not uncommon to catch more than 100 a day. The lake also provides good fishing for small and largemouth bass, catfish, crappie, carp and bluegill.

Naciemento Falls

Naciemento Falls isn't grandeur. Its a mere 20 feet tall, has little volume and only flows in the rainy season. Yet, I think the peaceful ride into the Narrows makes the trip worth it. Also, the grassy clearing below the falls' base, which thrives with colorful wildflowers in the spring, is a perfect picnic spot.

The Narrows is a narrow channel (hence it's name) on the west end of the lake, where boaters go to anchor up and avoid the wakes in the busier parts of the lake. Here, they swim, catch a few rays, and jump off rocks and cliffs. Teenagers come to the Narrows just to make a day out of jumping off the cliffs that are scattered about. Before jumping, do yourself a favor and make sure the water is deep enough and there are no underwater obstacles. People have died cliff jumping in the Narrows. Although jumping is legal, lake management urges you to think before jumping. Better yet, dont jump at all.

The Narrows is also popular with nature lovers and snorkelers. Nature lovers come to watch birds and admire the dozens of assorted wildflowers that blanket grassy banks at the base of the cliffs. Snorkelers swim in the clear creek inlets, chasing fish. I even saw a guy with a spear gun chasing carp.

If you plan to make the trip, supplies are available at the lake. There is a day-use fee.

Also nearby are San Antonio Lake, Naciemento River, Pinnacles National Monument, Arroyo Seco Lakes and Arroyo Seco River.

Directions: *From Paso Robles, drive north on the 101 Freeway to Road G-14. Exit G-14 and drive 16 miles west to the lake.*

Some teenagers leap off cliffs in The Narrows   *A lupine*

Santa Margarita Lake Falls

Rating: 4

How Short? Boat To

How Easy? 1

Best Time to View:
January to March

Need Information?
Contact: Santa
Margarita Lake (805)
788-2397, Santa
Margarita Marina
(805) 438-4682

Are you tired of hiking to waterfalls? Need a change? Want to work some different muscles? Then Santa Margarita Lake Falls is perfect for you. Although you can reach the falls on a hiking trail, it's best visited in a boat or kayak.

If you hug the shoreline, it takes about 3.5 miles of paddling to reach the falls. Kayakers have to stick close to the shoreline or the other boaters will run them off the lake. For boaters, it's an easy straight shot across the lake to the falls. Both boaters and kayakers can launch at the boat launch near the marina.

After putting your craft in the water, head east to the far end of the lake. Once you hit the Narrows, a 5 mph speed limit is in effect. After passing through the Narrows, the lake widens into an open area surrounded by lush green foothills sprinkled with oak trees. Stay on the south side of the lake and motor or paddle into the first cove on the right. About 50 yards back in the cove, the canyon forks. Take the left branch and head all the way to the end of the cove.

The waterfall can be a bit difficult to see from a boat, because there is a fallen tree in the water that partially blocks its view. Although kayakers can paddle under the tree, most boats are too high to get under it. You probably won't want to take a whole roll of photos of this waterfall, anyway. It's an unimpressive 25-foot cascade that empties into the lake over a rock ledge. There's also a trail that accesses the falls from the Santa Margarita Lake Natural Area. It can be accessed via River Road.

If it weren't for the scant area of runoff that restricts the falls' power, it might be one of the lake's main attractions. If it hasn't rained in the preceding few weeks, the waterfall could be dry. Yet, even if the waterfall is dry, the pleasant ride around the lake is worth the visit.

If you plan to make the trip, supplies are available at the lake. There is a day-use and boat-launch fee.

Also nearby are Atascadero Lake, Lopez Lake, Laguna Lake, Big Falls and Little Falls.

Directions: *From the 101 Freeway in San Luis Obispo, drive eight miles north to Highway 58. Drive four miles east on Highway 58 to Pozo Road. Turn right and drive seven miles on Pozo Road to Santa Margarita Lake Road. Turn left and drive two miles to the lake.*

Big Falls

Rating: 8

How Short? 3.0 Miles

How Easy? 2

Best Time to View:
December to June

Need Information?
Contact: Los Padres
National Forest
(805) 925-9538

There are three waterfalls along a 1.5-mile stretch of Big Creek, all quite different from one another. It isn't just the waterfalls, however, that attract visitors to this section of the Los Padres National Forest, near Arroyo Grande. Tourists come to Big Falls so they can drive their vehicles through Lopez Creek, which guides you to the trailhead for Big Falls.

From December to June, Lopez Creek averages two to three feet deep in most spots, and people love to drive their pickups and sports utility vehicles through it, splashing water off their tires the way you do when you drive through flooded streets. I saw many drivers making three-point turns on the road, just so they could drive through the water again. After most people have satisfied this inexplicable splashing urge, they make the short trip to Big Falls.

Locating all three of the falls is easy and requires little effort. From the dirt pullout, pick up the unsigned trailhead by walking towards the stream, which is on the right side of the road. The three-foot wide dirt path immediately crosses Lopez Creek and then leads into Big Canyon and the Santa Lucia Wilderness, while paralleling Big Creek along the way. The first half-mile of the hike goes by fast, as the shaded path follows Big Creek, bringing you to the base of Lower Big Falls.

Lower Big Falls is a 30-foot limestone waterfall, whose face is covered in moss. The pool below the falls is large, yet shallow and a haven for snakes, frogs and small rainbow trout. In order to reach the falls you'll need to follow a side spur that breaks off the main trail 25 yards before the path leads uphill.

If you don't take the side spur that path continues on to an overlook of the middle falls. In order to reach the base of middle falls, instead of settling from the view from

Lower Big Falls

the path, you'll need to do a little scrambling. Right after the path breaks off the main route and heads to the lower falls keep an eye out for another trail spur that skirts up the limestone to the base of the middle falls.

Middle Falls is a 25-foot cascade that empties into a deep, inviting pool. When I last visited, a few teenagers made an afternoon out of jumping off the cliffs to the right of the falls. It didn't look safe to me, though. To land safely they had to clear a few trees below the rock they were jumping from, and miss a few rocks that stuck out of the water. Play it safe, stick to swimming. Swimming, on the other hand, can be refreshing on this pool which is deeper than 10 feet in some spots.

Paralleling Big Creek the last three-quarters of a mile, the trail twists into switchbacks above the falls, bringing you to 80-foot Big Falls. Many hikers never make it to Big Falls, partly because they don't know about it, but also because they can't pull themselves away from swimming in Middle Falls. Due to it's height, Big Falls is the most impressive of the three and also has an inviting wading pool at its base.

Although I'm a waterfall enthusiast, I don't come to Big Creek for the waterfalls; I visit for the fishing and the newts. Although small (most of the wild rainbows range from five to seven inches), the fish are a blast to catch. The creek averages about five feet wide and is home to thousands of newts, which are found in most coastal streams in California. Fishing is catch and release only.

If you plan to make the trip, supplies are available at Lopez Lake. A Forest Service Adventure Pass is required to park in the Los Padres National Forest. In spring, a high-clearance vehicle is required to reach Big Falls. The stream crossings can be deep.

Also nearby are Little Falls, Lopez Lake, Santa Margarita Lake, Laguna Lake and Atascadero Lake.

Directions: *From the 101 Freeway in San Luis Obispo, drive south to Arroyo Grande. In Arroyo Grande, take the Lopez Lake/Highway 227 exit and drive approximately 10 miles east to Hi Mountain Road, just before the turnoff to Lopez Lake. Turn right on Hi Mountain Road and drive eight-tenths of a mile to Upper Lopez Canyon Road. Turn left, drive 6.3 miles and turn right on an unsigned road. (On the left there will be a sign that says "Road Ends, 500 Feet.") One-tenth of a mile after turning on the unsigned dirt road (past the Lopez Canyon Conference Grounds and the Coastal Mountain Bible Grounds), the pavement becomes dirt. Continue 3.8 miles to pullouts on both sides of the road There is a no camping sign here. (From the point where the road becomes dirt, it makes 13 stream crossings.)*

Big Falls at extremely low flow

Little Falls

Rating: 7

How Short? 1.0 Mile

How Easy? 1

Best Time to Visit:
December to June

Need Information?
Contact: Los Padres
National Forest
(805) 925-9538

Lets start by saying Little Falls isn't all that little. Compared to its nearby neighbor, Big Falls, perhaps Little Falls is little. Yet compared to the rest of the waterfalls in the region, Little Falls is just average.

Thirty five-foot Little Falls is a 45-minute drive east of Arroyo Grande in the Santa Lucia Wilderness. Partly because Big Falls is just up the road, and also because of its diminutive name, visitors tend to overlook Little Falls. That's not a good idea.

The falls has a lot to offer. For example, you'll encounter a well-established trail through a shaded oak forest and a stream brimming with salamanders. No strenuous climbing is required, because the trail only gains 150 feet to the base of the falls, and you'll probably have it all to yourself. How can you beat that?

When you're driving to the trailhead, the path can be found on the right side of road. It crosses Little Falls Creek before passing a sign for the Santa Lucia Wilderness. Then, it straightens out through a flat, grassy area filled with ferns, wildflowers and poison oak. In the spring, the two-foot wide dirt path is overgrown with three-to-four-foot high plants. At times poison oak extends over the trail. Use caution not to brush up against it.

Most of the trail is dappled by the shade of oaks and sycamores. After 15 minutes or so of walking along it, you'll near the falls. Begin to listen for it on the left. Since the trail doesn't lead to its base, abandon it when you hear the falls and begin bushwhacking your way upstream. From this point, Little Falls is fewer than 30 yards away. If you begin to head uphill out of the canyon, you've gone too far. Turn around and backtrack.

With its glistening limestone face, Little Falls is most remarkable in early spring when Little Falls Creek runs at full force. At peak flow, the stream splits into three branches, which all cascade off the rocks, hugging Little's face and splashing into a five-foot deep clear pool. What I like most about this pool are the dozens of salamanders hiding under its submerged rocks. Plant lovers enjoy the ferns that thrive here, hanging from the canyon walls around the waterfall.

For those who desire, there is another waterfall upstream. Backtrack to the point where the trail ascends and continue uphill for one-tenth of a mile. Although the mountain is too steep to scramble down to its base the 40-foot drop is admirable from this vantage.

If you plan to make the trip, supplies are available at Lopez Lake. A Forest Service Adventure Pass is required to park in the Los Padres National Forest. In spring, a high-clearance vehicle is needed to reach Little Falls. The stream crossings can be deep.

Also nearby are Big Falls, Lopez Lake, Santa Margarita Lake, Laguna Lake and Atascadero Lake.

Directions: *From the 101 Freeway in San Luis Obispo, drive south to Arroyo Grande. In Arroyo Grande, take the Lopez Lake/Highway 227 exit and drive approximately 10 miles east to Hi Mountain Road, just before the turnoff to Lopez Lake. Turn right on Hi Mountain Road and drive eight-tenths of a mile to Upper Lopez Canyon Road. Turn left, drive 6.6 miles and turn right on Upper Lopez Creek Road. (On the left there will be a "Road Ends, 500 Feet" sign.) Pass the Lopez Canyon Conference Grounds and the Coastal Mountain Bible Grounds. One-tenth of a mile from where you turned on the unsigned dirt road, the pavement becomes dirt. Continue 1.6 miles to a pullout on the right. (From the point where the road becomes dirt, it makes eight stream crossings.)*

Little Falls

Nojoqui Falls

Rating: 7

How Short? 0.50 Miles

How Easy? 1

Best Time to View:
January to April

Need Information?
Contact: Nojoqui
County Park
(805) 688-4217

Sitting on a rock at the Dough Flat Observation Area of the Sespe Condor Sanctuary, looking through my binoculars trying to spot a condor, a man came up to me and tapped me on the shoulder. "Have you seen any condors?" He gestured to his son and daughter. "I've brought the kids here every weekend and we've never seen one."

After a brief chat about the birds, he asked me if there was anything else around that his kids might like. When I told him Condor Falls was just down the road, he was thrilled. "My kids love waterfalls. Hey, have you ever heard of Nojoqui Falls?"

I think he was shocked when my response showed that I knew what he was talking about. "You mean the one in that little county park on the way to San Luis Obispo. I've been there." He said he visits relatives in Paso Robles, and on the way he stops at the falls to give his kids a chance to burn off some steam.

If you're smart, you'll do the same thing and use Nojoqui as a quick rest stop. Although the waterfall doesn't warrant a special trip, it makes for a great side trip. This seasonal waterfall is perfect for kids, too, because the walk is a measly 20-minute round-tripper on a wide, easy trail.

Pick up the trail from the day-use parking lot and follow the path into the canyon. The oak tree-filled canyon begins to narrow with each step, as the stream that was only a trickle near the parking area grows and gains volume. The trail is a fun walk. The five to 10 minutes goes by fast when you're walking up flights of stone steps and crossing bridges over the stream.

Nojoqui Falls is a 75-foot tall sandstone waterfall set in the back of a canyon. This vertical waterfall has hundreds of ferns hugging tightly to its sheer face and surrounding walls. Unless a storm has passed through the area in the last few days, the water will cling close to Nojoqui's moss-covered sandstone walls. Rainfall causes the water to shoot off the top.

If you plan to make the trip, supplies are available in Buellton.

Also nearby are Little Falls and Big Falls.

Directions: *From Santa Barbara, drive approximately 40 miles north on the 101 Freeway to the turnoff for Nojoqui Park on the right. Exit and drive just under one mile east on Old Coast Highway to Alisal Road. Turn right on Alisal Road and drive less than a mile to the park entrance on the right. Follow signs to the trailhead for Nojoqui Falls.*

Nojoqui Falls

Region

11

Los Padres National Forest

Seven Falls
Mission Falls
West Fork Cold Springs Falls
San Ysidro Falls
Chorro Grande Falls
Potrero John Falls
Rose Valley Falls
Highway 33 Falls
Middle Matilija Falls
Matilija Falls
Matilija Road Falls
Santa Paula Canyon Falls
Tar Creek Falls
Tar Creek Falls (Upper)
Four Fork & Oat Mountain Falls
Dough Flat Falls
Drill Hole Falls
Condor Falls

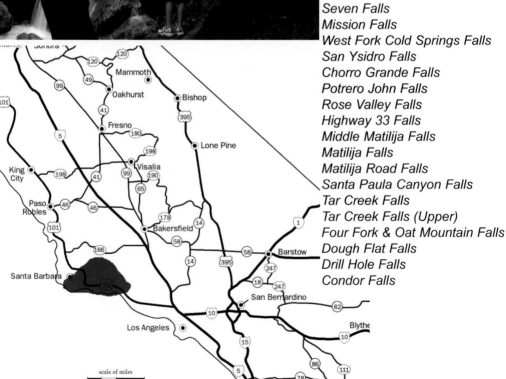

Seven Falls

Rating: 6

How Short? 3.0 Miles

How Easy? 1 to 4

Best Time to View:
December to May

Need Information?
Contact: Los Padres
National Forest
(805) 967-3481

Seven Falls is precisely what its name suggests, a series of seven waterfalls along Mission Creek near the Santa Barbara Mission. Ideal for hikers, swimmers and waders, because this is the most popular waterfall in the Santa Barbara area, its biggest problem is crowds.

There are often dozens of college kids downing beers and tanning themselves on the sandstone ledges above the falls. Climbers sometimes attempt to scale the steep sandstone that juts out and breaks up the falls' drops. Often, families who hike out to explore the stream try to capture the little newts that inhabit the water. There is no room for solitude here. The way you do at the popular California beaches, you have to be willing to share your space here.

The main reason Seven Falls is so popular is due to its swimming holes. Although there are many mountain streams that offer lovely swimming holes both nearby and inland all over Southern California, Seven Falls is in a class by itself. From Mexico to Santa Maria, there is no other place along the coast with swimming holes like Seven's.

There are seven pools ranging from two to 10 feet deep, and all are crystal clear and superlative for wading. Mission Creek looks like effervescent soda spilling out of the spout of a pitcher as it skips from one drop to the next. Beginning from the bottom and working your way up, the first two drops are located 20 yards downstream from the third, which at 15 feet is the tallest. The fourth through seventh drops are nearly identical four- to six-foot cascades.

When you come to Seven Falls, the first thing you're going to have to worry about is finding a parking spot, because Tunnel Road has limited parking. Although there is no parking permitted

Christian Perez attemps to surmount Seven Falls

on the left side of the road, parking is permitted on the right, but there aren't many spots available. If you arrive later than 9 a.m. on a weekend, you may end up having to park much further from the trailhead than you wanted.

Once you nab a parking spot, make sure to follow the directions below carefully. There is a fork at the end of Tunnel Road, offering three options. You'll want to take the middle one, a paved road that leads into the canyon. If you don't see a locked gate at the beginning of the path, you've gone the wrong way.

Follow the dirt road roughly three-fourths of a mile to a bridge over Mission Creek. While crossing the bridge, look downstream for a view of a 25-foot cascade. Immediately after crossing the bridge, a trail breaks off to the left, paralleling the creek. You can take this trail, but be forewarned it is overgrown and takes about 10 minutes longer than the established trail most hikers take. If you still choose to follow this trail along the stream, continue upstream for approximately a half-mile to the falls.

For the easier route, continue on the paved road as it angles off to the left, passing a small building and a fence on the right. You'll come to a fork where the paved road becomes dirt. The right fork breaks away from Mission Creek. Stay left, and in fewer than 100 yards, you'll come to a signed junction. The right fork is the Tunnel Trail. Go left on the Jesusista Trail. In fewer than five minutes the trail forks again. Stay left and continue another few-hundred yards to Mission Creek.

When you hit the creek, there will be two ways to get to Seven Falls, which is nearly 200 yards upstream. The easiest is to walk along the left side of the stream, following a partially worn path. You can also rock-hop upstream. Either way, it should take 15 to 20 minutes to reach Seven Falls.

Because they are fewer than 10 feet tall, most people walk past the first two falls. You can't miss the third, which has a 10-foot deep pool at its base, because the trail ends there. The only way to continue to the next four falls is by rock climbing.

Although climbing above the third drop is easily doable by hiking up the right side of the falls, continuing past to the fourth falls is trickier. Even though hoards of amateurs take their chances climbing them everyday, it's only recommended for experienced rock climbers. Swimming in the fourth pool is popular, but crowds develop quickly. The pool is 10 yards long, five yards wide and can be as deep as five feet.

The last three drops, all fewer than five feet tall, have inviting pools at their bases. If you want to continue on to them, walk to the far left end of the fourth pool. Look for crevices in the sandstone offering handholds and footholds, which begin about two feet above the waterline and progress up the rock face. Over the years, climbers have chiseled holes in the rock for climbing further up the canyon. After climbing above the fourth fall, you'll have to do more climbing at the fifth. You can wade from the sixth to the seventh.

As late May approaches flows dissipate, although the water in Mission Creek turns to a trickle, the pools remain all year.

If you plan to make the trip, supplies are available in Santa Barbara. Use extreme caution while swimming in Seven Falls. There are many rocks in the pools, and while the water tends to be clear most of the time, swimmers can stir up dirt and leaves, which make it difficult to see under the water.

Also nearby is Mission Falls.

Directions: *From the 101 Freeway in Santa Barbara, exit east on Mission Street and drive nine-tenths of a mile to Laguna Street. Turn left and drive one-tenth of a mile to Los Olivos. Turn right, drive another one-tenth of a mile and veer left on Mission Canyon Road. At the first stop sign, turn right onto Foothill Blvd. In one-tenth of a mile, turn left on Mission Canyon Road. Veer left on Tunnel Road and drive to its end. Park alongside the road.*

A few of Seven Falls' cascades

Mission Falls

Rating: 5

How Short? 4.0 Miles

How Easy? 4

Best Time to View:
December to May

Need Information?
Contact: Los Padres
National Forest
(805) 967-3481

Like Seven Falls, which is located a half-mile downstream, Mission Falls suffers from overuse. Mission is a series of four waterfalls along Mission Creek, all of which offer great swimming holes that are surrounded by slabs of sandstone perfect for tanning. Each sunny weekend, Mission is mobbed by hundreds of college students from Santa Barbara City College and UCSB. With towels laid out on the rocks and radios blaring, this place can look like a swim-party on sunny days.

Hiking to Mission Falls can take a lot of effort; it requires some difficult rock climbing and possibly even swimming during high water levels. Although the trip is not easy, it is well worth it.

To get to Mission Falls, first follow the instructions to Seven Falls in the previous write-up. Once you've done all the work getting to Seven Falls, reaching Mission is easy. From the top of Seven, continue upstream, following Mission Creek. There is a trail on the left side of the stream that fades in and out, frustrating hikers who would rather follow a path than rock-hop.

A few-hundred yards above Seven, you'll arrive at the first of Mission's four drops, a 20-foot cascade. Continuing on, walk to the left of the cascade, up and over a small hill. Another 200 yards of scrambling takes you to the base of the second drop, a 15-foot cascade with a seven-foot deep pool at its base. Directly above is the third drop, a 20-foot cascade that empties into an eight-foot deep pool.

The best swimming hole, 50 yards upstream, is 15 feet deep and looks like a crater. Mission Creek glides down a chute into this pool. Although many teenagers slide down the chute, it can be dangerous. After the first 10 feet, there is a small ledge, and those who pick up too much speed launch off it, slapping their backsides on the smooth sandstone as they land on the lower portion of the slide. The easiest way to avoid the problem is to only use the lower portion of the slide. To reach the top of Mission Falls, hike along the left side of the second and third falls to the fourth drop.

Directions *and trip info for Seven Falls also apply to Mission Falls.*

Sliding down one of Mission's cascades

West Fork Cold Springs Falls

Rating: 7

How Short? 2.0 Miles

How Easy? 2

Best Time to View:
January to May

Need Information?
Contact: Los Padres
National Forest
(805) 967-3481

The West Fork Cold Springs Falls is one of Santa Barbara's most popular outdoor attractions. This becomes immediately apparent when you arrive on a weekend and have trouble finding a parking spot. Sometimes you need to park a half-mile from the trailhead.

There are two ways to reach West Fork Cold Springs Falls: One takes roughly an hour and the other can take up to a few hours. One offers a comfortable, well-maintained trail. The other rock-hopping.

Most people choose their route based on the amount of time they have. If you have plenty of time, I recommend following the stream to the falls, rather than taking the quicker route with a trail. By following the stream, you have the option of enjoying some great swimming holes; whereas, the trail stays well above the stream until it nears the falls.

The trek begins on the south side of Mountain Drive where Cold Springs Creek flows over the road. The shaded dirt path that begins at the road and enters the wilderness. For the first two-tenths of a mile, the path is fairly straight, and then it reaches a trail junction near the convergence of the West and East Forks of Cold Springs Creek. This trail junction has a sign, which instructs you to cross the stream just before reaching a bench alongside the path. Follow the sign. If you reach the bench you've gone a few feet too far, and if you continue you'll be following the East Fork of Cold Springs Creek.

After crossing the stream, the path follows the West Fork, on which the waterfall is located. Now it's time to make a choice: streambed or trail? If you opt to stick to the trail, keep walking along it. For those brave souls who want to rock-hop to the falls, abandon the trail and continue three-quarters of a mile upstream to the base of the falls. It will take at least an hour, and while dodging poison oak, you're bound to get your feet

Swimming holes are an option at Mission Falls (pictured below), however, not at West Fork Cold Springs Falls

wet.

Back to the trail: the path continues briefly along the creek, before climbing 100 feet above it. You'll parallel the stream for the next 15 to 20 minutes. Keep an eye out for a clearing in the trees above. This is the first chance to see the waterfall. After the waterfall comes into view, start looking for an unsigned trail junction. At the junction, take the right fork, which descends to the West Fork. I counted 1,100 steps from the first trail junction to this junction, but the steps vary depending upon your stride.

There is a path all the way to the base of the waterfall; however, it can be difficult to follow at times. Several stream crossings, hoards of poison oak, large boulders and overgrown trees all pose obstacles. If you lose the trail, simply continue upstream.

Before reaching the waterfall, there are series of small

West Fork Cold Springs Falls

cascades along the creek, many of which are inviting on warm days. Once you reach these cascades, be sure to stay on the left side of the stream. Because of steep hillsides, the right side isn't traversable. In fewer than 10 minutes from the smaller waterfalls, you'll arrive at the base of West Fork Cold Springs Falls. When I arrived at this point in Cold Springs Canyon, I pondered which was better, the waterfall or the stunning view of the Pacific Ocean.

The waterfall is a 90-foot drop cascading down a slab of limestone. There is also a huge slab of limestone at the base, which many hikers use as a tanning salon. Look out! I ran into a group of men who bared it all! Not a pretty sight to say the least, especially when there are kids around.

If you plan to make the trip, supplies are available in Santa Barbara.

Also nearby are Seven Falls and Mission Falls.

Directions: *From the 101 Freeway in Santa Barbara, drive south to Hot Springs Road. Turn left on Hot Springs Road and drive approximately 2.5 miles to Mountain Drive. Turn left and drive 1.1 miles to the trailhead, where Cold Springs Creek crosses the road.*

San Ysidro Falls

Rating: 4

How Short? 3.6 Miles

How Easy? 2

Best Time to View?
December to June

Need Information?
Contact: Los Padres
National Forest
(805) 367-3481

San Ysidro Falls is one of those waterfalls where you'll remember the trail a lot longer than the waterfall. While the trail is well maintained and the coastal scenery is excellent you can't say the same for the waterfall. San Ysidro Creek maintains a substantial volume of water, however, the waterfall you are headed to is located on a smaller tributary, not the creek you follow the entire way. Nonetheless, if not for the waterfall come for the lush green setting found here in the Los Padres National Forest.

The trips begins along paved East Mountain Drive and threads between several houses for the first one-tenth of a mile before spitting you out on a paved dirt road. Now, again between rich homes follow the paved road. Soon it will become dirt. Paralleling the creek continue on the wide, dirt road uphill. In seven-tenths of a mile a signed path breaks off to the right. Ignore it. Stay on the dirt road.

In fewer than two-tenths of a mile, just before the path veers to the left keep an eye out for a small single track path that breaks off to the right. If you reach a stream crossing you went too far. Backtrack 20 yards and look for a trail that heads upstream. Now heavily shaded, again parallel the creek and get light of excellent wading holes, lush greenery and small cascades along this clear creek rich with ferns and other foliage.

Many people often mistake two small cascades for San Ysidro Falls. A good marker to judge your position on the trail is a single switchback, the only one on the trip. Once you hit this point you'll be forced to do some climbing. It's not hard, just much steeper than the rest of the path. However, many hikers stop here thinking this small waterfall and the 20-foot drop 40 yards upstream are San Ysidro Falls. Don't be mistaken.

Continue on the path. The trail switches from a dirt bottom to rock and to aid hikers when the path is moist metal guardrails have been installed. From this point it's three-tenths of a mile to your first stream crossing. Cross the stream and in less than 100 yards (make sure you stay left instead of following the path up the stream you just crossed) you'll come to the base of the waterfall.

Unless you arrive right after a rainstorm the disappointment will be evident. San Ysidro Falls stands 50 feet; however, this waterfall doesn't have the force you'd expect to see after witnessing San Ysidro Creek the entire way. The waterfall dribbles most of the year. Its face is more likely to be enjoyed by a botanist than a waterfall lover. Heartbroken by the lack of volume many hikers salvage the day by taking their time back to their cars, wading through the stream and picnicking.

If you plan to make the trip, supplies are available in Montecito.

Also nearby are Seven Falls, Mission Falls and West Fork Cold Springs Falls.

Directions: From the 101 Freeway in Santa Barbara drive south to Montecito and take the San Ysidro Road exit. Drive east for one mile to East Valley Road and turn right. Drive eight-tenths of a mile and turn left on Park Lane. Continue four-tenths of a mile and veer left on East Mountain Drive. Continue a quarter-mile to the end of the road and the trailhead.

Chorro Grande Falls

Rating: 6

How Short? 1.7 Miles

How Easy? 1

Best Time to View:
February to April

Need Information?
Contact: Los Padres
National Forest
(805) 646-4348

Let's start with the meaning of "Chorro." In Spanish, the word has two meanings: "diarrhea" and "the way water drips out of a faucet or nozzle." It's obvious which meaning we'll use for the purposes of this book. And, in regards to Chorro Grande Creek, the meaning is close to literal.

Most of the year, the Chorro Grande Creek is small, like a drip of water; however, if you visit it in late winter or early spring, snowmelt from above in the Pine Mountain Ridge changes things a bit. During the rainy season, the dribble, which is present most of the year, becomes a nice-sized seasonal stream. The rain and snowmelt also bring to life two waterfalls, which can be viewed by an easy hike along the Chorro Grande Trail.

Chorro Grande Falls

The trail that begins at Highway 33, 11 miles north of the Rose Valley turnoff, and ends atop Pine Mountain at Reyes Peak Campground, is popular in late spring and summer, when outdoor enthusiasts walk the five-mile trip, with a 3,000-foot elevation gain. Lucky for your legs the falls are close to the road, long before the path begins its ascent.

Although the elevation of Chorro Grande Creek and the two waterfalls is 4,300 feet, only one of the falls is fed by water from Chorro Grande. An unnamed tributary that runs parallel to Chorro Grande feeds the other. Only Chorro Grande's waterfall, however, is clearly visible from the trail.

From a dirt pullout on the right, signed for the Chorro Grande Trail, pick up the trail, which gradually climbs 200 feet over the course of the eight-tenths of a mile to the falls. This flat, unattractive dirt trail leads through small hills, blanketed with hundreds of yucca, small shrubs and bushes.

After hiking six-tenths of a mile (approximately 15 minutes) across a canyon on the right, you'll get your first glimpse of the waterfall from the unnamed stream, which freefalls 25 feet off its grayish sandstone lip. Because of tall trees below, you'll only be able to see the upper portion of this falls. Chorro Grande Falls, however, is difficult to see from this vantage.

The best way to view the waterfall that is

Look for these murals carved into the sandstone 273

fed by the unnamed stream is to use three sandstone boulders as markers to locate it. Each is about the size of a two-bedroom house. Located just below a small peak across the canyon, they are arranged in the shape of a triangle. The waterfall can be sighted between the boulder in the middle and the one on the left.

Chorro Grande Falls is 50 yards northwest, tucked below a large rock formation. To see it, continue two-tenths of a mile along the trail, until you are just above the falls. Walk out onto the rocks for a view of Chorro Grande from above. If you look carefully, you'll see plastic pipes in Chorro Grande Creek. They are used to divert water to the households that lie downstream near Highway 33.

The best view of the waterfall is from below. Chorro Grande appears to be a freefall, however, after the short scramble down the rocks to the base of the falls, you'll discover it's not. At the base, you'll see a congregation of large rocks, similar in shape to stalagmites. These rocks create a grotto. You can walk behind the rock formation and be directly under the waterfall. While you are here, keep walking past the falls to the unnamed waterfall. There is a level, heavily shaded campsite between the two falls.

The fun isn't over yet. If you search the sandstone rocks above the falls, you'll see numerous murals painted hundreds of years ago by early explorers.

If you plan to make the trip, supplies are available in Ojai. A Forest Service Adventure Pass is required to park in the Los Padres National Forest.

Also nearby are Highway 33 Falls, Rose Valley Lakes, Sespe River, Rose Valley Falls, Reyes Creek and the Matilija Wilderness.

Directions: *From the 101 Freeway in Ventura, exit north on Highway 33 and drive 14 miles to Ojai. In Ojai, turn left, staying on Highway 33, and continue approximately eight miles to Wheeler Gorge Campground. Reset your odometer and drive 6.6 miles to the Rose Valley turnoff. Continue 11 miles past the turnoff to the sign for the Chorro Grande Trail on the right.*

Located in the center of the picture, Chorro Grande Falls spills off a sandstone ledge

Potrero John Falls

Rating: 9

How Short? 5.5 Miles

How Easy? 3

Best Time to View:
January to July

Need Information?
Contact: Los Padres
National Forest
(805) 646-4348

Potrero John Falls is the type of waterfall you'd expect to see in Yosemite National Park, not in the Los Padres National Forest. At 4,800 feet, Potrero is a dazzling 80-foot freefall, visible after a 2.75-mile hike that has more than a 1,000-foot elevation gain. Sounds like a great waterfall, right? Well, few know it exists.

To prove my point, when I phoned the Ojai Ranger District, the receptionist told me she knew nothing about a waterfall on Potrero Creek. She did, however, know there was a popular walk-in campground along the creek. And she wasn't the only person who'd never heard of the falls. When I arrived at the trailhead and saw a dozen or so cars, I figured some of these people must be going to visit the falls, right? Wrong!

It turned out seven of the cars belonged to a Boy Scout Troop that was learning to rappel on the sandstone cliffs near the trailhead. Then, there was the couple that was camping at Potrero John. The final four were two husband and wife teams who'd heard Potrero was a nice canyon for a hike, so they'd walked to the campground and then back to their cars. Wasn't anybody going to the waterfall? Not on this busy Saturday.

Potrero John Falls

Except for the last few-hundred yards, getting to the waterfall is easy. The trail begins along Highway 33, where Potrero John Creek empties into Sespe River. Although the sign at the trailhead says that Potrero John Campsite is 2.5 miles ahead, both the topo maps I used, as well as my GPS, had the hike at 1.6 miles.

The path is easy to follow from the trailhead to the camp, but it does gain more than 500 feet before reaching the campground. For the first three-fourths of a mile, it twists and turns through a narrow canyon, crossing Potrero Creek nearly a half-dozen times. After leaving the narrow canyon walls, the route guides you out into a flat area. The landscape consists mostly of shrubs for the final eight-tenths of a mile, before reaching the camp here.

The final quarter-mile before the camp, the trail parallels the left side of Potrero Creek. There is a post in the dirt in the middle of the path pointing to Potrero Camp, which is on the far side of the creek. Although maps don't show a trail past the campground, there is one. Boy Scouts made it.

For the next three-fourths of a mile, continue along the trail, which is heavily shaded by tall oaks, pines and alders, as well as shorter manzanita and willow trees. At times the trail becomes faint. Don't get stressed about it. Simply follow the stream; you can't get lost. There are no tributaries that enter the stream, nor any canyons that meet up with Potrero, to lead you astray.

The last half-mile is like walking through a demolished maze. The path disappears, leaving you to forge a trail of your own. It can be a little difficult. Think of a cornfield in which the stalks are so high, you could play hide and seek and never find the hiders. This canyon is just that thick with fallen trees, dead branches, and 50-pound-plus boulders from rockslides. On a more positive note, however, I didn't see any poison oak.

The narrower the canyon gets, the closer you're getting to the falls. Just before the falls, there's a 20-foot cascade. From the base of this cascade, Potrero Falls will be visible. Because of the steep hillsides, it may look impossible to scramble to Potrero's base, but it's not. On the left side of the stream there are a few trees that hug the hillside. You can use the live and fallen trees to climb to the base, or use the rocks next to the trees for handholds.

From the get-go you'll be in awe of Potrero Falls. It's one of the few waterfalls in Southern California with both power and volume. Potrero Creek spills out from a narrow gorge, forming the waterfall, which freefalls for the first 10 feet, before slamming into a ledge. Above the ledge the stream is a mere two feet wide, but the impact causes the water to fan out and freefall the final 70 feet, splashing into a shallow pool. At peak flow, the waterfall can swell as wide as 20 feet after hitting the ledge.

Potrero is located at the base of a narrow canyon, which has sandstone walls that soar more than 200 feet above its brink. A half-dozen alders keep the small area below the falls shaded at all times. While we were there, the mist from the falls was so strong I was soaked in less than a minute.

If you plan to make the trip, supplies are available in Ojai. A Forest Service Adventure Pass is required to park in the Los Padres National Forest.

Also nearby are Chorro Grande Falls, Rose Valley Falls, Reyes Creek, Rose Valley Lakes, Sespe Creek and Highway 33 Falls.

Directions: From the 101 Freeway in Ventura, turn north on Highway 33 and drive 14 miles to Ojai. In Ojai, turn left, staying on Highway 33, and continue approximately eight miles to Wheeler Gorge Campground. Reset your odometer and drive 6.6 miles to the Rose Valley turnoff. Continue approximately 6.4 miles past the turnoff to the sign for the Potrero Grande Trail on the right.

Potrero John Falls

Rose Valley Falls

Rating: 8

How Short? Drive-To or Hike-In 1.0 Miles

How Easy? 1 or 3

Best Time to View: January to April

Need Information? Contact: Los Padres National Forest (805) 646-4348

When it comes to outdoor activities, Rose Valley is one of the most lively areas in the Los Padres National Forest. No other part of the forest has so many things to do in such a compact area. Nearby, there are four waterfalls, three ponds for fishing, the Ojai Gun Club, campgrounds, two streams that also offer good fishing and dozens of hiking trails. There are so many choices, chances are you won't have enough time to fit them all into one weekend.

If you visit from late winter through mid-spring, don't overlook Rose Valley Falls, which can be enjoyed two different ways. The first is by hiking to its base. The second, a bit more appealing to those who don't enjoy hiking, is admiring it from a distance. Both are rewarding in different ways.

The latter is much more peaceful. Rose Valley Lakes No. 2 and 3 are splendid places to view the falls with little to no work. Imagine this: You spread out a wool blanket along the shore and cast a line out into the pond. While waiting for a rainbow trout to bite, you watch mallards cruise the shoreline. Several other species of birds bask in the warm sun and chirp from branches of trees whose trunks are submerged in the lake.

The sloped sand shoreline, ornamented with tall grass and bushes, is the perfect spot to view snowcapped mountains in the distance. These conical mountains are mostly topped with smaller trees and overgrown brush, rather than pines. Two hundred feet below the top of the ridge, two small mountains gradually slope down to meet each other in a perfectly symmetrical v-shape. Right in the heart of that "v," Rose Creek gently tumbles off the limestone canyon walls, forming Rose Valley Falls. While you're enjoying the waterfall and clear blue sky, your bobber gets sucked underwater. Fish on!

If this doesn't sound appealing to you, viewing the waterfall while barbecuing hamburgers and hot dogs at Rose Valley Campground might. All of the campsites offer an unobstructed portrait-like vista of the falls. Picnic tables make picnicking easy and enjoyable.

Although beautiful vistas aren't for everyone, the hike is also exceptional and might be more to your liking. If not staying at the campground, park at Rose Valley Lake No. 3 and walk the 50 yards to the campground.

At the end of the campground, a sign resting on a wooden post points in the direction of the falls. The path makes one quick stream crossing and then parallels Rose Creek, staying to the right of the stream for the duration of the trip. After 10 minutes of walking the trail, sheltered mostly by coastal live oak, you'll come to Lower Rose Falls.

Surprise! This isn't the same waterfall seen

Upper Rose Valley Falls

from the parking area. From that vantage, the lower falls is hidden under the trees. Here, the water rushes down a limestone and sandstone face, hugging closely to it while spilling over moss that clings to the rock. The waterfall stands more than 90 feet tall.

For those who'd prefer to see the upper falls up close, it's possible. From the lower falls, backtrack about 25 yards and look for a trail spur that leads up the mountain. There are two short switchbacks before the trail climbs above the oaks and the lower falls. At an unsigned junction, stay left, walking towards the upper falls, which are visible from here. The trail ends at a 50-foot waterfall that can't be seen from below.

This waterfall is a lot like Lehamite Falls in Yosemite National Park. Its light water flows cut through a narrow canyon composed of dark jagged rocks. When you see this waterfall, make a left on a small, unsigned trail that leads down to Rose Creek. Again, those sharp, pointed lava-like rocks are scattered along the banks.

The base of Upper Rose Valley Falls is less than 100 yards from this waterfall. There is no better view of the waterfall than from here. The water, which appears to be frozen in a freefall, looks almost motionless. It actually glitters like snow hanging in the sky.

The thrill isn't over yet. On the way back, take time to absorb the panorama of Rose Valley. From this vantage Rose Valley Lake No. 3, the Ojai Gun Club, the Sespe River and Pine Mountain can be seen. Take a last look at the upper falls. Does it remind you of Bridalveil Falls in Yosemite National Park? If you came after a hard rainfall, it should.

On the way back down, keep an eye out about 50 yards downstream from the lower waterfall. There is a nice swimming hole along Rose Creek. Also, another 20 yards downstream is a 20-foot waterfall.

If you plan to make the trip, supplies are available in Ojai. A Forest Service Adventure Pass is required to park in the Los Padres National Forest.

Also nearby are Highway 33 Falls, Rose Valley Lakes, Sespe River, Chorro Grande Falls, Reyes Creek and Matilija Wilderness.

Directions: From the 101 Freeway in Ventura, drive north on Highway 33 and drive 14 miles to Ojai. In Ojai, turn left, staying on Highway 33, and continue approximately eight miles to Wheeler Gorge Campground. Reset your odometer and drive 6.6 miles to the Rose Valley turnoff. Turn right and drive 3.1 miles to an unsigned intersection. Turn right and continue to Rose Valley Campground.

Lower Rose Valley Falls

Upper Rose Valley Falls

Highway 33 Falls

Rating: 5

How Short? Drive-To

How Easy? 1

Best Time to View:
January to June

Need Information?
Contact: Los Padres
National Forest
(805) 646-4348

Some waterfalls weren't meant to spend a lot of time at. Highway 33 Falls, between Rose Valley and Wheeler Gorge in the Los Padres National Forest, is one of them. Highway 33 Falls is a perfect pit stop, where you pull the car over to the side of the road, step out for a quick stretch, grab a snack for the kids, take a few pictures and keep on driving. There just isn't much else to do.

Highway 33 Falls is a 50-foot cascade, broken into several tiers, some of which are hidden back in a canyon and can't be seen from the road. Although the cascade has some appeal when it rushes forcefully after winter storms, winding along its narrow canyon, its surroundings aren't attractive.

At only 2,700 feet in the Los Padres National Forest, Highway 33 Falls is below the pines, and the surrounding area looks bland. The hillsides are sparsely covered with scraggly brush and a few stubby trees that grow over the stream, obstructing a clear view of the cascade.

Highway 33 Falls flows year-round, but its force is frequently reduced greatly by summer and throughout fall. If desired, walk 20 yards from your car to the base of the falls, where you'll find a metal gate. If you walk to the left of the gate, you'll see a faint dirt trail that leads to less obstructed view of the upper cascade.

Okay, the pit stop is over. Get back in your car and continue up the winding road to more spectacular waterfalls, such as Rose Valley Falls, Potrero John Falls and Chorro Grande Falls. These waterfalls won't disappoint you.

Highway 33 Falls

If you plan to make the trip, supplies are available in Ojai. A Forest Service Adventure Pass is required to park in the Los Padres National Forest.

Also nearby are Rose Valley Falls, Rose Valley Lakes, Sespe River, Chorro Grande Falls, Reyes Creek and Matilija Wilderness.

Directions: *From the 101 Freeway in Ventura, turn north on Highway 33 and drive 14 miles to Ojai. In Ojai, turn left, staying on Highway 33, and continue approximately eight miles to Wheeler Gorge Campground. Reset your odometer and drive 3.2 miles to a dirt pullout on the left side of the road.*

Middle Matilija Falls

Rating: 3

How Short? 9.0 Miles

How Easy? 3

Best Time to View:
February to April

Need Information?
Contact: Los Padres
National Forest
(805) 646-4348

There are waterfalls hikers come to see and others they stumble upon while walking popular trails. Middle Matilija Falls is one of the latter. Middle Matilija isn't the kind of waterfall to plan a separate trip to see - it isn't worth it. But if you were planning a hike in the Matilija Wilderness, it wouldn't be a bad idea to make the waterfall one of your resting points.

The Matilija Wilderness isn't one of the region's premier hiking destinations. Yet, considering that it's located in a coastal mountain range, it does offer relatively uncrowded trails, as well as seasonal and year-round streams. Extending from the end of Matilija Road to Highway 33, a distance of 10 miles, the Middle Matilija Trail is one of the more popular paths in the wilderness.

The trail starts at the end of the paved Matilija Road. Walk past the locked gate and proceed on the paved road through Peacock Ranch. The trail becomes dirt, crosses a small stream and then bends to the right, before coming to a second stream crossing over Matilija Creek.

Warning! If there has been a powerful rainstorm during the previous week, this stream will be impassable. I tried to cross it in high water, but made it only five feet before the water level reached my chest and I had to turn back. I hadn't even made it one-fourth of the way across. Once the high water recedes, you can rock-hop across the stream.

After the stream crossing, there is a wooden trailhead sign for Trail 23W07 on the right. Following the sign, make a right, and in 10 yards the path again crosses Matilija Creek. At this point, you will have traveled less than a half-mile. After a brief 40-yard trek on land, the path crosses the Upper North Fork of Matilija Creek and then enters Matilija Wilderness. For the next quarter-mile, the trail parallels the right side of the

creek. Another stream crossing awaits before reaching Matilija Campground, one mile from where you parked. In the months of March and April, there is a 25-foot waterfall above the campground.

Over the next quarter-mile, the path crosses the stream five times before leading into a 1.1 mile straightaway on the left side of the creek. About halfway through the straightaway, the path meanders through an area overgrown with poison oak that hangs over the trail. You'll need to twist your body to avoid brushing against it. Near the end of the 1.1 miles, the path crosses a

Jackie Fodor uses a rope to cross Matilija Creek

small feeder stream, before making two more crossings of Matilija Creek.

Roughly 2.75 miles from the parking area, the path leads uphill into a number of switchbacks, then climbs above the right side of Matilija for the next half-mile, before crossing another feeder stream, 3.35 miles from the parking area. It would be a good idea to wear long pants through this section. The trail is severely overgrown with thick brush that will cut up your legs if they are not properly protected. A half-mile of gradual uphill walking and two more stream crossings brings you to Middle Matilija Campground, a small hike-in site shaded by oaks.

After leaving the camp, the trail ascends for the first one-tenth of a mile. The path then descends back down to the stream, where a canopy of trees keep you shaded while making at least half-a-dozen more stream crossings. At seven-tenths of a mile from Middle

Middle Matilija Falls

Matilija Camp, you'll see the waterfall on the left. It's easy to miss, so use the trail as a marker: the waterfall immediately precedes the place where the trail zigzags into a series of long switchbacks.

Middle Matilija Falls isn't on the Upper North Fork of Matilija Creek; as a matter of fact, it's not on Matilija Creek at all. The waterfall comes from a small, unnamed tributary whose lack of volume, as well as the fact that the view of the waterfall is partially blocked by alder trees, keeps it from being impressive. Although the waterfall is more than 100 feet high, only the final 30-foot cascade can be seen from the trail. Before emptying into Matilija, the water splashes over a jagged sandstone ledge with exposed sedimentary layers. To see the upper tiers, continue on the trail up the switchbacks. Once you've climbed above the trees, the upper tiers will come into view.

If you plan to make the trip, supplies are available in Ojai. A Forest Service Adventure Pass is required to park in the Los Padres National Forest. After heavy rains, many of the stream crossings may be difficult. Use caution when attempting these stream crossings. If the water is too high or swift, don't attempt them.

Also nearby are the North Fork Ventura River, Matilija Road Falls, Highway 33 Falls, Rose Valley Lakes, Rose Valley Falls and Lake Casitas.

Directions: *From the 101 Freeway in Ventura, turn north on Highway 33 and drive 14 miles to Ojai. In Ojai, turn left, staying on Highway 33, and continue approximately five miles to Matilija Road. Turn left, drive 4.9 miles to a locked gate at the end of the dirt parking area.*

The water was too deep for Ross Greeney to cross Matilija Creek

Matilija Falls

Rating: 6

How Short? 8.2 Miles

How Easy? 3

Best Time to View:
December to July

Need Information?
Contact: Los Padres
National Forest
(805) 646-4348

No matter what shape you're in, it's a long walk to Matilija Falls. Many hikers probably ask themselves if it's worth it. In the winter and early spring, it's a tossup. In spring and early summer, however, the answer is definitely yes; the hike is worth it. I emphasize the word "hike," because even better than the waterfall itself are the fantastic swimming holes located along Matilija Creek. They are deep, clear and inviting; so much so, many never make it all the way to the falls. Unfortunately, because I hiked to the falls in the winter after a recent storm, I didn't get the chance to take advantage of the pools. I can assure you, however, I'll be back when it's warmer to give them a try.

This section of the Matilija Wilderness abounds with water. After the first section of the hike, which runs a few hundred yards west of Matilija Creek, the trail parallels the stream's edge, giving a bird's-eye view of all the great pools to take a dip in. The creek spills off sandstone ledges, gets held up in clear pools two to 10 feet deep and sometimes as wide as 20 feet, and then flows into the next pool. The bottoms of many of these pools are perfectly rounded for swimming.

By now, I'm sure you want to know how to get there. Begin at the end of Matilija Road and walk through the wildlife sanctuary. About 100 yards past the sanctuary, the path crosses a stream and then angles to the right, before coming to a second, much larger stream crossing. Cross Matilija Creek, and in about 20 yards a trail signed for Middle Matilija Campground veers off to the right. Pass that trail and continue on the dirt road.

The dirt road splits in another 100 yards. Follow the left fork signed for hikers. The right fork leads to a few residences. In a few yards, when the road splits again, follow the right fork. The route travels through a ranch with two-foot high stone walls built on each side to keep you on the path. After passing through the ranch, the path begins to narrow and the bushes on each side become increasingly taller.

In 2.2 miles from the locked gate at Matilija Road, the path makes its third stream crossing, before bending to the right and running parallel to, while staying about 20 feet above, Matilija Creek. For the next seven-tenths of a mile, the path continues to follow along the stream; however, about three miles from the trailhead, the trail begins to disappear and reappear. Your best bet is to stay close to the stream, along its west side, which is much easier to follow.

The Matilija Wilderness

At this point, the deep swimming holes come into sight, tempting you to leave the trail and take a dip. These holes continue for about a half-mile before the creek bends to the left and the canyon walls close in. No trail exists for the next half-mile, challenging you with numerous stream crossings and fallen trees to clamber over. Watch out for poison oak, too. It's everywhere in this part of the canyon.

After 4.1 miles and a good three hours of hiking, Matilija Falls comes into view. Although it's not an eye-grabber, it does have some unique characteristics. For example, Matilija Creek tumbles down a series of layered sheets of sandstone before emptying into a four-foot deep pool. These sedimentary rocks make up the canyon walls on both sides of the falls. The right side is steep, while a mix of poison oak and ferns cover the left, which makes climbing to the fall's brink from here nearly impossible.

If you want to climb to the top of the falls, you're going to have to swim, because the only canyon wall that can be climbed is in the back of the pool. Why would you want to climb to the brink? Well, there is another taller waterfall upstream. I didn't go that far, because I wasn't about to swim the pool in the dead of winter, but my topo map showed a much larger waterfall less than a quarter-mile upstream.

If you plan to make the trip, supplies are available in Ojai. A Forest Service Adventure Pass is required to park in the Los Padres National Forest. After heavy rains many of the stream crossings may be difficult. Use caution when attempting to cross the stream. If the water is too high or swift don't attempt it.

Also nearby are North Fork Ventura River, Matilija Road Falls, Highway 33 Falls, Middle Matilija Falls, Rose Valley Lakes, Rose Valley Falls and Lake Casitas.

Directions *and trip info for Middle Matilija Falls also apply to Matilija Falls.*

Matilija Road Falls

Rating: 4

How Short? Drive-To

How Easy? 1

Best Time to View:
March and April

Need Information?
Contact: Los Padres
National Forest
(805) 646-4348

Some people don't enjoy hiking. They simply want to drive to a waterfall and be able to view it from their car. Matilija Road Falls is that kind of place. Located near Ojai, only a 30-minute drive from the Pacific Ocean and Highway 101, Matilija Road leads to dozens of waterfalls hidden in canyons that branch out from it. Looking out the window of your car, you can see six waterfalls in the Los Padres National Forest. No walking is required. Some are striking, others just so-so. Yet, because this place is so easily accessible, few sightseers complain.

When you turn off Highway 33 onto Matilija Road, reset your odometer and drive four-tenths of a mile uphill on the paved road. There are no pullouts along the road here, so you'll need to keep an eye out for the waterfall on the left. Matilija Reservoir is visible off to the left with rolling mountains above it. Matilija Dam is all the way over to the left side of the reservoir. Waterfall No. 1 is 10 yards to the right of the dam.

This waterfall tumbles off rocks, down a narrow crevice in the canyon and empties into the reservoir. There are two tiers visible from this vantage point, each about 20 feet tall, however, more tiers can be seen further up the road. Don't spend too much time here. The tall cliffs on the right side of the road are covered with loose rocks and soil, and rockslides are common. Also, have someone keep an eye out for cars coming from behind.

Better yet, move on to waterfall No 2. Don't reset the odometer again. Simply continue on the road until the odometer reads "2.6." Then park in a small pullout on the left. Look across Matilija Creek for a 30-foot drop. The stream that feeds the waterfall isn't named. It's actually a collection of water from several different streams along a ridge in the Santa Ynez Mountains. Only a 20-foot section of the falls can be seen, because tall trees growing up from Matilija Creek's banks hide the lower portion. The waterfall is a lot like Rose Valley Falls. Both are fed by small, narrow streams that fan out as they cascade over their brinks, hugging rock faces on the way down.

For No. 3, continue three-tenths of a mile from No. 2, to a canyon on the right. Looking up the treeless mountainside, which is partly covered with small bushes that surround large bare areas of light brown dirt, you'll see a 40-foot freefall. Even during the

Waterfall No. 5

heaviest rainy season, it has little volume spilling over its v-shaped face.

No. 4 is located above No. 3, but you can't see it from here. Drive two-tenths of a mile further and then look up the canyon, three-fourths of the way from the road to the top of mountain. This waterfall is nearly identical to No. 3, but much taller, nearly 70 feet. It also only flows after heavy rainfall.

The fifth waterfall, which can be viewed four-tenths of a mile further up the road, is my favorite. About 50 yards from the road, this cascade has the most volume of all the waterfalls along this stretch. Emerging from a heavily overgrown narrow canyon across the creek, this 40-foot drop is the most impressive. Its waters form a narrow chute that looks like it's been vacuumed off the lip and sucked down into Matilija Creek.

The final waterfall is 4.1 miles from Highway 33, this time on the right side of the road, hidden about a quarter-mile back in a canyon. This waterfall is taller than 100 feet, however, only 40-feet can be seen from the road. And the waterfall is on private property, so you can't walk to its base.

All the waterfalls along this stretch require rainfall to flow. If there hasn't been a normal or above normal rain year, they may not flow at all. Try to come a few days after a hard rain. It's dangerous to come right after or during a rainfall, because the road floods and rockslides become a problem. It wouldn't be a bad idea to check with the Forest Service before heading out. If measurable rain hasn't fallen in the past few days, the waterfalls will dry up. Their life is that short!

If you plan to make the trip, supplies are available in Ojai. A Forest Service Adventure Pass is required to park in the Los Padres National Forest.

Also nearby are North Fork Ventura River, Middle Matilija Falls, Matilija Falls, Highway 33 Falls, Rose Valley Lakes, Rose Valley Falls and Lake Casitas.

Directions: *From the 101 Freeway in Ventura, turn north on Highway 33 and drive 14 miles to Ojai. In Ojai, turn left, staying on Highway 33, and continue approximately five miles to Matilija Road. Turn left and drive four-tenths of a mile to the first waterfall. Follow the directions below to reach the next five waterfalls.*

Waterfall No. 4

Santa Paula Canyon Falls

Rating: 6

How Short? 6.0 Miles

How Easy? 3

Best Time to View:
Year-Round

Need Information?
Contact: Los Padres
National Forest
(805) 646-4348

Contrary to popular belief, there are a few places with a nice waterfall and swimming holes in Southern California. Santa Paula Canyon Falls, also known as Devils Punchbowl, is one of four places in the southern portion of the state with a deep and wide swimming hole at the base of the waterfall. Cedar Creek Falls in San Diego County and Murray Canyon Falls near Palm Springs, Seven Falls in Santa Barbara and are the others.

Jumping and swimming are popular here, but outdoors lovers come for more than that. A short drive from anywhere in Ventura or western Los Angeles County, the falls offers a quick getaway from city life. Unless you visit on a weekday morning, however, don't bank on being the only one there.

The falls is a popular attraction that lures all sorts of recreationists, including backpackers, hikers, anglers and rowdy teenagers. For backpackers, there is a developed campground, Big Cone Camp, less than one-eighth of a mile from the falls, and there are also primitive sites along Santa Paula Creek.

For those who enjoy cliff jumping, you may have to wait in line. Teenagers with stereos, sandwiches, chips and coolers filled with beer raid the area on weekends. There is usually a line to jump, because to get up to the 20-foot-high rock platform adjacent to the falls, you'll need to use the rope that's provided.

It's such a popular jump, you'll usually have to tread water in the pool below the falls while you wait for others to complete the climb to the jumping platform. The clear, emerald pool below the falls is about 20 feet deep at its deepest and is large enough for both jumpers and swimmers to enjoy at the same time. Where most people jump, some crazies dive off the granite platform, but it's not recommended because of the pool's depth.

Located near Santa Paula in the Los Padres National Forest, the waterfall is about 20 feet high and flows year-round. Usually people jump off the platform adjacent to the falls, because jumping off the waterfall is extremely dangerous. It's slippery up there and tough to get solid footing to properly launch yourself. Also, there are rocks below the falls that must be cleared to make it safely down into the pool. In the early Nineties, a student from Thomas Aquinas College died when she slipped and fell off the cliff above the falls. Please be careful.

Fishing is also an option, but with all the commotion, catching fish can be difficult. Although there are wild rainbow trout in the pool below the falls, anglers who fish either upstream or downstream from the falls have better luck.

My favorite activity here is snorkeling. There are lots of trout under a small underwater rock outcropping below the falls, which can be seen best with a mask. I tried to feed some with a few worms, but they

Jerry Weeks uses a rope to reach Upper Santa Paula Canyon Falls

Upper Santa Paula Canyon Falls

didn't budge. The cliff jumpers must have spooked them. If you bring a mask along, why not search for hidden treasure on the bottom? My friend Jerry Weeks did and finished the day with three watches and some cash. Don't try it, however, if people are jumping off the cliffs. You wouldn't want them to land on you.

The trail to the falls is easy to follow. The hike takes a little over an hour there and 45 minutes back to your car. Begin by following the signs through Thomas Aquinas College.

Leaving the college, walk through an opening in the fence and pass by some oil wells, before coming to a dirt trail that follows Santa Paula Creek. When you get to the creek, veer right. Stay on the south side of the creek until the trail ends.

Cross the stream. On the other side, pick up the trail and continue up the canyon to the second stream crossing. After crossing the stream, it's time to climb - up, up and up the path - now a fire road that curves around the mountain before coming to Big Cone Camp. From here, follow the trail down a switchback to the East Fork of Santa Paula Creek, which soon joins with the main branch of Santa Paula Creek. Head downstream. In minutes, you'll see the falls on the right.

Got extra time? Follow the trail past the falls, working your way further up the creek. Just above the falls, there is a smaller waterfall with a fairly deep, but narrow swimming hole at its base.

If you plan to make the trip, supplies are available in Santa Paula and Ojai. Keep any eye out for rattlesnakes. Because the weather stays warm from April through October, they can frequently be seen in the area. Keep any eye out for steelhead, too. Recently placed on the endangered species list, these fish are known to spawn in the stream.

Also nearby are Lake Casitas, North Fork of the Ventura River and Matilija Creek.

Directions: From Highway 101 in Ventura, drive east on Highway 126 to the city of Santa Paula. Take the Highway 150 exit and turn left. Drive through Santa Paula and then parallel Santa Paula Creek through Santa Paula Canyon. Just past Thomas Aquinas College, turn into a large pullout on the right. Park your car in the parking lot and walk across the bridge over Santa Paula Creek to the paved road that leads through the college.

Santa Paula Canyon Falls

Tar Creek Falls

Rating: 7
How Short? 5.2 Miles
How Easy? 4
Best Time to View? January to May
Need Information? Contact: Los Padres National Forest (805) 646-4348

Tar Creek Falls isn't for everyone. In reality, unless you have a full arsenal of climbing gear and know how to use it forget about getting to the fall's base. Tar Creek Falls is an excellent waterfall, one of the best in the Los Padres National Forest. And, at 1,920 feet, inside the Sespe Condor Sanctuary it's situated in a remote, seldom visited and hard to reach canyon. Basically, other than a few hard core rock climbers, few come here.

Follow the directions in the previous write-up to reach the base of Upper Tar Creek Falls. At this point, half of the excursion is over, actually, 90 percent of it is. However, now it's time for the tough part. Although Tar Creek Falls is fewer than a quarter-mile downstream of the upper falls there is no path, flat ground is impossible to find and house-size boulders litter the streambed. As you guessed, it's time to rock hop, swim, rock climb and do whatever helps you to surmount these obstacles.

The scramble isn't as difficult as it may seem. Just be prepared to work a bit. Your task is simple. Get downstream! That's it. It doesn't matter how you do it. Some places you'll need to wade, others require climbing rocks, some jumping from one rock to another and in some places you'll sit on the rock and ponder over which route to take. The trek should take about 20 minutes if you are in good shape. If you take your time allow 45 minutes.

Is all this trouble worth it? If you need adventure, yes. If you are a leisure hiker who enjoys easy strolls through the woods, no. While the hike to Tar Creek Falls is doable, it's no walk in the park.

Tar Creek Falls

And, unfortunately the view comes from its brink, not the base. Don't even think of trying to climb to the bottom either. Without extensive climbing skills and the proper equipment it's not happening. Sheer and unstable cliffs pose a massive problem for those seeking a better view.

Regrettably, you'll have to settle for the view from above. This isn't so bad. Tar Creek Falls is an 80-foot, two-tier drop. The first is a 40-foot freefall, which slams onto a granite ledge before splashing down into a clear, deep, emerald pool we'd all love to swim in.

Rather than risking injury trying to get a closer peek of the falls enjoy the peace and quiet and set up a picnic on the slabs of granite that make up the topography near the brink. If you get hot the pools above the falls are excellent for wading.

If you plan to make the trip, supplies are available in Fillmore. A Forest Service Adventure Pass is required to park in the Los Padres National Forest. In winter and early spring check on road conditions. If measurable rainfall has accumulated in the past few weeks the roads will be wet and muddy. In this case a high clearance vehicle is recommended. Call ahead for updated conditions.

Also nearby are Condor Falls, Dough Flat Falls and Drill Hole Falls.

Directions: From Fillmore drive 4.8 miles on A Street and veer right at the end of the road. Continue 4.8 miles to a dirt pullout and locked gate on the left. The pullout is 2.1 miles from the Los Padres National Forest sign and 1.5 miles from the Fire Station.

Upper Tar Creek Falls (pictured above) offers better swimming holes than Tar Creek Falls

Tar Creek Falls (Upper)

Rating: 5

How Short? 5.0 Miles

How Easy? 2

Best Time to View:
January to April

Need Information?
Contact: Los Padres
National Forest
(805) 646-4340

In one word Tar Creek Falls is an exception. Tar Creek Falls is an oasis in the low lying dry coastal mountains. In a shrub and chaparral infested area of Ventura County, Tar Creek Falls is an undiscovered jewel that has yet to be destroyed by irresponsible hikers who leave their trash basking on sandstone

Upper Tar Creek Falls has great swimming holes

rocks, destroy natural vegetation for fires and tag all over house size rocks and delicate canyons. To all but a few, Tar Creek Falls doesn't exist.

In a dry, arid and seldom used section of the Los Padres National Forest there are no signs acknowledging the trailhead to the falls, no hidden parking lots, or even words on a map stating the waterfall's existence. Without following these instructions carefully, good luck. You'll have trouble finding it. I know I did.

Here's how to ensure you don't get lost. When you get to the Los Padres National Forest sign, which will be on your right, reset the odometer, and drive exactly 2.1 miles. Paying close attention to roadside landmarks, you'll see a locked gate roughly 20 yards to the left of the dirt road and a small, unmarked dirt parking area. Most likely, there will be other cars parked. If you found the gate you're in business. Finding the trailhead is the hardest part. The rest is a synch.

Walk through the gate and proceed on the wide dirt road for 1.4 miles before coming to another parking area, which you, or I unfortunately don't have a key for. Someone, however, does because there have been cars parked overnight here every time I visit. At this point, the wide path turns into an overgrown single track trail. Continue another eight-tenths of a mile downhill to where the trail intersects Tar Creek. The path loses nearly 600 feet; however, you won't notice it

Tar Creek Falls

Cooling off at Upper Tar Creek Falls

till the way back.

Let's abandon the trail; it's time to rock hop and wade downstream. It's a mere quarter-mile to the falls. On the other hand, there's no trail so expect it to take a half-hour or so. The stream is overgrown. We found the easiest path being as close to the water as possible. The first tenth of a mile is pretty easy going, but expect to get wet. As you near the falls the pools get bigger and deeper. There is no way around getting wet.

Tar Creek Falls is a series of waterslides, cascades and freefalls, four in all, that provide a water park atmosphere, minus the crowds. The first cascade is the best. The cascade is a small, 10-foot waterslide that many use to launch themselves into the 20-foot deep pool. While chilly, the water is in great shape for swimming through April in most years. Later on, the water turns stagnant an unsafe for human contact. Getting to this pool takes some work. Walk down the left side of the falls. There's a small crevice you'll be forced to crawl through (it's like a small tunnel) to reach the base of the pool. It will be evident when you arrive what I'm talking about.

The next drop is a 15-foot freefall; however, without a little struggle it's not easily reached. It would be possible to hike along the left side of the drop here; unfortunately that space is covered by a field of poison oak. Here's what you need to do. Walk to the edge of the pool and then take a few steps to the left, that's walking away from the water. You'll be standing on a fairly steep rock ledge, roughly 15 feet high. Just below you is a fallen log. You'll need to walk across the log and then carefully lower yourself down to the ground to be able to reach the next pool. Below the log is a small cave that many people walk through to reach the waterfall.

This pool is nearly 10 feet deep. The highlight is being able to swim underneath the falls. The water is sparkling clear and emerald green making for perfect swimming opportunities. The next waterfall is a pitiful five-foot freefall. However, what's below it is important. In this case, the bathtub shaped pools are what makes the waterfall and there are two of them here. To reach them again stay to the left crawling your way down the steep rocks.

The last pool is the largest. Fed by two small cascades this hole is the size of a backyard swimming pool. Fortunately, there's a sandy beach to go with it. Plan on laying out and catching some rays here. It's worth it.

***Directions** and trip info for Tar Creek Falls also apply to Upper Tar Creek Falls.*

Sliding down Upper Tar Creek Falls

Four Fork Creek and Oat Mountain Falls

Rating: 5

How Short? Drive-To

How Easy? 1

Best Time to View:
February to April

Need Information?
Contact: Los Padres
National Forest
(805) 646-4348

Many Fillmore residents are aware of the vast recreational opportunities available in the mountains north of town. Few, however, venture there in the winter and spring, when high clearance or four-wheel drive vehicles are required to reach national forest lands. Little do these residents know that Four Fork Creek and Oat Mountain Falls can be visited without an off-road vehicle, in less than 45-minutes roundtrip. But there is one downfall to both drive-to waterfalls: they only flow during the rainy season and in above normal rain years.

Lets get started. If we wait any longer, they may dry up! At the intersection of Goodenough Road and A Street, reset your odometer and drive exactly 5.3 miles on the narrow, winding mountain road. Just before the falls, the road curves to the right and crosses over an unnamed stream. Park on the dirt pullout on the left, just after the road crosses over the stream.

Oat Mountain Falls is fed by runoff from Oat Mountain. The falls cascades down an almost vertical cliff that is covered from February to April with tall grass, wildflowers and weeds. The best view is from the road, on either side of the falls. Don't attempt to climb to its base. The canyon is too steep to climb down.

Oat Mountain Falls is on private land in oil drilling country. Four Fork Creek is in the Los Padres National Forest, where it's often difficult to tell who owns what land. The oil companies own some of the land; private individuals who lease it out to the oil companies own other sections; and the remainder belongs to the Forest Service.

To get to Four Fork Creek Falls, continue one mile along the road to a Los Padres National Forest sign. Park on the dirt pullout on the left. Four Fork Creek Falls is fed by water from Four Fork Creek and can be viewed by looking down the canyon walls, which are composed of loose sand. There is a series of small cascades that tumble down to a 25-foot freefall. As I said previously, don't try to hike to the base; it's impossible to maintain stable footing down the canyon walls.

If you plan to make the trip, supplies are available in Fillmore. A Forest Service Adventure Pass is required to park in the Los Padres National Forest. The road to the falls requires extremely slow driving. There are dozens of blind turns. Use Caution!

Also nearby are Dough Flat Falls, Drill Hole Falls and Lake Piru.

Directions: *From Interstate 5 in Santa Clarita, drive north to Highway 126. Exit Highway 126 west and drive to Fillmore. In Fillmore, turn right on A Street and drive 1.1 miles to Goodenough Road. To get to Oat Mountain Falls, veer right on Goodenough Road and drive 5.3 miles to a dirt pullout on the left. For Four Fork Creek, continue one mile past Oak Mountain Falls to the sign for the Los Padres National Forest.*

Four Fork Creek Falls

Dough Flat Falls

Rating: 4

How Short? Drive-To

How Easy? 1

Best Time to View:
February to April

Need Information?
Contact: Los Padres
National Forest
(805) 646-4348

The California condor, a member of the endangered species list, is the largest bird in North America. According to the US Fish & Wildlife Service, the condor can weigh up to 25 pounds, have a maximum wingspan of 9.5 feet and fly up to 55 mph. Although there aren't many condors left in the world, some of the few that still exist in the wild (as opposed to the captivity of zoos) are near Fillmore in Southern California.

In 1947, the 53,000-acre Sespe Condor Sanctuary was established to help protect these birds. Although the sanctuary is closed to the public, there is an observation site where visitors with binoculars can hope for a chance to see a wild condor soar free in the sky.

Most likely, you won't see a condor if you come here; however, if you visit in late winter and early spring, the trip can be spiced up with a long-distance view of two waterfalls. These waterfalls are clearly visible from the Dough Flat Observation Site. Depending on rainfall, the waterfalls can either trickle or soar down the sandstone cliffs.

To see the waterfalls, park in the parking area on the left, signed for the Alder Creek Trailhead. To protect the birds, hiking to the base of the falls is prohibited; but they're better viewed from afar, anyway. You won't even need binoculars to see them. Just find the bathrooms and look east about halfway up the sandstone cliffs.

Surrounded mostly by dirt and brush, the waterfalls are about 200 yards apart, and both are fed by unnamed streams. Nestled in the canyon, these 20-foot cascades make more of a whimper than a roar, rolling lazily into areas dominated by trees and shrubs.

Don't be too disappointed. Remember, you didn't come for the waterfalls; you came for the condors. While you're here, walk to the parking lot on the right, pick up a trail from the south end of the lot and continue to a nice picnic area. Okay, you missed the condors and weren't impressed by the waterfalls, but at least you brought a good lunch, didn't you?

If you plan to make the trip, supplies are available in Fillmore. A Forest Service Adventure Pass is required to park in the Los Padres National Forest. If coming in the winter or spring, bring a high-clearance or four-wheel drive vehicle. The road gets flooded in many spots and most likely will be impassable for low-clearance vehicles.

Also nearby are Drill Hole Falls, Condor Falls, Four Fork Creek Fall, Oat Mountain Falls and Cow Spring Falls.

Directions: From Interstate 5 in Santa Clarita, drive north to Highway 126. Exit Highway 126 west and drive to Fillmore. In Fillmore, turn right on A Street and drive 1.1 miles to Goodenough Road. Veer right and drive 12.6 miles to Dough Flat.

Dough Flat Falls

Drill Hole Falls

Rating: 3

How Short? 6.0 Miles

How Easy? 2

Best Time to View:
February to April

Need Information?
Contact: Los Padres
National Forest
(805) 646-4348

Contrary to popular belief, bear country still exists in Southern California. Black bears are plentiful east of the Sespe River drainage and west of Pyramid Lake in the Los Padres National Forest. This area, however, is rarely visited by anyone other than a few hunters who target 200- to 300-pound bears in the fall.

Most of these hunters begin tracking around Ant Campground, nearly two miles and a 900-foot drop in elevation from an abandoned drilling site. This drilling site isn't quite in bear country, but it's close enough. Although I've seen bear droppings all along the trail, I've never seen a bear here.

This former oil-drilling site isn't a popular hiking area. At 3,600 feet, two drill holes are still visible, along with rusty old poles and splintered sheets of plywood. I also saw hundreds of dented and rusted beer cans last time I was here.

Aside from the drill holes, the flat area where they are located has little to offer except for two waterfalls. Neither of the falls is appealing; both stand atop rugged, brush-covered mountains and only flow in the rainy season. Also, they must be viewed from a distance, because the hills around them are much too thick with overgrown brush to approach them.

Okay, here's how to get to the falls: from the Alder Creek Trailhead, follow the wide dirt trail north from the parking lot, entering the Sespe Wilderness soon after leaving your car. After a brief uphill walk, the trail bends to the right, crosses a stream and then makes its way uphill, again crossing a few streams before leveling out in Squaw Flat.

This area isn't signed, however, it's easy to spot, because there are two 20-foot waterfalls on the right, spraying off the tall, bare sandstone mountains. (The waterfalls only flow in February, March and April, unless there's significant rainfall in December; in that case, they'll begin to flow in January.) You can't see the two drill holes from this point, but they are over a small hill on the right.

From Squaw Flat, the trail climbs again before coming to an old, rusted trail sign that is difficult to read because of bullet holes and weather damage. Take the right fork, and in three-tenths of a mile you'll come to the first of the two unnamed waterfalls. You'll see the first waterfall when you arrive at a small stream crossing in a wide-open dirt area without any trees. It's to the right, less than a quarter-mile up the mountain. Fed by an unnamed stream, the drop is only about 15-feet.

Continuing on the trail, less than 50 yards ahead, is a point where two streams meet. Look to the left, there will be some rusty old poles sticking out of the ground. That is the old drill site. Instead of walking to the drill holes, cross the stream and walk another 50 yards along the trail. To the right, 100 yards up the canyon, is the second waterfall. This waterfall is about 20 feet tall and is set in the same bushy surroundings. It has twice the volume of the other waterfall.

Directions *and trip info for Dough Flat Falls also apply to Drill Hole Falls.*

Drill Hole Falls

Condor Falls

Rating: 8

How Short? Drive-To

How Easy? 1

Best Time to View:
February to April

Need Information?
Contact: Los Padres
National Forest
(805) 646-4348

When it comes to accessibility, drive-to waterfalls may be good for some people. In most cases, however, along with the ease it takes to view the falls, come crowds. That's not the case at Condor Falls in the Los Padres National Forest. Hardly anyone comes here. This section of the national forest isn't popular with Southern California residents, except for the few that come with binoculars, eager for the chance to see condors.

At 2,800 feet, Condor Falls is located in the Sespe Condor Sanctuary and can be reached via a long drive on a dirt road. The long drive is worth it, as long as you visit from January to April, when runoff and snow melt keep water flowing through the region.

Unlike most other waterfalls near the sanctuary, Condor Falls is noteworthy, taking a superb plunge with tremendous force off a sandstone lip. Like many of its neighbors, the stream that creates Condor Falls is unnamed, most likely because it's a seasonal stream. It's mostly dry from May to December; however, with even the slightest rain, it comes to life.

Several streams meet near Dough Flat, creating Condor's feeder stream. Above Condor, the stream's banks are mostly bare, with only a few trees, but below the falls, the foliage thickens, and ferns cling to the sandstone walls adjacent to the falls. In the spring, wildflowers are scattered around its base. Because of the dense foliage, only the top 15 feet of the 40-foot waterfall can be clearly seen. Below that, the view is obstructed.

There are three good viewing points. The best is from the dirt pullout, which provides a view of Condor plummeting directly in front of you off the sandstone cliff. Less than one-tenth of a mile upstream, Condor can be observed from above. For those who desire, hiking up the creek to the base is doable. To do this, walk back to the dirt pullout, locate a trail spur that leads down to the creek and bushwhack upstream.

Directions *and trip info for Dough Flat Falls also apply to Condor Falls.*

Condor Falls

Coastal Falls (LA to Ventura)

12

Temescal Canyon Falls
Santa Ynez Canyon Falls
Escondido Canyon Falls
Solstice Canyon Falls
Dry Creek Falls
Zuma Canyon Falls
Newton Canyon Falls
The Grotto
Circle X Ranch Falls
La Jolla Canyon Falls
Sycamore Canyon Falls

Temescal Canyon Falls

Rating: 4

How Short? 2.4 Miles

How Easy? 1

Best Time to View:
December to April

Need Information?
Contact: Temescal
Canyon Gateway Park
(310) 454-1395

People don't come to Temescal Canyon for its waterfall, which is one of the poorest in Southern California. Hikers, families, outdoor enthusiasts and others visit the park year-round for outstanding scenic views. From the trail on the way back from the falls, visitors can see the Pacific Ocean, Santa Monica Pier, factories in San Pedro, planes taking off from LAX and sailboats cruising the ocean. It's awe-inspiring and a damn good reason to come here. The waterfall by itself, however, is not worth the trip. There are two cascades along Temescal Canyon Creek, neither of which are taller than 10 feet.

The trail that escorts you to the falls is well kept up and easy to follow. Begin near the self-pay station at the parking lot and follow the signs down to the stream. Cross the stream and take the trail about 100 yards upstream to a trail junction. The left fork is signed for the Temescal Canyon and Leacock Memorial Trails. Stay right, following signs to the Waterfall and Temescal Ridge Trails. The waterfall is only 1.1 miles from the junction, although the route continues far above the stream, paralleling it for the first half-mile.

In a half-mile, the route makes its only stream crossing, after which it gradually works its way uphill to the signed boundary of Topanga State Park. From this point, the waterfall is just four-tenths of a mile ahead, but the trail will get you huffing and puffing as the ascent becomes steeper.

Once you've reached the metal bridge that crosses over the stream, you've gone far enough. The smaller of the two cascades empties into the pool above and bridge, and the larger cascade empties into the pool below. There are trails that descend to the lower cascade's base, but the hillsides are steep with loose dirt and stones, so use caution not to lose your footing.

Another interesting side note is that the cross-country and track teams from Palisades High School sometimes use the trails to train on. When I last visited in winter I was almost run over by a group of kids who were wearing Palisades Track & Field T-shirts.

If you plan to make the trip, supplies are available at the Temescal Canyon General Store located in the park. A day-use fee is charged.

Also nearby are Santa Ynez Canyon Falls, the Santa Monica Pier and the Pacific Ocean.

Directions: *From Highway 1 in Santa Monica, drive (towards Malibu) to Temescal Canyon Road. Turn right and drive 1.1 miles to the entrance of Temescal Canyon State Park. Park in the day-use parking area at the end of the access road.*

Temescal Canyon Falls

Santa Ynez Canyon Falls

Rating: 6

How Short? 2.4 Miles

How Easy? 2

Best Time to View:
January to May

Need Information?
Contact: Topanga State
Park (310) 455-2465 or
(310) 454-8212

Most L.A. couples have heard of the romantic restaurant called Gladstone's on Pacific Coast Highway between Santa Monica and Malibu. Here, you and your better half can eat lunch while admiring the surf, smelling the fresh scent of salty air and feeling the cool ocean breeze.

But, little did you know there is another nearby activity that can be enjoyed together after lunch. One that will even burn off a few of those calories you gobbled down at Gladstone's. I'm talking about a short nature walk into Santa Ynez Canyon to see a 25-foot waterfall. The trailhead is close to the restaurant, too- only about five minutes away.

Santa Ynez Canyon Falls are located in Topanga State Park, just a short distance from the gated communities in Pacific Palisades. As a matter of fact, the trailhead begins directly across from the entrance to one of these gated communities. The path guides you down a few steps, passes a concrete flood control channel on the left and then leads over a giant concrete slab that looks like a skateboarder's dream.

Then, the trail becomes dirt, directs you through thick foliage and leaves behind most reminders of civilization. There are willows, oaks and sycamores to keep you shaded, as well as poison oak creeping over the edges of the path that need to be avoided.

Over the next half mile, the path crosses the stream four times before coming to a fork in the trail, just past a metal gate on the right. At this junction a sign that reads, "Trail," points to the left. Follow the trail across the stream once more. In fewer than 50 yards, the final trail junction awaits.

Again, this junction is signed. The left fork leads to Trippet Ranch and the right is signed for the waterfall. Veer right, crossing over the stream, and continue upstream along the trail, making four more stream crossings along the way. Where the trail disappears into the stream, a little rock-hopping is necessary. The falls is about 30

Middle Santa Ynez Canyon Falls

yards upstream, and if there is high water, you may have to get your feet wet to reach it.

There are several waterfalls located in this part of the canyon, but the lower one, a 25-foot narrow shoot, is the only one that is suitably accessible for after-lunch couples or families with children. The rest require difficult off-trail scrambles. Depending upon the intensity of Southern California's rainy season, these falls can be spectacular or a trickle.

There are two ways to reach the second set of waterfalls. The quickest is by climbing over the boulders adjacent to the lower falls. There is a rope to aid you, but the boulders are extremely slippery, so the climb can be difficult. Once you get over the boulders, the next set of waterfalls is fewer than 10 yards upstream.

The second group of waterfalls begins with a short cascade and ends with a 15-foot-high freefall. Getting to the base of the waterfall can be fun. There are ropes hanging over the stream to help you navigate the water without getting wet, and another set of ropes that can be used to assist you in climbing over the falls to the next group of cascades.

If climbing over boulders seems too tough, there is an easier way. Where the trail disappears into the stream, there is another trail on the right side of the stream that ascends the hillside. It winds over the rocks on the top of the ridge and then down to the streambed, positioning you between the two falls.

There are other waterfalls upstream, but they can be even more challenging to reach. Most of the other falls require rappelling gear to reach. Use caution. All of these waterfalls flow over loose sandstone, which provides precarious footing at best.

If you plan to make the trip, supplies are available in Pacific Palisades.

Also nearby are Temescal Canyon Falls, the Santa Monica Pier and the Pacific Ocean.

Directions: *From Highway 1 in Santa Monica, drive north (towards Malibu) to Sunset Blvd. and turn right. Drive a half-mile and turn left on Palisades Drive. Continue 2.4 miles to Verde de la Montura and turn left. Drive to the end of the road and park at the trailhead.*

Upper Santa Ynez Canyon Falls

Escondido Canyon Falls (Upper & Lower)

Rating: 8

How Short? 4.2 Miles

How Easy? 2

Best Time to View:
December to May

Need Information?
Contact: Santa Monica
Mountains National
Conservation Authority
(310) 454-1395

Providing you visit shortly after a rainfall, Escondido Canyon's waterfalls are two of the best coastal falls in Southern California. In fact, I'd go so far to say that Upper and Lower Escondido Canyon Falls could inspire you to become a waterfall lover. To sum it up, these waterfalls, set back in Escondido Canyon in the Santa Monica Mountains National Recreation Area, are absolutely striking in the rainy season.

The trek begins on a paved road. After parking in the Winding Way Trail parking area at the intersection of Highway 1 and Winding Way Road, walk roughly one mile up the road as it gradually climbs uphill, passing multimillion-dollar homes that overlook the ocean. Even without seeing the waterfalls, many sightseers would be satisfied with the splendid view of these magnificent homes.

You'll come to a sign at a small plateau on the road, which reads "Santa Monica Mountains Conservancy Parkland." Continue on the road another 100 yards past the sign to a locked gate and another sign that reads "Escondido Canyon Natural Area." Make a left at this sign and walk down to the stream. Cross the stream and make a left, heading up Escondido Canyon. Although five stream crossings are required to reach the Lower Falls, steppingstones in the creek make most of these crossings easy.

A few trails break off the main path, but don't let them lead you astray. If in doubt, follow the stream. Just before reaching Lower Escondido Falls, you'll be able to glimpse the upper portion of Upper Escondido Falls in the canyon above. Fewer than 100 yards ahead, the trail ends at the lower falls.

Hugging a limestone face covered in ferns and mosses, the frothy water cascades down the 60-foot drop, emptying into a pool too shallow for wading. As splendid as the lower falls may be, remember it is the smaller of the two. Twice as tall, Upper Escondido Falls awaits approval upstream.

To reach the upper falls, follow a trail that begins on the south side of the stream and ascends the mountain. It first passes a series of small cascades and then crosses the stream, finally leading to the base of the upper falls, also a limestone waterfall.

The lip of the upper waterfall reminds me of a small spoon that extends over the side of a cliff. The stream spills off its end, freefalling about five feet before crashing onto another ledge and cascading into a small wading pool.

If you plan to make the trip, supplies are available in Malibu.

Also nearby are Zuma Falls and Solstice Canyon Falls.

Directions: *From Los Angeles drive north on the 101 Freeway to Agoura Hills, exit Kanan Road and turn left. Continue on Kanan Road to Highway 1 and turn left. Drive approximately 1.5 miles to Winding Way Road. Turn left in the parking lot for the Winding Way Trail.*

Upper Escondido Canyon Falls

Christian Perez in front of Escondido Canyon Falls

Solstice Canyon Falls

Rating: 4

How Short? 2.1 Miles

How Easy? 1

Best Time to View:
January to May

Need Information?
Contact: Santa Monica
Mountains National
Recreation Area
(805) 370-2301

Many of the waterfalls on Southern and Central California's coast are located in state parks, which means that biking and/or walking your dog to the falls is prohibited. Solstice Canyon Falls is an exception. Located in Solstice Canyon Park, part of the Santa Monica National Recreation Area, the trail to the waterfall is paved, well signed, easy to follow and fairly flat. Also, it's ideal for a short bike ride or a nice run with the family dog, providing it's on a leash.

Solstice Canyon Falls is not an imposing waterfall, however, it's easy to reach and so close to Highway 1 that many hikers and nature lovers visit it regularly. It's just over a mile to the falls, which is a suitable walk for even the smallest child.

The walk begins next to the Solstice Canyon information board in the day-use parking area. The path follows Solstice Canyon Creek the entire way, crossing the creek only once via a bridge before reaching the falls. Just after the bridge, the trail splits. Follow it to the right, heading up Solstice Canyon.

A little more than halfway to the falls, the Keller House can be seen on the left. According to the park brochure put out by the National Park Service, it's the oldest existing stone building in Malibu. Beyond this point the trail splits, but it doesn't matter which fork you take. They both end up in the same place.

The next trail marker is the Tropical Terrace. The Tropical Terrace was once the home of the Roberts Family, who resided on what was formerly called Roberts' Ranch. Although the home burned in a fire in 1982, remnants of it and its surrounding ranch are still visible. A park ranger told me giraffes, camels and buffalo used to roam the ranch.

The waterfall is just past the terrace, directly behind a chimney that still stands on the house's foundation. This 25-foot high cascade is the parks main attraction. There are many other small cascades and waterfalls to explore upstream, but most people choose to nose around the Tropical Terrace, searching through the rubble of the burned house.

Solstice Canyon Park has many other trails to explore, including the TWR Loop Trail, Deer Valley Loop Trail, Rising Sun Trail and Sostomo Trail.

***Directions** and trip info for Dry Creek Falls also apply to Solstice Canyon Falls.*

Solstice Canyon Falls

Dry Creek Falls

| Rating: 3 |
| How Short? 1.2 Miles |
| How Easy? 1 |
| Best Time to View: January to April |
| Need Information? Contact: Santa Monica Mountains National Recreation Area (805) 370-2301 |

Throughout most of the year, Dry Creek is just that: bone dry. If you rush to the creek shortly after a rain, however, it can leave a much different impression.

The Dry Canyon Trail follows Dry Canyon Creek six-tenths of a mile to this 150-foot waterfall. Although the height of the waterfall may sound grandeur, the waterfall itself most likely won't be. Because the stream that feeds the waterfall is surrounded by a small watershed, it struggles to stay alive most of the year.

Of all the hiking trails in Solstice Canyon Park, Dry Canyon Trail is the least used. Yet it is well maintained. The signed trail begins in the day-use parking area. Hiking the trail requires two easy stream crossings. Then, it gradually works its way uphill, back into the canyon. Because of homes that can be seen on the hillsides, hikers aren't exposed to the wilderness on this trail the way they are on other trails in the park. On a more positive note, however, this trail is dirt, whereas the other trails are mostly paved.

When the trail ends near the back of the canyon, you'll see the waterfall on the left. Most likely only a dribble of water will be coming down the mountainside. It doesn't

become spectacular until immediately after a large rainfall. There is a trail spur that breaks off from the main trail down to the falls' base, but the view is best from the main path. Also, the trip to the base is a bit tricky, because the foliage that grows over the trail includes some poison oak.

If you plan to make the trip, supplies are available in Malibu. The park is opened to day-use only.

Also nearby are Solstice Canyon Falls, Escondido Canyon Falls, Circle X Ranch Falls, the Grotto, Malibu Creek State Park, Zuma Canyon Falls and Newton Canyon Falls.

Directions: *From the intersection of Highway 1 and Kanan Road in Malibu, drive approximately 3.5 miles south to Corral Canyon Road. Turn left and drive three-tenths of a mile to the entrance on the left for Solstice Canyon Park. Turn left and continue to the day-use parking area at the end of the road.*

Dry Canyon Falls with a mere sliver of water trickling down its face

Zuma Canyon Falls

Rating: 6

How Short? 1.0 Mile

How Easy? 3

Best Time to Visit:
January to April

Need Information?
Contact: Santa Monica
Mountains National
Recreation Area
(805) 370-2300

If you want to take a short, rugged hike through the Santa Monica Mountains National Recreation Area and see three great waterfalls in one trip, Zuma Canyon Falls and Upper and Lower Newton Canyon Falls can all be seen on a one-mile excursion. This is not, however, a good place to bring kids.

Viewing Lower Newton Falls is effortless, but getting to the base of Upper Newton and Zuma Falls can take some work. After the easy hike to Lower Newton, the trail disappears. There's so much poison oak in its place, however, you'll be tempted to walk in the stream to escape it. And to get to the base of Upper Newton, some tough downhill climbing is required.

So, if you're still ready to begin, lets get started: From the parking lot, pick up the Backbone Trail signed for Zuma Ridge Motorway. The trailhead is directly behind the information kiosk, where you can read about the Backbone Trail and the Santa Monica Mountains. After one switchback, the trail enters Newton Canyon and crosses over Newton Canyon Creek before curving to the left. After this bend, look for a few trail spurs that veer to the left and take one of these spurs down to the stream.

If you choose to view Upper Newton Canyon Falls (see Newton Canyon Falls write-up), make a left at the stream. For Lower Newton Canyon and Zuma Falls, continue downstream. When you reach the stream, the trail is faint, and in most places it can't be see at all. After about 100 yards of rock-hopping is the brink of Lower Newton.

To reach Lower Newton's base and gain access to Zuma Canyon, follow the trail along the left side of the falls. Here's where things get a little hairy. There is a vertical descent to the base, and if it's rained in the past few weeks it will be difficult, because the steep hillside will have loose, slippery mud. Carefully scramble down to the base. From this point, continue downstream about 40 yards, where Newton Canyon Creek meets Zuma Canyon Creek.

Although there are many falls in Zuma Canyon, Zuma Canyon Falls is the only one I recommend. Take a right at Zuma Canyon Creek, and in approximately 10 minutes you'll be staring at the falls. Not as dramatic as Upper and Lower Newton Falls, 30-foot Zuma flows over a sandstone face. In high water, it crashes down onto a trash can-sized boulder, forming two drops.

For experienced hikers in great physical condition, there are several other waterfalls downstream. There is no trail leading to them, nor are they shown on any maps. They're located about 10 minutes downstream from where Zuma and Newton Canyons connect. If you try the hike, you will get wet because several stream crossings are required. Reaching these waterfalls is extremely difficult and not generally recommended.

Directions and trip info for Newton Canyon Falls also applies to Zuma Canyon Falls.

Zuma Canyon Falls

Newton Canyon Falls

Rating: 7

How Short? 1.0 Mile

How Easy? 2

Best Time to View:
January to April

Need Information?
Contact: Santa Monica
Mountains National
Recreation Area
(805) 370-2300

It's 11 a.m. You and a few friends are traveling west on Kanan Road on the way to Zuma Beach, however, the marine layer has yet to lift, and the day is beginning to look gloomy. You need to kill some time before the sun breaks through the clouds, but are having trouble deciding what to do. I'll make the decision for you. Take the short, but worthwhile trip to Upper and Lower Newton Canyon Falls. It will cut less than an hour off your schedule, and, providing you visit in the winter or spring, chances are you won't be disappointed with what you see.

The two waterfalls located in the Santa Monica Mountains National Recreation Area are perfect for a short, but rewarding side trip. Upper Newton Canyon Falls is simple to reach. The trail to the falls is well-maintained, easy to follow and short. It begins from the north end of the parking lot, works its way down a switchback, and then crosses the stream a few yards above the falls.

The falls can't be reached from this point, though. Continue on the trail as it bends to the left and look for a few trail spurs that work down into the canyon on the left. Take any of the spurs and continue down to the stream. Once you've reached the stream, walk upstream to the falls.

Although Upper Newton Falls is most impressive after a rainstorm, it usually flows year-round. The falls is only 25 feet tall, but can be pretty when water races over its limestone face.

Locating Lower Newton Canyon Falls is a pushover, but getting to its base can be a little tricky. The feat requires confidence in your hiking abilities. To reach Lower Newton Falls, walk approximately 100 yards downstream to the brink of the falls. There is no maintained trail on this section of the hike, so bushwhacking is required. Chances are you'll get your feet wet to avoid brushing up against poison oak.

Once at the top of the falls, it's time to use caution.

Upper Newton Canyon Falls

At this point, the narrow trail arcs around the left side of the falls and descends to its base, however, in the rainy season the terrain can get wet and muddy, causing unsafe trail conditions. Even excellent climbers can slip, lose their balance and fall. While on this section of the trail, make sure you always have hold on a tree or rock to keep your balance. The vertical descent may only be 25 yards, but it's not an easy

The path to Newton Canyon Falls

climb.

   Lower Newton Falls is far more dazzling than its upper counterpart. It's wider, at least 20 feet taller and has an assortment of mosses and ferns hugging its face. From here, either continue downstream to Zuma Canyon or begin climbing back to your car. Remember, the marine layer has burned off, and now it's time to hit the waves.

If you plan to make the trip, supplies are available in Malibu.

Also nearby are Zuma Canyon Falls, Escondido Falls, La Jolla Canyon Falls, The Grotto, Sycamore Canyon Falls and Troutdale.

Directions: *From Highway 1 in Malibu, drive north to Kanan Road. Turn right and drive 4.3 miles to a dirt pullout on the left side of the road, just after the first tunnel. If coming from Agoura Hills, take the Kanan exit off the 101 Freeway and drive west approximately eight miles (through two tunnels) to a dirt pullout on the left.*

Lower Newton Canyon Falls

The Grotto

Rating: 5

How Short? 3.5 Miles

How Easy? 2

Best Time to View:
January to May

Need Information?
Contact: Santa Monica
Mountains National
Recreation Area
(805) 370-2301

Over the last few years, access to the Grotto has changed, although the Grotto itself hasn't been altered. The Grotto used to be a popular drive-to waterfall set near a campground, but visitors who have visited regularly over the past couple of decades often find themselves shocked upon their return in the 21st-century.

One big shocker is that Happy Hollow Road, which used to extend from the ranger station to Happy Hollow Campground, is no longer in service. Because the road continually got washed out in the winter, the National Park Service grew tired of paying $10,000 a year to repair it, and opted to close it for good.

You can still walk the road to Happy Hollow Campground, but it might look different than you remember. Trees and plants have been placed on the road to rehabilitate the area from the effects of the road. Happy Hollow Campground is also closed. There is a new group camp near the ranger station, and it is opened for camping.

The best way to reach the Grotto is by taking the Grotto Trail. Park at the ranger station and walk down Happy Hollow Road to the group camp. (If the road is opened, you can save two-tenths of a mile by driving to this point.) Walk through the group camp to the Grotto Trailhead. The path gradually descends four-tenths of a mile to a junction with the Canyon View Trail. Stay right, cross the stream, and as the trail curves to the left, you'll

get a view of 40-foot high Botsford Falls over your left shoulder.

After Botsford Falls, the trail gradually works its way up a hill for a short period of time, before descending to the West Fork of the Arroyo Sequit Creek. On the way down, keep an eye out for H.H. Falls on the left and Triunfo Falls straight across the canyon. The trail descends to a flat area that looks ideal for a campsite. It once was a parking lot for an old Boy Scout camp, but is no longer in use.

The path then crosses the creek and angles off to the right, working its way down to where Happy Hollow Campground used to be. In fewer than 10 minutes, the trail begins to fade in and out, requiring numerous stream crossings. This is the area just above the Grotto.

Stay along the right side of the stream. The left side is too steep to navigate. Fifty yards downstream, the Grotto awaits. The Grotto got its name because of the cave-like (grotto) area that sits behind two side-by-side freefalls dropping some 20 feet each. There is a giant boulder splitting the water's descent into two parallel drops. The pool

below the waterfalls can be deep enough for a swim, providing there is still enough water in the stream for the falls to flow forcefully.

There are many other small cascades downstream, which require a steep climb, but none are as striking as the Grotto. A few-hundred yards downstream, the creek leaves Circle X Ranch and enters private property. The boundary isn't marked, so be careful not to wander too far. A ranger told us that a resident hangs out down there and shoots at hikers who wander onto her property.

If you plan to make the trip, supplies are available in Malibu.

Also nearby are Circle X Ranch Falls, Escondido Canyon Fall, Zuma Canyon Falls, Newton Canyon Falls, Troutdale, Dry Canyon Falls, Solstice Canyon Falls and Malibu Creek State Park.

Directions: From the intersection of Kanan Road and Highway 1in Malibu, drive north on Highway 1 to Yerba Buena Road, less than two miles past Leo Carrillo State Beach. Turn right on Yerba Buena Road and drive approximately 5.5 miles to Circle X Ranch on the right.

The Grotto Falls

Circle X Ranch Falls (Botsford, H.H., and Triunfo Falls)

Rating: 6

How Short? 2.0 Miles

How Easy? 2

Best Time to View:
January to April

Need Information?
Contact: Santa Monica
Mountains National
Recreation Area
(805) 370-2301

For decades, hikers visited Circle X Ranch to hike down to the Grotto and explore it. Prior to spring of 2000, campers were able to drive to Happy Hollow Campground and walk less than 100 yards to get to the Grotto. Since then, the road to Happy Hollow has been closed, the campground has been shut down, and the Grotto has become far less popular, because it requires a longer walk to reach.

Although it's true the road closure has been the reason why fewer people visit the campground and Grotto, it has also increased visitation to three waterfalls that visitors previously overlooked. The Grotto Trail has been in existence as long as the road, yet hikers used to drive down the road instead of walking down the trail, preferring the shorter trip. Now, visitors hike along both the road and the Grotto Trail to get to Happy Hollow Campground. By taking the Grotto Trail, hikers are

now exposed to three waterfalls along the path. The waterfalls are on the way to the campground, and are thrilling in late winter and spring.

To reach these waterfalls from the visitor center at Circle X Ranch, drive two-tenths of a mile down the access road to the group camp. Walk through the campground to the Grotto Trailhead. From this point, it's 1.3 miles to the Grotto, but the falls are located well before reaching it.

The trail gradually descends four-tenths of a mile, before coming to the junction with the Canyon View Trail. Stay right at this junction; shortly, you'll be standing at the top of Botsford Falls. The path crosses over the stream just above the falls. The waterfall is about 40 feet tall and looks a lot like Trail Canyon Falls in the Angeles National Forest. There is no trail to its base.

The Grotto Trail continues, bending to the left and then briefly ascending, providing a superb view of the canyon below. After sloping downhill, the path comes to the unofficial H.H. Waterfall Overlook. Look to the left, you can't miss H.H. Falls. It's twice as tall as Botsford Falls. H.H. and

H.H. Falls

Botsford Falls were both named by Boy Scout Troops, and together they form the headwaters of the West Fork of Arroyo Sequit Creek.

You can also see Triunfo Falls from H.H. Waterfall Overlook. Triunfo Falls is fed by water from Big Buck Spring, as well as by runoff from the mountains above Triunfo Pass. Triunfo Falls is a freefall that drops some 50 feet before hitting the canyon bottom. The freefall is pretty, but rarely is its volume equal to the amount of water that would come out of a large garden hose. The spring that feeds it usually dries up by summer, and after a long dry spell, the waterfall dries up.

If desired, a trip to the base of Triunfo Falls is possible, but it's a long trek. Continue on the trail to the bottom of the canyon, where you'll come to a stream crossing. This area used to be a campground, however, camping is now off-limits here. Head upstream, following the creek to a small tributary that feeds the main stem. Follow the

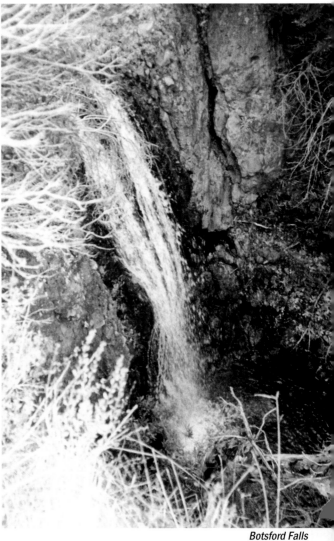

Botsford Falls

tributary to the base of the falls. If you scramble up the main stem, you'll end up at H.H. Falls. Reaching both of the falls requires quite a bit of bushwhacking; unfortunately there's a lot of poison oak and no trail.

If you plan to make the trip, supplies are available in Malibu.

Also nearby are the Grotto, Escondido Canyon Falls, Zuma Canyon Falls, Newton Canyon Falls, Troutdale, Dry Canyon Falls, Solstice Canyon Falls and Malibu Creek State Park.

Directions: *From the intersection of Kanan Road and Highway 1 in Malibu, drive north on Highway 1 to Yerba Buena Road. (It's less than two miles past Leo Carrillo State Beach.) Turn right on Yerba Buena Road and drive approximately 5.5 miles to Circle X Ranch on the right.*

La Jolla Canyon Falls

Rating: 4

How Short? 1.5 Miles

How Easy? 1

Best Time to View:
January to April

Need Information?
Contact: Point
Mugu State Park
(805) 488-5223

The Santa Monica Mountains National Recreation Area and Point Mugu State Park rival each other for great hiking trails. Both are located in the coastal mountains close to the beach, and receive heavy visitation. Most waterfall lovers, however, choose to hike in Point Mugu State Park.

Two of Point Mugu State Park's waterfalls are located at the Ray Miller Trailhead, between Oxnard and Malibu, directly across from Thornhill Broome State Beach in La Jolla Canyon. Strolling to these easy-to-reach falls requires little effort, and hikers of all ages can enjoy the well-maintained trails.

Two trails set out into the wilderness from the parking lot. The right one is the Backbone Trail, and the much wider one on the left is the La Jolla Canyon Trail. There is a locked gate you'll need to walk around to access the La Jolla Canyon Trail. From the trailhead sign, about 10 yards past the gate, the trail briefly swoops downhill and crosses the stream, which will most likely be dry even during the rainy season. The path then bends to the left and parallels the streambed, but never drops down into it.

In a few hundred yards, follow the canyon as the trail curves to the right, dips downhill and then crosses the stream again. Now, the trail stays on the north side of the canyon. From this point, it's less than a five-minute walk to the falls.

The waterfalls, mere trickles most of the year, are far from spectacular, especially from June through December when the stream struggles to stay alive. Even during the rainy months the stream is hardly impressive. I arrived a week after a heavy rainstorm, and there was no water in the stream below the falls, nor were the falls flowing. The scant runoff hugged the falls' faces and dribbled down to their bases, brushing through thick algae and moss that blanketed the rocks.

The two waterfalls, both about 20 feet tall, are clearly visible from the trail. Both have small pools at their bases. If you choose to hike past the falls, well-maintained La Jolla Canyon Campground, which is commonly used by boy scouts, is less than a mile away.

A side note: After driving into the parking lot and passing over a dry streambed that is fed by the falls, many visitors decide not to go see them. Don't assume that just because this streambed is dry, the falls will also be dry. Downstream from the falls, the water travels underground.

If you plan to make the trip, supplies are available in Malibu.

Also nearby is Solstice Canyon Falls.

Directions: *From the 101 Freeway in Ventura, drive south and exit Highway 1. Drive south on Highway 1 through Oxnard and continue to the signed turnoff for La Jolla Canyon. Turn left on La Jolla Canyon. Then, veer left at the first fork in the road and park in the parking lot. The trailhead can also be reached by driving approximately 20 miles north of Malibu on Highway 101.*

A dry La Jolla Canyon Falls

Sycamore Canyon Falls

Rating: 3

How Short? 2.4 Miles

How Easy? 2

Best Time to View:
January to April

Need Information?
Contact: Santa Monica
Mountains National
Recreation Area
(805) 370-2301

While hikers dominate the western and coastal accesses to Point Mugu State Park, the eastern access is mostly used by mountain bikers. The non-coastal section of the park near Newbury Park is ideal for these bikers, with scenic trails that both beginners and more experienced mountain bikers can enjoy. There's even a trail to the Pacific Ocean. One of the few trails these bikers aren't permitted on, however, is the one where waterfall enthusiasts go. And you have to be an "enthusiast" to visit the waterfall in Sycamore Canyon, because its volume is almost always a trickle.

Not only waterfall lovers take the hike to the falls. It's also popular with those looking for a wilderness experience in an area close to the city. In fact, the trip to the waterfall is perfect for a family walk. It's short enough for young kids to handle, and has a wide variety of scenery to keep them occupied the entire trip.

From the day-use parking area, follow signs to the Satwiwa Cultural Center, a quarter-mile away. Where the gravel trail becomes a paved road, the Cultural Center and Chumash Demonstration Area are on the left. Continue uphill on the paved road for another quarter-mile to a water tank on the right.

At this point, turn left on the Old Boney Trail, leaving the paved road and taking a much narrower dirt trail. There are two turnoffs for the Satwiwa Loop Trail that will beckon you to leave the Old Boney Trail. Continue straight. At the top of the hill, is a "y" in the trail. The left fork goes to the Hidden Valley Overlook, 1.1 miles ahead. Stay right, following signs to the waterfall, six-tenths of a mile away.

In another 15 feet, is the boundary of Pt. Mugu State Park. Continue downhill on the wide dirt trail. Just before crossing the stream, there's a trail on the right that guides hikers downstream. Don't take it; it leads away from the waterfall. Cross the stream and climb uphill. Pass a sharp right turn in the trail, continuing straight along the much narrower path that parallels the stream. There's a sign that says "No Horses"

Sycamore Canyon Falls

at this juncture. Partially overgrown in places by poison oak, the trail continues another 75 yards to the base of the falls.

At approximately 100 feet tall, although Sycamore Canyon Falls is grand in size, it suffers from low water levels. Its stream runs year-round, but is kept to a trickle most months. Following a downpour, however, the falls can be moving as the stream swells and cascades off its sandstone ledges.

The falls' first few drops are the most dramatic. Each is 10 to 15 feet tall, emptying into wading pools. The last drop is a cascade that is nearly 50 feet, but due to the lack of volume, its thin trickle of water hardly causes a glisten on the sandstone face,

making it lackluster to most visitors.

From the end of the trail at the base of the falls, a little rock-hopping is required to reach the upper cascades. The only way to do it is to cross over to the right side of the stream and then follow a faint hiker's trail winding through the slippery rocks. Use caution not to slip. This section of Sycamore Canyon is heavily shaded and rich with ferns and other foliage. As you take time to enjoy it, remember the city is a mere two miles away.

If you plan to make the trip, supplies are available in Newbury Park. No bikes or dogs are permitted on the last half-mile of the trail to the falls.

Also nearby are Wildwood Falls, La Jolla Canyon Falls and Malibu Creek State Park.

Directions: *From the 101 Freeway in Thousand Oaks, exit Lynn Road. Turn south and drive 5.4 miles to Via Goleta. Turn left and drive to the last parking lot, where you can pick up the trailhead.*

Maytal Schvartz at the base of Sycamore Canyon Falls

Region Angeles National Forest/ LA Basin

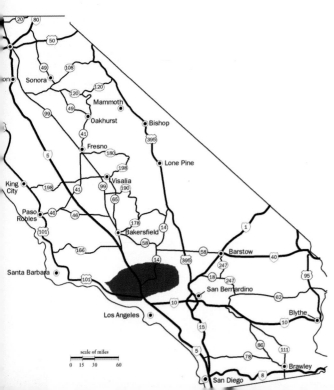

Paradise Falls
Piru Creek Falls
Bouquet Canyon Creek Falls
Placerita Canyon Falls
Devils Punchbowl Falls
Lower Punchbowl Falls
Earthquake Falls
Trail Canyon Falls
Fox Creek Falls
Fall Creek Falls
Fall Creek Road Falls
Lucas Creek Falls
Upper Big Tujunga Falls
Cooper Canyon Falls
Buckhorn Falls
Switzer Falls
Millard Canyon Falls
Rubio Canyon Falls
Bailey Canyon Falls
Sturtevant Falls
Hermit Falls
Eaton Canyon Falls
Monrovia Canyon Falls
Soldier Creek Falls
San Antonio Falls

Paradise Falls

Rating: 7

How Short? 2.4 Miles

How Easy? 1

Best Time to View:
December to May

Need Information?
Contact: The Conejo
Park District
(805) 495-6471

Residents of Thousand Oaks aren't used to seeing water in the form of a stream, lake or even runoff in drains. So, when they're told there's a waterfall less than a five-minute drive from the Thousand Oaks Mall, they're usually stunned.

"No way," said a person who overheard me talking about the waterfall in a sporting goods store in the mall. "There can't be. I live in Thousand Oaks. There are houses here. How could there be a waterfall?"

There is, and a damn good one. Located in Wildwood Park, near Lynn Road, Wildwood Falls in one of the best in the region, and it's also one of the easiest to reach. It's a 1.2-mile walk to the base of the falls, and worth the trip.

From the day-use parking area off Avenida de los Arboles, pick up the trailhead behind the kiosk and follow the Mesa Trail away from the sign pointing towards parking lot No. 1. The trail (more of a dirt road) continues straight for nearly a half-mile, gaining maybe 20 feet in elevation. There is thick grass on both sides of the path, and also tall, rocky mountains on the right.

Where the road intersects a signed turnoff for the Teepee Overlook and Paradise Falls, veer away from Lizard Rock and Box Canyon, taking the left fork towards the Teepee Overlook. The path arcs around a mountain, and in a few hundred yards, brings you to a large teepee that overlooks the canyon below.

Near the teepee, veer right at a signed junction pointing towards Wildwood Canyon, Paradise

The path to Paradise can get pretty muddy after a rainstorm

Falls, Skunk Hollow, Sycamore Flats and Oakgrove Area. A wide dirt path winds down into the canyon. As the route begins to level out and angles off to the left, a small trail spur breaks off to the left. Follow the trail spur down to the Wildwood Picnic Area, just above the falls.

To the left of the picnic area, the path comes to the Wildwood Falls Overlook. (Paradise is also known as Wildwood.) This will be your first glimpse of 70-foot Paradise Falls, but this side view isn't as rewarding as the observation point from below. So, continue back towards the picnic area and veer left on a side trail that descends to the base of the falls.

The freefall has a powerful flow in the winter and spring as it plunges off a sandstone cliff. Paradise has a wide, deep foam-covered pool below, lined with tules. I've seen people wade in the pool, but the water looked too murky to me. After storms, the water takes on a brownish color, and with all the trash I saw in the stream, both above and below the falls, I didn't think it was a good idea to take a swim.

Instead of taking the same route back to the parking lot, try continuing past the overlook. The path parallels the stream up the canyon and leads to picnic areas and a few small caves. It makes for a great loop trip. There are signs pointing back to the parking lot, so you don't have to fret about getting lost.

If you have a chance, take the Indian Creek Trail back to the parking lot. Near where the trail meets up with Avenue de los Arboles, keep an eye out on the right for a 30-foot drop over a rock ledge, situated in a dark canyon below a group of houses. It can be inspiring in the spring.

If you plan to make the trip, supplies are available in Thousand Oaks. Depending on road and trail conditions, the park is sometimes closed after winter storms to protect trails. Call ahead for information. If the road into the park is open, you can bypass the first part of the hike by driving a half-mile to a lower parking area and following signs to the falls.

Also nearby are Sycamore Canyon Falls, Malibu Creek State Park, Point Mugu State Park and La Jolla Canyon Falls.

Directions: From the 101 Freeway in Thousand Oaks, exit Lynn Road and drive 2.5 miles north to Avenida de los Aroboles. Turn left and drive about a mile to the parking area on the left.

Paradise Falls

Piru Creek Falls

Rating: 4

How Short? 1.5 Miles

How Easy? 1

Best Time to View?
Year-Round

Need Information?
Contact: Angeles
National Forest
(661) 296-9710

Piru Creek Falls isn't a great waterfall. In fact, personally, I would never plan a hike to it with the sole purpose of viewing the waterfall. There are two reasons why I chose to include the waterfall in this book; the first, the waterfall is listed in the California Department of Fish and Game's regulations book, and second, it's used by many anglers as a land marker. Hundreds of anglers have heard of the waterfall, yet few can put a picture to its name.

Piru Creek Falls is situated in the Angeles National Forest, roughly one mile below Pyramid Lake Dam and a half-mile upstream of Frenchmans Flat. The waterfall was created by a huge slab of concrete poured back in the days before Interstate 5 was built. In those days Highway 99 was the main gateway from the Central Valley to Southern California. The falls rests alongside Old Highway 99.

Over the years, a purpose has evolved for the concrete. The falls designates the start of the wild trout section of Piru Creek. The CA DFG stocks Piru Creek with rainbow trout below the falls, however, upstream only wild trout reside. No plants are made here and the creek is governed by special fishing regulations.

Piru Creek Falls is a 15 foot freefall that is fed by cold water from the base of Pyramid Dam. Releases are maintained year-round to ensure the wild trout have sufficient water conditions to maintain their population.

Reaching the waterfall takes little work. All the hiking is done on a paved road. Begin at the locked gate at Frenchmans Flat. Walk through the gate and continue upstream, following the four lane road. In four-tenths of a mile, you'll come to a footbridge over Piru Creek. Push on. In another quarter-mile you'll see a small pond on the left. Two-tenths of a mile ahead is the waterfall on the right.

The pool below the falls is deep enough to wade in. I don't recommend it though. Not only are there hundreds of fishing hooks and lures stuck on the rocks in the water, there's also broken glass and trash everywhere. Its unfortunate people can't clean up after themselves, and their lack of respect for the environment is truly evident here.

If you plan to make the trip, supplies are available in Castaic. A Forest Service Adventure Pass is required to park in the Angeles National Forest.

Also nearby are Quail Lake and Castaic Lake.

Directions: *From Interstate 5 in the San Fernando Valley, drive north through the Santa Clarita Valley and past Castaic to the Templin Highway exit. Exit and make a left. You'll drive under the freeway and come to a stop sign. Turn right and continue to the locked gate and parking area at the end of the road.*

Piru Creek Falls

Bouquet Canyon Falls

Rating: 4

How Short? Drive-To

How Easy? 1

Best Time to View:
February to June

Facilities: None

Need Information?
Contact: Angeles
National Forest
(661) 296-9710

If you ask yourself why you made the trip to Bouquet Canyon Falls, it's got to be because you have small children who aren't ready for the big falls yet, right? Bouquet Canyon Falls is an easily accessible waterfall that can be enjoyed by people of all ages. Reached by a short 10-minute drive from Valencia and Saugus to its location in the Angeles National Forest the small cataract is one of the few drive-to waterfalls in the region.

The waterfall is less than 20 yards from Bouquet Canyon Road, which connects the Santa Clarita and Antelope Valleys. Fed by Bouquet Reservoir, which is closed to the public, this 20-foot freefall almost never dries up. It provides local residents with a nearby adventure; the roundtrip to the falls, including stopping to enjoy it, is doable in less than two hours, if you start out from anywhere in the Santa Clarita Valley.

Surprisingly, the falls isn't heavily visited, with the exception of the late spring and summer, when people wade in the stream. Most of Bouquet Canyon Creek's visitors are anglers who show up in the spring and summer to catch stocked trout. They inadvertently stumble upon the falls, only to find out they're fishing in the wrong place; fish aren't stocked here. They can, however, be caught about a mile downstream.

Although the falls is heavily shaded by tall trees, it isn't spectacular in any way. It's just a good place to bring kids to see their first waterfall. Walking to the brink or the base of the falls from your car should take no more than three minutes.

Bring along a camera; you'll probably want to take some shots of your kids cooling off beneath the falls. There's always enough water for them to play around in, but never too much to make things dangerous.

If you plan to make the trip, supplies are available from the general store just downstream of Streamside Campground. A Forest Service Adventure Pass is required to park in the Angeles National Forest.

Also nearby are Castaic Lake, Castaic Lagoon and Magic Mountain.

Directions: From Interstate 5 in Santa Clarita, drive north to Valencia Blvd. Turn right and continue to Bouquet Canyon Road. Turn left and follow the road past Saugus High School, to about a mile downstream of Bouquet Reservoir. The waterfall is on the left side of the road.

Rick Spadaro at Bouquet Canyon Falls

Placerita Creek Falls

Rating: 4

How Short? 2.0 Miles

How Easy? 1

Best Time to View:
January to April

Need Information?
Contact: Placerita
Canyon County Park
(661) 259-7721

Many parents would love to educate their children about the trees, plants and shrubs that grow in the wild. Most children, however, don't enjoy walking through nature centers to learn about poison oak and other poisonous plants. Kids are hands-on; they want to learn by exploring on a trail in the "real" outdoors.

Only a five-minute drive from Canyon Country in the Santa Clarita Valley, Placerita Canyon Park is the perfect place to teach children about nature. The signed trails are well groomed and easy to walk. One trail even escorts you to a small waterfall, giving kids an added incentive to get out and learn about nature.

So, how is this trail different from other trails in the wilderness? Where's the learning experience? The last half-mile of the trail has signs on both sides of the path pointing out different plants that are commonly found in the wild. Signs point to poison oak, which is found all around the path, and distinguish the different types of trees, ferns and other flora.

Interested? How do you sign up? The trail begins at the Walker Ranch Gate of Placerita County Park. Since no bikes are allowed, walk through the park entrance, following a dirt road as it bends to the right and descends to a stream crossing through Placerita Creek. After crossing the creek, continue another 100 yards uphill.

On the left, there's a rock wall about two feet high that marks the signed Waterfall Trail. Take a left at the junction and walk about 150 yards over the grassy hills to a sign that says: "Waterfall Trail 1/3 Mile." From this point, the trail narrows and escorts you into the canyon. The waterfall is a short 15-minute walk away. Nearing the falls, the greenery thickens, the path makes a few more stream crossings and the trail changes from packed dirt to a rocky base that meanders through the streambed. There are several stream crossings before you reach the end of the trail at the base of 25-foot Placerita Creek Falls.

Although the waterfall isn't fantastic, it is a great place to get your children excited about the outdoors. The falls is formed by Placerita Creek, which cascades down a dark rock face into a cool canyon below. Oaks heavily shade this canyon, and moist ferns glisten along its fertile hillsides.

If you plan to make the trip, supplies are available in Canyon Country. There is a day-use fee to park in the main entrance, but not at the Walker Gate.

Also nearby is Earthquake Falls.

Directions: *From the San Fernando Valley, drive north on Interstate 5 to the 14 Freeway and exit Placerita Canyon Road. Drive four miles to the Walker Ranch entrance of Placerita Canyon Park.*

Tom Bomar atop Placerita Canyon Falls

Devils Punchbowl Falls

Rating: 3

How Short? 1.4 Miles

How Easy? 1

Best Time to View?
December to April

Need Information?
Contact: Devil's
Punchbowl Natural
Area (661) 944-2743

It would be safe to say Devils Punchbowl County Park offers some of the most vibrant and intriguing rock formations in California. However, to say the park's waterfalls are worthwhile is out of the question. Hiking at the park for my first time I asked the man working at the visitor center (which is excellent I might add) if there were any waterfalls in the park. I was kidding. His answer, however, stunned me.

"Yes," he said. "We have several. One of them is spectacular." I was speechless. "Spectacular," I thought to myself. There was no way. There was no flowing water around here. Well, nothing more than a trickle. Spectacular was no doubt out of the question.

The visitor center was exceptional, as was the wildlife on display, including a hawk that had a broken wing after being hit by a car and an owl that was also injured. The

Devils Punchbowl County Park

waterfalls, on the other hand, were pathetic. By definition there were a few waterfalls in the county park. I sure as heck wouldn't send anyone here to see them. Their flow was limited to the amount that comes out of a three liter bottle of Dr. Pepper. If I put my foot atop the falls I could have stopped the flow altogether. Yes, in most years it does only run in the late winter and spring.

At any rate, it is remarkable there were waterfalls in this arid desert, but don't come for the water. Come for the rocks formations, the desert wildlife, and the natural arches of course.

If you are coming for the waterfall, start at the visitor center and pick up the well signed Loop Trail. The path descends for a half-mile to the bottom of the canyon where it meets the stream. Abandon the path and scramble downstream. You'll pass a smaller nine-foot waterfall and then the one-tenth of a mile downstream you'll get a glimpse of the "spectacular" waterfall, a 17-foot freefall. Unfortunately, steep banks prohibit you from reaching the base of this sandstone waterfall. No biggie. Head back to the trail and complete the one mile loop trip.

If you plan to make the trip, supplies are available in Pearblossom.

Sandstone formations in Lower Devils Punchbowl Canyon

Also nearby are Little Rock Reservoir, Lower Devils Punchbowl Canyon Falls and Big Rock Creek.

Directions: *From the junction of the 14 and 5 Freeways just north of the San Fernando Valley take the 14 Freeway north and take the Pearblossom Highway/Angeles Forest Highway exit. After exiting, veer left onto Pearblossom Highway and drive 5.8 miles to Highway 138. Turn right and continue 8.6 miles to Longview Road and turn right again. Drive 2.2 miles and turn left on Fort Tejon Road. Continue three-tenths of a mile and make a right to get back onto Longview Road. Drive 2.2 miles to Tumbleweed Road and turn left. Continue three miles to the county park.*

This hawk can be seen on display at Devils Punchbowl County Park

Lower Devils Punchbowl Falls

Rating: 3

How Short? 2.0 Miles

How Easy? 1

Best Time to View?
January to April

Need Information?
Contact: Angeles
National Forest
(661) 944-2187

Unlike Devils Punchbowl, Lower Devils Punchbowl Canyon gets few visitors and is rarely publicized. The waterfall is even more pitiful than the ones at Devils Punchbowl. They can't be found on any maps, nor will you hear people talk about them. I first heard about the waterfall here, while fishing Big Rock Creek for trout.

I was approached by a hiker who was rock-hopping the creek asking anglers about a waterfall on one of Big Rock's tributaries. He said he read about it in a hiking book, but was unable to locate the falls. This intrigued me, and being the thrill seeker I am, I headed back the next weekend after scanning my topo maps to find this "waterfall" the man had heard of.

He was able to tell me where the trailhead was, that the waterfall was said to be small and somewhere in Lower Devil's Punchbowl Canyon. It didn't take us long to find the waterfall, if that's what you really want to call it. Located on an unnamed creek, which is more or less a seasonal trickle the word pitiful would be describe this uneventful drop. Lower Devils Punchbowl Falls isn't worth visiting if you are hiking solely to see a waterfall. However, the rock climbing and sandstone rock formations are hard to beat.

Minus the crowds, Lower Devils Punchbowl offers some of the coolest sandstone formations in Southern California. Reaching them isn't that difficult. Begin at the dirt pullout on the east side of Big Rock Creek Road. Carefully cross the road and then rock hop across the stream. Just downstream of where the bridge is (and the abandon graffiti shacks) you'll see a small stream dumping into Big Rock Creek on the west side. Follow this stream for three-tenths of a mile to a fork in the canyon. There is no path so don't waste time trying to find one. Stay right, and continue upstream for six-tenths a mile to a point where you can't continue further upstream because of steep sandstone ledges and a small four-foot waterfall. Keep in mind that if it hasn't rained hard recently this stream may not run at all.

Now that you've come to realize that a 4,300 feet in the Angeles National Forest, this waterfall is one of the worst you've ever seen, enjoy the rock climbing, because it won't disappoint you.

If you plan to make the trip, supplies are available in Pearblossom. A Forest Service Adventure Pass is required to park in the Angeles National Forest.

Also nearby are Little Rock Reservoir and Jackson Lake.

Directions: *From the junction of the 14 and 5 Freeways just north of the San Fernando Valley take the 14 Freeway north and take the Pearblossom Highway/Angeles Forest Highway exit. After exiting, veer left onto Pearblossom Highway and drive 5.8 miles to Highway 138. Turn right and continue 8.6 miles to Longview Road and turn right again. Drive one-half mile to Avenue W and turn left. In a half-mile Avenue W becomes Valyermo Road. Drive 6.1 miles and turn right on Big Rock Creek Road. Drive eight-tenths of a mile to a dirt pullout on the left.*

Earthquake Falls

Rating: 5

How Short? Drive-To

How Easy? 1

Best Time to View:
January to April

Need Information?
Contact: Angeles
National Forest
(818) 899-1900

Although earthquakes are common in Southern California, waterfalls that tumble down earthquake faults are almost unheard of. Located near Sylmar in Little Tujunga Canyon, north of the 118 Freeway, Earthquake Falls is located directly on the San Gabriel Fault, approximately seven miles from the epicenter of the 1971 San Fernando Earthquake.

The fault line is visible in the jagged gneiss cliff face. The water slides down the mountainside only partially following this unusual vertical fissure, because the fissure loops in and out of the waters path. And after a heavy rainfall, the fissure is difficult to see under the thick blanket of water.

Although not breathtaking in any way, the falls is an easy drive for residents of the

Santa Clarita and San Fernando Valleys. Because it's one of only two drive-to waterfalls in Los Angeles County, it's a good place to bring children. The waterfall can be seen from the car, however, by walking less than 20 yards along a path, you can be standing at its base.

Earthquake Falls is 70 feet tall. The upper tier is 15 feet and the lower some 55 feet high. Although most of the time water dribbles down its rock face, it can be remarkable for a few days after a hard rainfall. Visit anytime later than early May and the waterfall may be dry.

If you plan to make the trip, a Forest Service Adventure Pass is required to park in the Angeles National Forest.

Also nearby are Hansen Dam Lake and Hansen Ponds.

Directions: *From the 405 Freeway at the north end of the San Fernando Valley, exit east on the 118 Freeway and drive to Osborne Street in Lake View Terrace. Exit Osborne and turn left on Foothill Blvd. Drive two-tenths of a mile to Osborne Street and turn left. Drive 9.8 miles to a dirt pullout on the right. There is a sign with a write-up about earthquake faults that are visible from the pullout.*

Earthquake Falls

Trail Canyon Falls

Rating: 8
How Short? 4.0 Miles
How Easy? 2
Best Time to View: January to July
Need Information? Contact: Angeles National Forest (818) 790-1151

Los Angeles is a monstrous metropolis that encompasses a wide variety of terrains and ecosystems, offering Southern Californians a unique lifestyle. It is also home to a national forest with boundaries so diverse they span from pine-covered mountains to barren deserts. For sheer variety, this forest rivals any other in the nation. The Angeles National Forest encompasses a significant portion of the county as well as the majority of its open space, boasting snow-capped mountains that abound with spectacular waterfalls, high dry deserts and trout-filled rivers and streams. Sadly, millions of Angelinos take it for granted, ignoring it from year to year.

Trail Canyon Falls is a good place to begin taking advantage of the forest's resources. Only a 10-minute drive from Sunland, this waterfall's stunning beauty will quickly transport you away from thoughts of nearby congested freeways, trash-lined streets and crowded shopping malls. Located in Lower Big Tujunga Canyon, the trail to the falls is popular among those who do venture into the outdoors, especially on spring weekends.

Trail Canyon Falls

Scott Wiessner cools off at Trail Canyon Falls

From the dirt parking area, pick up the trail near the stream. The first stretch of the path is a dirt road that steadily climbs uphill through a group of cabins. After about three-fourths of a mile, it makes a sharp left turn, and a spur breaks off to the right. Leaving the fire road, follow the spur and head down into the canyon to Trail Canyon Creek.

Now, under a canopy of sycamores, alders and cottonwoods, the path crosses the creek a few times before ascending a hillside and leaving the stream. Having abandoned the trees, there is no cover to protect you from the hot sun. The trail is overgrown with chaparral and brush, so wearing long pants would be smart. Well above the stream, the path follows a straightaway for roughly 200 yards before bending to the left, working its way up the canyon. Shortly, you'll get your first glimpse of the lip of Trail Canyon Falls. The rest is hidden in the canyon below.

There are two ways to view the falls. One is to continue on the path to the top of the falls, where a few trails lead to its brink. The view from its base, however, is much better. To get there, walk 20 yards back down the trail to a path that descends the canyon. Take this steep path to the base of 50-foot Trail Canyon Falls. This freefall is one of the best in the forest. Even in June, when many of the other falls in the forest have turned to a dribble, Trail Canyon has a consistent flow. Also, there is a gravel-bottom pool about waist deep at its base. It feels great to take a dip on hot days.

If you plan to make the trip, supplies are available in Sunland. A Forest Service Adventure Pass is required to park in the Angeles National Forest.

Also nearby are Upper and Lower Big Tujunga Creek, Fox Creek Falls, Lucas Creek Falls, Fall Creek Falls, Fox Falls, Upper Big Tujunga Falls and Fall Creek Road Falls.

Directions: *From the 210 Freeway in Sunland, exit Sunland Blvd. and turn left. Continue east on Foothill (Sunland Blvd. becomes Foothill) to Oro Vista. Turn left and drive to Big Tujunga Canyon Road. (Oro Vista becomes Big Tujunga Canyon Road.) Continue north on Big Tujunga Road to Trail Canyon Road. Turn left on the dirt road. After a quarter-mile, there is a locked gate on the left. Veer right and continue to the dirt parking area. The trail is on the northwest side of the lot.*

Trail Canyon Falls on July 4th, 1998

Fox Creek Falls

Rating: 8

How Short? 7.0 Miles

How Easy: 4

Best Time to View:
February to April

Need Information?
Contact: Angeles
National Forest
(818) 790-1151

Fox Creek Falls is the best waterfall in the Angeles National Forest. Among the millions of Los Angeles residents, ironically, probably fewer than 500 have seen it. Part of the reason it is so rarely visited is because people don't know it exists. Also, viewing the waterfall up close requires an enduring off-trail hike with numerous stream crossings. I can guarantee you'll get wet!

At 2,300 feet in the Angeles National Forest, Fox Creek Falls is hidden at the back of one of Big Tujunga's Reservoir's arms. Although it would be easy to reach with a boat, watercraft is forbidden at the reservoir. As a matter of fact, there is no way down to the reservoir's banks.

In heavy rain years, such as the El Nino season in 1998, the waterfall can't be reached at all. Reservoir keepers let Big Tujunga overflow, and the water backs up so far into the canyon that the arm leading to Fox Creek Falls becomes flooded. It is rare, however, for the reservoir to become this full. In the first few years of the 21st Century, earthquake repairs are planned for the dam, which will require that the reservoir be left nearly empty. Then, reaching the waterfall won't be a problem.

If there has been measurable rainfall in the months of December and January, 60-foot Fox Creek Falls is worth the trip. Sometimes it freefalls and other times it slides down the smooth gneiss cliff face, depending on the volume of water in the stream.

Brett Ross crosses Big Tujunga Creek in the winter of 2002

Getting to the falls takes at least two hours of hiking and climbing, and it can take up to three if you take breaks. Chances are you'll take a lot of breaks. There are opportunities to fish for wild rainbow trout in Big Tujunga Creek. You'll also pass Fall Creek Falls and Lower Fall Creek Road Falls, not to mention dozens of swimming holes. Plan on spending the entire day to do the trip right.

Although there are lots of activities to keep you busy, the trip is not one for inexperienced hikers or young children. An array of obstacles, including heavy brush, poison oak, ticks, dangerous stream crossings and rattlesnakes (as the weather begins to warm in early spring) must be overcome.

The adventure begins at a locked gate at Fall Creek Road, less than a mile north of the Big Tujunga Reservoir Overlook. Walk along the wide, open trail down to the Big Tujunga Creek crossing, descending 700 feet over 1.8 miles.

On the way you'll pass Upper Fall Creek Road Falls, which is 1.15 miles from the trailhead. It's a small series of cascades on the right as you cross over the first and only stream before coming to Big Tujunga Creek. Beyond crossing the stream, the trail bends to the left and then begins to straighten out.

At the end of the straightaway, before the trail bends back to the right, look down into the canyon on your left. The same stream you crossed produces a 30-foot freefall, but because of the steep mountainside, it's too difficult to reach. In another half-mile, scan the canyon to your left for a view of all four tiers of Fall Creek Falls.

When the trail intersects Big Tujunga Creek, abandon the road and head downstream. From this point on, there is no trail. After 10 minutes of boulder-hopping, the four-tier Fall Creek Falls will be on the right. From this vantage, however, only the bottom tier can be seen. After passing Fall Creek Falls, another 15 minutes of scrambling is required to reach the next landmark, a small hill between the canyon walls. Behind that hill is Lower Fall Creek Road Falls, a 60-foot drop.

Now things get difficult. The canyon narrows, and the easy stream crossings found in the first part of the trip, where there were boulders to step on, are no longer an option. Don't bother taking your time to search up and down the stream for stepping-stones, just walk through the stream. In other words, you are going to have to get wet.

At times, the canyon is so thick with brush, bushwhacking is required. A fire hasn't swept through this canyon since the 1975 Mill Creek Fire, so the trees, poison oak and brush have had more than 25 years to grow. It would be wise to check yourself often for ticks, too. You will frequently be rubbing up against brush, and the chances of picking them up are good.

Now the canyon begins to open up into a wide, flat area, and it's time to keep an eye out for a sizable stream entering from the right. This is Fox Creek, 3.15 miles from the trailhead. Veer right, following the creek upstream. This stream is also heavily overgrown and has steep, sandy hillsides. Follow upstream for less than four-tenths of a mile to the falls, where you'll find a small wading pool, which is not deep enough to swim in. Take a break, eat a sandwich, and remember it's a long climb back to the car.

Viewing Fox Creek Falls is possible without the long hike, but it's far less rewarding. From the trailhead, walk about 50 yards past the locked gate to the end of the straightaway. Looking across the canyon, in the back of one of the canyon arms you'll see the upper portion of the falls. It can be best seen with a pair of binoculars.

If you plan to make the trip, supplies are available in Sunland. A Forest Service Adventure Pass is required to park in the Angeles National Forest. Call the Forest Service in advance to check on water conditions.

Also nearby is Lucas Crreek Falls.

Directions: *From the 210 Freeway in Sunland, exit Sunland Blvd. and turn east. Continue east on Foothill (Sunland Blvd. becomes Foothill) to Oro Vista. Turn left and continue to Big Tujunga Canyon Road. (Oro Vista becomes Big Tujunga Canyon Road.) Drive approximately one mile past Big Tujunga Reservoir to a locked gate on the left side of the road.*

Fox Creek Falls

Fall Creek Falls

Rating: 7

How Short? 4.0 Miles

How Easy? 3

Best Time to View:
February to April

Need Information?
Contact: Angeles
National Forest
(818) 790-1151

Hidden in Big Tujunga Canyon just above Big Tujunga Reservoir, Fall Creek Falls is one of only a few waterfalls in Southern California that has more than one tier. Actually, it has four, and its total height is more than 250 feet, making it the tallest waterfall in the Angeles National Forest. Despite its enormous height, however, Fall Creek Falls isn't a popular destination. Few hikers know it exists.

Fall Creek Road provides the only view of all four tiers of the waterfall, but the road is closed to vehicular traffic, so you'll have to travel on foot. The walk to the waterfall is easy, except for the last three-tenths of a mile where some bushwhacking is required. The view from the road, however, is much better than from its base and requires a lot less energy.

If you decide to walk to the falls, the trip begins at the locked gate on the left side of the road, less than a mile past the Big Tujunga Reservoir Overlook. Walk around the gate and follow the dirt road as it descends, dropping 700 feet over 1.8 miles. When the path hits Big Tujunga Creek, leave the dirt road and begin walking downstream. There is no path here, and a few stream crossings are required. The final three-tenths of a mile should take roughly 10 minutes.

From this point in Big Tujunga Canyon, only the bottom tier of the waterfall is visible. Dodging dozens of yucca plants, bushwhack your way to the base of the falls. Give or take a few feet, the lower tier is 80 feet tall. I saw a rope hanging from the top of the waterfall to its base, but I couldn't figure out its purpose; it was overgrown with moss and too slippery to climb.

To see the upper three tiers, climb back to Fall Creek Road. After less than five minutes of ascending, look across the canyon to view the lower tier of the waterfall. Above the lower tier there is a small grouping of mostly alder trees. Tucked behind the trees is a 30-foot waterfall, which can be difficult to see without a pair of binoculars.

Above this 30-footer are a 55-footer and a 40-footer; both are easy to spot. There are more waterfalls higher up, but they can't be seen from here. The only downfall with Fall Creek Falls is that it is fed by a seasonal stream and only becomes dramatic after a consistent rainy season.

Directions *and trip info for Fox Creek Falls also applies to Fall Creek Falls.*

The base of Fall Creek Falls

Fall Creek Falls from a half-mile away

Fall Creek Road Falls

Rating: 6

How Short? 5.0 Miles

How Easy? 3

Best Time to View:
February to April

Need Information?
Contact: Angeles
National Forest
(818) 790-1151

Upper Fall Creek Road Falls used to be a drive-to waterfall. When Fall Creek Road was closed to vehicular traffic in the early Eighties, however, the waterfall stopped being as big of an attraction. Although Fall Creek Road passes by the waterfall, the Forest Service closed it because Southern California Edison could not maintain it for passenger cars. Fall Creek Road was mostly used by those heading to Fall Creek Campground on the other side of Big Tujunga Creek, but the road kept getting washed out at the stream crossing. Now called "Fall Creek Trail Camp," the campground is rarely used, except by a few Boy Scout troops.

Fall Creek Road Falls consists of two waterfalls, both fed by an unnamed stream that crosses under Fall Creek Road. The upper waterfall is the easiest to reach, but it's the less notable of the two. It's made up of a series of small cascades, none taller than 20 feet, and because it's hidden back in the canyon, it's difficult to see.

To reach these cascades from the locked gate on Big Tujunga Road, walk around the gate and continue 1.15 miles down the road to the first and only stream crossing. No rock-hopping is required. The stream is channeled through a tunnel under the road, and the cascades are visible on the right.

Lower Fall Creek Road Falls is the better of the two. This waterfall requires a bit of off-trail hiking, but it's worth it, providing there is a sufficient amount of water in the stream. Unless there has recently been a decent rainfall, the stream will turn to a trickle, and the waterfalls won't be worth visiting.

From the upper falls, continue just over a half-mile, where the road runs into Big Tujunga Creek. Just before the road drops down into the canyon, look across the canyon, to the left for a view of all four tiers of Fall Creek Falls. At the stream, leave the road, heading downstream. Although there is no trail to follow, there are a few markers to use. The first marker is Fall Creek Falls, which can be seen on the right side of the canyon after 10 to 15 minutes of rock-hopping.

After passing Fall Creek Falls, another 10 minutes of stream crossings and bush whacking are required before coming to Lower Fall Creek Road Falls. A small mountain between the two canyons is the best marker to let you know you've reached the right spot. Once you pass the mountain, look for a small stream on the left side of Big Tujunga Creek. There is a lot of overgrown brush where the stream enters the creek, but if you look above the brush, the waterfall should be easy to spot.

If desired, a trip to the base is doable. Simply follow the stream, dodging the many yucca plants to the waterfall. It's a 2.5-mile trip to the falls, that has a 60-foot drop.

Directions *and trip into for Fox Creek Falls also apply to Fall Creek Road Falls.*

Lower Fall Creek Road Falls

Lucas Creek Falls

Rating: 6

How Short? 1.8 Miles

How Easy? 4

Best Time to View:
February to March

Need Information?
Contact: Angeles
National Forest
(818) 790-1151

On our way to Lucas Creek Falls, my friend Manny Martins suddenly stopped dead in his tracks. "I thought you said we were going hiking. This isn't hiking. This is a damn adventure," he said. "Next time you call and ask me to go hiking, the first thing I'm going to find out is whether there's a trail or not. If you say there isn't, I'm going to tell you I'm sick." He took a few more steps and continued, "I'm going to be dead tired for at least a few days after this." Manny couldn't have picked better words to put our "adventure" in perspective.

North of Sunland, in the Angeles National Forest, the hike to Lucas Creek Falls isn't for everyone. Actually, few can handle it. For me, that's what makes the trip so rewarding. Hardly anyone's seen Lucas Creek Falls, and it will probably remain that way forever.

This is the only book in which you'll be able to read about the hike to Lucas Creek Falls, because it's such a well-kept secret and I'm sure will remain so even after the printing of this write-up. The waterfall is just too difficult to reach; and the fact that there is no trail and there are several major obstacles to overcome before reaching the falls makes things even tougher. You have to be determined to make it to this waterfall.

You ask what's so difficult that I would risk talking you out of a trip to the falls? Where should I start? Hmm… Let's begin with all the threats you'll face along the way. There are fields of poison oak, ticks, yucca plants and mosquitoes, not to mention hundreds of downed trees and slippery boulders to climb over, as well as difficult clambering through a steep narrow canyon.

Still interested in going to the falls? For those thrill-seekers who are, here are a few tips before attempting to locate the trailhead. Because of the brush, poison oak and ticks, wearing long pants and a long-sleeved shirt is a must. Also, wear pants that don't get heavy when waterlogged. Unless you can walk on water, you will get wet. There is no way around it. In fact, for much of the way the stream is the trail.

Lets get started. Finding the trailhead can be a little tricky. From the dirt pullout, carefully cross Angeles Forest Highway and locate a metal guardrail. From the west end of the guardrail, walk about 20 steps (to the right, passing by the end of the guardrail). Then look for a small clearing between the brush and small trees. Walk through the opening (which will be overgrown) and follow the trail 30 yards as it twists and turns down to the stream.

On the left you'll see 30-foot Upper Lucas Creek Falls. This waterfall cascades down a narrow chute of gneiss, which, over the years, seasonal flows of water have carved into sharp jagged points. After the first 20 feet of the drop, the water crashes onto a small rock ledge and fans out, splashing against the surrounding

The base of Upper Lucas Creek Falls

canyon walls before tumbling to the base. But this isn't the main attraction. Just make sure your shoes are laced up, and let's keep moving.

There are several markers that can be used to let you know how far away the falls are. First, 20 yards downstream there's another 20-foot freefall. To get around it, scramble down its right side. The canyon then bends to the left, and within ten minutes, a small feeder stream enters from the right. Making it to this point without getting your feet wet is easily doable, but past here, chances dim from slim to none.

Now, the canyon begins to look like a war zone. Hundreds of fallen trees lie across a stream that is less than a foot deep and three feet wide. Debris from rockslides is piled up in the stream, looking like stone breakwaters in the ocean. Thousands of dead branches cover the ground, and each time you take a step, it sounds like walking on Coco Puffs cereal. Every 10 yards or so, mosquitoes suddenly swarm as if you've stepped on a beehive. Still having fun? Good, things get better.

path can be wet!

Now that you've abandoned the game of trying to keep your shoes dry, a few hundred yards of twisting and turning through the canyon brings you to Fern Canyon No. 1. This is one of my favorite parts of the hike. By now, hopefully you've realized that the stream is your only chance of a trail. If not, well, then check your body for poison oak in the morning.

The streambed is now one solid slab of rock, and the nearly vertical canyon on the left will be alive with hundreds of maidenhair, lady and polypody ferns that cling to its face from the stream upwards to 20 feet. Continuing downstream, the next marker will be a 20-foot high cascade. Steep mountains on both sides force you to walk along the slippery rock in the three-foot deep pool below.

Now, using the stream as the path, it's time to be extra careful. Not only will the bottoms of your shoes be wet, but the rocks will also be extremely slippery. Not a good combination for keeping solid footing; and let me tell you, it's not a great feeling when you know you're going to be slip-sliding along the rocks and can't to do a damn thing about it. It feels like ice-skating. Yes, many of the rocks are that slippery.

Another 10 minutes brings you to the toughest part thus far. After the stream bends to the left, the canyon narrows and becomes fewer than 10 feet wide. The stream cascades down into a five-foot-deep pool, and unless you have Spiderman abilities to cling to the surrounding cliffs, you are going swimming. The good news is that at this point on the way back, you can avoid the pool by walking up over the hill on the south side of the cascade. The bad news is that there is no way to help you identify where this point is on the way back.

Shortly after reaching the pool, the stream passes Fern Canyon No. 2, which is identical to No. 1, and then zigzags further down the canyon. The last major marker is a group of three small cascades you must wade through. (The water is waist high.) From this point, the top of the falls is about five minutes away. You'll know you've reached it when a 30-foot freefall prohibits further travel downstream. Wait! You aren't done yet!

From the brink, backtrack a few steps and look at the hill on the left. There is a small trail that cuts through the brush. Follow the trail, pushing your way through hundreds of overgrown bushes, then climb down the steep mountainside. The trail disappears and reappears, but if you keep working down the mountain, you'll come to an area shaded by oaks.

Now, having emerged from Lucas Canyon, you'll be along the banks of Big Tujunga Creek. Make a right and walk about 30 yards to Lucas Creek. Take a right at Lucas Creek and walk 20 yards to the base of Lower Lucas Creek Falls. This 20-foot freefall also tumbles over a ridge of gneiss. Just above, is Middle Lucas Falls, a 30-foot freefall, however, from this point, only the top 10 feet can be seen. Unless you have rappelling gear, the middle falls can't be seen in its entirety.

The entire walk to the lower falls should take from 45 minutes to an hour and 15 minutes, and now that you've come all this way, you might as well make a day out of it. Just upstream on Big Tujunga Creek, there is a sandy beach ideal for tanning. And anglers can be kept occupied by small wild rainbow trout.

Leave yourself at least an hour and 15 minutes to walk back up the canyon. Your body will be pretty tired, so the climb back out with its 600-foot elevation gain should take a lot longer than the hike in.

There are a few more things to keep in mind when coming to Lucas Creek Falls. Although there is still plenty of water in the stream well into early May, I strongly discourage you from coming after March. Walking the trail after this time isn't safe. I came once in early April and saw three baby rattlesnakes in the first 100 yards of the hike. Also, the stream dries up by summer and doesn't start to flow again until February.

If you reach the base of Upper Lucas Falls and don't see any water, the lower and middle falls will also be dry.

If you plan to make the trip, supplies are available in Sunland. A Forest Service Adventure Pass is required to park in the Angeles National Forest. In poor rain years, Lucas Creek Falls may not run long. Plan your trip accordingly.

Also nearby are Upper and Lower Big Tujunga Creek, Upper Big Tujunga Falls, Fox Creek Falls, Falls Creek Falls and Fall Creek Road Falls.

Directions: *From the 210 Freeway in Sunland, exit Sunland Blvd. and turn east. Continue east on Foothill (Sunland Blvd. becomes Foothill) to Oro Vista. Turn left and continue to Big Tujunga Canyon Road. (Oro Vista becomes Big Tujunga Canyon Road.) Drive north on Big Tujunga Road past the Big Tujunga Reservoir Overlook to a stop sign. At the stop sign, turn left on Angeles Forest Highway and drive 1.1 miles to a dirt pullout on the right.*

Manny Martins at Lower Lucas Creek Falls

Upper Big Tujunga Falls

Rating: 5

How Short? 1.0 Mile

How Easy? 2

Best Time to View:
February to June

Need Information?
Contact: Angeles
National Forest
(818) 899-1900

You live in Southern California and enjoy adventures, but don't like driving several hours to find a nice juicy one? For the residents of the San Fernando and San Gabriel Valleys, less than an hour away, a great adventure awaits with open arms. Upper Big Tujunga Falls gives the feeling of being remote, but it's an easy hike that's worthy of a half-day trip. The falls may only be 20 feet tall, but in a region scarce on wilderness, where waterfalls are rare, who's complaining?

Upper Big Tujunga Falls is found along a quiet, heavily shaded scenic stretch of Upper Big Tujunga Creek. The route to the falls is a fun-filled escapade for those who don't mind getting their feet wet. There are nice swimming holes, fishing opportunities and wildflowers along the way.

Before going, however, make sure you know what poison oak looks like, because it flourishes all along the stream's banks. Also, be alert for rattlesnakes. The combination of greenery and water make it prime habitat.

Depending on the time of the year, the falls can either flow forcefully or present a more delicate drop. In spring of 1998 during El Nino year, the falls were 10 feet wide and plummeted over the cliff; but in the springs of '99, '00 and '01, the width rarely extended more than three feet, and the stream rolled gently over the falls' lip. The strength of the falls depends on rainfall and the snow pack in the San Gabriel Mountains. In most years, the falls dries up by late July.

Fishing for planted rainbow trout can be good in the pool below Upper Big Tujunga Falls

Begin the hike at the bridge that crosses over Upper Big Tujunga Creek, and descend down the trail on the north side of the stream. This trail leads less than one-tenth of a mile downstream, before crossing the creek and continuing south another one-tenth of a mile to a stream crossing. After this crossing, it is nearly impossible to avoid getting your feet wet.

When the trail disappears, follow the stream to the falls. There are several useful markers to let you know that you're heading in the right direction. First, on the left is a small stream that cascades down the mountainside into the creek. Then, as the stream curves to the right, there is a lovely sandy beach that's perfect for swimming. Finally, just beyond the beach, are a series of fallen logs over the stream.

After passing these markers, you'll be directly above the falls. Stay on the left side of the stream and continue another three minutes to the base of the falls. There are also smaller cascades downstream, but because of slippery rocks and difficult terrain, they can be difficult to reach.

If you want to do a little fishing while you're here, there are many rainbow trout in the stream and in the pool below the falls. The California Department of Fish and Game stocks the creek several times during the spring.

Still have some energy to burn? Try climbing Strawberry Peak, the tallest peak on the western part of the San Gabriel Mountain Range. The trailhead is in the parking lot behind the trash cans.

If you plan to make the trip, supplies are available in Sunland. A Forest Service Adventure Pass is required to park in the Angeles National Forest.

Also nearby are Big Tujunga Dam, Lower Big Tujunga Creek, Copper Canyon Falls, Buckhorn Falls, Switzer Falls, Trail Canyon Falls and Arroyo Seco Creek.

Directions: *From Pasadena, drive west on the 210 Freeway to Highway 2 (Angeles Crest Highway) and turn right. Drive nine miles to Clear Creek Ranger Station and turn left on County Road N-3. Continue 12 miles Angeles Forest Highway and turn right. Continue to Upper Big Tujunga Road and turn right. Drive approximately three miles to a sign for Colby Camp. Turn right and follow the winding road to the stream.*

Travis Tikugawa poses next to a seasonal waterfall downstream of Upper Big Tujunga Falls

Cooper Canyon Falls

Rating: 7

How Short? 3.2 Miles

How Easy? 3

Best Time to View:
January to July

Need Information?
Contact: Angeles
National Forest
818-790-1151

It was on New Years Day in 1999 that I learned there is a real winter in Los Angeles. A few friends and I decided to do something different and go camping on New Year's Eve. Our destination, Buckhorn Campground, was covered in snow; the ground was frozen and nighttime temperatures dipped into the teens. What intrigued me most, however, was discovering a partially frozen Cooper Canyon Falls on our hike the next morning.

Cooper Canyon Falls' face was covered in thick ice. The ice was so dense that throwing a rock at it wouldn't break it. Beneath the ice, Cooper Canyon Creek dribbled down the face of the falls, maintaining a small but consistent flow in the stream, and keeping the pool below the falls from freezing solid. There were also dozens of icicles hanging from the rocks around the falls.

At 5,775 feet in the Angeles National Forest, less than an hour's drive from Pasadena, Cooper Canyon Falls is one of the San Gabriel Mountain's prettiest waterfalls; yet it's also one of the least visited. Watching the lustrous water glide down the glistening rock face into a sparkling emerald pool, I couldn't help but wonder why so few people come to view it. The falls is just minutes from Mt. Waterman Ski Area and can be reached via a hike that is achievable for people of all ages. The trail is well marked, maintained regularly and easy to follow. Somehow, crowds rarely form, and if you arrive in the winter, chances are only a few other two legged creatures will be around.

After crossing Buckhorn Creek, the trip begins on the Burkhart Trail, just beyond the campsites at the end of the access road to Buckhorn Campground. The trail parallels Buckhorn Creek, running above it for the first 1.1 miles. In spring and summer, wildflowers bloom along this part of the path, and towering cedars and pines shade the trail. After 15 minutes, keep an eye out for a few trails on the right that lead down into the canyon to seldom-visited Burckhorn Falls.

After 1.1 miles, the trail narrows and makes a sharp left turn, descending down a long switchback into Cooper Canyon. Then, the trail follows Cooper Canyon Creek, crosses over Buckhorn Creek and parallels Cooper Canyon Creek the rest of the way to the falls.

A few minutes after crossing Buckhorn Creek, a trail veers off to the left, towards Cooper Canyon Campground. Don't take this turnoff; continue on the Burkhart Trail for approximately 10 minutes to the falls. First, is the unsigned falls overlook, where a series of small cascades can be seen prior to your arrival at the main waterfall. The smaller cascades are approximately 20 feet tall, and the main waterfall stands at 25 feet tall.

Take note of the large clear pool below. Only those who can tolerate cold water dare to swim in it; but, aside from its frigid temperatures, the pool is ideal for swimming. There are also wild rainbow trout in the pool.

Reaching the falls' base can be difficult. There is a spur trail down to it, but the first 20 yards are steep and there are loose rocks and dirt that make it difficult to get secure footing. Because of slippery rocks and a steep slope, the use of a rope is needed to complete the last part of the trail, and one is provided.

Depending on the season you arrive, the falls changes character. Most of the time in winter, Cooper Canyon Falls is partially frozen over. In spring and early summer, it flows fast and is spectacular. From late summer through fall, it subsides. No matter what time of year, however, it's always worth visiting. Just keep in mind that on the way back to your car the climb consists of a 675-foot elevation gain. Take the trip slow, enjoy the forest, and you won't even notice it.

If you plan to make the trip, a Forest Service Adventure Pass is required to park in the Angeles National Forest. In winter, the access road to the campground closes, so you'll have to park at the gate located along Highway 2, signed for Buckhorn Campground, and walk through the campground to the trailhead. It adds an extra four-tenths of a mile to your trip. Also, in winter, call ahead for road conditions. Chains may be required.

Also nearby are Buckhorn Falls, Mt. Waterman, Pacific Crest Trail, Upper Big Tujunga Creek and Mt. Wilson.

Directions: From the 210 Freeway in Pasadena, drive west to Highway 2. Exit north on Highway 2 and drive approximately 34 miles to Buckhorn Campground on the left. Turn left into the campground and follow the signs to the trailhead.

Cooper Canyon Falls on New Years Day in 1999

Buckhorn Falls

Rating: 6

How Short? 1.2 Miles

How Easy? 4

Best Time to View:
January to June

Need Information?
Contact: Angeles
National Forest
(626) 796-5541

Quiet campsites are hard to come by in Southern California. Litter-free Buckhorn Campground, near Mt. Waterman in the Angeles National Forest, however, is one of the few remaining campsites not battered by overuse. Buckhorn Creek flows through this campground that is heavily shaded by cedar and pine trees.

Buckhorn Campground is also a favorite spot for Boy Scout troops. Because of the vast array of flora and fauna found in and around the campground, troops use it as a kind of nature center. Although the scouts make regular visits to Cooper Canyon Falls, few of them know about Buckhorn Falls, which, at 6,300 feet, is on the way to Cooper Canyon Falls. That's probably because steep cliffs make it difficult to reach and no signed trails lead to it. Yet, if you have some route-finding skills, Buckhorn Falls is worth a peek.

There are two ways to get to the falls, and they differ drastically in difficulty. The easiest way is by walking up Buckhorn Creek from Cooper Canyon. The hike begins at the end of the access road to Buckhorn Campground on the Burkhart Trail, just beyond the campsites, after crossing Buckhorn Creek. It's the same trail that leads to Cooper Canyon Falls.

The trail runs above Buckhorn Creek, paralleling it for the first 1.1 miles. After that, it narrows, makes a sharp left turn and drops down a long switchback into Cooper Canyon. It then follows Cooper Canyon Creek and crosses Buckhorn Creek. At this point, make a right and begin rock-hopping up the creek. There is no trail, but you won't get lost if you continue seven-tenths of a mile upstream to the base.

The shorter but more difficult way requires some route-finding skills. From the same trailhead, follow the Burkhart Trail approximately a half-mile. It should take 10 to 15 minutes. Begin looking for a small, unsigned trail spur on the right, descending the canyon.

Buckhorn Falls

The spur appears after a few small waterfalls that can be seen and heard from the trail. Follow the spur down to Buckhorn Creek. Cross the creek, climb over a small hill and carefully scramble down the mountainside to the base of the falls. A word of caution: this route is only recommended for experienced hikers. It is extremely difficult to find secure footing on the loose rocks and soil.

There is a small pool below the falls, perfect for wading, but it's not deep enough for swimming. Buckhorn Falls is 70 feet tall, however, due to a lack of volume in its stream, water normally clings to the falls' face, as opposed to shooting out forcefully. Unfortunately, it can be reduced to a dribble by early summer.

***Directions** and trip info for Cooper Canyon Falls also apply to Buckhorn Falls.*

Switzer Falls

Hands down, Switzer Falls is the most popular waterfall in the Angeles National Forest. Located downstream from the overused Switzer Picnic Area, the waterfall gets more visitors than any other waterfall in the San Gabriel Mountain Range, and for a good reason: Less than 20 minutes from La Canada, the trail to the falls is short and easy, allowing parents to bring their children and pets to the waterfall.

There are two waterfalls for you to enjoy. Both the upper and lower falls can be seen from the same trail, which is shaded by large trees keeping you cool on even the hottest days. But before heading down to the falls, it might be a good idea to do a little fishing. The California Department of Fish and Game stocks the creek with rainbow trout each spring.

Begin your descent at the day-use picnic area and cross the bridge over Arroyo Seco Creek. Walk downstream on the paved trail, following the creek until you come to Commodore Switzer Camp, about 10 minutes after the trail changes from cement to dirt. There is no actual campground here, just a few remains of one that was used years ago.

Cross the stream and head uphill. Shortly, you'll get a view of Upper Switzer Falls. For those who wish to continue to the bottom of the falls, at the junction of the Gabrielino and Bear Canyon Trails, veer left, heading down to the stream. When you reach the stream, turn left and walk a quarter-mile to Lower Switzer Falls. Lower Switzer is comprised of two drops: a 15-foot cascade piggybacked on a taller 20-footer.

There's also a great swimming hole below the falls. If you attempt to climb above the lower falls to the upper falls, be aware that the route is slippery and dangerous. If you're a skilled hiker, however, it's doable, and will bring you to the bottom of 50-foot Switzer Falls.

A side view of Switzer Falls

If you plan to make the trip, supplies are available in La Canada. A Forest Service Adventure Pass is required to park in the Angeles National Forest. Switzer Picnic Area is open for day-use only.

Also nearby are Upper Big Tujunga Creek, the Royal Gorge, Upper Big Tujunga Creek Falls, Mt. Wilson, Cooper Canyon Falls, Mt. Waterman and Buckhorn Falls.

Directions: *From the 210 Freeway in La Canada, take Highway 2 north and drive 9.8 miles to the Switzer Picnic Area on the right.*

Millard Canyon Falls

Rating: 5

How Short? 1.0 Mile

How Easy? 1

Best Time to View:
January to April

Need Information?
Contact: Angeles
National Forest
(626) 574-5200 or
(818) 790-1151

Most parents have a hard time dragging their kids away from the TV, but a trip to Millard Canyon Falls might do the trick. A 10-minute drive from La Canada, Millard Canyon Falls is a 60-foot freefall in the Angeles National Forest, and a recreational area heavily used by families. It provides a close, but real getaway from city life, which won't take more than an hour or two out of the day to visit.

The trail is short, easy, well maintained and suitable for even the smallest child. Because the waterfall is fed by Millard Creek, there is one big downfall: the short window of time when you can see it in full bloom. Millard flows in the early spring or right after a rainstorm, otherwise, there are just a few drips of water dribbling down its face. The falls usually totally dries up by late April.

Millard Canyon Creek, which finds its origins at the bottom of the falls, is fed by an extremely small watershed and is dependent on heavy rainfall before it flows. Two small streams, Grand Canyon Creek and Saucer Branch Creek, merge at the end of Millard Canyon and form the freefall, which is framed by canyon walls covered in moss.

For those who want to make a day out of it, there are also campgrounds and picnic areas near the parking lot. From the parking lot, pick up Millard Creek and follow it upstream through the campgrounds into Millard Canyon. Passing a few cabins, the canyon walls begin to narrow. Continue upstream, crossing the creek several times to the falls. You can't miss it. The stream ends at the falls, where vertical walls prohibit further passage.

If you plan to make the trip, supplies are available in La Canada. A Forest Service Adventure Pass is required to park in the Angeles National Forest.

Also nearby are Eaton Canyon Falls and Rubio Canyon Falls.

Directions: *From the 210 Freeway in Pasadena, exit Lake Avenue and turn north. Drive 3.5 miles to Loma Alta Drive and turn left. In one mile you'll come to a flashing yellow light and see a sign for the Chaney Trail. Turn right and drive approximately 1.5 miles to Millard Campground.*

Millard Canyon Falls can be dry most of the year

Rubio Canyon Falls

Rating: 1

How Short? 2.0 Miles

How Easy? 4

Best Time to View:
None

Need Information?
Contact: Angeles
National Forest
(818) 790-1151

During most of the 20th Century, Rubio Canyon was rich with waterfalls, the richest waterfall canyon in the Los Angeles Basin. It has been reported that as many as nine waterfalls could be seen in Lower Rubio Canyon. Things, however, have taken a turn for the worse in this canyon, and hikers and outdoor enthusiasts have put the blame for the disaster on the Rubio Water Company.

WARNING HAZARD AREA LANDSLIDE AND PERSONAL INJURY MAY OCCUR

Here's what we know for sure (the rest are pure allegations and will not be discussed in this book): In the 1994 Northridge Earthquake, a small rockslide in Rubio Canyon damaged one of the Rubio Canyon Water Companies pipes that was located in the lower canyon. Rubio Canyon Water Company received money from the Federal Emergency Management Agency to fix the pipe. While blasting a hole in Lower Rubio Canyon to create a ledge to lay the new pipe on, more than a quarter-mile of the canyon became covered in dirt and boulders.

According to several reports, five of the canyon's nine waterfalls were covered in rubble and completely destroyed, and a sixth was partially damaged.

I contacted the Forest Service for further details, but they refused to go on the record with a comment. I hiked into the canyon to see for myself what had occurred. Someone created a giant mess up here, that's for sure. Although I'd never seen the waterfalls before they were obliterated, I did bring along old photos of what the canyon looked like before the blast. All evidence of any of the first five waterfalls was completely eradicated.

The blast that destroyed the canyon also made it unsafe for hiking. The streambed is now hidden below thousands of boulders; and the waterfalls, well, they're hidden, too. It looks like a mining dump where dirt and boulders that were dug out of the

This rockslide destroyed several waterfalls in Rubio Canyon

ground got deposited.

According to maps I consulted, as well as a few knowledgeable hikers I ran into on the trail, these are the names of the five waterfalls that were destroyed: Roaring Rift, Lodged Boulder, Moss Grotto, Ribbon Rock and Grand Chasm. I can't, however, absolutely verify these names, because I've never seen the waterfalls myself.

Hiking in Rubio Canyon is still permitted, but strongly discouraged. The hillsides are extremely unstable. Not only is the canyon completely overgrown, the trail has all but disappeared and rockslides occur daily. There is nothing to see anyway.

Many hikers have called for a massive cleanup effort to restore

The view of Glendale from the top of the rockslide can be inspiring

the canyon, but it would costs millions of dollars, which no one seems willing to pay. As for now, put plans for visiting this canyon on the back burner. It may take a decade for anything to change here.

If you plan to make the trip, supplies are available in Pasadena. Don't venture into the canyon after a storm. There is always the threat of rockslides.

Also nearby are Eaton Canyon Falls, Monrovia Canyon Falls, Hermit Falls, Sturtevant Falls and Millard Canyon Falls.

Directions: *From the 210 Freeway in Pasadena, exit Lake Avenue and drive north to Delores Drive. Turn right, drive to Maiden Lane and turn left. Drive less than one-tenth of a mile to Rubio Canyon Road and turn right. Continue to Rubio Crest Drive and turn left. In one-tenth of a mile, turn right on Rubio Vista. The trailhead is located between two houses at the intersection of Rubio Vista and Pleasantridge.*

This waterfall is the only drop remaining in this section of Rubio

Bailey Canyon Falls

Rating: 4

How Short? 1

How Easy? 1

Best Time to View?
January to April

Need Information?
Contact: Sierra Madre
Parks and Recreation
(626) 355-7135

Many Southern California waterfalls are found on intermittent streams, those which flow during heavy rainy seasons and remain dry the rest of the year. Bailey Canyon Falls in the mountains above Sierra Madre needs heavy rain to come alive. The waterfall is located in Sierra Madre city limits just outside the boundary of the Angeles National Forest.

The hike to the falls shouldn't tire you out. The route begins in the parking area. The path can be picked up between the sign board and the restroom. Only 50 yards of the trail is found within Bailey Canyon Wilderness Park. The path begins on grass and is sheltered by trees before quickly leading you through a chain link fence. Make a right on the paved access road. Shortly, you'll pass by a flood control basin on the right and a monastery on the left. The route passes the flood control basin and comes to a junction. To the right is a bridge that crosses over Bailey Canyon Creek, which will most likely be dry. Ignore the signs for the Bailey Canyon Trail and continue on the path, which will have narrowed and become a single track path. Passing overgrown trees, bushes and poison oak the path winds through the canyon bringing you to the base of 25-foot Bailey Canyon Falls.

From this point you'll follow the Canyon View Natural Trail to the waterfall, which the trail ends at a quarter-mile ahead. The path narrows and crosses Bailey Canyon Creek several times. However, because the stream rarely flows with any force the crossings are easy.

Unfortunately, Bailey Canyon Falls' life is short. Its watershed is even shorter. If there hasn't been a steady downpour recently Bailey Canyon Falls will be dry. In the early rainy season even after a steady rain the waterfall may be dry. The hillsides need to be saturated before the stream begins to flow.

If you plan to make the trip, supplies are available in Sierra Madre.

Also nearby are Eaton Canyon Falls and Monrovia Canyon Falls.

Directions: *From the 210 Freeway in Pasadena drive east and take the Baldwin exit. Turn left, drive under the freeway and in one-tenth of a mile you'll come to a three way intersection. Turn left on Foothill and drive one-tenth of a mile to Baldwin. Turn right on Baldwin and drive 1.4 miles to Carter Avenue. Turn left on Carter and continue a half-mile to the intersection of Carter and Oak Crest Drive. Park in the day-use area.*

Bailey Canyon Falls was dry when Chris Cocoles visited in January of 2003

Sturtevant Falls

Rating: 7

How Short? 3.2 Miles

How Easy? 2

Best Time to View:
January to July

Need Information?
Contact: Angeles
National Forest
(626) 574-5200

The first time I ventured to Sturtevant Falls (just minutes north of Arcadia in the Angeles National Forest) and saw all the racket, I thought I was in the wrong place. I figured there would be fewer people as I drove further up the mountain away from the city, but I was wrong.

Arriving at Chantry Flat, I was stunned to see all the cars and people. The three parking lots and overflow parking were full, and both sides of the road were loaded with cars. In fact, there was nowhere to park. Did I mention it was drizzling, foggy and cold? I'd hate to see this place on a sunny day. What were all these people doing here? But the first time I got a glimpse of 60-foot Sturtevant Falls, my questions were answered.

Sturtevant Falls isn't your average waterfall hikers are accustomed to stumbling upon while exploring the trails of the San Gabriel Mountains. The trail to the waterfall follows Santa Anita Creek through a lush green canyon dappled with ferns, vines and wildflowers and shaded mostly by alders, with a sprinkling of oaks.

Although the thriving plant life is worth admiring, Sturtevant serves as the main attraction. The magnificent freefall draws visitors from all over the San Gabriel and surrounding valleys. The falls is best viewed from late winter through the spring, but flows year-round.

With a canopy of trees keeping you cool on even the hottest days, the hike is fairly easy. After a brief downhill walk from the parking lot, it follows Santa Anita Creek the entire way. The only part that is remotely tough is the walk back, up the paved road.

Begin your stroll at the locked gate across the street from the parking area at Chantry Flat. Pass the gate and begin the descent to Santa Anita Creek. The trail is paved for the first six-tenths of a mile, until you cross the bridge over Winter Creek (about halfway to the Santa Anita Creek).

Once you reach the creek, follow the trail as it bends to the left. You'll see small cabins on both sides of the path. From here, the trail is fairly flat with a few gradual uphill climbs. There are many smaller waterfalls and cascades on the way to the falls, but don't mistake them for Sturtevant.

Sturtevant Falls

After crossing the stream, you should arrive at the base of the falls in approximately five minutes. For those who want to continue, the trail leads above the falls and on to Mt. Wilson. In the spring, the California Department of Fish and Game plants rainbow trout in the creek, giving anglers a chance to visit a waterfall and do some fishing in the same trip.

Directions *and trip info for Hermit Falls also apply to Sturtevant Falls.*

Hermit Falls

Rating: 5

How Short? 2.4 Miles

How Easy? 2

Best Time to View:
February to June

Need Information?
Contact: Angeles
National Forest
(626) 574-5200

There was a time, hundreds of years ago, when all the canyons on the western slope of the San Gabriel Mountain Range remained untouched. Now, because of trash, graffiti, roads, power lines and downed trees, the fact that humans have left their mark here could not be clearer.

No evidence tells the story of "man vs. nature" more strongly than the flood control dams built in Santa Anita Canyon. Walking along the canyon bottom, you can't miss several of the 20-foot high dams that form artificial waterfalls, but at least they provide some benefit to go along with their blight upon these once pristine mountains.

So, why are these dams here? They were built in response to floods in the Twenties and Thirties, which washed away homes in the canyon and near Arcadia. Their purpose is to slow the flow of the Santa Anita Creek and reduce damage inflicted by trees, boulders and mud carried swiftly downstream during floods. Prior to the construction of these dams, even car-sized boulders were swept downstream, destroying everything in sight. By slowing the velocity of the creek and its loose debris, these dams greatly reduce the threat of damaging floods. Similar dams are now in nearly every canyon on the western slope of the San Gabriel Mountains.

Except during the rare occurrence of these potentially damaging floods, which happens perhaps once a decade, Santa Anita Canyon is one of the most popular hiking destinations in the San Gabriel Mountains. Most hikers come to see Sturtevant Falls on Santa Anita Creek, upstream from Hermit Falls. Those who want to avoid the crowds, however, head downstream to the less-splendid Hermit Falls. While Sturtevant is a 60-foot freefall, Hermit is a smaller 20-foot cascade. Both falls are in the Angeles National Forest and can be reached from the Gabrielino National Recreation Trail at Chantry Flat. From the trailhead, walk past the locked gate and proceed down the paved road. The trail first winds downhill and curves to the left, then makes a sharp turn and bends back to the right.

Hermit Falls

Before the route makes another sharp turn back to the left, there is a trail junction you'll need to keep any eye out for. A sign on the right side of the road marks this junction. Following signs to Hermit Falls, walk onto the First Water Trail. The trail becomes dirt and descends into switchbacks, through chaparral and yucca-covered hillsides. By the time you reach the canyon bottom, the flora will consist mostly of alders and oaks.

At the bottom, you'll see a small green outhouse and a trail that breaks off to the right. Take this trail to the right, which descends to Santa Anita Creek and crosses the stream. After crossing the stream, you'll come to a trail sign along Santa Anita Creek that reads "First Water ¾ Junction." From this point, Chantry Flat, the Gabrielino Trail and Hermit Falls are three-fourths of a mile away.

Continue downstream along the First Water Trail, passing a few artificial dams and making a few easy stream crossings. The streambed is kept cool by oaks, ferns, wildflowers and hundreds of tall alders. The foliage is thick and green year-round. The path continues downhill, and in another 10 minutes you'll see a circular metal pipe that bolts five feet out of the ground. Below the pipe is a series of granite boulders through which Santa Anita Creek flows.

Walk down to the boulders and you'll be standing on top of Hermit Falls. There are a few small cascades above the falls; however, the big drop is best seen from the falls' base. To reach the base, walk downstream along the boulders to a small crevice between two large rocks. The 20-foot climb down is a little steep, but there are plenty of rocks to hold onto.

The pool below Hermit Falls is actually better than the waterfall itself. It's like a giant swimming pool and is warm enough to swim in by early spring. Because the California Department of Fish and Game stocks Santa Anita Creek upstream, some of the rainbow trout make their way down to this pool that also provides good fishing. The waterfall isn't wonderful, but it's a perfect spot to perch on a boulder and munch some lunch, while admiring the water as it gently slides down the smooth, moss-covered rocks into the clear, inviting pool.

Directions *and trip info for Sturtevant Falls also apply to Hermit Falls.*

Brett Ross at the First Water 3/4 Junction upstream of Hermit Falls

Eaton Canyon Falls

Rating: 6
How Short? 3.0 Miles
How Easy? 1
Best Time to View: December to July
Need Information? Contact: Eaton County Park (626) 398-5420

When it gets hot in the Los Angeles Basin, people look for water. Some stay home and swim in their backyard swimming pools, while others drive to the beach or the mountains. The Angeles National Forest has a lot of water, although many of the streams do dry up (or are at least reduced to a mere trickle) by early summer. Because Eaton Canyon Falls almost never dries up, it has become popular to visit when the thermometer rises.

Located in a little county park north of Altadena, Eaton Canyon actually stays crowded almost year-round, getting a lot of use from families, runners, dog walkers and nature lovers. Pretty much everyone in the area knows about this place, and they all keep coming back. Because the trail is undemanding and easy to navigate, it is also suitable for all ages.

To pick up the trailhead, walk to the end of the parking lot and follow the dirt road to the right. The path crosses the stream, which, unless you visit in the rainy season, will most likely be dry. It then begins to parallel the creek, heading upstream to the Mt. Wilson Toll Road.

Cross the bridge on the Mt. Wilson Toll Road and follow the trail down to the stream. From this point, the route crosses the stream at least a dozen times. Nearing the falls, the canyon narrows, alders and oaks appear along the shore, and the boulders along the streambed increase in size. Just before reaching the falls, the stream angles off to the left, and another stream crossing is required before the falls appears.

Eaton Canyon Falls

There is a reason why this place is always crowded. The 40-foot freefall is stunning, plunging out from a gorge into a small, shallow pool. You can't see Eaton Canyon Creek above the falls, because the stream is hidden in the canyon. Not seeing where the water came from baffled one of the youngsters, and I overheard the four-year-old say, "Mommy, how does that rock spit out that water like that?" It it going to do that all day?

If you plan to make the trip, supplies are available in Altadena.

Also nearby are Monrovia Canyon Falls, Hermit Falls and Sturtevant Falls.

Directions: *From the 210 Freeway in Pasadena, drive east and exit Altadena Drive. Continue 1.6 miles north on Altadena to Eaton County Park.*

Monrovia Canyon Falls

Rating: 5

How Short? 1.3 Miles

How Easy? 1

Best Time to View:
December to June

Need Information?
Contact: Monrovia
Canyon Park
(626) 256-8282

Are you sick of dodging poison oak on small single-track trails? Do you have a fear of getting lost because of a poor sense of direction? Do you not enjoy long hikes? If you answered yes to the above, Monrovia Canyon Falls is the ideal destination for you.

In the foothills above Monrovia, this waterfall is a cinch to reach, requiring little effort. There are no confusing trail junctions, dangerous stream crossings or exhausting uphill climbs. Except for a few small hills, the 1.3-mile roundtrip path is relatively flat. I even saw a woman pushing a stroller to the falls! It's that easy.

From the picnic area next to the nature center, pick up the signed trail, which immediately descends into the canyon. Within about two minutes, comes a junction at the bottom of the hill; take the right fork, heading upstream. Oaks and alders keep you cool and shaded for the full six-tenths of a mile to the falls. The trail makes a few easy stream crossings, while passing some artificial concrete falls on the way to Monrovia Canyon Falls.

Don't let the concrete waterfalls fool you. These are not Monrovia Canyon Falls. At the end of Monrovia Canyon, after about 20 minutes of leisurely walking, the trail dead-ends at the base of the falls.

Monrovia is a two-tiered waterfall with a tiny pool at its base, far too shallow for even youngsters to wade in. The waterfall is 40 feet tall and cascades over a rock face. Although the entire 15 feet of the lower tier can be seen from its base, a portion of the upper tier is hidden in the canyon above.

If you plan to make the trip, supplies are available in Monrovia. There is a day-use fee. The park is opened to day-use only. At the time of publication, the park is opened from Wednesday to Monday. Call ahead to verify park hours.

Also nearby are Santa Anita Creek, Sturtevant Falls, Hermit Falls and Eaton Canyon Falls.

Monrovia Canyon Falls

Directions: *From the 210 Freeway in Pasadena, drive east to the Myrtle Avenue exit in Monrovia. Turn left on Myrtle and drive 1.8 miles to Scenic Drive. After turning right on Scenic, drive less than one-tenth of a mile and turn right on Encinitas Drive. On Encinitas, make a quick left back onto Scenic. Stay on Scenic, which becomes Canyon Boulevard, and turn right at the sign for Monrovia Canyon Park. Drive to the nature center.*

Soldier Creek Falls

Rating: 6

How Short? 1.25 Miles

How Easy? 1

Best Time to View:
December to June

Need Information?
Contact: Angeles
National Forest
(626) 335-1251

For those who visit the San Gabriel Mountains north of Azusa, you have probably driven past Soldier Creek Falls numerous times and never realized it. I know I did. Once you find Soldier Creek Falls, however, you'll keep coming back, if for no other reason than it's the only easily accessible waterfall in the San Gabriel River Drainage.

Soldier Creek Falls, sometimes referred to as Lewis Falls, is a 40-foot waterfall that shoots out over the rim of a canyon. Nestled at more than 4,000 feet in the Angeles National Forest, the falls is far enough from the city to get you away from the urban population, and remote enough to keep you secluded from the crowds that visit the forest year-round.

It requires only a 20-minute walk, including a 400-foot elevation gain, to find yourself at the base of the falls. The trail is suitable for all ages, with only a few stream crossings and a little rock-hopping. Pick up the trail on the north side of the stream and follow it past a few cabins. After you pass these cabins, the trail gradually climbs and begins to bend to the right, following the stream the entire way to the falls.

As the canyon narrows and the trail disappears, you'll come to a few easy stream crossings. Don't mistake the small cascades along the creek for the falls. You'll know you're at the falls when a steep cliff inhibits you from continuing upstream. The entire roundtrip should take no more than an hour, even if you choose to relax at the fall's base and take a few pictures.

Don't panic: there's much more for you to do than just taking pictures. For starters, you can visit Crystal Lake a few miles up the road or fish for stocked trout in the West and North Forks of the San Gabriel River. How about gold mining? People do it every day along the East Fork. As you might have guessed, the possibilities are endless.

If you plan to make the trip, make sure to obtain supplies in Azusa. A Forest Adventure Pass is required to park in the Angeles National Forest.

Also nearby are East, West and North Forks of the San Gabriel River and Crystal Lake.

Travis Kikugawa at Soldier Creek Falls

Directions: *From Pasadena, drive east on the 210 Freeway to the city of Azusa. In Azusa, exit Azusa Ave (39) and turn left. Just before entering the canyon, the road becomes San Gabriel Canyon Road. Continue 18 miles to Coldbrook Camp on the left. Reset your odometer and drive 2.4 miles to an unmarked turnout on the right side of the road, where Soldier Creek runs under the highway. If you reach Falling Springs Resort, you've driven two-tenths of a mile too far.*

San Antonio Falls

Rating: 7

How Short? 1.5 Miles

How Easy?

Best Time to View:
January to May

Need Information?
Contact: Angeles
National Forest
(626) 335-1251

There were children throwing snowballs, sledding down hills and building snowmen, while a few others were on the sidelines putting on their warm wear so they could get in on the action. It was only 9 a.m. and the Forest Service wasn't letting any other cars up Mt Baldy Road. Both sides of the road were already lined with cars; the parking lots were full as was overflow parking. All of these people were enjoying the great outdoors on the slopes of Mt. Baldy, yet not one of them knew about one of its best points of interest.

Just around the bend, near where the cars were parked, was San Antonio Falls, a stunning freefall near the Mt. Baldy ski area in the Angeles National Forest. You think perhaps these people knew about the waterfall, but instead chose to play in the snow?

"There's no waterfall around here," said a 17-year old high school kid. The skies where blue and temperatures were in the sixties, but he was dressed like he was preparing for a blizzard. "I've been coming here with my family for years. I would have heard about it."

Well, there is a waterfall, but in the winter, particularly after a snowfall, there is so much commotion, few see the sign for it. Because of all the vehicular traffic when snow is on the gound, the best time to visit is in the spring when snowmelt from Mt. Baldy keeps San Antonio Falls at peak flow.

At 6,000 feet, about a 20-minute drive from Upland, the falls is made up of three separate tiers. The first tier is a freefall and the other two are cascades. In all, the falls is roughly 90 feet tall.

The trail to the falls is short and easy to follow. Begin at the locked gate behind the sign for Falls

Fabian Espinosa at San Antonio Falls

Road. Walk past the gate and follow the trail as it bends to the right. (It's actually the maintenance road for the ski area.) In fewer than 10 minutes you'll come to an overlook where the falls can be seen. If desired, continue to the falls' base. In the winter the trail may be covered in snow.

If you plan to make the trip, supplies are available in Mt. Baldy Village. A Forest Service Adventure Pass is required to park in the Angeles National Forest. In winter call ahead for road conditions. Chains may be required.

Also nearby are Mt. Baldy Trout Pools and Mt. Baldy ski area.

Directions: *From Interstate 10 in Upland, exit Monte Vista Ave. and turn left. Drive to Mt. Baldy Road and turn right. Continue a mile past Manker Flats Camp to Falls Road on the left. Park and walk through the gate.*

Region

14

San Bernardino National Forest

Third Stream Falls

Rating: 8

How Short? 4.8 Miles

How Easy? 2

Best Time to View?
December to July

Need Information?
Contact: San
Bernardino National
Forest (909) 887-2576

Third Stream Falls is a rare gem in the San Bernardino National Forest. The waterfall is one of the best in the forest, and what makes it even more amazing to me is that it's located on an unnamed stream. Its name can't be found on a map. The stream is a year-round tributary to the Middle Fork of Lytle Creek. How did I find it? I'm fortunate to have an uncle who is an Eagle Scout. His son's troop stumbled upon the falls while camping at Third Stream Crossing on a recent backpacking trip.

The waterfall is comprised of three tiers, the bottom of which is the most inspiring. The drop is more than 40 feet, and is preceded by two other falls that can't be seen from the base, but can be viewed further downstream in the canyon. The upper tiers are between 20-30 feet tall, giving the total drop a height of nearly 100 feet.

The route to the falls gains roughly 1,200 feet, however, most of elevation gain is gradual. The path begins in a high desert like setting where shrubs dominate the terrain as you begin on the dirt track that gradually climbs into Middle Fork Canyon while paralleling the creek, but remaining high above it. After the initial climb you'll pass a left turnoff for Stone House Camp. Stay right and continue as the path emerges into a pine forest and dips down into a dry streambed at one mile in.

Over the next 1.2 miles the path treads closer to the Middle Fork of Lytle Creek. The canyon narrows, while the trees and undergrowth also get thicker. In one mile from the dry up streambed the path crosses the Middle Fork at Third Stream Crossing. The campground is located across the stream, opposite of the side you've been hiking on.

At this point, leave the path and walk downstream. In one-tenth of a mile you'll come to a small tributary. Follow that tributary upstream for two-tenths of a mile to the base of Third Stream Falls. At first, scrambling to the falls is easy. However, the topography gets steeper as you near the falls and climbing over slippery rocks is necessary.

At 5,200 feet in the Cucamonga Wilderness the waterfall can be tough to reach in the winter. Oftentimes snow blankets the trail and thick ice can make traversing the rocks below Third Stream Falls dangerous. Be careful out there. For those who wish, you can also walk the river to the falls instead of taking the high trail. However, this takes more time and a lot more energy.

If you plan to make the trip, supplies are available in Rancho Cucamonga. A Forest Service Adventure Pass is required to park in the San Bernardino National Forest.

Also nearby are Bonita Falls and Lytle Creek.

Directions: *From the junction of Interstate's 10 and 15 in Ontario take Interstate 15 north to the Sierra Highway-Lytle Creek Road exit. Turn left and drive 6.3 miles to Middle Fork Road. Turn left and drive 2.8 miles to the end of the road.*

Third Stream Falls

Bonita Falls

Rating: 7

How Short? 1.5 Miles

How Easy? 3 or 5

Best Time to View:
January to May

Need Information?
Contact: San
Bernardino National
Forest (909) 887-2576

If Bonita Falls were located along California's Central Coast, it would have its own state park named after it. Yet, because it's located in the San Bernardino National Forest, it receives little attention.

Due to extremely poor access, this tall three-tier waterfall isn't tops on most tourists' list of places to visit. Bonita Falls, however, can also be viewed from the road near where the Middle and South Forks of Lytle Creek converge, a short five-minute drive from Interstate 15 near Devore. Although this spot is the easiest place to drive to see the waterfall, much of the roadside access is either closed to parking or located on private property.

The best way to view the falls is from the base. In order to reach it, you first have to figure out a way to cross Lytle Creek, which can be difficult in the rainy season. When crossing the creek, plan on getting your feet wet.

To reach the base, from the dirt pullout on Lytle Creek Road, walk down to the Middle Fork of Lytle Creek and find a safe place to cross the stream. After crossing the Middle Fork, cross the narrower South Fork and begin walking upstream. There's no flat ground or trail here. The path is like the bottom of a large wash, covered with boulders ranging in size from baseballs to medicine balls.

After crossing both streams, hike a quarter-mile upstream. The best way to do this is to hug the canyon wall on the left. Not only are there are fewer rocks here, but you're going to want to be on this side when you locate the canyon on the left that Bonita's outlet stream trickles out of. It's the only canyon on this side of the creek. A trail will appear at the mouth of the canyon. Once you've reached it, leave the wash and enter the canyon. Follow the trail fewer than 100 yards to the base of Lower Bonita Falls.

Because only the top tier can be seen from Lytle Creek Road, most passersby viewing the falls from the road think Bonita only has one tier. Don't be fooled. Bonita is 230 feet tall; however, reaching the upper two tiers is only doable by rappelling.

The lower tier, which you can walk to, is approximately 90 feet tall. This drop is a lot like Escondido Falls near Malibu

Lower Bonita Falls

and Limekiln, and Pfeiffer Falls along the Central Coast. It's a near plumb drop, and the stream hugs the waterfall's face, brushing against ferns as it cascades down. If you walk back down the canyon and look above the lower falls, the middle tier will come into view. Because you can only see part of the 50-foot drop from here, it doesn't appear as impressive as the lower tier.

The upper tier, a 90-foot drop, is best viewed from Lytle Creek, rather than from inside the canyon. From the creek, near the mouth of the canyon, look about 150 feet up the mountainside to view the drop. For those who aren't inclined to rappel, the upper tier can also be viewed from the intersection of South Fork Road and Lytle Creek Road, but from this distance, its height and beauty are too far away to fully appreciate. The waterfall is located behind a private trailer park, and you're not allowed to park your car inside it; the trailer park doesn't want non-customers blocking access.

The biggest problem with Bonita is that it suffers because it is fed by a small watershed, which never seems to convey enough water to give the falls extraordinary force. It's best to come shortly after a rain, or risk being disappointed.

If you plan to make the trip, supplies are available in Devore. A Forest Service Adventure Pass is required to park in the San Bernardino National Forest.

Also nearby are Green Mountain Ranch, Glen Helen Park Lake and Lytle Creek.

Directions: *From Interstate 15 in Rancho Cucamonga, drive 7.6 miles north to the Sierra Highway-Lytle Creek Road exit. Turn left and drive 6.2 miles to South Fork Road. Turn left on South Fork Road. To reach the waterfall, you must backtrack one-tenth of a mile on Lytle Creek Road to a dirt pullout on the right.*

Trout like these caught by Brett Ermilio are common in Lytle Creek

Heart Rock Falls

Rating: 4

How Short? 1.8 Miles

How Easy? 1

Best Time to View:
January to June

Need Information?
Contact: San
Bernardino National
Forest (909) 337-2444

Love is on display on the rocks of Heart Rock Falls in the San Bernardino National Forest. The waterfall may be small, but a naturally carved heart in a large, smooth granite boulder two feet to the left of the waterfall gives lovers a reason to visit.

Last time I visited, I saw a couple standing in the three-foot deep hole beneath the approximately three-foot wide heart. They stood waist-deep in stagnant water and kissed, as another couple took their picture. Too bad for the couple in the picture that they were blocking the view of the heart-shaped rock. After hiking downstream to look for more waterfalls, I came back and found another couple taking a somewhat better picture. They were both about 16, lying on their stomachs with their lips touching just above the heart. It appeared one of their moms was taking the photo.

At 3,600 feet, downstream from Camp Seeley, Heart Rock Falls requires little to no effort to reach. From the dirt parking area, walk downstream along the creek, passing Camp Seeley, which is on the right of the stream. The trail may not appear for the first 100 yards. Don't panic. Just keep walking downstream. It will appear.

No stream crossings are required. The trail parallels the creek the entire way. After 15 to 20 minutes of downhill walking through a cedar and pine forest, begin listening for the waterfall on the right. A trail spur descends to the top of the falls. The waterfall is only a 20-foot tall freefall; but you came for the granite heart, not the falls, right? Although it's possible to maneuver down to the base, the view is best from above.

Make sure to visit Heart Rock Falls by late June. Come any later and the freefall may have turned into a trickle, dribbling down the granite face. Don't forget to bring a loved one along, or risk returning with a picture of yourself alone next to the heart. That would feel lonely.

Heart Rock

If you plan to make the trip, supplies are available at Silverwood Lake and Crestline. A Forest Service Adventure Pass is required to park in the San Bernardino National Forest.

Also nearby are Silverwood Lake, Miller Canyon Creek and Cleghorn Creek.

Directions: *From Ontario, drive east on Interstate 10 to Interstate 15. Drive north on Interstate 15 over the Cajon Pass to the Silverwood Lake exit (Highway 138) at the Cajon Junction. Exit Highway 138 and drive east. Continue approximately19 miles to the sign for Camp Seeley. Turn right, cross the stream and park alongside the road.*

Cold Creek Falls

Rating: 4

How Short? Drive-To or Hike-In 1.2 Miles

How Easy? 1 or 4

Best Time to View: February to June

Need Information? Contact: San Bernardino National Forest (909) 794-1123

For those readers who actually take the time to open a map at home to locate the waterfall you're going to see, you might get confused when trying to pinpoint Cold Creek Falls. Don't get me wrong, it's easy enough to get to Cold Creek Falls, but it might baffle you that Cold Creek Falls is located off Mill Creek Road, since there is no Mill Creek around. I searched several different maps looking for a Mill Creek nearby, but the nearest one was down the mountain in a different canyon.

So, why was the road to Cold Creek Falls named Mill Creek Road when Mill Creek is more than five miles away? Did someone name the road incorrectly? I asked three different Forest Service rangers and none could provide an answer.

"Are you sure the waterfall is on Cold Creek, and there is no Mill Creek anywhere along the road?" one ranger asked. "If there is no Mill Creek around here, well, then I don't' know what to tell you. These roads were named long before I was working here."

I scanned the map again to make absolutely sure there was no Mill Creek along Mill Creek Road. There were the Santa Ana River and Mile, Forsee, Scheider, Kilpecker and Metcalf Creeks, but no Mill Creek. Driving through Big Bear City a few hours later, I saw another sign for Mill Creek Road. "Oh no!" I thought. "Another sign for Mill Creek Road. Great! Here we go again." After looking on the map, it turned out this was the same Mill Creek Road that began in Angelus Oaks. I thought of driving the road all the way through, but it was closed because of snow.

Getting away from the mystery of Mill Creek Road, at 5,650 feet in the San Bernardino National Forest, near Angelus Oaks, along Mill Creek Road, Cold Creek Falls is a pretty little waterfall, which receives only modest attention from tourists..

Although the best time to view the falls is in February, March and April, when snow is melting on the mountaintops, this is also the same time the road is closed. Since the road isn't plowed by Cal Trans the Forest Service closes it for your safety.

A friend and I made the trek through three feet of snow, happy to find we had the falls all to ourselves. It was a perfect spot to sit back, relax and enjoy the small 25-foot waterfall, which spills down jagged grayish rocks. There are alders, tall pines and oak trees above the waterfall, which cast shade across it on a sunny day. Unlike most waterfalls, Cold Creek doesn't have a pool at its base. Instead, the water runs through a drainage pipe and flows under the ubiquitous Mill Creek Road.

By April, the road should be opened, and you can take an easy drive to the falls. It's a tad more than a half-mile down the dirt road. There's only enough space on the right side of the road for two cars.

Trip info for Monkeyface Falls also applies to Cold Creek Falls.

Directions: *From Interstate 10 in Redlands, exit Highway 38 and drive 14 miles northeast. At the junction with Forest Home Road, veer left and continue approximately five miles to Angelus Oaks. At the edge of town, on the right side of Highway 38, you'll come to a mileage sign for Barton Flat, Big Bear and Fawnskin. On the left side of the road, opposite the sign, turn left on Mill Creek Road. Continue six-tenths of a mile to the waterfall.*

Monkeyface Falls

Rating: 4

How Short? Drive-To

How Easy? 1

Best Time to View:
January to April

Need Information?
Contact: San
Bernardino National
Forest (909) 794-1123

The name alone makes many people want to visit Monkeyface Falls. The curiosity "Monkeyface" engenders, however, isn't rewarded when you finally see it: Monkeyface in no way resembles a monkey's face. The waterfall acquired its name from being on Monkeyface Creek. Located in a remote, dark gorge, the falls benefits little from the scant runoff coming off the 9,000-foot peaks in the San Bernardino National Forest. Like the waterfall, the surrounding canyon is also not very rewarding, and it offers no recreational opportunities.

So, if Monkeyface is so visitor unfriendly, why did anyone bother to name it? And why am I writing about it? Because a lot of people do end up viewing it. During the rainy season, visitors on their way to Big Bear can see Monkeyface Falls without leaving their cars. As a matter of fact, there's no other way to view it. You can't hike to the waterfall's base, because it's located on private property.

The best place to view the falls is right next to the deer crossing sign along Forest Home Road. Another good spot is next to the tow-away sign for vehicles blocking snowplows. To see the waterfall, look north in the narrow gorge 100 yards ahead. There are two sections of the falls, but the upper section is difficult to see without binoculars. Because Monkeyface's flow is so dark and narrow, the waterfall can be difficult to see. When the sun hits the lower cascade, it's easier to spot. All the drops total about 100 feet. If you don't have the time, don't fret over not stopping. Monkeyface isn't exciting even after a downpour.

Plan on continuing to Big Bear? Back on Highway 38, drive six-tenths of a mile towards Big Bear to a large, dirt pullout on the left. Across the highway, there is another waterfall in a canyon that is well lit, and there is a trail that leads 30 yards from the highway to its base. Although Frustration Creek Falls suffers from the same lack of runoff as Monkeyface, its 60-foot drop can be impressive right after a winter storm.

If you plan to make the trip, supplies are available in Angelus Oaks and Redlands. A Forest Service Adventure Pass is required to park in the San Bernardino National Forest.

Also nearby are Big Falls, Mill Creek and Cold Creek Falls

Directions: *From Interstate 10 in Redlands, exit Highway 38 and drive 14 miles northeast. Veer right at the junction with Forest Home Road and continue fewer than 50 yards to a small pullout on the right.*

Cold Creek Falls

Monkeyface Falls

Big Falls

Rating: 7

How Short? Drive-To or Hike-In 0.50 Miles

How Easy? 2

Best Time to View: February to August

Need Information? Contact: San Bernardino National Forest (909) 794-1123

When I read there was a 500-foot waterfall only 20 minutes from Interstate 10 in Redlands, I hurried to find it, only to be disappointed on arrival. There are 500-foot waterfalls and then there are waterfalls like Big Falls, which measures 500 feet, but doesn't offer the full experience that a 500-foot waterfall should. The US Forest Service told me the waterfall is 500 feet, yet in my mind 100 feet is far more realistic for most people.

While many 500-foot waterfalls can be seen in their entirety, Big Falls, the San Bernardino National Forest's tallest waterfall, cannot. Merely a 50-foot portion of the drop is visible. The other 450 feet are tucked back in a canyon, not visible to visitors. In other words, you might as well think of Big Falls as a 50-foot waterfall near Forest Falls, a small mountain community in the forest.

The hardest thing about viewing the falls is finding a parking spot. In February and March, if you don't arrive before 9 a.m., you're out of luck. The lot fills early and no roadside parking is allowed. Once the spots are gone, park rangers stop cars from coming in until others leave. It's worse than standing in line at Disneyland, where at least you know how long the wait is going to be.

If you are fortunate enough to snag a parking spot, the rest is easy. There are signs in the lot pointing to the trail, which is easy to follow but provides no shade until the last 100 yards. The trail runs parallel to Mill Creek for the first two-tenths of a mile, opposite sheer cliffs on the far side of the stream.

Some hikers make the mistake of walking through the stream, but I consider doing so an ankle injury waiting to happen. It's like walking in a dry wash. There are hundreds of thousands of softball-sized boulders on top of gravel and sand, all guaranteed to wobble underfoot.

After about five minutes of easy walking, two cabins will appear downstream on the left. Time to cross the stream. If you forget, there is a sign just after the first cabin that reminds you to cross the stream. Two signs on the other side warn of the danger that exists for those who attempt to leave the trail. Take this seriously.

Although it might look possible to make your own trail, there are too many loose rocks in the cliffs above to attempt it. I've seen rocks suddenly fall here for seemingly no reason, without any movement in the canyon. Be safe and stay on the trail. The route takes on an upward slope for the next 100 yards, bringing you through an oak and cedar forest and ending at the falls' overlook. Only a small portion of Big Falls can be seen from here.

Big Falls is a freefall and a cascade, however, the 50 feet you can see is all freefall. Situated in a narrow winding gorge, the first 400 feet of the waterfall is located back in a canyon, behind where you see water catapulting off the cliff. The last 50 feet is obstructed by a small hill in front of the drop, so it can't be seen either.

One thing to take into consideration before leaving the parking lot and beginning the journey to the falls is the thickness of the snowpack at the Falls Recreation Area. In the winter, snow accumulates here and can completely cover the trail and the trailhead signs. In that case, walk to the north end of the parking lot and locate the canyon walls, 30 yards away. Mill Creek is down in the canyon.

Hike down to the creek and use the streambed as the trail, walking five minutes downstream. If the snowpack is as heavy as it was when I last visited, you won't have to worry about the boulders in the streambed. The deep snowpack will have covered them. Soon, you'll be able to see a portion of the falls on the right.

If you couldn't find a parking spot, don't fret. Here's what you do: from the Falls Parking Area, backtrack three-tenths of a mile to the intersection of Valley of the Falls Road and Rock Drive. The same view of the falls can be seen here from your car as from the falls' overlook.

If you plan to make the trip, supplies are available in Forest Falls. A Forest Service Adventure Pass is required to park in the San Bernardino National Forest. In winter, call ahead for road conditions. Chains may be required.

Also nearby are Monkeyface Falls, Cold Creek Falls, Mill Creek, Santa Ana River, Jenks Lake and Big Bear Lake.

Directions: *From Interstate 10 in Redlands, exit Highway 38 and drive 14 miles northeast. At the junction with Forest Home Road, veer right and continue 4.3 miles to the road's end at the Falls Recreation Area. (The road becomes Valley of the Falls Drive).*

Fuller Mill Creek Falls

Rating: 4

How Short? 0.60 Miles

How Easy? 1

Best Time to View:
April to May

Need Information?
Contact: San
Bernardino National
Forest (909) 659-2117

From January through March, Idyllwild is one of Southern California's most popular snow-play areas. The town thrives on visitors coming to ride sleds, cross-country ski, build snowmen, throw snowballs and just generally goof around in the snow. Traffic jams are common in the winter, and the lines at restaurants and gas stations can test your patience.

But what happens when the snow melts? For waterfalls lovers, things begin to brighten. The crowds disperse, the streams flow at full force, wildflowers bloom and waterfalls come to life.

At 5,700 feet in the San Bernardino National Forest, less than a 15-minute drive from the cabins, pizza parlors and motels in Idyllwild, Fuller Mill Creek Falls is a pleasant, relaxing destination; a great place to bring the family for the day, especially in springtime. Although it doesn't compare to the better waterfalls in the region, it offers what Idyllwild can't: a chance to be alone.

The falls is also easy to reach. Pick up the trail by walking across Highway 243 to Fuller Mill Creek. Then, it's just a 30-minute roundtrip walk from Highway 243, ideal for kids who have trouble coping with long hikes. There are some nice wading pools along the way to this 30-foot waterfall, if you can tolerate the cold water.

Fuller Mill is a series of small cascades. Creating the largest drop, Fuller Mill Creek gets funneled through a narrow chute, and the water splashes off granite rocks into a shallow pool below. There are other cascades above, but rock-climbing skills are required to reach them. While walking along the right bank (the Idyllwild side) of the creek to the cascades, keep an eye open for some smaller cascades along the trail.

After enjoying the waterfall, walk back past your car down to the Fuller Mill Creek Picnic Area, located on the other side of the highway. Shaded by tall pines, there are picnic tables spread along the stream, providing great places to eat lunch.

A note: If coming in the winter, skip the journey to the waterfall. The trail can be covered with snow, and although the hike is short, it's too dangerous to hop through the stream with no trail to follow. Most of the rocks are coated with ice, and, more importantly, there will only be a dribble of water coming down the cascades, anyway. In poor rain years Fuller Mill Creek can nearly dry up by mid-June. Try fishing for rainbow trout instead.

If you plan to make the trip, supplies are available in Idyllwild and Banning. A Forest Service Adventure Pass is required to park in the San Bernardino National Forest.

Also nearby are Strawberry Creek and Fulmor Lake.

Directions: *From Interstate 10 in Banning, exit Banning/Idyllwild Road (Highway 243) and continue 22 miles south to Fuller Mill Creek Picnic Area on the right.*

Fuller Mill Creek Falls is a trickle in the winter

Dark Canyon Falls

Rating: 5

How Short? 2.0 Miles

How Easy? 2

Best Time to View:
May through August

Need Information?
Contact: San
Bernardino National
Forest (909) 659-2117

A winter wonderland? Hardly anymore. Dark Canyon Falls used to be a fabulous winter destination, but things have changed. For years, many Southern Californians made Dark Canyon Campground, on the banks of the North Fork of the San Jacinto River, a favorite cold weather destination. Frozen water lines and an abundance of vehicles getting stuck in the snow and ice, however, caused the Forest Service to close the road to the campground in the winter and early spring.

Now (and most likely for the rest of our lives), Dark Canyon Campground will remain opened only to seasonal use. The Forest Service targets the Thursday preceding Memorial Day weekend as the yearly opener, but sometimes opens the campground earlier. It all depends on how badly winter hits the San Jacinto Mountains.

Located 6,900 feet up in Mt. San Jacinto State Park, just a short distance from Idyllwild, Dark Canyon is a pretty campground shaded mostly by pine trees. It provides its visitors with many options, including swimming (if you can handle the brisk temperatures), fishing, hiking and visiting a series of waterfalls.

The river, which is really more the size of a stream, is stocked in early summer with rainbow trout by the California Department of Fish and Game. The cascades are in a dark, narrow granite canyon, upstream from where the trout are planted. Pines on the mountainsides above the falls add a little character, but none of the cascades are taller than 20 feet, so they are neither dramatic nor breathtaking.

The North Fork of the San Jacinto River is less than a mile from Fuller Mill Creek, but it has much more water in it. A trail that leads to the base of the first of a series of cascades can be picked up in Dark Canyon Campground. After the first cascade, however, you're on your own. Rock-hopping, rock climbing and wading is required to continue upstream to the other cascades.

If you plan to make the trip, supplies are available in Idyllwild. In winter, chains may be required. Call ahead for road conditions. A Forest Service Adventure Pass is required to park in the San Bernardino National Forest.

Also nearby are Fuller-Mill Creek, Fulmor Lake, Fuller Mill Creek Falls, Strawberry Creek and Hemet Lake.

Directions: *From Interstate 10 in Banning, exit Banning-Idyllwild Road (Highway 243) and turn south. Follow Highway 243 approximately 22 miles to the turnoff for Dark Valley Campground on the left. Turn left, entering San Jacinto State Park, and continue eight-tenths of a mile. Veer left, following signs to the campground. Drive another 3.4 miles to the campground.*

Roaring River Falls, for more information see page 188

Region

15

Palm Springs/ Anza Borrego

Whitewater Falls

Rating: 3

How Short? Drive To

How Easy? 1

Best Time to View:
February to April

Need Information?
Contact: Whitewater
Trout Company (760)
325-5570 or
(760) 320-7875

Whitewater Falls isn't the ideal waterfall to visit. Its flows are usually non-existent, even in the rainy season; it isn't very tall, only about 30 feet high; and it has no distinctive characteristics. What does make it a good destination, however, is that it's located next to Whitewater Trout Farm.

Whitewater Trout Farm is a fish hatchery that raises rainbow trout for many lakes in San Bernardino, Riverside and San Diego Counties, and opens its grounds for fishing to the public. The in-thing to do is visit the falls and then head over to Whitewater to do a little fishing.

As for the falls themselves, it's the kind of place you drive to, get out, take a few pictures and move on. Since the falls only flows after a recent rainfall, it's best to call ahead to make sure it's flowing before you make the trip.

Located in the high desert of Riverside County, at least once a year the area gets snow, and you can get some great photos of the frosty falls. If you don't arrive soon after a snowfall, however, the snow will have melted. Then the falls reverts to a slow, boring dribble.

If you plan to make the trip, supplies are available in Banning. There is a fishing fee at Whitewater Trout Farms. No fishing license is required, however, there is a charge for each fish you catch. Whitewater is opened from Wednesday through Sunday.

Also nearby are Murray Canyon Falls, the Cabazon Outlets and Palm Springs.

Directions: *From Interstate 10 in Banning, drive east to the Whitewater exit and turn left, crossing over the freeway. Continue four-tenths of a mile to Whitewater Canyon Road and turn left. Follow the road 4.3 miles to the falls on the right.*

Tahquitz Falls

Rating: 7

How Short? 2.0 Miles

How Easy? 1

Best Time to View:
January to June

Need Information?
Contact: Agua Caliente
Indian Reservation
(800) 790-3398,
Tahquitz Visitor Center
(760) 416-7044

New tourist attractions are constantly popping up all over the Palm Desert area. Unlike most of these attractions, Tahquitz Canyon doesn't involve golf courses, fancy restaurants, outdoor shopping malls, or spending lots of money. What it does offer is a guided tour to a waterfall. Yes, I said waterfall. A few actually exist in this blazing-hot dry desert.

You may have seen Tahquitz Falls on TV. In the early Fifties, it was featured in the movie "Lost Horizon." I'm sure it was chosen because there is no better desert waterfall in California. Yet, as good as it is, most people have never seen it. And there's an excellent reason why: Tahquitz is located on the Aqua Caliente Indian Reservation, and up until January of 2001, the canyon was closed to the public.

Just because the canyon was closed, however, doesn't mean that some people didn't illegally enter to visit the waterfall. A park ranger told me that those who unlawfully entered the canyon misused it. Several people actually took up residence in the canyon; others used it as a place to dispose of trash; and to add insult to injury, taggers used the stone canyon walls to practice their writing style. It cost the reservation thousands of dollars to clean it up. Now it looks great and is fast becoming popular.

Hiking in Tahquiz Canyon

The only authorized way into the canyon is with a park ranger. Tours leave each hour from the Tahquitz Canyon Visitor Center and cost $10 a person. The tour begins in an air-conditioned room where you are shown a 10-minute video about the legend of Tahquitz, whom the locals believe still lives in the canyon.

Following the video, the tour heads out into the desert. The two-mile roundtrip loop takes about two hours. It could be done in less than 45 minutes, but the rangers stop to talk about different plants, animals and wildflowers encountered along the trail, and to elaborate on the history of the canyon. It's a true educational experience.

If you can bear the heat, the hike is well worth it. The dirt path only gains 300 feet over the mile to the falls. One advantage is that you don't need to bring any maps or have a clue where you're going; simply follow the ranger.

There are two waterfalls in Tahquitz Canyon. The first is a small 10-foot drop along the left side of the path.

The ranger usually stops at this waterfall so you can snap a few pictures. Shortly after, you'll come to Tahquitz Falls. Fed by springs and snow runoff from Mt. San Gorgonio, this 60-foot waterfall spills over a sheer white-granite cliff. The rocks near the waterfall are also granite, however, the mountains above the falls are composed of brick-red gneiss. There's a nice wading pool below, but the reservation prohibits visitors from contact with the water.

One of the stops on the hike back is a place called Green Tree. It has

Tahquiz Falls

a gorgeous swimming hole, but, again, you're required to stay on the trail. Instead of taking a dip, look north. You'll get a fabulous view of Palm Springs.

Although Tahquitz flows from December through July, most visitors choose to come before May. Later in the year, the temperatures could top 120, making the trip far less enjoyable. It's best to visit during the week when crowds are light.

If you plan to make the trip, supplies are available in Palm Springs. There is a fee to participate in the waterfall tour. Tours are by reservation only. Bring along lots of water. It's important to keep yourself hydrated.

Also nearby are Murray Canyon Falls, Lake Cahuilla, Whitewater Falls and Whitewater Trout Farm.

Directions: *From Banning, drive east on Interstate 10 to Highway 111. Take Highway 111 east to Palm Springs and turn right on Mesquite Avenue. Continue to the parking area.*

Tahquiz Falls

Murray Canyon Falls

Rating: 6

How Short? 3.5 Miles

How Easy? 2

Best Time to View:
December to May

Need Information?
Contact: Agua Caliente
Indian Reservation
(800) 790-3398

Contrary to popular belief, Palm Springs has more to offer than suntans, golf courses, gated communities, trendy shops and palm trees. Murray Canyon Falls is proof. What? A waterfall in the desert? Yes, and an impressive one too!

Murray Canyon Falls is located on the Agua Caliente Indian Reservation, not more than a five-minute drive from Palm Springs. Although dozens of tour buses visit the reservation each week, few of their sightseers stray far enough away from the tour buses' cushioned seats and air conditioned interiors to appreciate what the reservation has to offer. Most of the buses make a brief stop at Andreas Canyon, but to really see the best the grounds have to offer, you'll need to walk east to Murray Canyon, the next canyon over.

In Murray Canyon, a mirage literally comes to life: poof! waterfalls in the desert. Throughout winter and early spring, Murray Canyon Creek will change the way you look at the desert. Wildflowers sprout along the streambed; the shade of palm trees keeps you from sweltering; and crystal clear water sparkles under the bright desert sun. There is no escaping the absolute awe felt when you reach Murray Canyon Falls, a series of spectacular freefalls in the back of a wondrous canyon.

Iguanas and lizards can be found in Murray Canyon

The hike begins next to the tour buses, in the day-use parking area at Andreas Canyon. Cross Andreas Canyon Creek, following signs to Murray Canyon. After crossing the stream, pass through two parking areas and a picnic area, all shaded by palms. Then, all of a sudden, the trees disappear, and you'll be standing on a dirt trail in the middle of the desert.

Yup, you're in the right place. Although the path offers no shade as it works its way to Murray Canyon, there are plenty of bushes and frequent visits from lizards. The trail angles to the right towards palm trees that stand in the distance. Smile, those palm trees line Murray Canyon Creek, and you're getting close to shade again. Once at the stream, you will have been walking through the desert for a half-mile: time for a change of scenery.

The final 1.5 miles can take as little as a half-hour, or as much as a few hours. Several easy stream crossings are required, but it's the wildlife and scenery that keep you occupied and slow you down. Tall, impressive rock formations tower above, as the trail threads through the canyon and continues to crisscross the stream.

Keep an eye out for are rattlesnakes; we saw a few on our way to the falls in the morning. Desert iguanas more than a foot long are also abundant. A park ranger told me that bighorn sheep can sometimes be seen in the canyon. But, what most hikers come for is Murray Canyon Falls.

Although small, Murray Canyon Falls is one of the finest desert waterfalls in the state. It consists of three tiers, but only the bottom one can be seen from the trail. This 15-foot freefall empties into a swimmer-friendly pool with a sandy bottom. The pool is only about four-and-a-half feet deep, but that doesn't stop people from jumping off its brink, although it's not safe to do so.

For the adventurous, a trip to the upper two tiers is possible. I did it, but it's a dangerous climb back down to the trail. The hikers ahead on me swam back to the trail, however, that is far too dangerous and against park regulations. First, they jumped off the top of the upper waterfall and swam to the middle falls. Then, they jumped again, swam and jumped once more off the lower falls. It's dangerous. The pools aren't deep enough for jumping. On a more positive note, the water is as clear as glass, so you can see the deeper areas where you should land. Check with the park in regards to jumping. Some years, water contact is prohibited. I've had one park rangers tell me water contact is illegal and saw the same ranger jumping off the falls. You figure!

To reach the upper falls, walk to the left side of the lower waterfall and climb up the slippery, water-polished rocks to the top of the ridge. Then, carefully scramble down to the stream.

If you plan to make the trip, supplies are available in Palm Springs. There is a day-use fee for each person to enter the reservation. Call ahead for water conditions. In poor rain years, the stream may dry up before May. The trail is opened for day-use only. If you aren't out by 5 p.m., you'll be locked in for the night. You might end up with an iguana licking your face in the morning.

Also nearby are Lake Cahuilla, Palm Springs and the Salton Sea.

Directions: *From Banning, drive east on Interstate 10 to Highway 111. Take Highway 111 towards Palm Springs and continue 12.3 miles to a fork in the road. Stay right, following the signs for Palm Canyon Drive, and drive to the tollgate at the reservation.*

A small waterfall below Murray Canyon Falls

Borrego Palm Canyon Falls

Rating: 3

How Short? 2.50 Miles

How Easy? 2

Best Time to View:
December to May

Need Information?
Contact: Anza-Borrego
State Park (760) 767-
5311, Anza Borrego
State Park Visitor
Center (760) 767-4205

After a fun-filled day of fishing the Salton Sea, an evening visit to Anza-Borrego State Park seemed fitting. We packed the fishing rods in the back of the truck, and I began driving west on Highway S22 out of Salton City.

As we crossed the eastern boundary of the state park, my friend burst out, "You aren't going to believe this, but there's a waterfall up here."

I was almost sure he was reading the map wrong, so I pulled over to take a look for myself. After all, we were in the desert: how could there be a waterfall? It was early spring and all the streambeds we'd seen were dry. Sure enough, my friend was right! It said "Falls" on the map.

The sun was beginning to set, and I figured we had about an hour of light left. So, we decided to visit the falls. When we arrived at Borrego/Palm Canyon Campground, there was less than a half-hour of light left.

My friend estimated the distance to the falls to be a mile and a quarter, so we had some decisions to make. Should we save the waterfall for the morning when we knew there would be plenty of light, or risk getting lost in the desert under total darkness? Since we were in a state park, I figured the trail would be well signed and maintained, so my vote was to go to the falls. My friend, Blake Lezak, chose to play it safe and wait in the car.

A desert wildflower

I scanned the map, grabbed a walk-talkie, strapped a headlamp on, put a bottle of water in my pocket and started running along the trail into the canyon. I hadn't gone a half-mile when an old man with his grandson stopped me. "Slow down, son," he said. "You need to be careful around here. It's the evening, and the snakes are coming out. We've seen two sidewinders already."

Wait a minute. Did that guy just say "snakes"? Now, I've stood toe-to-toe with a hungry bear picking food out of my backpack; I've stared a nine-pound bass in the eye while I was unhooking it; I've chased coyotes out of my campground; but the only thing I'd just as soon avoid is a snake.

I decided it was better to run to the falls and risk encountering a snake when it was still light, rather than walking slowly and not being able to see the snake in the dark. So, I kept running. I reached the falls about 15 minutes before sunset and thankfully didn't see any snakes.

Although the waterfall I'd been so eager to see didn't satisfy me (Borrego Palm Canyon Falls was far from remarkable), what did astonish me was that there was water here at all. The landscape was arid and it hadn't rained in months. I later learned that the waterfall is created both by runoff and a spring located further up Borrego Canyon that flows year-round.

The 15-foot cataract, which empties into a small wading pool shaded by palms, never becomes spectacular. Although the spring that feeds the waterfall flows year-round, it doesn't flow with enough force all year to keep the waterfall also flowing year-round, so the falls is usually dry from May to November.

The route to the falls is easy, well signed and suitable for all ages. The toughest obstacle to overcome is the blazing heat. The trail begins at the day-use parking lot near the campground at the Borrego Palm Canyon Trailhead. It's sandy and lined with rocks in most places, and there is absolutely no shade, so wear a hat and bring lots of water.

Another good idea is to pick up a brochure at the visitor center before setting out on the hike. The brochure describes many of the hundreds of different plants you'll see along the trail. The walk through the desert to the falls should take about a half-hour, maybe even less.

If you plan to make the trip, supplies are available in Borrego Springs. Make sure to bring lots of water, because none is available on the trail. A day-use fee is required at the state park.

Also nearby are the Salton Sea, Maidenhair Falls and Oriflamme Canyon Falls.

Directions: From Highway 78 in Julian, drive 19 miles east to Highway S3/Yaqui Pass Road. Turn left and drive 12 miles to Borrego Springs. In Borrego Springs, turn left on S22/Palm Canyon Drive and continue one mile to a signed turnoff for Borrego Palm Canyon Campground. Turn right and drive to the day-use parking area.

Cactus is common on the path to Borrego Palm Canyon Falls 369

Maidenhair Falls

Rating: 3

How Short? 5.4 Miles

How Easy? 2

Best Time to View:
January to May

Need Information?
Contact: Anza-Borrego
State Park (760) 767-
5311, Anza Borrego
State Park Visitor
Center (760) 767-4205

If you are visiting Anza/Borrego State Park for its waterfalls, you're coming for the wrong reason. The park's waterfalls are admittedly pitiful, but the hikes to them are often exhilarating. For example, take Maidenhair Falls: the waterfall is small and definitely not impressive, but the trek through the hot, dry desert, which ends in a virtual oasis, is a journey worth taking.

The hike begins south of Borrego Springs on a five-foot-wide sandy trail that enters Hellhole Canyon. Because there's no shade for the first two miles, as the trail passes cacti, wildflowers, dry streambeds and an abundance of wildlife, the best time to complete this hike is in the early morning or late evening, when it's cooler and animals are roaming the trail.

We saw rabbits dart across our path, hummingbirds flit from bush to bush, bees pollinate flowers, heard birds singing in the trees and coyotes howling in the distance. At times, so much was going on around us, we stopped and perched on boulders just to take a moment to watch nature take its course. If you're lucky, there's a chance you might even see a bighorn sheep on the trail.

As the canyon begins to narrow, several trails can be seen on both sides of the dry streambed. It doesn't matter which you take. They eventually merge. Often, when hikers see there isn't any water in this stream, they worry that Maidenhair Falls will also be dry. Don't let it bother you. The stream that feeds Maidenhair doesn't show up until you are about 300 yards from the falls.

Near a palm tree grove is a small 15-foot freefall. This isn't Maidenhair. Follow the trail to the

A small waterfall downstream of Maidenhair Falls

right of the cataract and continue another 100 yards upstream to Maidenhair Falls. This last section of the hike requires a lot of boulder hopping and stream crossings.

Maidenhair Falls is located in a cool, damp area of the desert, under a canopy of sycamores and willows. Wildflowers grow around the falls in fertile soil in crevices between the rocks. Although 20-foot Maidenhair Falls is hidden in the back of a grotto, the surrounding ferns and moss growing in the canyon will probably divert your attention. You may even be more impressed with the foliage than the waterfall; I was. Hikers are usually first drawn to the canyon because of the phenomenon of a waterfall in the desert, but they return here because this desert oasis in the canyon, filled with dense foliage, is truly a mysterious and wonderful place.

If you plan to make the trip, supplies are available in Borrego Springs. Brings lots of water. Temperatures can soar well above 100 on a daily basis. Don't let yourself get dehydrated.

Also nearby are Borrego/Palm Canyon Falls, Oriflamme Falls, Salton Sea and Lake Cuyamaca.

Directions: *From the Anza/Borrego Visitor Center near Borrego Springs, drive east on Highway S22 (Palm Canyon Drive) to Montezuma Road and turn right. Drive less than half a mile to an unsigned dirt pullout on the right. The trailhead is located directly behind the information sign.*

Brett Ross cools off near the ferns at the base of Maidenhair Falls

Oriflamme Falls

Rating: 5

How Short? 2.6 Miles

How Easy?

Best Time to View:
January to June

Need Information?
Contact: Anza-Borrego
State Park (760) 767-
5311, Anza Borrego
State Park Visitor
Center (760) 767-4205

Most people think the desert is a hot, dry sandy place. Typically, they're right. But Oriflamme Canyon, a remote area of Anza-Borrego State Park, smack in the middle of the desert, is lush, cool and moist. That's right. Unlike most deserts, or even like the rest of the state park, the canyon is filled with greenery and an abundance of water.

Oriflamme is the only waterfall with significant volume in Anza-Borrego; it truly looks like a waterfall, not just a teeny cascade. One of the few drawbacks to visiting Oriflamme is an overgrown trail. To solve this problem, I wore a pair of long pants, and the hike became enjoyable.

After parking near the primitive camping area, walk back up the dirt road you drove in on. At the point where the road forks, take the left fork and begin walking down the wide access road. In about 20 yards, the road splits again. Stay left and follow the road as it drops down towards the streambed.

The road will soon become a three-foot-wide trail. It stays above the stream and travels through an area of shrubs, yucca, cacti and other desert plantlife, before leading through an opening in a fence and descending to the stream. From this point, the path crisscrosses the stream numerous times, bringing you in and out of areas shaded by trees.

After about 45 minutes of hiking, when the trail brings you to the right side of the stream, begin looking to the left for the waterfall. Oriflamme is tucked under the shade of willow trees, but can be seen and heard from the trail. The path doesn't go down to the falls, but a faint side spur does. Just beware of the poison oak on the way down; it's thick in places. There's really no need to scramble to the base, though, because the view is better from above.

Oriflamme is a 20-foot waterfall that plummets off a rock ledge into a clear pool about three feet deep. The pool would be a nice wading hole if it weren't filled with silt.

If you plan to make the trip, supplies are available in Julian. It's recommended that you have a high-clearance vehicle to drive to the trailhead.

Also nearby are Borrego Palm Canyon Falls, Maidenhair Falls, Green Valley Falls and Lake Cuyamaca.

Directions: *From Highway 78 in Julian, drive east to Highway S2 and turn right. Drive approximately nine miles to the Oriflamme Canyon turnoff and turn right. Drive two-tenths of a mile and bear right at a fork. Reset your odometer and just under two miles bear left. Drive another mile and bear left again. Continue 100 yards to the parking area along the stream.*

Oriflamme Falls

For Tar Creek Falls see page 288-289

Region 16 Cleveland National Forest

Tenaja Falls
Falls Canyon Falls
Holy Jim Falls
San Juan Falls
Ortega Falls
Prisoner Creek Falls
Black Canyon Falls
Cedar Creek Falls
Green Valley Falls
Cottonwood Creek Falls
Kitchen Creek Falls

Tenaja Creek Falls

Rating: 6

How Short? 1.4 Miles

How Easy? 1

Best Time to View:
January to April

Need Information?
Contact: Cleveland
National Forest
(909) 736-1811

I call Tenaja Creek Falls "Trash Falls." Unless the area has been combed by a large group of cleanup workers, the waterfall will have more trash on its banks than any other I've seen. It's an embarrassing sight. I find it disgusting, as I'm sure you will, too. There's more trash here than along the banks of the Los Angeles River. It isn't just fast food wrappers and soda cans, either. There are diapers, old clothes, torn rafts, poop-stained underwear, broken beer bottles, empty cigarette packs and dirty socks. It's a sight I'd love to forget.

Aside from the constant reminders of visitors' lack of respect, Tenaja Creek Falls can be exciting in the spring. Although the waterfall is comprised of five main tiers, at no single vantage point along the trail can all five be seen at once.

Reaching the cascades is easy. Walk around the locked gate near your car, cross the creek and continue upstream, following the dirt road. Initially, the path is composed of soft dirt, but closer to the falls it's made up of small, loose rocks. The road parallels the stream the entire route to the falls, however, after the crossing you'll remain far above its banks.

The first cascade you'll come to is the tallest. It stands higher than 60 feet and can be quite eye-catching in February and March when the stream is at peak flow. Continue up the trail to the top of the waterfall, and the upper two cascades will come into view. All the cascades glide down slippery polished rock. Each of the top two cascades are taller than 40 feet, whereas the two middle cascades are not even 20 feet. The entire height of Tenaja Creek Falls is 160 feet.

Located at roughly 1,500 feet in the San Mateo Canyon Wilderness, the waterfall is situated in the foothills, and the terrain can become extremely dry if rain hasn't fallen in recent weeks. Plan your trip accordingly.

If you plan to make the trip, supplies are available in Murietta. A Forest Service Adventure Pass is required to park in the Cleveland National Forest.

Also nearby are Lake Elsinore, San Juan Creek Falls and Ortega Falls.

Tenaja Falls

Directions: *From Interstate 15 in Lake Elsinore, drive east to Murietta and exit Clinton Keith Road. Drive approximately 4.3 miles south on Clinton Keith Road (which becomes Tenaja Road) to a signed intersection with Tenaja Road. Turn right on Tenaja Road and continue four miles to Cleveland Forest Road. Turn right and drive nine-tenths of a mile to the Tenaja Trailhead sign and parking area. Stay right, passing the parking area, and continue 4.3 miles to a dirt pullout on the left. You'll see a Forest Service Adventure Pass sign and metal fence.*

Falls Canyon Falls

Rating: 6

How Short? 0.50 Miles

How Easy? 2

Best Time to View:
January to June

Need Information?
Contact: Cleveland
National Forest
(909) 736-1811

You say you don't have a lot of time to spare, but you need to get out of the city and burn some energy? You must be having trouble finding a place close by to visit. Orange County residents need wait no longer. Just a short drive from Mission Viejo, Falls Canyon Falls is a perfect destination.

Located in the Cleveland National Forest near Trabuco Creek, Falls Canyon Falls can give you an all-around great outdoor experience, without having to endure a long drive from home. The hike, which takes fewer than 45 minutes, is short enough to be undertaken by children. Supervising adults, however, might need to help them dodge poison oak.

The hardest part about visiting Falls Canyon is the last 3.4 miles of the drive on Trabuco Canyon Road: it's horrible! The dirt road is so bad, it's impossible to drive faster than 10 mph without banging your head on the roof and windshield. Once you reach the trailhead, however, things get much easier.

There are two ways down to Trabuco Creek, which you'll need to cross to enter Falls Canyon. Both are dirt trails visible from the pullout, however, you should take the one on the left when facing the stream. Although the one on the right is wider and less steep, it is also overgrown with poison oak. The path on the left, although steeper, has no poison oak creeping over it.

Newts

Walk down the path and cross Trabuco Creek. Proceed downstream a few yards to a tributary that feeds Trabuco. Head upstream on the path that parallels this tributary, which is Falls Canyon Creek. The path makes at least 10 stream crossings, all of which require little effort. It should take no longer than 20 minutes to reach the falls. It's impossible to get lost by passing it by, because the steep cliffs prohibit travel upstream.

A side note: stay on the trail near the stream. Many paths along the way lead up the canyon's hillsides, but they are all overgrown with poison oak, and most eventually lead back down to the stream anyway.

The path ends at 35-foot Falls Canyon Falls; a

narrow drop, its water clings to a mossy, sandstone cliff face, before emptying into a small, shallow pool. The waterfall is pretty, but the true rewards can be found in and along Falls Canyon Creek.

The creek is rich with salamanders. We saw dozens in each pool, not to mention frogs, water bugs and the occasional garter snake. The fertile canyon hillsides are adorned with several species of ferns, wildflowers, tall grass and moss, all growing under large oaks. The greenery is extremely thick and keeps the canyon cool.

If you plan to make the trip, supplies are available in Mission Viejo. A Forest Service Adventure Pass is required to park in the Cleveland National Forest. In the rainy season, a high clearance vehicle is needed on the dirt road.

Also nearby are Holy Jim Falls, Trabuco Creek, San Juan Falls and Ortega Falls.

Directions: From Interstate 5 in Mission Viejo, exit El Toro Road and drive 7.1 miles east to Live Oak Canyon Road. Turn right and drive 4.2 miles. Just after crossing Trabuco Creek, turn left on an unsigned dirt road. Drive 3.4 miles to a dirt pullout on the right side of the road.

Falls Canyon Falls

Holy Jim Falls

Rating: 6

How Short? 2.5 Miles

How Easy? 2

Best Time to View:
December to May

Need Information?
Contact: Cleveland
National Forest
(909) 736-1811

Holy Jim Falls is a small waterfall with no outstanding characteristics, but in this part of Orange County any waterfall is appreciated. Because it is so close to numerous residential neighborhoods, this section of the Cleveland National Forest is mostly visited by nearby residents. Just ten minutes from Mission Viejo, reaching Holy Jim Falls simply requires a short drive on a winding mountain road.

Although the overall drive from the city is mostly short and easy, if it weren't for the final brutal 4.4 miles of the drive on Trabuco Creek Road, the hike would be much more popular. From the point where the road turns from concrete to dirt, it's difficult to drive faster than 10 mph. Press the gas down any harder, and it feels like the wheels are going to burst off your car. I put my car in four-wheel drive and it didn't do any good. I was driving less than 10 mph; our sodas were falling out of the cup holders; the CD player wouldn't stop skipping; and all sorts of things were tossed all over the car out of compartments.

The walk to the falls is much easier than the drive. The trail is fairly flat, well maintained, short and easy to follow. Pick up the path directly behind the information board and walk uphill for a few minutes to a sign for the Holy Jim Trailhead and a Forest Service gate. Cross Holy Jim Creek and continue upstream, passing some cabins. Although there are several stream crossings required, there is one important one to keep an eye out for.

While walking along the right side of the stream, you'll pass two large oak trees and a group of boulders. At this point, take a left, following the trail as it crosses the stream. It's 23 steps from the stream crossing to a fork in the trail. Veer left and you'll remain on the Holy Jim Trail, eventually ending up at the top of Santiago Peak. Take the right fork and continue to the base of the falls.

Holy Jim Falls might only be a mere 18 feet tall, but it's good enough to make the young ones cheer at first sight. It's no freefall, just a portion of Holy Jim Creek that cascades down a channel cut through the rocks.

If you plan to make the trip, supplies are available in Mission Viejo and Rancho Santa Margarita. A Forest Service Adventure Pass is required to park in the Cleveland National Forest.

Also nearby are Laguna Niguel Lake and Holy Jim Falls.

Directions: *From Interstate 5 in San Juan Capistrano, drive nine miles north to the El Toro Road turnoff and turn right. Drive seven miles to Live Oak Canyon Road and bear right. Follow the road 3.3 miles to Trabuco Canyon Road. Turn left and continue another 4.4 miles past where the concrete road becomes dirt. Park in the dirt pullout on the left. There is a trailhead sign in the parking area, just after crossing over Holy Jim Creek.*

San Juan Falls

Rating: 3

How Short? 0.50 Miles

How Easy? 1

Best Time to View:
January to March

Need Information?
Contact: Cleveland
National Forest (909)
736-1811, Ortega
General Store
(909) 678-2774

Start preparing a rain dance, because if you can't convince the rain gods to make it rain, there will be no reason to visit San Juan Falls: it will be dry. Between Lake Elsinore and San Juan Capistrano, San Juan Falls is a small waterfall that is easy to reach, however, its life is short, very short. In poor rain years, San Juan Creek won't start flowing until late January and may cease by early March. When there is sufficient rain in winter and spring, the stream can still dry up by April, but even at peak flow it never seems to have any real force to it.

San Juan Canyon

San Juan Falls is located in the coastal mountains between the Pacific Ocean and the desert lands near Lake Elsinore. In this area it's amazing there are any waterfalls at all. San Juan Creek only gushes after a good rain, when it gets forced through a crevice in a jagged rock face and cascades over its ledge down a tiny break in the rocks into a small pool. The waterfall is only about as wide as a free throw line in basketball.

I've been to the waterfall twice now in late March. The first time the stream wasn't flowing, but there was still water trapped in pools at the base of the falls. Although the second time the stream was barely struggling to stay alive, I did get a chance to view this small 15-foot drop from the San Juan Loop Trail. There are also other small waterfalls below San Juan's base, but unless you're an expert rock climber, don't attempt to scramble down to the base to view them.

If you're not that interested in this small waterfall, then come to the San Juan Loop Trail to learn about the coastal mountains. Although the wildlife is limited to birds, ground squirrels and snakes, the flora is much more diverse. An array of shrubs, bushes and wildflowers decorate the hills on the way to the falls. A few oaks keep the route shaded some of the way, but the rest is exposed to the sun.

The trail begins at the east end of the parking lot on a path about three feet wide made of rocks riprapped in packed dirt. The path guides downhill, and before you get a feel for it, the path angles off to the left, becomes rocky and parallels San Juan Creek.

SAN JUAN LOOP TRAIL 6W05
CLEVELAND National Forest

In fewer than 100 yards, you'll arrive at the San Juan Creek overlook, marked by a metal fence bolted into rocks to keep visitors from falling down the steep hillside. From here, there are two options: continue on the loop back to the parking lot or backtrack the way you came in.

If you plan to make the trip, supplies are available across the trailhead at the Ortega Oaks Store. A Forest Service Adventure Pass is required to park in the Cleveland National Forest.

Also nearby are Ortega Falls, Trabuco Creek, Falls Canyon Falls, Holy Jim Falls and Lake Elsinore.

Directions: From Interstate 5 in San Juan Capistrano, take Ortega Highway (Highway 74) 18.9 miles east to the parking area on the left for the San Juan Loop Trail. It's directly across from the Ortega Store.

San Juan Falls

Ortega Falls

Rating: 5

How Short? 0.40 Miles

How Easy? 1

Best Time to View:
January to March

Need Information?
Contact: Cleveland
National Forest (909)
736-1811, Ortega
General Store
(909) 678-2774

In the coastal mountains above San Juan Capistrano, Ortega Falls is a mountain climber's waterfall. Although it's in a location that is visitor friendly, the unnamed stream that creates Ortega doesn't flow long or strong enough to keep the waterfall noteworthy more than a few months each year. Yet, climbers come year-round to the waterfall for its granite cliffs, not to view the falls. When Ortega is flowing, it simply adds to the climbing experience.

So, if Ortega is a climber's waterfall, why is it visitor friendly? Along Ortega Highway in the Cleveland National Forest, the waterfall can be seen from the road, and it's an easy walk to its base. It's the kind of place Orange County residents bring their kids to walk around on the rocks, even though most of the time the falls isn't more than dribble.

If you arrive soon after a downpour, the waterfall can be impressive, unfortunately the water levels subside within a few days of the rain. The 35-foot waterfall cascades over granite with jagged outcroppings that have been carved by millions of years of flowing water. Ortega's pool is wide, but less than a foot deep, perfect for the little ones to splash around in.

There is no signed trail to the base. From the parking area, locate the falls to the northeast, and then look for dirt trails that descend through the brush and rocks down to the stream. It doesn't matter which trail you take; they all go to the same place. Once at the stream, make a right and rock-hop to the base of the falls.

Because of the rock climbing opportunities, Ortega can get crowded on the weekends. To avoid the crowds, walk upstream or downstream from the falls. Smaller cascades exist in both places.

If you plan to make the trip, supplies are available at the Ortega Store. A Forest Service Adventure Pass is required to park in the Cleveland National Forest. In poor rain years Ortega Falls may dry up by March.

Ortega Falls

Also nearby are San Juan Falls, San Juan Creek and Lake Elsinore.

Directions: *From Interstate 5 in San Juan Capistrano, take the Highway 74/Ortega Highway exit and continue 22.4 miles to a dirt pullout on the left, 1.4 miles past the Ortega Store.*

Prisoner Creek Falls

Rating: 5

How Short? 3.0 Miles

How Easy? 4

Best Time to View:
February to April

Need Information?
Contact: Cleveland
National Forest
(760) 788-0250

You think you have patience? Getting to Prisoner Creek Falls will definitely test it. If you survive the entire trip to the falls without getting frustrated and/or angry, you are a patient person. Few can complete the trip to the falls, however, without honestly admitting that somewhere during the adventure they lost their patience.

Four miles west of Lake Henshaw and just minutes from the San Luis Rey River, Prisoner Creek Falls is a small remote waterfall in the Cleveland National Forest. The trip to the falls can make even the most avid hiker not want to hike anymore.

The fact that there is no trail is only a small annoyance compared to the other hazards you'll encounter.

Since there is no trail, the only way to reach the falls is to follow the stream, but overgrown trees, brush, grass and thorn bushes make doing so difficult. Expect to encounter plenty of poison oak, ticks, spiders, flies, mosquitoes and rattlesnakes. All of these are present at most streams, but the difference here is that there is no trail protecting you from them. There are few things worse than walking into spider webs every 10 yards! Another downfall is that the falls and the creek only have water in them from January to April. Arrive any later and you'll never find the falls, because it won't exist.

If you think you can handle Prisoner Creek's hazards, here's what to do: Park in the parking lot near the San Luis Rey River (across the street from the Denver C. Fox Outdoor Education School) and walk down to the creek. Cross the creek and walk east, paralleling it until you come to a small tributary. This feeder stream is Prisoner Creek. Cross Prisoner Creek and follow it upstream.

There will be a trail for about 100 yards, but then it disappears and you're on your own. There are no specific landmarks or trail markers you can use. The only way to know you're nearing the falls is when the canyon begins to narrow. After a little more than an hour, you'll come to the 50-foot cascade, which is split into three tiers. Just keep in mind that rock-hopping takes much longer than walking on a maintained trail, so give yourself plenty of extra time to complete the trip.

If you plan to make the trip, supplies are available at Lake Henshaw. A Forest Service Adventure Pass is required to park in the Cleveland National Forest.

Also nearby are Lake Henshaw, Palomar State Park, San Luis Rey River and Doane Pond.

Directions: *From San Diego, drive north on Interstate 15 to the city of Escondido. Continue past Escondido and turn east on Highway 76. Drive approximately 26 miles to a dirt pullout across the street from Denver C. Fox Outdoor Education School. The trail leads to the stream.*

Black Canyon Falls

Rating: 6

How Short? 0.25 Miles

How Easy? 1

Best Time to View:
January to April

Need Information?
Contact: Cleveland
National Forest
(760) 788-0250

Less than a mile downstream from the Mesa Grande Indian Reservation, Black Canyon Falls has suffered from the kind of "outsider" desecration that is not unfamiliar to the native inhabitants of these wilderness areas. A beautiful granite waterfall had been destroyed by the obliviousness of visitors who seem to have no notion that our national forests are home to us all.

I met a young man from the San Isabel Tribe who explained his version of the story. He said his father told him how the canyon in this part of the Cleveland National Forest used to be clean and free of litter. Over the years, however, as San Diego and its suburbs grew, more people discovered the waterfall. Hikers and swimmers made it a habit to visit the falls on the weekends, but when they left, their trash stayed behind.

More recently, the problem has escalated from trash to graffiti. It seems that all the graffiti writers from the surrounding cities have made Black Canyon Falls another one of their victims. The Forest Service sent in crews to blast graffiti off the canyon walls, but it has become a chronic blight. Some thought the closure of Black Canyon Campground in 1982 would deter people from going to the falls. Unfortunately, due to a population influx in San Diego County and the surrounding suburban areas, the closure was ineffective.

Alcohol poses another big problem here. Too often, people have become intoxicated in the canyon; a few even had to be airlifted out after they slipped off rocks and injured themselves. I confirmed reports with the Forest Service that several people have died here attempting to dive off the waterfall. "My daddy died here," is spray painted on one of the rocks above the waterfall. It's a sad reminder of what alcohol can do. Because there is a lot of broken glass, open cans and other trash, be sure to wear shoes around the falls. There's so much garbage, I don't even think it's safe to wear sandals.

Aside from the reminders that disrespectful visitors have left behind, a lot of fun can be had at the falls. Black Canyon Falls isn't a grand display of rushing water; it's usually limited to a small 20-foot cascade about three feet wide, which clings to large slabs of smooth granite and empties into an ideal swimming hole.

Directly below the waterfall, the pool is about 20 feet deep, but it does get shallower as you swim downstream. I saw a few guys sliding down the waterfall into the pool. There are also rope swings hanging off tree branches that extend over the pool, which

A rope swing at Black Canyon Falls

are used for Tarzan-like antics. And huge granite boulders surround the pool, making perfect tanning rocks or great places to eat lunch.

Besides trash and graffiti, one of the biggest problems here are low water levels. The guy from the San Isabel Tribe blamed it on ranchers diverting a lot of water off the stream into stock ponds. This may be partly true, however, I think a simple lack of rain in the region is the most critical reason.

Trash is abundant around Black Canyon Falls

The only time water seems to flow fast in Black Canyon Creek is during El Nino seasons, and they don't occur that often. If you arrive after late April, Black Canyon Creek will most likely have stopped flowing, and the water will be stagnant from having been held up in pools.

If you plan to make the trip, supplies are available in Ramona. A Forest Service Adventure Pass is required to park in the Cleveland National Forest.

Also nearby are Lake Henshaw, San Luis Rey River, Lake Sutherland, Cedar Creek Falls and Green Valley Falls.

Directions: *From San Diego, drive north on Interstate 15 to the city of Escondido. In Escondido, exit Highway 78 and drive east to Sutherland Dam Road. Turn left and drive 3.4 miles past Sutherland Dam to a three-way fork in the road. The right fork is signed as a private road; the left leads towards a horse staging area. Take the middle fork. At the base of the mountain, veer right at another fork, crossing over a bridge. After crossing the bridge, continue approximately two miles on the dirt road to a dirt pullout on the left. If you reach Hallyeyaaw Road, you've gone one mile too far.*

Black Canyon Falls in March during a low rain year

Cedar Creek Falls

Rating: 8

How Short? 4.5 Miles

How Easy? 3

Best Time to View:
January to May

Need Information?
Contact: Cleveland
National Forest
(760) 788-0250

Like neighboring Los Angeles County, San Diego is one of the few counties in the country that can offer its residents almost any type of recreational opportunity imaginable. Within an hour's drive, you can visit sunny beaches with warm water, go snow sledding in the mountains, take bike rides along the beach or in the country, roller blade down a boardwalk, camp along a trout-filled mountain stream, take scenic drives through the desert, or hike to a waterfall with an inviting pool at its base.

One of San Diego's best waterfalls is often overlooked because of everything else there is to do in the county. Located between Ramona and Julian, 100-foot Cedar Creek Falls is easy to hike to, however, San Diegans don't take advantage of it the way they should. If a waterfall of this height were located in Los Angeles County, it would have a state park named after it. Yet, located in the Cleveland National Forest, Cedar Creek Falls rarely sees more than 20 visitors at a time. This means there's room for you to visit and enjoy the waterfall.

Cedar Creek Falls

It is possible to ride a mountain bike to the falls, but the trip loses 1,100 feet on the way, so it could be tough coming out, and you'd have to lock the bike above the falls before heading down the steep trail to its base. Walking may take longer, but I found it to be easier.

The route begins at the point where Cedar Creek Road and Eagle Peak Road converge. Stay right, following Eagle Peak Road, which is opened to vehicular traffic; however, it really isn't wide enough or in good enough condition for most cars, even four-wheel drive vehicles. Because the county doesn't maintain the road, it isn't recommended you travel on it. It's safer to park your car and use your feet.

The path is a dirt road all the way to the top of the falls. It stays high above the San Diego River and parallels it for the first 1.6 miles, before veering left on a trail spur that leads towards Cedar Creek. It then ascends uphill, and at a plateau breaks into several smaller trails. No worries. Follow any of them; they all lead to the same place. Shortly, one of these trails will lead you Cedar Creek.

Continue fewer than 50 yards downstream to the top of the falls. There is no signed overlook, just a sheer cliff, so use caution not to get too close to its lip. The view of the waterfall isn't great from here. It's best appreciated from the base. There are two ways to get there, and climbing down the lip is not one of them! There are narrow trails that traverse both cliffs adjacent to the falls, however, they are steep and require careful footing.

After a good rain, Cedar Creek Falls plummets down the sheer granite cliff into a grand pool, ideal for swimming, jumping and swinging from rope swings. The water isn't clear; partly because of its depth, it's a dark green color. I failed to touch bottom, trying to get near where the water enters the pool. The pool remains full year-round, however, the stream can stop flowing by early June, leaving its dark water stagnant for the rest of the year. When I last arrived in late June, the waterfall was dry, but the fun and games in the pool were alive and well.

It was Sunday, and the place was packed with about 20 teenagers and young adults. Many of them were intoxicated, jumping from the cliffs adjacent to the falls. I thought most of the jumps were unsafe, because the water was too cloudy to check for rocks, but they told me they'd been jumping for years and never hit a rock. It still didn't make it safe. My advice: play it safe and don't jump. While I didn't take any wild jumps I watched a few guys leap from rock ledges about 70 feet high, and they hit the water like missiles. It was too hot and dry outside to resist a dip in the cool pool, but I did check for rocks first before that refreshing swim.

Cedar Creek Falls is a great place to visit, but there were a few things that bothered me on that last visit. The wildflowers scattered around the pool were trashed with broken glass, which I guessed was a result of the drunken teenagers throwing bottles. A group of kids dragged three coolers with them to the falls' base (and I have no problem with people of age relaxing with a beer); on their way back, however, they decided to leave the bottles at the base of the falls to take some weight out of the coolers. I saw the same group earlier trying to catch a rattlesnake with a few sticks. It wasn't the smartest bunch of dudes I've ever run across. The best thing to do is arrive early in the morning or during the week, and hopefully similar annoyances won't arise.

If you plan to make the trip, supplies are available in Julian. A Forest Service Adventure Pass is required to park in the Cleveland National Forest.

Also nearby are Lake Cuyamaca, San Luis Rey River and Green Valley Falls.

Directions: From Julian, drive two miles west on Highway 78/79 and turn left on Pine Hills Road. Drive 1.5 miles and veer right on Eagle Peak Road. Continue 1.4 miles and veer right again, staying on Eagle Peak Road. Drive eight miles on a mostly dirt road to the junction of Eagle Peak and Cedar Creek Roads. Park and follow Eagle Peak Road.

In the middle of the picture look for a man jumping off Cedar Creek Falls

Green Valley Falls

Rating: 4
How Short? 0.25 Miles
How Easy? 1
Best Time to View: January to May
Need Information? Contact: Cuyamaca State Park (760) 765-0755

Green Valley Falls is not spectacular, but for residents of San Diego County, it offers a place to escape city life and enjoy nature, just a short, easy drive away. Located in Cuyamaca State Park, Green Valley Falls is a series of small cascades that can be enjoyed from December to May. These cascades are located along a portion of the Sweetwater River, less than a 10-minute drive from popular Lake Cuyamaca.

Other activities are also available for visitors who prefer to come for the entire day, and for campers making a weekend trip out of it. Although most hikers choose to make a brief appearance at the falls, there are plenty of campsites and picnic areas a short walk away, for those planning a family outing. These easily accessible areas are heavily shaded, mostly by oak trees, and are kept clean.

Green Valley Falls

Reaching the falls is simple. Drive to the end of Green Valley Campground and park in the dirt parking area signed for day-use parking. Pick up the trail in the parking lot and follow it to the stream. Less than five minutes away awaits the first of a series of cascades.

The tallest cascade stands fewer than 25 feet, but after a winter storm it can be quite impressive, with water splashing off granite boulders into small, shallow pools. For the next 100 yards downstream there are more cascades. In late spring and early summer, many visitors choose to cool off in the pools below these cascades.

Another good idea is fishing. From February to May, the California Department of Fish and Game stocks the stream with 4,500 rainbow trout. The rainbows are small, usually from seven to nine inches, however, there aren't many other streams in the region that offer trout fishing, so take advantage of it.

If visiting after a storm, use caution on the rocks near the cascades. The polished granite becomes extremely slippery and dangerous. Better to be safe than sorry.

If you plan to make the trip, supplies are available at Lake Cuyamaca. There is a day-use fee to enter Cuyamaca State Park.

Also nearby are Lake Cuyamaca, Julian, Anza-Borrego State Park, Cedar Creek Falls, Lake Henshaw, Doane Pond, San Luis Rey River and Prisoner Creek Falls.

Directions: *From Interstate 8 in San Diego, drive 30 miles east to Highway 79. Turn north and continue seven miles to Green Valley Campground. Turn left into the campground.*

Cottonwood Creek Falls

Rating: 5

How Short? 2.0 Miles

How Easy: 2

Best Time to View:
January to June

Need Information?
Contact: Cleveland
National Forest
(619) 445-6235

In an area where waterfalls are scarce, Cottonwood Creek Falls shines; however, placed next to some of San Diego's more spectacular waterfalls, Cottonwood Creek Falls ranks among the worst.

Located at 4,350 feet in the Cleveland National Forest, Cottonwood Creek Falls is a series of five small cascades that can be reached by an easy and short drive from San Diego. The falls is close to the Vejas Casino and Outlet Center, and after visiting the scanty falls, many people opt to stick with gambling and shopping on their next trip. Others are just happy to have a waterfall close by and continue coming back.

Being in an arid desert terrain, the falls just don't have much to offer. It's a good thing only a short hike is required. After parking in the large dirt pullout along Highway S1, walk across the road and pick up the trail. Gradually working your way downhill the narrow trail is overgrown with shrubs and chaparral. Be careful not to sprain your ankle. There are thousands of loose softball-sized rocks that can easily cause injury if you aren't careful.

Near the stream, the trail begins to widen. At the bottom of the canyon you'll reach the stream and make a left turn. In less than 100 yards is the first cascade. Four others follow upstream, with the final one being the longest and prettiest. None are taller than 20 feet, nor are any of their pools deep enough for wading.

If you plan to make the trip, supplies are available in Alpine. A Forest Service Adventure Pass is required to park in the Cleveland National Forest.

Also nearby are Kitchen Creek Falls, Loveland Reservoir and El Capitan Reservoir.

Directions: *From Interstate 5 in San Diego, take Interstate 8 east approximately 45 miles to Highway S1. Drive two miles north on Highway S1 to a large dirt pullout on the west side of the highway. (There is a large rock wall in the pullout.)*

Cottonwood Creek Falls

Kitchen Creek Falls

Rating: 7

How Short? 4.5 Miles

How Easy? 3

Best Time to View:
January to April

Need Information?
Contact: Cleveland
National Forest
(619) 445-6235

The Pacific Crest is probably the most renowned trail in the United States. It begins at the California/Mexico border and continues through Oregon and Washington into Canada. Because of its length (2,650 miles) and the time it takes to hike the entire trail, most hikers only trek along sections of it, sticking to the more popular areas near Sequoia, Kings Canyon, Lake Tahoe, the Eastern Sierra, and Yosemite and Lassen National Parks.

Outdoor enthusiasts who don't have time to hike the entire trail are seldom attracted to the areas in the most southerly portions of California where the PCT cuts across the desert. Diehard backpackers who do set out to walk the entire trail often begin near Campo and shortly find themselves a few hundred feet above Kitchen Creek. Yet, not many of them take the time to leave the main trail and walk a few hundred yards down to the creek to see Kitchen Creek Falls.

Most hikers don't even know the falls exists. It is not named on maps, and there are no signs acknowledging it along the trail. Also, since there isn't a lot of water in this hot, dry area, hikers don't expect to encounter a tall waterfall, the way they might in Central and Northern California. That's why Kitchen Creek Falls is such a shocker.

Lake Morena is located near Kitchen Creek Falls

Although residents of San Diego can enjoy Kitchen Creek Falls via a simple day trip, they don't often taken advantage of it. Part of the reason is that Border Patrol vehicles positioned near the trailhead and close to Interstate 8 underpasses deter many possible visitors. Also, people wanting to visit have difficulty locating the trailhead. The Boulder Oaks Store used to be a good landmark for locating the trail, however, it recently burned down.

To become one of the few who does take advantage of Kitchen Creek Falls, here is what to do: First, follow the above directions to the sign for the Pacific Crest Trail, which breaks away from the road and crosses under Interstate 8. To follow the trail, hop (or crawl) through two fences, one which has a barbed gate. After getting around the gate, take the shadeless path, which bends to the left and begins gradually climbing uphill. Although many hikers don't notice, on the left you can see the canyon that

Kitchen Creek cuts through.

After nearly an hour of hiking, the trail makes a sharp right and ascends more steeply. Begin looking for trail spurs leading off the path down into the canyon. When you reach these spurs (usually marked by small piles of rocks or outlined by rock trails), follow one down to the stream. Depending on which spur you take, you'll end up at either the brink or the base of the falls.

Kitchen Creek Falls is a series of cascades formed by Kitchen Creek. The falls splashes over granite boulders through a series of separate tiers, none of which look alike. If there has been measurable rain in recent weeks, the falls can be stirring. Although it feeds the falls year-round, most of the time the creek's lack of volume diminishes the cascades. This 120-foot fall is most notable from late winter through early spring. I last arrived in March of 2000 and found the stream at low flow. The pools below the cascades were filled with algae and moss, a sign that the stream hadn't been flowing strongly anytime in the recent past.

If you plan to make the trip, supplies are available in Morena Village. A Forest Service Adventure Pass is required to park in the Cleveland National Forest. Bring along lots of water. None is available along the path.

Also nearby are Cottonwood Creek Falls, Lake Morena and Loveland Reservoir.

Directions: *From San Diego, drive approximately 50 miles east on Interstate 8 and exit the Buckman Springs Road turnoff. Turn left on Old Highway 80 and drive 2.3 miles to the Boulder Oaks Campground. Look opposite the campground for a sign for the Pacific Crest Trail. Park alongside the road and pick up the trailhead.*

The lip of Kitchen Creek Falls as seen from the ridge above the canyon

About the Author

The founder of the "Definitive Guides" to California outdoors, Chris Shaffer has spent the last seven years of his life exploring, investigating and documenting more than 1,200 lakes, rivers, streams, ponds and waterfalls throughout California. The California native is a graduate of Cal State Northridge and Crespi High School in Encino.

Shaffer has taken an active role reporting on and photographing California outdoors. Currently in print, ***The Definitive Guide to Fishing in Southern California*** and ***The Definitive Guide to Fishing Central California*** are followed by his third book, ***The Definitive Guide to the Waterfalls of Southern and Central California***. A former LA Times sportswriter, Shaffer is also working on two more books. ***The Definitive Guide to the Waterfalls of Northern California*** and ***The Definitive Guide to Fishing Northern California*** are poised for a 2004 release. More than 1,300 of Shaffer's photographs have been printed in newspapers and magazines worldwide.

Shaffer's work extends far beyond the book business. Aside from running a publishing company and writing books he is a regular guest on California Sportsmen radio with Sep Hendrickson and other local radio shows. Shaffer also is a columnist and contributor for Fishing and Hunting News and The Sportsman's Series, a freelance consultant for the California Department of Fish and Game and performs seminars at several International Sportsmen's Exposition and Fred Hall Fishing Shows.

A member of the Outdoor Writers Association of California and Outdoor Writer Association of America Shaffer also contributes to several newspapers and magazines, including the Los Angeles Daily News, Fish Taco Chronicles, Ojai Valley News, California Game and Fish, ESPN.com Outdoors and Outdoor California magazine.

Index

G

H

I

J

M

Also available from Shafdog Publications

The Definitive Guide to Fishing in Southern California

The Definitive Guide to Fishing in Central California

www.fishingcalifornia.net

The Definitive Guide to the Waterfalls of Northern California

www.californiawaterfalls.com

www.californiawaterfalls.com

Available in 2004
The Definitive Guide to Fishing Northern California

www.fishingcalifornia.net

www.californiawaterfalls.com